Religions of Asia Today

Religions

# of Asia Today

JOHN L. ESPOSITO
Georgetown University

DARRELL J. FASCHING
University of South Florida

TODD LEWIS
College of the Holy Cross

New York   Oxford
OXFORD UNIVERSITY PRESS
2009

Oxford University Press, Inc., publishes works that further Oxford University's
objective of excellence in research, scholarship, and education.

Oxford   New York
Auckland   Cape Town   Dar es Salaam   Hong Kong   Karachi
Kuala Lumpur   Madrid   Melbourne   Mexico City   Nairobi
New Delhi   Shanghai   Taipei   Toronto

With offices in
Argentina   Austria   Brazil   Chile   Czech Republic   France   Greece
Guatemala   Hungary   Italy   Japan   Poland   Portugal   Singapore
South Korea   Switzerland   Thailand   Turkey   Ukraine   Vietnam

Published by Oxford University Press, Inc.
198 Madison Avenue, New York, New York 10016
http://www.oup.com

Oxford is a registered trademark of Oxford University Press

Library of Congress Cataloging-in-Publication Data

Esposito, John L.
    Religions of Asia today / John L. Esposito, Darrell J. Fasching, Todd
Lewis.
        p. cm.
    Includes bibliographical references and index.
    ISBN 978-0-19-537360-8 (alk. paper)
1. Asia—Religion.   I. Fasching, Darrell J., 1944–   II. Lewis, Todd
Vernon, 1949–   III.   Title.
    BL1033.E87   2009
    200.95—dc22

2008043008

Printing number: 9 8 7 6 5 4 3 2 1

Printed in the United States of America
on acid-free paper

For
Jean Esposito
Melissa and Nathan Lewis
and in memory of Harold Gushin

Contents

Chapter 3 ✤ Hinduism: Myriad Paths to Salvation   75

Preface

Religion is unquestionably a dynamic spiritual and political force in the world today. Around the globe religious experiences and beliefs profoundly change individual lives even as they influence politics and play a powerful role in international affairs. This new volume, *Religions of Asia Today*, comprises one-half of the new, third edition of our textbook *World Religions Today* and addresses this reality by providing an introductory volume for college and university students.

Although this is a multiauthored text with each of us taking primary authorship of different chapters (John Esposito: Islam; Darrell Fasching: New Religions and Globalization; and Todd Lewis: Asian traditions and Primal Religions), it has truly been a collaborative project from start to finish. Throughout the entire process we shared and commented on each other's material.

Religions of Asia Today grew out of our several decades of experience in teaching world religions. It is a product of our conviction that, for our students to understand the daily news accounts of religions in our global situation, they need more than just the ancient foundations of the world's religions. Textbooks on world religions too have often tended to emphasize historical origins and doctrinal developments, focusing on the past and giving short shrift to the "modern" world. Many stressed a textual, theological/philosophical, or legal approach, one that gave insufficient attention to the modern vicissitudes of these traditions. Most gave little attention to their social institutions and their connections to political power. As a result, students came away with a maximum appreciation for the origins and development of the classical traditions but a minimal awareness of the continued dynamism and relevance of religious traditions today. So, despite the growing visibility and impact of a global religious resurgence and of the unprecedented globalization of all world religions, most textbooks have not quite caught up. *Religions of Asia Today* extends our commitment to address this situation for

Hinduism, Buddhism, Daoism, Confucianism, and new age religious movements and globalization, with short chapters also devoted to indigenous religions and Islam.

Religions of Asia Today continues the approach of the previous two editions of *World Religions Today*, using historical coverage of religious traditions as a framework to help students understand how faiths have evolved to the present day. Indeed, we open most chapters with an *Encounter with Modernity*. These encounters illustrate the tension between the premodern religious views and modernity. Each chapter then returns to the origins of the tradition to trace the path that led to this confrontation with "modernity." We attempt to show not only how each tradition has been changed by its encounter with modernity but also how each religion in turn has influenced modernity. We would like to point out that we have included the short chapter "Indigenous Traditions," in this new edition. While we realize that many instructors do not cover indigenous religions in their courses, growing numbers do; however, those who wish can skip this chapter without negative impact.

A short comment on the selection of this volume's title, *Religions of Asia Today*, and that of its companion volume, *Religions of the West Today*. These titles, while illustrating our contemporary emphasis, also highlight the difficulties of choosing apt language in our postmodern, globalized world. The authors engaged in a spirited debate to find agreement on the question of what terms to use as titles of the two new volumes. Going back to the nineteenth century, a Eurocentric vantage point on the world created the dichotomy "Western" religions versus "Eastern" (or "Oriental") religions. While it is true that any geographic, directional terms are arbitrary, the fact remains that the power of imperial Europe and its creation of the new field of knowledge of religious studies coined these terms. As Kipling wrote, "East is East, and West is West, and never the twain shall meet." In so doing, Islam was commonly—and erroneously—shunted away from the "West" and distanced from the "Western" monotheisms of Christianity and Judaism. All of Asia was likewise lumped together, misleadingly, as "Eastern Religions," despite the extraordinary diversity found there.

So we, as authors, found it problematic either to assent to this now-archaic dichotomy or to find a completely satisfactory alternative. How could we craft a textbook for the twenty-first century that highlights postcolonial and postmodern perspectives while labeling our textbooks with nineteenth-century, colonialist terms? Such words recall stereotypes of the mysterious, mystical, and unchanging (and therefore backward and unscientific) East. And yet today, in an age of globalization, our students learn advanced mathematics, chemistry, and physics from their professors from India, China, Japan, and other Asian countries. Moreover, they are most likely to associate the term *the East* with the superiority of Japanese and Korean automobiles, cutting-edge electronic technology, and the growing international dominance of the Chinese economy. Nevertheless, there are those who remember the preglobalization era and fear that the old colonial stereotypes may still linger.

Our solution is an awkward one that suggests we are still in transition to a new way of looking at the world. We chose to mix geographic metaphors. So we have *Religions of the West Today* to highlight the grouping of the Abrahamic faiths together; and we grouped Hinduism, Buddhism, and the traditions of East Asia all under the title *Religions of Asia Today*, with the plural word *religions* underlining their plurality. One of the problems with this choice is that Islam today is also a major religion in Asia, with substantial communities in Pakistan, Bangladesh, India, Indonesia, Malaysia, and China. We include a chapter on Islam in *Religions of Asia Today* to reflect this reality. We believe that this addition empowers instructors to include in their courses the discussion of Islam in Asia, a possibility that recent events in the world certainly justifies. Of course, this still leaves the growing role of Christianity in China and the major social and political role of Christianity in South Korea, treated only in passing (in the "East Asian Religions" chapter). One can see why we, as authors, had an extended and not fully resolved conversation about both content and titles. It is a conversation that mirrors the complexities and perplexities of our new global situation.

The major theme and chapter structure of the earlier editions of *World Religions Today* have been retained, though they have been updated and revised. Chapter 2, on "Indigenous Religions," has been revised to reflect current scholarship on the faith practices that predate or live outside the global traditions that make up the bulk of this book. Each of these indigenous practices could fill an entire book on its own, but we hope this chapter strikes manages to survey the range of traditions without making artificial generalizations.

Each chapter is enriched by four kinds of thematic boxes. "Teachings of Religious Wisdom" are designed to offer examples of the primary texts and formal teachings of the faiths. The "Tales of Spiritual Transformation" describe the religious experiences of believers in their own words. The "Contrasting Religious Visions" boxes compare the beliefs of two significant adherents of a faith who each see the demands of their religion calling believers in very different directions in the modern age. These demonstrate that, no matter what religion we are examining, that very same religious tradition can used to promote both peacemaking and conflict. Finally, each chapter features a wide variety of special-topic boxes to explore particular ideas or practices in some depth.

SUPPLEMENTARY MATERIALS

For the instructor: The following rich set of supplements is available to aid in preparing to teach this course. These materials are also available as Blackboard/WebCT® cartridges.

❖ *Instructor's Resource CD*
- Chapter overviews
- Chapter summaries
- Chapter learning goals
- Lecture outlines
- PowerPoint® lecture slides

- Essay/Discussion questions
- Fill-in-the-blank, multiple-choice, and true/false test questions
- Key Terms list
- Suggested reading, viewing, and Web links
- Electronic test bank

❧ *Instructor's Manual (Print)*

[N.B.: Content of *all* items identical to Instructor's Resource CD.]
- Chapter overviews, summaries, and learning goals
- Lecture outlines
- Essay/Discussion questions
- Fill-in-the-blank, multiple-choice, and true/false test questions
- Key Terms list
- Suggested reading, viewing, and Web links

❧ *Password-Protected Website* (http://www.oup.com/us/esposito)

- Chapter overviews
- Chapter summaries
- Chapter learning goals
- Lecture outlines
- PowerPoint® lecture slides
- Essay/Discussion questions
- Fill-in-the-blank, multiple-choice, and true/false test questions
- Key Terms list
- Suggested reading, viewing, and Web links

For the student: A website study guide is available (http://www.oup.com/us/esposito) containing:

- Chapter overviews and learning goals
- Sample essay/discussion questions
- Self-quiz fill-in-the-blank practice questions
- Self-quiz multiple-choice practice questions
- Self-quiz true/false practice questions
- Flash cards of Key Terms
- Suggested reading, viewing, and Web links

ACKNOWLEDGMENTS

Religions of Asia Today has been substantially improved in light of the valuable comments on *World Religions Today* we received from colleagues across the country who have used it and in light of our own subsequent experiences and reflections. We offer special thanks to the following professors and to the other, anonymous, reviewers. This book is much stronger because of their thoughtful comments.

Constantina Rhodes Bailly, Eckerd College

Sheila Briggs, University of Southern California

Terry L. Burden, University of Louisville

Dexter E. Callender, Jr., University of Miami

James E. Deitrick, University of Central Arkansas

James Egge, Eastern Michigan University

John Farina, George Mason University

Debora Y. Fonteneau, Savannah State University

William Hutchins, Appalachian State University

Father Brad Karelius, Saddleback Community College

Sean McCloud, University of North Carolina at Charlotte

Tim Murphy, The University of Alabama

Patrick Nnoromele, Eastern Kentucky University

Barry R. Sang, Catawba College

D. Neil Schmid, North Carolina State University

Martha Ann Selby, The University of Texas at Austin

Theresa S. Smith, Indiana University of Pennsylvania

Hugh B. Urban, Ohio State University

Anne Vallely, University of Ottawa

Glenn Wallis, University of Georgia

Tammie Wanta, University of North Carolina at Charlotte

We have been fortunate to work with an excellent, supportive, and creative team at Oxford University Press, led by Robert Miller, Executive Editor in Oxford's Higher Education Group. Senior Production Editors Christine D'Antonio and Lisa Grzan, Associate Editor Sarah Calabi, Editorial Assistant Yelena Bromberg, and Development Editors Linda Harris and Danielle Christensen have been extraordinarily supportive throughout the writing process. Our thanks also to Robin Tuthill, who prepared the student and instructor support materials for the book.

John L. Esposito
Darrell J. Fasching
Todd Lewis

World population by Religion	
Christian	1,965,993,000
Muslim	1,179,326,000
Hindu	767,424,000
Non-religious	766,672,000
Buddhist	356,875,000
Tribal Religion	244,164,000
Atheist	146,406,000
New Religions	99,191,000
Sikh	22,874,000
Daoist	20,050,000
Jewish	15,050,000
Baha'i	6,251,000
Confucian	5,067,000
Jain	4,152,000
Shinto	3,571,000
Parsi (Zoroastrian)	479,000

1. MACEDONIA	16. GERMANY
2. ALBANIA	17. DENMARK
3. BOSNIA	18. POLAND
4. SERBIA	19. GREECE
5. CROATIA	20. BULGARIA
6. SLOVENIA	21. ROMANIA
7. HUNGARY	22. MOLDOVA
8. SLOVAK REPUBLIC	23. UKRAINE
9. CZECH REPUBLIC	24. BELARUS
10. AUSTRIA	25. LITHUANIA
11. SWITZERLAND	26. LATVIA
12. ITALY	27. ESTONIA
13. LUXEMBOURG	28. GEORGIA
14. BELGIUM	29. ARMENIA
15. NETHERLANDS	30. AZERBAIJAN

Religions of Asia Today

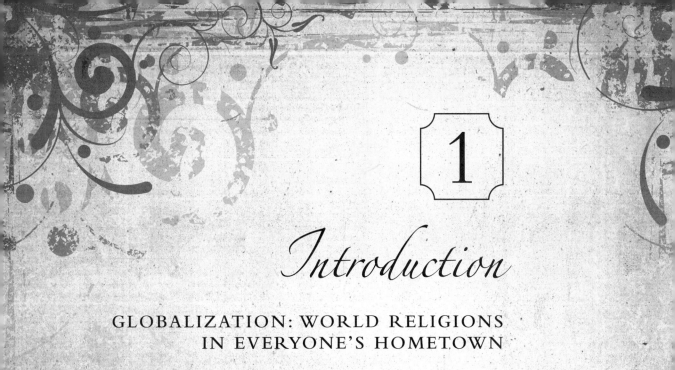

1

Introduction

GLOBALIZATION: WORLD RELIGIONS IN EVERYONE'S HOMETOWN

In the 1950s, if you walked down the streets of almost any city in the United States, you would have expected to find churches, both Catholic and Protestant, and Jewish synagogues. When people thought about religious diversity, it was limited largely to Protestants, Catholics, and Jews. In the twenty-first century, a new millennium, the situation is dramatically different. Almost daily the newspapers take note of new religious members of the community—announcing a meditation retreat at a Korean Zen center in the suburbs of Providence, Rhode Island; the opening of an Islamic mosque in St. Louis, Missouri; or the dedication of a Hindu temple in Tampa, Florida.

The beliefs and practices of world religions have become part of the mosaic of American society. *Karma* has become part of the American vocabulary, Hindu visualization practices are used in sports training, and Buddhist meditation techniques have been adopted in programs of stress management. No matter where we live today, it is more and more likely that our next-door neighbors are ethnically, politically, and, yes, even religiously diverse—coming from many parts of the globe (see Map 1.1). In an emerging global economy, most neighborhoods, workplaces, and schools reflect this diversity as well.

In this book we focus on the diverse ways in which we humans have been religious in the past and are religious today. Indeed, the last decades of the twentieth century brought a global religious resurgence, a development that defies countless theorists who predicted that the irresistible secularization of civilization would lead to the disappearance of religion. Religions, it was thought, are tied to ancient premodern worldviews that have been replaced by a modern scientific worldview. Indeed, the clash of traditional religions with modern scientific and secular society is a major concern of

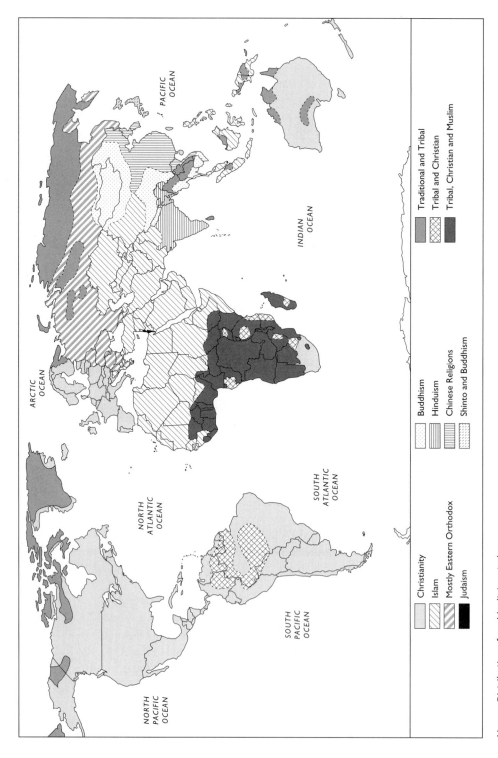

Map 1.1 Distribution of world religions today.

Christianity

Islam

Mostly Eastern Orthodox

Judaism

Buddhism

Hinduism

Chinese Religions

Shinto and Buddhism

Traditional and Tribal

Tribal and Christian

Tribal, Christian and Muslim

ARCTIC OCEAN

PACIFIC OCEAN

INDIAN OCEAN

NORTH ATLANTIC OCEAN

SOUTH ATLANTIC OCEAN

SOUTH PACIFIC OCEAN

NORTH PACIFIC OCEAN

this textbook. Awareness of this is essential if we are to understand the interactions between religions and cultures in the world today. We will begin every chapter not with a discussion of the origins and early history of each religious tradition, but with examples of a major controversy or significant tension each religion faces in the world today.

We describe our present time as one in transition between "modernity" and a new, or "postmodern," era that seems to be emerging. To understand what is "new" about our situation, we will have to understand the premodern period of the different religious traditions and how the premodern worldview of each relates to and contrasts with the modern period. In particular we will have to compare the premodern period in each tradition with the changes brought about by an era that began with the rise of modern science after 1500 and declined after World War II. In surveying world religions today, we shall not be able to cover everything that could be said about them. Our selection will be governed primarily by the following question: What do we need to know about the past to understand the role of religion in the world we live in today? To begin, we must introduce some core concepts.

With the Space Age, awareness that all humans share life in a global village has come to the religions and cultures of the earth.

Understanding Religious Experience and Its Expressions

First we need a working definition of the term **religion**. To help explain how we are using the term, let's suppose we have a time machine and can transport ourselves back to the city of Rome in the first century. Why are we interested in that time and place? The word *religion* has its roots in Latin, the language of the Romans, so understanding how the Romans defined the concept should help us understand our topic.

Imagine yourself now walking down a street in Rome in the first century BCE. You approach a small group of people on a street corner and ask them: "What religion are you?" They look at you strangely. They understand the individual words you have spoken, but they don't normally put those words together as you have done. Some give you blank stares, while others just look puzzled. Frustrated, you try rephrasing your question: "Are you religious?" Suddenly their faces light up and they smile and say, "Of course, isn't everyone?"

By its wording, the original question assumes that religion is a noun applied to distinct social bodies in the world, such that you can be a member of one only if you are not a member of another. So the question seeks to find out the distinct religious group to which you belong. This way of understanding religion naturally arises among monotheists, who by definition have chosen one god and excluded all others. However, such an exclusiveness was foreign to antiquity, and it also is not appropriate today for studying religious traditions among many African and Asian peoples.

In rephrasing the original question as "Are you religious?" you are no longer treating *religion* as a noun, describing something you join. Instead, you are treating it as an adjective, describing an attitude toward the human condition—a way of seeing, acting, and experiencing all things. In most times and places throughout history, religion and culture were like two sides of the same coin. Therefore people did not think of their practices as "a religion"—a separate reality they had to choose over and against another. Today in Japan, for instance, it is possible to follow Buddhism, Daoism, Confucianism, and Shintoism at the same time. This seems odd from the monotheistic perspective of Western religions, where one can be, for instance, either a Muslim or a Jew but not both at the same time. And yet, paradoxically, Jews and Muslims claim to worship the same God.

In first-century Rome, with very few exceptions, people didn't belong to a religion in any exclusive sense. They were, however, religious. Our first-century respondents would probably continue the discussion you had started something like this: "Am I religious? Of course I am. Isn't everyone? It's simply a matter of common sense. I respect all those powers that govern my destiny. Therefore I worship all the gods and goddesses. It would be stupid not to. If I must go to war I want the god of war on my side. So I would perform the correct ritual sacrifices before going into battle. And when I looked for someone to marry, I petitioned the goddess of love to help me. And needless to say, when I plant my crops every spring, I do everything possible to ensure that the goddess of fertility and the gods of wind and rain are on my side. I am not a complete idiot. To ignore or antagonize the gods would be stupid."

What does this tell us? For the ancient Romans, and nearly all other human beings in all places and all times throughout history, religion has been about power and meaning in relation to human destiny. Although its exact root is uncertain, the word *religion* is probably derived from the Latin *religare*, which literally means "to tie or bind," and the root *religere*, which has the connotation of "acting with care." It expresses our sense of being "tied and bound" by relations of obligation to whatever powers we believe govern our destiny—whether these powers be natural or supernatural, personal or impersonal, one or many. Ancient peoples everywhere believed that the powers governing their destiny were the forces of nature. Why? Because nature was experienced as that awesome collection of powers that surround and, at times, overwhelm human beings. On the one hand, nature provides life and all its necessities (food, clothing, shelter, etc.); but on the other hand, nature may turn on people, destroying them quite capriciously through earthquakes, storms, floods, and so on. Therefore the forces of nature evoke in human beings the ambivalent feelings of fascination and dread. Rudolf Otto, the great twentieth-century pioneer of the study of comparative religions, argued that the presence of these two ambivalent emotions is a sure sign that one is in the presence of the sacred. They are a defining mark of religious experience across cultures. They are the emotions that are elicited by the uncanny experience of being in the presence of that power or powers one believes have the ability to determine whether one lives or dies and, beyond that, how well one lives and dies.

Religion as a form of human experience and behavior, therefore, is not just about purely "spiritual" things. Religion is not just about gods or God. People's religiousness over the millennia and across the earth has proven to be as diverse as the forms of power they believe govern human destiny. These powers have ranged from gods as forces of nature to the unseen ancestral spirits or spirits associated with sacred places, to more impersonal sacred forces or energies; or finally the mysterious power(s) that govern history (including the seemingly secular powers associated with wealth and politics that get treated as if "sacred"). Religious attitudes in the modern world can be discerned even in what many people would consider to be purely secular and very "unspiritual" attitudes and behaviors in relation to power. Hence, whatever powers we believe govern our destiny will elicit a religious response from us and inspire us to wish "to tie or bind" ourselves to these powers in relations of ritual obligation. Thus tied or bound, we will act respectfully and carefully in relation to the powers, to ensure that they will be on our side. How do we know what our obligations to these powers are? Throughout history this knowledge has been communicated through myth and ritual.

MYTH AND RITUAL

Our word **myth** comes from the Greek *mythos*, which means "story." Myth, we could say, is a symbolic story about the origins and destiny of human beings and their world; myth relates human beings to whatever powers they believe ultimately govern their destiny and explains to them what the powers expect of them. Unlike the contemporary English use of *myth* to indicate an untrue story or a misunderstanding based on

A Shinto priest and believers purify their bodies in icy water for the New Year's ceremony at the Teppozu Shrine in Tokyo.

ignorance, in every religious tradition *myth* conveys the essential truths of life. These truths, in turn, are embedded in grand stories of origin and destiny rather than in abstract theoretical and scientific theories. The world's major religions have preserved their mythic accounts in the most durable material available in each age: first on stone, parchment, and tree bark, later on paper, and today in CD-ROM format.

Ritual actions connect the individual and the community to the sacred. Such actions often involve the symbolic reenactment of the stories that are passed on from one generation to the next. Myth and ritual are closely tied to the major festivals or holy days of a religious tradition and illuminate the meaning of human destiny in relation to sacred powers. By celebrating a cycle of festivals spread throughout the year, people come to dwell in the stories that tell them who they are, where they came from, and where they are going.

Naturally the leaders of religious communities over many generations have sought to make myth and ritual, worldview and ethos, belief and practice, idea and emotion, mutually reinforcing. Yet some of the great schisms within the faiths of the world have been based more on practice than on belief. Rituals often precede the myths used to explain them, with the result that over centuries a ritual may continue, but the mythic explanation may change. In many cases it is difficult to discern which came first—the myth or the ritual.

We should not assume that rituals communicate only ideas or beliefs. Religions are not confined to doctrines regarding the sacred. Rather, they include many *careful acts* that, in their own right, *tie and bind* people to each other and to cosmic meaning. Being religious thus entails taking decisive action at times, abstaining from certain acts at others—offering, for instance, precious gifts to supernatural beings, making pilgrimages to sacred places, or engaging in meditation or other disciplines of spiritual practice.

For devout persons of many faiths, acting in the prescribed manner, called **orthopraxy**, is more important than **orthodoxy**—acceptance of the often intricate doctrines set forth in texts and formulated by scholars. Performing the five daily Muslim prayers, visiting a Buddhist or Hindu temple to offer flowers on the full moon day, cleaning a Chinese family's ancestral grave during the spring festival, or being baptized as a Christian—all these acts are as central to "being religious" as is adopting the beliefs defined as orthodox.

To live well, have many descendants, and live a long life—these are three great treasures in Chinese culture. A Chinese woman prays for prosperity, posterity, and longevity at a Buddhist temple on the island of Lantau.

Dashara

Dashara is one of the most important festivals in Hinduism. Family members return home each fall to share in a ten-day festival. In the temple art displayed and in the ancient texts read by devout Hindu families during Dashara, the community returns to the myth recounting how the goddess Durga once rescued the world from Mahisha, a giant demon who had won the boon of not being killed by any male, human or divine.

As a result, this demon expelled the gods from heaven and began to despoil the earth. All the male gods, led by Shiva and Vishnu, seeing this threat to creation but knowing their own powerlessness in the face of the demon's special power, created the goddess Durga by merging of all their powers. Having armed her with their distinctive supernatural weapons, they begged her to end Mahisha's rampage. With relentless power and divine fury, she did so in a furious struggle, finally severing the demon's head and vowing to remain as creation's protector. During the Dashara festival, each family participates in this cosmic victory, celebrating and reconnecting with the myth of the goddess's triumph over evil. By sacrificially decapitating an animal so that its blood can be offered to Durga in her temple images, Hindu families seek to renew her protection from the demonic. Dashara is experienced by Hindus as reenacting the original event and renewing the goddess's blessings. This connection is literally made when Hindu families feast on the meat from the sacrificed carcass, for it is now imbued with the power and grace of Durga. The Dashara myth and ritual thus perform two religious functions—that is, they "tie or bind" the life of Hindus into a great cosmic drama, and they fulfill the Hindu wish to "be careful" regarding the potent divine powers that make life possible and give it meaning.

What we say of Hinduism is also true of the myths and rituals of all religions.

Hindu women pay homage to the god of the sun during the Chat Puja festival on the banks of the Hooghly River in the eastern Indian city of Calcutta. Thousands of Hindu devotees reached the riverside at sunset and will spend the night praying.

Carefully choreographed religious rituals recall important events in the history of each faith: the "Night Journey" of the Prophet, Muhammad, the enlightenment of the Buddha, the birthday of Krishna. In other rituals, the faithful donate gifts to the supernatural beings to whom they ascribe power to profoundly affect their lives. Still other rituals require circumcision, tattoos, or burn marks to set the believers off from nonbelievers, fostering in-group solidarity. The consumption of certain foods as part of some rituals suggests that the believer can acquire the "same essence" as the divine through ingestion, as in the Christian communion, Hindu puja, or tribal eating of a totemic animal to affirm common identity.

The great annual festivals in the world's religions give devotees a break from the profane time of normal working life, times for special rituals, for fasts or feasting, and periods of rest and reflection on the fundamental truths. These events also reinforce life's most important ties with family and fellow devotees. The need to orchestrate such crucial religious actions also leads followers to create institutions that occupy central places in their societies.

Pivotal figures of each world religion are the priests or ministers who mediate between the deity and the community. The world's oldest religious specialist is the shaman, a man or woman who goes into a trance to be able to leave his or her body to go to the spirit realm and communicate with sacred ancestors and supernatural beings (spirits, gods, demons, ghosts). Practitioners of this art (also called *mediums* or *oracles*) are depicted on cave walls across Eurasia from the Neolithic period 25,000 years ago. Shamans still exist in many parts of the world, not only among the remaining indigenous peoples but also within the great world religions.

Since all the modern world religions have relied on written materials, there have always been scholars who have learned to write and read and thereby interpret the sacred texts, translating them for the great majority of rank-and-file followers, most of whom, until the modern era, were illiterate. Among this group are those who specialize in being spiritual teachers (e.g., the Hindu guru, the Jewish rabbi, the Sufi Muslim shaykh). Although we can point to interesting comparative patterns among religious rituals and between religious teachers, it is also true to say that each tradition can be known by its own unique set of religious practitioners and institutions. To understand the great

A healer from Nepal seeks to enter a trance by donning the mask of the goddess Durga.

world religions thus entails not only knowing what believers believe but also how they are expected to act, what rituals are essential, what distinctive institutions have supported the community, and in what unique architectural settings (mosque, church, synagogue) individuals practice meditation, pray, venerate their ancestors, and praise or please their gods (or God).

MORALITY

In most religious traditions, ritual and morality have been closely intertwined. "Right" is often defined by "rite"—the ritual patterns of behavior that keep life sacred. Morality is an inherent dimension of religious experience, for religion is not only about sacred powers; it also describes the way of life the powers require and make possible.

The religious experience of the sacred—what matters most to a given community—provides the ground for the moral experience of the virtuous life. Whatever is sacred provides a yardstick for measuring the rightness of any human action. The blueprint for just what is right action, or **ethical**, is expressed in myth and ritual. For Muslims, the teachings of the Quran (Islam's sacred book) and *hadith* (stories or traditions about the Prophet, Muhammad) exemplify the moral way of life that God expects of human beings. These ideals and requirements have been communicated from one generation to the next through the ritual reenactment and the recitation of Islam's sacred stories of origin and destiny.

A 2-year-old Muslim boy, living in predominantly Catholic East Timor, prays alongside his father at a mosque in Dili.

This is just one example of how a religious tradition shapes morality. It is important to recognize that even the most secular and seemingly nonreligious morality, insofar as it treats anything as sacred, can be understood as having a religious dimension. In the former Soviet Union, May Day was a great national festival celebrating the Russian revolution of 1917 and the founding of an atheistic state. At this celebration, the values of the way of life in the U.S.S.R. were held up as sacred—worth living for and worth dying for. Although not connected in any way to one of the world's religions, this festival served a profound religious purpose: It told Soviet citizens that their individual lives were important, a part of the great historical drama that would inevitably lead to a pure and egalitarian communist society.

Once we realize that religion is about what people hold sacred and the way of life that is called for by such beliefs, then it makes sense to say that all religion requires morality. We can also say that every morality (no matter how nonreligious it appears) is grounded in religious experience, namely in the experience of what is held sacred (i.e., matters most) in a given community. Such an observation still leaves open the philosophical question of the degree to which a tradition's sacred morality is truly ethical, for ethics is the questioning of our sacred moralities, asking whether what people customarily say is good or virtuous really is good or virtuous.

Thus, we can see that myth and ritual tie and bind individuals in three ways: to whatever power(s) they believe govern their destiny; to each other in a community of identity; and to the cosmos in which they live. This is accomplished through both stories and ritual obligations that express a tradition's morality.

RELIGIOUS LANGUAGE

One of the most challenging tasks facing anyone trying to understand the diversity of religious experience is to grasp the nature of religious language. To interpret religious language literally will cause you to misunderstand it. This is because religious language is primarily symbolic. For example, in Asian religious traditions, images of Buddhas and Hindu gods are routinely shown seated on lotuses. We know that enlightened sages and the great gods are not literally flower blossoms, nor did they sit on them. This symbol is not meant to be taken literally. The Buddha is not literally a flower. When Buddhist or Hindu devotees speak like this they are speaking metaphorically. A metaphor uses things that are more familiar to help us understand what is less familiar. A water flower like the lotus is something Asians know about, but Shiva or Buddha is more mysterious. So the tradition draws on the known to help us understand the mysterious nature of the sacred. A person who observes a Buddha seated on a lotus in a monastery sees that just as a water flower rises from the mud and up through murky water to blossom with surpassing beauty, so does the sage (or the great gods) incarnate and serve humanity in the troubled, clouded, and messy human realm. Vishnu seated on a lotus implies the divine living in but not sullied by the defects and delusions of our world, a reality that can always be relied on.

Not all religious experiences, however, are theistic, reflecting belief in one or more gods. Theravada Buddhists in ancient India refused to use the Hindu words roughly equivalent to the English word *God* to describe their religious experiences. Instead they spoke of "the unconditioned" and the inadequacy of all spoken metaphors to explain their goal, the blissful state of *nirvana* (see Chapter 7). And yet they too used metaphors to try to help people understand what they had experienced as "the blissful," as "having suchness," or as "true awakening." In fact, the word *God*, which is so central to the Abrahamic Western religious traditions (Judaism, Christianity, Islam), is just one of a class of diverse terms used in different religions and cultures across the world to designate the **ultimate reality**, that which is the highest in value and meaning for the group. This class of terms includes not only the God of Western theism but also the impersonal Brahman of Hinduism, the transpersonal nirvana of Buddhism, and the impersonal power of the *Dao* at work in all things that is central to Chinese religions. At the same time one can find some parallels to Western theism in Asia, too: T'ien (Heaven) and Shang Di (Lord of Heaven) in China; incarnations of Brahman in gods such as Shiva and Krishna in devotional schools of Hinduism; and the cosmic Buddhas and bodhisattvas whom Mahayana Buddhists venerate and meditate on.

All these expressions for what is truly ultimate and meaningful may in fact refer to different forms of religious experience—or perhaps different people use language unique to their own cultures and times to point to what may ultimately be the same reality. Here lies the challenge, mystery, and fascination of studying the religions of the world: Do differences in religious terminology reflect experiences of different realities? Or are they different expressions of or ways of describing the same reality? Because religious metaphors come out of particular historical and cultural times and places and because they are symbolic forms of expression, to understand the religious languages and messages of different religious traditions, to put ourselves in the time and place of their origins, we must use empathy, or **sympathetic imagination.**

Metaphor and Symbol in Religious Language

If religious language is primarily symbolic, where do these metaphors and symbolic expressions come from? To answer this question requires a little sympathetic imagination. Think of a beautiful warm summer evening: The sky is clear, and millions of stars are shining brightly. The evening is so breathtaking that you decide to go for a walk in the rolling hills just outside the city. As you walk, you are suddenly in the grip of an experience so overwhelming that it cannot be expressed in words. After a short time, which seems in retrospect like an eternity, you return to your normal consciousness and wander back to the city, where you run into some friends at the local cafe. You order a latte and then you say to them: "You'll never guess what happened to me tonight. I had the most incredible experience, so incredible it defies description." Yet paradoxically, your friends immediately ask, "What was it like?" With that question, we have entered the realm of metaphor and symbolic language.

Your friends are asking you to describe what you have just said is indescribable. To answer at all, you must draw analogies to things they already know about. So you might say that the experience was like being in the presence of a shepherd who really cares for his flock. At least you might say that if you and your friends were nomads familiar with the raising of sheep, like the people of ancient Israel. Roughly a thousand years before the start of the Common Era, however, the people stopped being nomads and settled into a fixed territory under the rule of a king. Although many continued to raise sheep, they started speaking of God as a king who protects his subjects. Today some people seem unsure of how to speak of God. Women often point out that most images of God have been male. Some seek to shock their hearers into an awareness of the metaphorical nature of religious language by referring to God as "our Mother."

Religious language, as symbolic language, can take one of two forms: analogy or negation. The metaphors just quoted ("God is my shepherd" and "God is my rock") are examples of the way of analogy (*via analogia*). In these metaphors, we use familiar words to create an analogy that describes something less familiar. However, there is another form of religious language, the way of negation (*via negativa*). This way of speaking religiously proceeds not by asserting what God or ultimate reality is (or is like) but by saying what it is not. This approach is very typical of mystical traditions. The Muslim mystic declares that Allah is "nothing," stating that Allah (God) is beyond (i.e., transcends) or is different from anything in our material universe and experience. Allah is not this thing and not that thing. Allah is in fact no "thing" at all. Being beyond all finite things and thus **transcendent**, Allah must be said to be no-thing.

In general, Western monotheism has emphasized the way of analogy by saying that there is one God who is like humans, able to "know" and to "love," but in a superior fashion. Thus, God is described as all-knowing, all-loving, or all-powerful. By contrast, Buddhism, of all the religions, has emphasized most strongly the way of negation, insisting that what is most valuable cannot be either named or imaged. Yet both ways are found in all traditions. Some Jewish, Christian, and Muslim mystics have referred to God as a "Nothingness," even as some Hindus have referred to the ultimate reality as a cosmic person (*purusha*) rather than an impersonal power (Brahman). Moreover, we should note that these two ways are not really in conflict, for the way of analogy itself implies the way of negation. That is, every time we say God is *like* some thing, we are at the same time saying God is *not* literally that thing. Every analogy implies a negation.

Our discussion of religious language should help us to appreciate just how challenging and at times confusing it can be to study and compare various religious traditions. Just as religious communities and religious traditions from different parts of the world use different metaphors and symbols, they also mix the way of analogy and the way of negation in varying degrees. Therefore, two different traditions sometimes talk about the same human experience in ways that seem to be totally contradictory. For example, it may seem that a Jewish theist and a Theravada Buddhist hold diametrically opposed religious beliefs, for Jews believe in a personal God who created the universe and Theravada Buddhists do not. Yet, when we look more closely at Jewish beliefs, we discover that Jews believe that God can be neither named nor imaged, even as Theravada Buddhists believe that ultimate truth is beyond all names and images. And yet, in both traditions, experiencing the nameless is said to make one more human or compassionate, not less.

After learning about the traditions covered in this book, it might be the reader's conclusion that perhaps theistic and nontheistic experiences are really not far apart. However, it is also possible that they might be seen as truly different. To pursue this great human question, we must begin by withholding judgment and simply try to understand how stories and rituals shape people's lives—their views, values, and behavior. Perhaps the real measure of comparison should be how people live their lives rather than the apparently diverse images and concepts they hold. If both Jews and Buddhists, for example, are led by their religious experiences and beliefs to express compassion for those who suffer or are in need, then clearly the two faiths are similar in that very important respect.

The Great Transition: From Tribal Life to Urban Life and the Emergence of World Religions

From about 8000 BCE the domestication of plants and animals made village life possible. Acquisition of agricultural skill then allowed the development of the first great cities, from approximately 3000 BCE, bringing about a great transformation in human experience. Urban life drew people together out of different social groups, each with a different culture. In the earliest indigenous human groups, everyone lived close to the rhythms of nature, in extended families or clans that shared a common way of life and lived by the same myths and rituals. In the cities people came together from different groups, bringing with them different stories, different rituals, and different family identities.

The complexities and new possibilities of urban life led to the specialization of labor. Whereas in small-scale indigenous societies everyone shared the hunting and gathering or simple agriculture, in the cities the agricultural surplus created by peasant farmers made it possible for some to engage in diverse occupations such as carpentry, blacksmithing, and record keeping. Society became more complex and differentiated into classes (peasants, craftsmen, noblemen, priests, etc.). In a parallel fashion, elaborate and detailed new mythologies emerged in the cities, assigning special powers and tasks to each of the many gods and spirits of the different tribes now embraced as the gods of the city.

These changes, and others, fundamentally transformed the economies and cultures of the new urban centers. The human situation evolved. In the indigenous group, identity was collective because everybody shared the same stories and actions. The cities, by contrast, were communities of "others." People did not automatically share a collective consciousness. Indigenous persons who migrated to them were confronted with differences that forced them to individuate their identities. Urban life enhanced awareness of how one person differs from another.

The loss of indigenous collective life and the emergence of large, impersonal, and often-brutal urban city-states in Egypt, India, China, and Mesopotamia led to growing human populations for whom the experience of the world was marked by increasing suffering and cruelty. Populated by strangers and ruled by absolute emperors, kings, or Pharaohs considered **divine**, or representatives of the gods, these new city-states eventually faced a threefold crisis. First, experienced as eternal, the tribe never dies. Under the impact of urban individuation, however, humans began to think of themselves as individuals, and death suddenly loomed as a personal problem even as life seemed more cruel and uncertain. With the greater development of individual self-awareness, death presented people with a new and unsettling problem: What happens to my (individual) "self" when I die?

Second, urban individuation created the new problems of law and morality. In the isolated indigenous group the right thing to do was prescribed by ritual, and the same rites were known and respected by all. In the cities people from a variety of mythic and ritual traditions lived together, yet as individuals, each looked out for his or her own good, if necessary at the expense of others. Thus in the cities law emerged to set the minimum order necessary to sustain human life, and it became necessary to develop a system of ethics to persuade people to live up to even higher ideals. Too often city dwellers experienced themselves as living in a world without morality, the pawns of rulers who governed arbitrarily and waged wars of conquest at their expense. Third, the situation evoked a crisis of meaning. Can life really have any meaning if it is filled with injustice and ends in meaningless death? The first written expression of this great question appeared in the ancient Near East at the beginning of the urban period (c. 3000–1500 BCE). This tale, known as the *Epic of Gilgamesh*, expresses the anguish of the new urban individual.

It is to answer the questions raised by the crises of morality, mortality, and meaning that the great world religions emerged. Once city dwellers were individuated in their identities, the old answers provided by indigenous religions no longer worked. Once people became individuals, they could not deliberately return to the old collective sense of identity. The only possible response to the kind of loss of innocence represented by individuation was to move forward and discover deeper wells of religious meaning to account for the common humanity of diverse peoples. That is the challenge the great world religions faced as they emerged in the three great centers of civilization in the ancient world—China, India, and the Middle East. Between 1000 BCE and 1000 CE all the great world religions developed their classical expressions, dividing much of the world among them (see Map 1.2).

The world religions emerged in conjunction with the formation of great empires that united peoples of various tribes and city-states into larger political entities. These new political orders created a need for a new sense of what it means to be human. They redefined the meaning of being human in terms beyond the boundaries of the tribe and the city-state, seeing a higher unity to reality beyond the many local gods and spirits. In China, all humans were said to share in common the *Dao* (the hidden power of harmony that governs the universe); in India, for Hindus it was the reality of *Brahman* (the universal, impersonal, eternal spirit that is the source of all things), and for Buddhists, the causality of interdependent becoming; in the Middle East it was that all were children of the one God who created all things. These ideas about the meaning of being human remain central to an understanding of the world's great religions and the stories they tell.

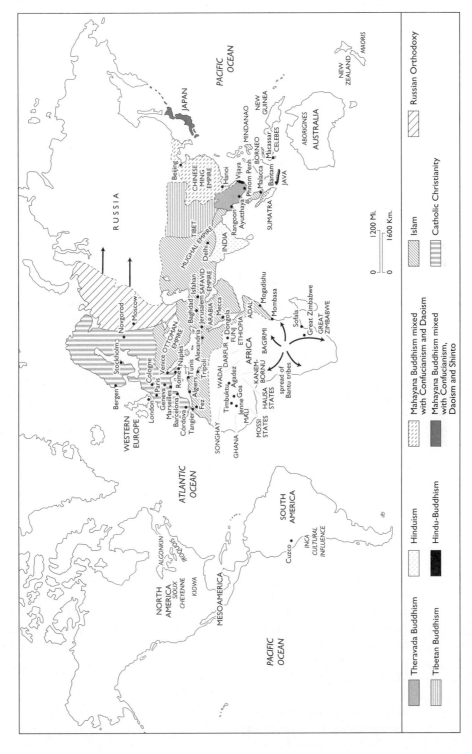

Map 1.2 Distribution of world religions circa 1500 BCE.

The Great Religious Stories of the World

Since the beginning of historical time people have told stories. We human beings are not just storytellers, we are "storydwellers." We live in our stories and see and understand the world through them. Even our understanding of what is good and evil, right and wrong, is shaped by the kind of story we see ourselves in and the role we see ourselves playing in that story. Although religious stories need not only be about gods and other spiritual beings, most of the earliest stories that have shaped human religious life have been.

While specific religious stories are indeed unique and diverse, we can group religious stories into four main types, each of which presents a symbolic story of the origins and destiny of human beings and the challenges they face in striving to realize their sacred destiny. These four main types of sacred story are the myths of nature, the myths of harmony, the myths of liberation, and the myths of history (see Chart 1.1).

THE MYTHS OF NATURE

If one goes back far enough into the history of any society, the earliest religious stories, found everywhere, are versions of the myths of nature. These are stories about the powers of nature that govern human destiny, which portray them as either personal beings (gods, spirits, and sacred ancestors) or impersonal powers. Such religions tend to see time as cyclical, always returning to the moment just before creation. Just as winter and death are followed by spring and new life, starting the earthly cycles all over again, time is an endless loop. Myth and ritual are the means to erase the distance between "now" and the time of origins, "in the beginning," when the gods or ancestral spirits first created the world fresh and new. In such stories the problem of life is time. Time is the enemy. Time brings decay. It brings old age, sickness, and inevitably death. The ideal in human life is to return to the newness of life at the beginning of creation, before time began.

The means for bringing about this return is the recitation of myths and the performance of ritual reenactments of the stories of creation. Hunter-gatherer stories emphasize the fertility of the earth, the relations with animals and plants, the need for the ritual renewal of life in harmony with the seasons, and the role the tribe plays in maintaining the eternal cosmic order. In many of these societies, a shaman is the spiritual leader; as will be seen in the next chapter, the shaman's trance journeys restore harmony between the human community, spirits, and the forces of nature.

Few groups that survive in the contemporary world have maintained such traditions, which we shall explore in Chapter 2. Nevertheless, belief in the spirit world and the shaman's ability to communicate with it did not vanish with the coming of the cities and empires. Instead, the shamanic trance continued into new settings, (in, for

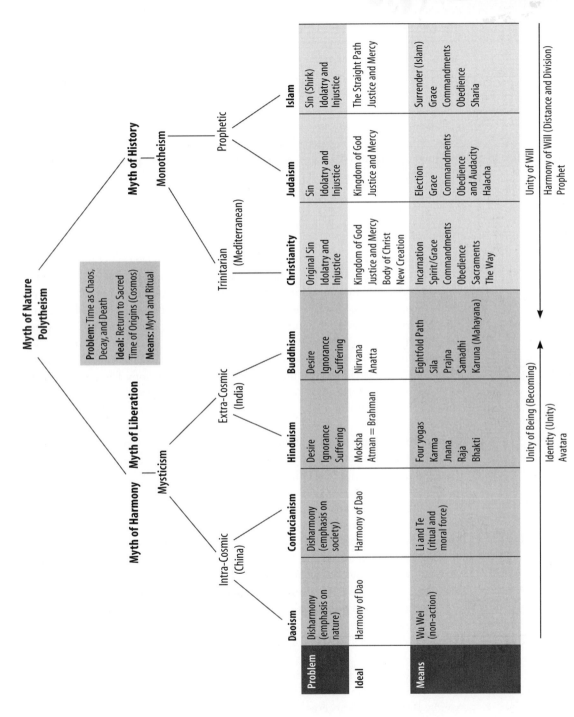

Myth of Nature
Polytheism

Problem: Time as Chaos, Decay, and Death
Ideal: Return to Sacred Time of Origins (Cosmos)
Means: Myth and Ritual

Myth of History
Monotheism

Myth of Harmony   **Myth of Liberation**

Mysticism

Intra-Cosmic (China)   Extra-Cosmic (India)   Trinitarian (Mediterranean)   Prophetic

	Daoism	Confucianism	Hinduism	Buddhism	Christianity	Judaism	Islam
Problem	Disharmony (emphasis on nature)	Disharmony (emphasis on society)	Desire Ignorance Suffering	Desire Ignorance Suffering	Original Sin Idolatry and Injustice	Sin Idolatry and Injustice	Sin (Shirk) Idolatry and Injustice
Ideal	Harmony of Dao	Harmony of Dao	Moksha Atman = Brahman	Nirvana Anatta	Kingdom of God Justice and Mercy Body of Christ New Creation	Kingdom of God Justice and Mercy	The Straight Path Justice and Mercy
Means	Wu Wei (non-action)	Li and Te (ritual and moral force)	Four yogas Karma Jnana Raja Bhakti	Eightfold Path Sila Prajna Samadhi Karuna (Mahayana)	Incarnation Spirit/Grace Commandments Obedience Sacraments The Way	Election Grace Commandments Obedience and Audacity Halacha	Surrender (Islam) Grace Commandments Obedience Sharia

Unity of Being (Becoming)
Identity (Unity)
Avatara

Unity of Will
Harmony of Will (Distance and Division)
Prophet

Chart 1.1 The world's religions in perspective.

example, the means of proclamations by the Hebrew prophets, the practice of "speaking in tongues" in Christianity, and in the trance states of Hinduism and Buddhism.) More recently, the "new religions" of nineteenth-century East Asia were based on the shamanic experiences by founders; global New Age Religions of the late twentieth century have also embraced many shamanistic practices, as we shall see in the final chapter.

The primacy of shamanistic and polytheistic forms of religion in prehistory yielded to the development of the great world religions in the ancient urban age. Out of this transition during this axial age emerged the great world religions, communicated through three new types of story.

CHINA AND THE MYTHS OF HARMONY

In China the great cosmic story that emerged was that of the Dao (sometimes rendered Tao). The universal Dao, which all beings share, is the source of harmony of the universe at work but hidden in all the forces of nature. One's true self is knowable only in relation to the Dao. All of creation works via the opposites of *yin* and *yang*, of dark and light, of earth and heaven, of female and male. Yin and yang are never polar opposites; rather, each flows into the other with no absolute division, the way day flows into night and night into day. There is a little day in every night, a little male in every female (and vice versa). The ideal for human life, then, is balance and harmony. The great problem of existence is the disharmony that occurs when the elements of society and/or the universe are out of balance.

To restore balance, two different religions emerged in China: Both Daoism and Confucianism sought to bring harmony between heaven and earth, self and society. These two traditions offered very different means to overcome the problem and realize the ideal. Daoist sages urged humans to seek harmony with the rhythms of nature through cultivating *wu-wei*, the art of "not doing," or not interfering with the natural flow of life. Out of that harmony, the harmony of society would flow spontaneously. By contrast, the Confucian sages urged humans to establish harmony in society through the practice of *li*, the ritual observance of obligations attached to one's station in society. They taught that people can be in harmony with the rhythms of the universe only when individuals know their place (as child, parent, citizen), cultivate their character, and sacrifice themselves for the good of the whole society.

INDIA AND THE MYTHS OF LIBERATION

In India, life was also seen in relationship to cycles and rhythms of nature, to enact careful, powerful rituals to control the gods behind all cosmic activity. But in India these worldly rhythms and concerns were ultimately to be escaped, not affirmed. Human existence was seen distorted by delusion and suffering, not because there is nothing good about life but because no matter how good it is, it is transient, it always ends in old age, sickness, and death. The problem of life is human entrapment in an endless cycle of suffering and rebirth; the highest goal was to overcome these bonds. The ultimate goal of Indian religions is to destroy the illusions fostered by our selfish desires, for only when these are mastered can humans be freed from the wheel of death and rebirth (*samsara*). In that moment of liberation or enlightenment, one will come to realize the ultimate reality and find union with it.

For most Hindus, the true self (*atman*) is merged with the eternal Brahman in either the personal or impersonal form. Buddhism offers the possibility of removing selfish attachments and realizing complete enlightenment (*samyak-sambodhi*) within the suffering and impermanence of life, achieving the indescribable and transpersonal reality called *nirvana*.

Hinduism and Buddhism, as two embodiments of the myth of liberation, developed a variety of means for achieving enlightenment. These include yoga, the selfless performance of one's duties, spiritual knowledge and insight through meditation, and selfless love or devotion toward a divine incarnation of the ultimate truth or reality.

THE MIDDLE EAST AND THE MYTHS OF HISTORY

The myths of nature, of harmony, and of liberation use the human experience of the rhythms and cycles of nature as the basis for religious metaphors and symbolic language expressed in sacred stories. In the myths of history, by contrast, it is not nature but history that comprises the realm of human experience from which the metaphors for religious experience are primarily drawn. While all religions communicate their traditions by telling stories, only the religions of the Middle East, beginning with Judaism, make "story" itself the central metaphor of religious expression. Unlike the eternally cyclical rhythms of nature, stories have a beginning and an end. Ancient Judaism conceived of the cosmos as a great unfolding story told by a great divine storyteller (God): In the beginning God spoke, the world was created, and the story began. The story is the story of the God who acts in time and leads his people through time toward a final fulfillment. The story begins with an initial harmony between God and humans, proceeds through a long period in which that harmony is disrupted by human idolatry and selfishness or sin, and looks with hope toward an end of time when all injustice, suffering, and death will be overcome and the wronged will be compensated—a time when the dead shall be raised and the whole of creation transformed.

Three versions of this story arose in the Middle East—first the Judaic, then the Christian, and finally the Islamic. For each of these, human beings are human by virtue of being children of the one God who created all things. All three traditions trace themselves back to the patriarch Abraham, whom each considers to be the true model of faith, and to Adam and Eve as the first human beings. In all three, the problem of life is viewed as "sin"—failing to follow God's will, a combination of idolatry and human selfishness that leads to injustice. The ideal goal of life is the restoration of human wills

All that remains of the great temple in Jerusalem, destroyed by the Romans in 70 BCE, is the Western Wall. It is considered to be the holiest of sites where observant Jews come to pray.

to be in harmony with the will of God, whereupon peace and justice will reign and death will be overcome. The means for bringing this about include but are not limited to obedience to the will of God, dialog and debate with God (Judaism), acceptance of divine grace or aid through the incarnation of God (Christianity), and submission to the will of God (Islam). Thus, although the story of the cosmos has many ups and downs, many trials and tragedies, it is seen as the story of a journey that is headed for a happy ending, though only for faithful believers. In contrast to the myths of nature, harmony, and liberation, traditions founded on myths of history regard time not as the enemy but as the vehicle for encountering the ultimate reality, which is God. The goal is not to escape time by returning to the beginning through myth and ritual, nor rising above time in mystical ecstasy, but of meeting the one God in time and making a journey with God through time. Time for the faithful is promising, and the future is ultimately hopeful.

RELIGIOUS DIVERSITY AND HISTORICAL CHANGE: THE STRUCTURE OF THIS BOOK

Each of the great narrative traditions sought to address the problem of mortality by going beyond collective individual identity of the indigenous religions. In India and China the ultimate answer was essentially mystical: All selves find their true identity through inner transformation, achieving union or harmony with the same ultimate reality (whether Brahman or the Dao) or, in the case of Buddhism, experiencing the same ultimate destiny of nirvana. In the Middle East, the answer was not primarily mystical but apocalyptic—the union with God at the end of time, which leads to the resurrection of the dead and paradise.

Each of these traditions speaks to the problem of morality as well, by helping the individual to get beyond the self-centeredness that came with urban individualism and to grasp the essential unity and interdependence of all human beings. And each sought to provide life with meaning by depicting individuals and communities as participating in a great cosmic story that gives drama and purpose to human life. These were stories that were not made absurd by death; rather, their purpose was to show individuals a way to transcend death.

Finally, it is necessary to qualify our statement about the unity and diversity of religions. When we stand back at a great distance we can use the four types of myth or story—those of nature, harmony, liberation, and history—to classify the various religions. As we get closer, we discover that each of these stories has variations, each expressing internal differences in doctrine and in practice. And as we draw even closer to any one of these religions, we will discover even more diversity. Those familiar with Christianity need only recall how many different kinds of Christianity there are. There is such a great difference between church rituals conducted by contemplative Quakers, enthusiastic Southern Baptists, and the more formal rituals of Anglicans that it is hard to believe they are all examples of the same religion. In fact, this range of diversity is true of every religious tradition. So the discovery of some forms of unity in the diversity of religions must not fool us into thinking that we have gotten rid of the diversity. The diversity is as important as the unity, and no form of human religiousness can be understood without taking both into account. As we will see, part of the challenge today for every religious tradition is to make sense of the seemingly irreducible multiplicity of paths by which humanity seeks ultimate meaning, value, and salvation.

In the chapters to come we will be examining how human beings struggle to continue the religiousness of their ancestors in a radically different and fast-changing world. We will see how Western civilization gave birth to modernity and, through its colonial expansion, spread its religious and cultural influence around the world, disrupting premodern religious cultures everywhere. By *colonialism* we mean the political, social, cultural, and economic domination of one society by another. Colonialism is as old as civilization and is part of the story of virtually all religions and civilizations, East and West. But after 1492, modern Western colonialism came closest to achieving global domination. Propelled by European colonialism, Christianity became the first faith to spread globally, forcing every religion to reckon with its beliefs, its practices, and its critiques of non-Christians.

We will also describe how colonialism, in turn, provoked a postcolonial reaction that has tended to divide those in each religious tradition into three groups. **Fundamentalists** reject important aspects of modernity and want to go back to what they perceive as the purity of an "authentic" social/political order manifested in the sacred way of life of their ancestors. Modernists adapt their religious tradition to the insights of science and modern life. The postmodernists, while rejecting the dominance of science and Western modernity, seek to go forward into a new situation that affirms both diversity and change in their religious tradition.

Among fundamentalists, a few religious movements reject everything modern, but most accept aspects they do not interpret as threatening the essential beliefs and purity of their religious tradition. Thus many embrace modern technology while rejecting changes suggested by the sciences that would call into question the fundamentalists' religious worldview. Among modernists and postmodernists, a few movements reject everything in their religious tradition that is not consistent with their understanding of the "modern worldview." Most pick and choose, however, arguing that some parts of the religious tradition must change while some must not. What is distinctive about the modernist end of the spectrum is the view that the human understanding of religious truth and practice is subject to historical change and development, a notion that the fundamentalist end of the spectrum finds abhorrent, even blasphemous.

Our treatment of these issues will be organized as follows:

- Overview
- Encounter with modernity
- Premodern
- Modern
- Postmodern
- Conclusion

The overview at the start of each chapter introduces the basic worldview of the religious tradition under discussion. The following section, *Encounter with Modernity*, describes a particular moment in which premodern religious traditions clashed with the modern worldview and explains the diverse responses that emerged from that encounter. Next, each chapter will shift back to the *premodern* period and begin to trace the origins and development of the tradition, to better understand why modernity represents a challenge to it. This period is accounted for in two phases—a *formative period*, which traces the origins of the traditions, and a *classical period*, which explains its fully developed premodern worldview (both beliefs and rituals).

The section on *modernity* traces the diverse fundamentalist and modernist responses that developed in each tradition as it was challenged and threatened by Western colonialism and its modern scientific/technological worldview. This material is followed by a *postmodern* section, in which we survey the most recent reactions to the adaptations each tradition has made to the modern world. These reactions tend to be postcolonial attempts (in most regions, after 1945) to reclaim religious and cultural identities that existed before the advent of modern Western colonialism. In this way we hope to promote understanding of why the world, with all its possibilities for coexistence and conflict, is the way it is today. The *conclusion* to each chapter addresses the implications of this history for the future of each tradition.

Modernization in Global Perspective

Before we can move on to explore the struggle of peoples everywhere to continue the religiousness of their ancestors in a new and radically different world, we need to be clear about the terms **premodern**, **modern**, and **postmodern**. In general, premodern history around the globe describes a wide range of cultures in which religion played the decisive role in explaining and ordering life. In premodern societies religion provided the most certain knowledge one could have of the world, and consequently religious authority played a central role in each culture's social, political, and economic ordering of public life. In this respect, all premodern cultures have more in common with each other than with modern **secular** (i.e., nonreligious) culture.

With the advances in science that began to gather steam in the eighteenth century, science itself came to replace religion as the most certain form of knowledge. The *modern* period is marked by a tendency to view religion as a matter of personal faith or opinion rather than objective knowledge. Gradually most areas of public life were secularized. That is, religion no longer played a governing role in politics, economics, or public education. The most dramatic institutional expression of this change in the West was the emergence of the separation of church and state. The secular state was the expression of "modern" reality—politics governed a society's public life and religion was a private matter for individuals and their families. From the end of the nineteenth century up until the early 1970s, many scholars even predicted the end of religion and a coming nonreligious, or *secular*, stage in world history. According to Max Muller, one of the pioneers of the comparative study of religions:

> Every day, every week, every month, every quarter, journals vie with one another in telling us that the time for religion is past, that faith is a hallucination or an infantile disease, that the gods have at last been found out and exploded.—Max Muller (1878)[1]

Every premodern culture saw its universe through explicitly religious eyes and pronounced its vision of life sacred. Since all premodern societies were dominated by the influence of religious authority, they all understood and ordered their worlds through myths and rituals that had been passed down for many generations. Modern culture, by contrast, understands its world through the myths and rituals of rational and empirical science. And, as we shall see in Chapter 4, the scientific worldview brought with it certain distinctive features, especially the tendency to reject the premodern past and to regard its beliefs and traditions as irrational and superstitious. In addition, history was understood as representing inevitable progress toward an ideal future, and the knowledge that would bring about this glorious future could be had only through science, with its "objective view" of the world, finally ending the centuries of human hatred and bloodshed caused by religions.

While much more can and will be said in the remaining chapters about the pre-modern/modern contrast, we have at least suggested that the contrast between pre-modern and modern is dramatic and clear. But a word needs to be said about our use of the third term in this sequence. Our *postmodern* situation, according to the post-modernist thinker Jean-François Lyotard, is characterized by the collapse of all **meta-narratives**, those grand, all-encompassing sacred stories through which human beings interpreted life in their respective cultures.[2] In ancient cultures, metanarratives were typically religious myths of the four types we have described, and the notion that they were true for all times and places went unquestioned in each culture. This is no longer the case. In modern culture the primary metanarrative has been the story of history as progress driven by science and technology. However, the globalization of religious and cultural interaction that began in the twentieth century has tended to relativize all such stories, including the modern one.

In the premodern world a single grand narrative or religious worldview was typi-cally experienced as true, valuable, and meaningful by the overwhelming majority of people in a given society. It is that kind of metanarrative that has collapsed in our day. However, our postmodern world of religious and cultural diversity is explained by a new metanarrative of religious and cultural pluralism. In this metanarrative, no single story is all encompassing for all people in a given culture—especially as a global cul-ture emerges and practitioners of the world's religions are found in everyone's home-town. The grand stories of the world religions have thereby become miniaturized. Everyone is left with his or her own stories, knowing full well that other people in one's neighborhood and around the world live by other stories.

The very creation of textbooks on world religions encourages just such a post-modern awareness of the diversity of all our stories. In this situation the adherents of each religious tradition have to deal with diversity within their own traditions as well as diversity among religious traditions. All, but especially those who follow the great missionary faiths—Christianity, Islam, Buddhism—are challenged to explain how it is that the world continues in this ever-multiplying religious pluralism and why their own ultimate reality (God, Allah, Brahman, Buddha nature, Dao) has not led all the world into their own path.

We suggest that there is a strong correlation between the postmodern challenge to modernity and the postcolonial challenge to colonialism. A postcolonial era typically begins with a rejection of the modern Western historical metanarrative of scientific-technological progress and in this way opens the door to postmodern awareness and cri-tiques. However, that door swings two ways, with some arguing for a return to pre-modern fundamental notions of religious truth and practice, insisting that there is only one true religious story and way of life, and others embracing the postmodern situation by welcoming diversity. What fundamentalisms and postmodern pluralisms have in common is a rejection of the earlier (i.e., modern) strategy of privatizing religion. Both insist that religion ought to play a role in influencing not only private but also public life. But fundamentalists advocate accomplishing this by returning to an absolute reli-gious metanarrative that should shape public life for everyone, whereas postmodernists, at least as we will use the term, reject such *totalism* in favor of the acceptance of a plurality of narratives, recognizing the public benefits of pluralism in contemporary society.

We do not use the contrast between *modern* and *postmodern* to describe either a philosophy or an existing historical period but, rather, a newly emerging historical trend. A postmodern trend deserves to be called "new" because it challenges the assumptions of modernity without simply reverting to premodern views of reality. In particular, postmodern pluralism challenges modern "science" as the single form of objective knowledge about the world and also the modern practice of privatizing religion. Today, virtually all the world's religions are caught up in the struggle between their premodern, modern, and possible postmodern interpretations.

Because Christianity is the dominant religion of the civilization that produced modernization, it went through the trauma of accommodation to modernity first, and in slower stages than those religions that did not encounter modernization until it had attained a more developed form. Chapter 4, on Christianity, will therefore also trace the history of the emergence of modernity in relation to Christianity and the West.

Some have charged that modernization is a form of Western cultural and perhaps even religious imperialism that has been forced on other cultures. However, modernization and secularization challenge all sacred traditions and identities, including those of Western religions. As we shall see in the remaining chapters of this book, the patterns of modernization's impact on diverse religions and cultures are quite variable, as are the responses elicited. Modernization did not have an impact on all religions simultaneously, nor did all react in exactly the same way, although there are striking similarities. Therefore, we should not expect all religions and societies to exhibit exactly the same patterns and responses.

A Catholic priest administers baptism to an infant in a temporary tent after the destruction of the parish church during Hurricane Katrina.

Modern Colonialism, the Socialist Challenge, and the End of Modernity

In the nineteenth century the synergy of Western science, economics (capitalism), and technology fostered among the dominant European nations, especially England and France, a thirst for building colonial empires. These colonial ambitions were paralleled in the modern period by those of only one Asian nation—Japan. By 1914 most of the world was under the domination of Western European culture. Geographically the Russians and the British controlled about a third of the globe. In terms of population, the British Empire controlled about a fifth of the human race—nearly 400 million people, while France controlled over 50 million colonial subjects. (See Map 1.3.)

The spread of science, technology, and capitalism along with colonial politics was accompanied by a strong sense of paternalism that was traumatic to indigenous cultures and their religious traditions. The impressive achievements of Western civilization often prompted an initial phase of emulation of Western ways, leading many to embrace such manifestations of modernization as the privatization of religion. Almost inevitably, however, there was a religious and political backlash, seen in struggles for national liberation as indigenous peoples sought to reclaim their independence and autonomy and to reaffirm the value of their original ways of life. This backlash often included a resurgence of religious influence as a force in anticolonial struggles. Most independence movements readily adopted a key element of Western civilization—nationalism—in their attempts to resist foreign occupation and to protect their religious and cultural identities by resisting exploitation.

Many of these movements paradoxically struck an alliance with socialism, the philosophical and political movement that arose in the nineteenth century in Europe among the new urban working class as a protest against the poverty and social dislocation created by early capitalism and the Industrial Revolution. Socialism was itself a modernist movement, sustained by a vision of scientific progress, and yet it also championed premodern values of community against the rampant individualism of modern capitalism. In Karl Marx's formulation of "scientific socialism," it became an international movement that had an impact on world history as profound as that of any world religion. Indeed, as religious societies around the globe revolted against European imperialism, most experimented with some form of socialism as a modern way of protesting and of dialing back modernity itself. The twentieth century produced examples around the world of Jewish, Christian, Islamic, Hindu, Buddhist, and neo-Confucian forms of socialism. In its secular form socialism or communism became the dominant element in Russian culture, spreading throughout Eastern Europe and across China, the largest country of Asia, as well.

Marx secularized the biblical myth of history by replacing the will of God as the directing force of history with what he maintained were "scientific" laws of social development that guide the progressive unfolding of history. Marx believed that capitalism depended on a large class of urban workers, who, once they were gathered

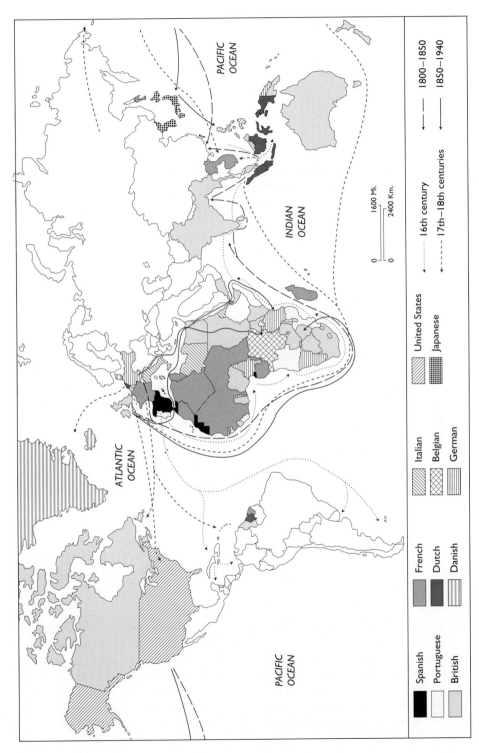

Legend:

Spanish
Portuguese
British

French
Dutch
Danish

Italian
Belgian
German

United States
Japanese

16th century
17th–18th centuries
1800–1850
1850–1940

0   1600 Mi.
0   2400 Km.

PACIFIC
OCEAN

ATLANTIC
OCEAN

PACIFIC
OCEAN

INDIAN
OCEAN

Map 1.3 Missions and colonialism.

together in the industrial cities of the modern world, would organize, creating an international workers union that would lead a worldwide revolution. This revolution would result in the replacement of capitalist societies, based on hereditary wealth and privileges, with a new, classless society of freedom, equality, and social justice for all.

Socialism represents an ambivalent rejection of a modern scientific world dominated by an economic system, capitalism, that seemed to make the rich richer and the poor poorer. Yet it claimed to be "modern," "secular," and "scientific." However, unlike capitalism, Marxism retained much of the religious and ethical power of biblical tradition, with its emphasis on justice for the poor, the widow, the orphan, and the stranger as the final outcome of history.

While socialism provided a vehicle to protest the impact of modernity on society, two world wars decisively undermined belief in inevitable progress toward greater scientific understanding, prosperity, and benevolent coexistence. World War I (1914–1918) and World War II (1939–1945) were the great wars of modern technology that shattered this myth. Science and technology, which had been viewed as the engines of progress, had become, as well, the means of unprecedented destruction. The utopian dream of technological progress ended as a nightmare in August 1945, when newly invented atomic bombs were dropped on Japanese civilians.

The use of nuclear weapons brought World War II to an end, only to usher in a "cold war" between the Soviet Union and the United States. Throughout the second half of the twentieth century, an armed standoff between these two superpowers threatened to plunge the whole human race into a third and final war of thermonuclear annihilation. The makers of the modern myth of progress had failed to foresee that a technology that increases efficiency can be applied not only to the production of less expensive consumer goods but also to the invention and manufacture of weapons of mass destruction. Indeed, since World War II progress in the means of destroying large number of humans has been staggering. It took the Nazis six years to kill 6 million Jews and others in their death camps. Today, nuclear war could destroy virtually the whole human race in a few days.

Finally, it is important to note that World War I and especially World War II not only called into question the "scientific age of progress" but also brought an end to

The Power of Modern Myth: Karl Marx's View of History

Consistent with the myth of modernity, the German socialist Karl Marx (1818–1883) saw history as progressively unfolding in three stages. He defined these stages in terms of a class theory of society that went from primitive communism (tribal societies), in which all were equal, through the rise of complex urban civilizations, which gave birth to societies ruled by bureaucracies, pitting privileged classes against the masses, to a final stage of history in which society would once more be communistic. In this last age all were again to be equal—for all complex, class-defined institutions would wither away, and people would live together in spontaneous harmony. As many who have studied Marx and his followers have suggested, this vision takes the biblical myth of history, culminating in the appearance of the messianic age, and recasts it in secular form as the coming to earth of a classless society in an earthly community.

the modern age of empires. The twentieth century saw the withdrawal of European powers from the Middle East, South Asia, Southeast Asia, East Asia, and Africa. European colonial powers left behind independent nation-states whose rulers were unelected. Many of these new political entities had arbitrarily drawn boundaries. Often, moreover, people were divided without regard to ethnic identity or religious communities, and the legacy of exploitative colonial practices was a series of underdeveloped local economies.

Postmodern Trends in a Postcolonial World

In the modern period the social authority of religion was undermined by the new scientific rationalists, whose descriptions of reality, they believed, explained how the world "really is," in contrast to the fanciful myths of religions. The postmodern world begins with the further loss of innocence, as many argued that not only religious knowledge but also scientific knowledge is relative in important ways. That is, science too is an imaginative interpretation of the world based on faith (faith in the intelligibility of the world) and does not offer the final truth about reality, either. Of course, many today dispute this understanding of science. Nevertheless, these arguments are similar to the arguments between premodern religious philosophers (defending religion) and the new secular scientists (challenging religion) at the beginning of the modern period. No matter who is right, the very existence of such disputes suggests that the postmodern situation is one in which unquestioning faith in science, which characterized the modern era, no longer exists.

From the perspective of postmodernists, all knowledge is relative, including religious and scientific knowledge. Postmodern trends seem to promote a radical cultural and ethical relativism. Some rejoice in this, arguing that it means the end of all the absolutes that have been used to justify violence by some against other people. Others are afraid that total relativism will lead to the end of civilization and the beginning of a new barbarism—that once we have relativized the absolute distinction between good and evil, we will plunge into an ethical void in which any atrocity can be justified.

Thus in the postmodern period scientific knowledge is on equal intellectual footing with religious knowledge: They are equally relative and equally subject to criticism by those who reject their main precepts. Therefore the position that scientific secularism is a source of public and certain knowledge while religious knowledge is mere private opinion no longer seems as valid as it once did. Consequently, the appearance of postmodern trends has been accompanied by a resurgence of religion in the public realm—a resurgence whose diverse forms are responses to both the threat and promise of postmodernity.

In the new, postmodern world and civilization, another stage in the history of religions has emerged, one in which the world religions encounter each other and undergo **globalization**. Until the modern period the great world religions had largely divided the globe among them, with some modest overlap. But in the postmodern world, more and more, all the world's religions have members in every country or society. For example, we find Hindus, Buddhists, and Muslims in significant numbers in virtually all large American and European cities and increasingly in smaller ones. Anyone using the Internet can view the major temples, shrines, churches, mosques, and monasteries from around the world and offer ritual prayers or make monetary offerings to them. This is globalization.

Conclusion: We Are All Heretics in the Postmodern Situation

In the premodern period, people, for the most part, acquired their religious identities because of where they were born. In the postmodern world, however, every individual is faced with what sociologist Peter Berger calls "the heretical imperative."[3] Berger notes that **heretic** comes from an ancient Greek word that means "to choose." In our postmodern world every religious person becomes a heretic, that is, one who is not simply born into a given religion or identity but must choose it, even if it is only to choose to retain the identity offered by the circumstances of his or her birth.

In this world of "heretics," all the world's religions, each of which originated to provide a universal answer to the question of human identity, have been forced to take account of the others. They have come face to face with their own particularism in a world of diverse faiths. Until postmodern trends set in, other people's religions could be readily dismissed in a series of negative stereotypes. When people of diverse religions are neighbors, this option is both more difficult and more dangerous. To the degree that stereotyping and discrimination persist, they promote prejudice, conflict, and violence. The alternative is to develop a new understanding of the relation between world religions and global cultures—one that allows the peoples of the earth to follow their respective faith traditions yet also share their wisdom with each other in an atmosphere of mutual respect and understanding. This alternative—to appreciate what we have in common as well as to acknowledge our distinctive differences—has been explored brilliantly by two of the great religious figures of the twentieth century, Mohandas K. Gandhi and Martin Luther King Jr. Each spiritual leader "passed over" from his native religion and culture to the religious world of the other and came back enriched by that second tradition without having abandoned his own. You are invited to embark on a similar journey through the study of the world's religions today.

Discussion Questions

1. Define religion, myth, and ritual, and explain the possible relations among them.
2. How do the authors understand the relationship between religion and morality?

3. In what way does religious language complicate the question of whether there is agreement or disagreement between religions on various issues? Describe in terms of the *via analogia* and the *via negativa*, giving examples of each.

4. Explain the four types of religious story and give an historical example of each.

5. Why did urbanization lead to the emergence of the great world religions? That is, what new urban problems did these religions address?

6. What is colonialism, and what is its significance for the religions and cultures in the modern period?

7. How are the terms *premodern, modern*, and *postmodern* being used in this text, and how are they related to modern colonialism?

8. According to the authors, modernization privatizes religion, whereas in premodern and postmodern religious movements religion plays a public role in society but in different ways. Explain.

9. Explain Marxist socialism, and tell why it was an attractive option to religious movements protesting modernity.

10. How might you justify the statement that both postmodernist and fundamentalist religious movements are examples of Peter Berger's "heretical imperative"?

Key Terms

divine	postmodern
ethical	premodern
fundamentalist	religion
globalization	ritual
heretic	secular
metanarrative	sympathetic imagination
modern	transcendent
myth	ultimate reality
orthodoxy	*via analogia*
orthopraxy	*via negativa*

Notes

1. F. Max Muller, *Lectures on the Origin and Growth of Religion as Illustrated by the Religions of India* (London: Longmans Green, 1880), p. 218.
2. Jean-François Lyotard, *The Postmodern Condition: A Report on Knowledge* (Minneapolis: University of Minnesota Press, 1984).
3. Peter Berger, *The Heretical Imperative* (New York: Doubleday, 1979), p. 60.

2

Indigenous Religions

⚜ Overview

Across all the earth's continents today are thousands of different *indigenous peoples*, ethnic groups whose ties to their group and the land go back a millennium or longer. Some have migrated to new homelands and changed their economies in recent centuries; others have been relocated in recent generations to "reservations" within modern states; still others (in growing numbers) live in two worlds, moving between life in their modern countries and their native group. Indigenous peoples today defy easy characterization: In remote Highland New Guinea, the village headman wears only a penis sheath as he performs a ritual to protect his home; more typical is a Kayapo chief in the Amazon rain forest who one day dresses in little more than body paint and on another wears western clothes; a visit to a Mongolian nomad today might find him out herding his Bactrian camels on a Honda motorcycle or off to visit a shaman whose day job is as a government official.

None of the indigenous peoples (or *first peoples*) that have survived until today are unaffected by the modern world and its trade, technologies, or communications. The cultural traditions and religious lives of these peoples in every instance have been altered, often dramatically, by outsiders encroaching on their lands, exposing them to new diseases, and imposing laws enacted by new, modern nations; the more numerous outsiders have used law and naked force to expropriate their land's resources by either isolating them or assimilating them into the majority citizenry. Around the world and over recent centuries, hundreds of indigenous groups have succumbed or been assimilated, their religions like their languages forever extinguished.

The religious traditions covered in this chapter stand in contrast, at least in part, to those of the great world religions covered in this volume. Yet these indigenous

Timeline

4 MILLION YEARS AGO	first hominids
2 MILLION	first tools
1/2 MILL	fire domesticated
100,000	*Homo sapiens*: Neanderthals and another line present evidence of ritual burial
40,000 BCE	Modern man biologically; hunting-gathering societies found across Africa and Eurasia
	Humans just "another animal" on earth
30,000	Human language and symbolic thought reach new level of advancement
15,000	Human burials across Africa and Eurasia with offerings, reflecting afterlife belief
10,000	Migrations of humans from Siberia disperse across North and South America via Bering Strait
9,000	Domestication of sheep/goats;
7,000	Beginnings of settled agriculture, first cities
5,000	Earliest archaeological evidence of Aboriginal belief connected with the Rainbow Serpent, perhaps the oldest continuing belief in the world
2,000	Major states arise on the Yellow River, China; Indus River, India; Babylon on Tigris-Euphrates; Nile in Egypt
800 BCE–**200** CE	Axial Age, era of lasting formulations of social-spiritual teachings defining ethical modes of human existence in cities
100 BCE	States expanding into wilderness frontiers; axial age traditions legitimate expansion, assimilation of indigenous peoples
1400	Growing populations in Americas live in hierarchically organized chiefdoms or small kingdoms
1492 CE	Columbus reaches America. He writes that the native peoples encountered "are the best people in the world and above all the gentlest." His record is nonetheless filled with accounts of enslavement, murder, and rape
1492–1600	Europeans make first contact with native peoples of Atlantic, then Pacific coasts of the western hemisphere continents
	Introduction of the horse alters human ecology across the "new world"
	Peoples having no natural immunological defenses to Eurasian microbes succumb to diseases in great numbers; 90 percent mortality in many settlements
	Christian missionaries travel on the networks of exploration and empire, making Christianity the world's first global religion
1546	The "New Laws" barring enslavement of indigenous peoples were repealed at the insistence of New World colonists, who developed societies and economies dependent on slave labor
1606	Earliest recorded contact between Europeans and Australian Aborigines
1616	Smallpox epidemic decimates native tribes in New England region

1709	A slave market erected on Wall Street in New York; negroes and Native American men, women, and children are daily declared the property of the highest cash bidder
1716	Alamo Mission in San Antonio is authorized by the viceroy of Mexico. The mission becomes an educational center for Native Americans who converted to Christianity
1746	From Boston, Massachusetts, call is issued to the Christians of the New World to enter into a seven-year "Concert of Prayer" for missionary work
1808–1811	Tecumseh, Chief of the Shawnees, organizes a defensive confederacy of Northwest frontier tribes to make the Ohio River a permanent boundary between the United States and Indian land
1811	William Henry Harrison, governor of Ohio, leads the ferocious Battle of Tippecanoe that destroys Tecumseh's town as well as the remnants of Tecumseh's indigenous confederacy
1830	Indian Removal Act passed, and from 1830 to 1840 thousands are forcibly removed west of the Mississippi
1838	"Trail of tears" when forced migration of Native Americans to Oklahoma enforced across the country by military
1850–1875	Hunting by American colonists leads to near-extermination of buffalo herds, endangering Plains Indians' survival
1871	1871 Indian Appropriation Act specifies that no tribe thereafter would be recognized as an independent nation
1876	Colonel George Custer leads army attack on assembled native tribes and all 250 soldiers are killed. The *New York Times* refers to the Native Americans who fought them as "red devils." Army orders, "Attack and kill every male Indian over twelve years of age."
1888	The phrase *White Australia Policy* articulated in Brisbane
1889–1890	Wovoka, the Paiute spiritual leader, has vision and spreads message of the Ghost Dance
1890	Massacre of Sioux at Wounded Knee, South Dakota
1910	Bwiti, a West Central African religion, is founded among the forest-dwelling Babongo and Mitsogo people of Gabon and the Fang people of Gabon and Cameroon. Modern Bwiti is syncretistic, incorporating animism, ancestor worship, and Christianity into its belief system
1918	Native American Church founded in Oklahoma. The church combines an ancient use of peyote with Christian beliefs of morality and self-respect. Church prohibits alcohol, requires monogamy and family responsibility, and promotes hard work
1920	Santo Daime, a syncretistic religion based on ceremonial ayahuasca (called *daime*) ingestion is begun in western Brazil by Raimundo Irineu Serra. He attracted followers in the 1930s, and the movement grows over the twentieth century throughout Brazil, now with affiliates in North America, Europe, and Japan
1930	Stalin begins Soviet repression of shamans in Siberia and in their satellite, Outer Mongolia, that lasts until 1989

Timeline (*continued*)

1950	People's Republic of China labels shamanism as "superstition" and represses spirit mediums of all sorts across China
1951	Australian government formally adopts a policy of assimilation in regard to aboriginal people.
1961	União do Vegetal is founded by Jose Porto Velho. A syncretistic religion based on the use of Ayahuasca and elements of folk Christianity, shamanism, and ancient Incan soul traditions. In 2007, it claims over 10,000 members, about 130 of whom are in the United States, with a branch in Santa Fe, New Mexico.
1975	The Australian Senate acknowledges prior ownership of country by aboriginal people and seeks compensation for their dispossession. The World Council of Indigenous People is founded.

peoples and their religions remain a noteworthy part of the world's religious landscape today, despite their small populations and each group's limited global dispersion. None possess the literary texts, complex institutions, or transregional diasporas that characterize, say, Islam or Buddhism. Each indigenous group, in its usually limited home territory, lives and perpetuates its traditions in relative isolation. While each group speaks a related dialect and may have some common traits in its religious tradition, the pluralism and diversity of the many indigenous peoples reflects their relative isolation.

These independent, ethnic, and land-bounded religions are themselves worthy of study; they also help us understand the general phenomenon of humanity as a religious species. The treatment of indigenous peoples by the great world religions gives us important insights about the latter's role in the historical expansion of early states and modern nations; and we can see beliefs and practices of the world's indigenous religions being assimilated into the new religions forming across the globe today.

This chapter will begin by looking back to prehistory to understand the long history of some of the common worldviews, religious roles, and ritual practices evident among early *Homo sapiens* and the world's last living hunter–gatherers and simple agriculturalists. We will then examine through case studies a representative sampling of indigenous religions across the globe today. The world's surviving indigenous religions would best be represented, due to their richness and diversity, by a series of chapters devoted to each one. The scope of this textbook precludes this, however; the short, introductory treatment here inevitably requires making generalizations and relies on somewhat arbitrary but representative case studies. Beyond conveying an awareness of the spiritual vitality and the neglected histories of these

1978	Religious Freedom Act promises to "protect and preserve" for Native Americans "freedom to believe, express, and exercise" traditional religions, "including but not limited to access to sites, use and possession of sacred objects, and the freedom to worship through ceremonial and traditional rites."
1989	Kayapo people joined by international indigenous group rights advocates to protest dam project at Altamira
1992	Australian High Court rules that native title to land has not been extinguished, rejecting 200-year settler claims that aboriginal lands *were terra nullius,* "no one's land."
2004	Smithsonian Institution's National Museum of the American Indian opens in Washington, DC.
2008	Australian and Canadian governments issue formal apologies to aboriginal peoples for policies detrimental to integrity of lives, including forcibly sending children to Christian boarding schools.

extraordinary indigenous traditions, we want to show that understanding religions today is enriched by seeing how all humanity, even in isolated nonliterate groups, has always been "religious:" through the vitality of group life, employing dance and song, alternating feasting and fasting, and by some individuals' periodically seeking extraordinary spiritual experiences.

Issues of Terminology and Imagination: Primitive, Indigenous

Writers who wish to refer to the peoples living in simple subsistence societies, both modern and prehistoric, face a problem of nomenclature. The term *primitive* was once popular, but it falsely suggests a lack of cultural development or factual understanding, since in fact many native peoples have complex languages and mythologies. In choosing the term *indigenous religions,* we are implying that the social and religious lives of a given people are rooted deeply in a given place. This first mode of religious life known in the record of human history is inextricably bound to the life of small groups. The reader should note that we are not equating modern hunter-gatherers with humans living in this mode of life 30,000 years ago or suggesting that these contemporary groups are "living fossils," since none today live isolated from the developed world and all have distinct histories. The term *indigenous religion* until recent times referred to peoples living in premodern modes of subsistence, either as hunter-gatherers or utilizing nonmechanical agricultural methods. In growing numbers, indigenous peoples today are quickly learning about the legal systems of modern states and selectively adopting modern technologies in an attempt to preserve their lands and to ensure their culture's adaptation and survival.

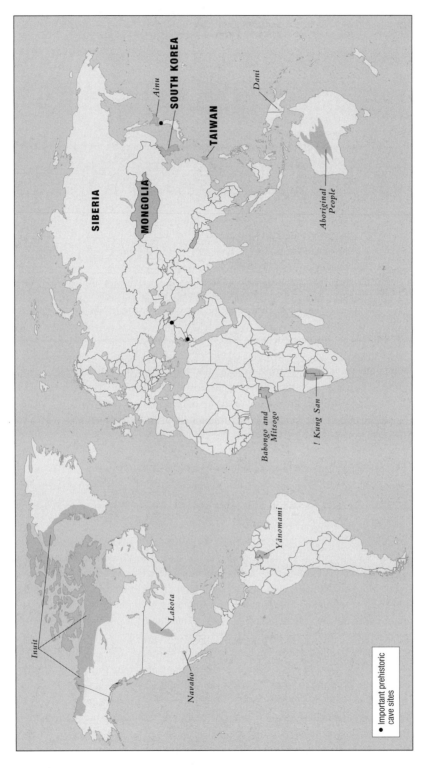

Map 2.1 Locations of some of the prehistoric and ethnographic cultural groups discussed in this book.

Origins of *Homo religiosus:* Prehistory

At some point around a hundred thousand years ago, *Homo sapiens* emerged from a 4-million-year process of hominid evolution to become the animal who speaks, makes tools, buries its dead, and thinks symbolically. Long before agriculture and urbanization, the first *Homo sapiens* lived in hunter-gatherer societies. By studying their artifacts as well as the small-scale societies that still subsist in this mode of life, we can imagine what their existence was like. We know our ancestors lived and ate well, yet without the material possessions and conveniences we now consider to be essential. We know they made efforts to communicate with the spirits of their ancestors and with animals. We also think that they regularly sought assistance from these spirits through trance and altered states of consciousness, which may have been the origins of religion.

Just as the core meanings of modern words can be discovered by uncovering their root derivations, so can our appreciation of world religions today be enriched by understanding religion's origins in prehistory, the characteristics of indigenous religions, and their existence in the world today.

Although the earliest humans used language, writing had not yet been invented. Consequently these societies had oral cultures in which everything that was known was known only because someone remembered it. And memories were made readily accessible because they were expressed in stories—stories of sacred ancestors, spirit beings, and heroes. These stories were not expressed in written texts but kept alive in song and dance.

Moreover, time and space were not cold abstractions but were reckoned according to ancestral myths and sacred experiences. Religion likely began at sites where people believed the powers that govern the universe first manifested themselves. Whether in sacred groves, on riverbanks, or on mountaintops, human beings experienced such places of revelation as "centers of the world" (*axes mundi*). Indeed, in the indigenous religions, most everything is spiritually alive, a collective of living entities to which people must relate. The trees, the mountains, the rivers, special stones, animals, and, of course, humans are said to have souls or spirits that give them life, or *animate,* them. Anthropologists once used the term **animism** to describe a worldview in which a measure of conscious life is attributed to a variety of entities.

Each of the thousands of indigenous peoples have (or had) a unique **cosmogony**, or account of the world's origins and the manifestation of its essential powers. Because in most cosmogonies the group was a part of the everlasting cycle of nature's rhythms, the group is assumed to be an integral part of the cosmos. Everything in premodern indigenous group life reinforced a collective sense of common identity: All shared the same occupations (hunting and gathering, simple agriculture), the same myths, and the same rituals; and all were integral to the group. As a result, a person's identity was not tied primarily to unique and transitory individual experiences but deeply embedded in the collective identity and fate of the group. The group lives on and the individual can stay connected to it, even after his or her own death.

This collective worldview is radically different from the extreme individualism, and social fragmentation that has evolved in many modern global contexts today. In the following chapters on the world's great religions, we will show how each in its own way pushed humanity, at least in part, out of the collective community mind-set and toward greater individualism. Comprehending the features of indigenous religions will make it clear how the world religions have some of the basic features of the earliest religious traditions, yet also how they have simultaneously reinterpreted and transposed them as the details of human existence have changed.

Our human nature endows us with certain qualities that underlie the most basic expressions of religion. These include a propensity for repetitive behaviors (ritual), a virtually unique cognitive ability to create meaning (symbols, ritual acts), the enhancement of survival by identification with land or territory (sacred space), and a strong mother-offspring bond (devotion).

Archaeologists have ascertained that about 30,000 years ago humans—who possessed the same physiology and cognitive capacity as we do—established themselves across Eurasia. They wove cloth for clothes, used finely wrought fishhooks, constructed boats that crossed large bodies of water, and were experts in subsistence wherever they lived, from the tropics up to the edge of the Ice Age glaciers. The record of human life indicates that in every society over the last 100,000 years, a progressive complexity in the mastery of tools was accompanied by the development of language ability and the unmistakable presence of religion.

The universality of religion in human societies even led Mircea Eliade, a pioneering scholar of comparative religions, to call our species **Homo religiosus**, or "religious humanity." In fact, now as well as from the earliest days of the modern species, religion has been at the center of human culture, reshaping social life. Thus, we can say that religion has always been an integral, at times even essential part of humanity's evolutionary path, from supporting the success of small hunter-gatherer groups to the domestication of plants and animals and on to affecting humanity's prodigious efforts to create cities, empires, and superpowers. We now turn to the very beginning of this extraordinary story.

Religion's Origins Among Hunter-Gatherers

For 99 percent of our species' history, all our ancestors lived as nomadic hunter-gatherers. However, our world has been transformed in so thoroughgoing a manner that few if any people anywhere on the planet still live in this mode of life.

The earliest *Homo sapiens* were much like the people we refer to today as belonging to indigenous or *simple subsistence* societies. Small groups of related individuals (usually fewer than fifty) "lived off the land and ocean," moving with the seasons to find wild fruits and vegetables and to be close to the animals or fish they hunted. Close-knit bonds within these living groups were essential to everyone's survival, with all individuals sharing the food and relying on the others for protection. Also typical was a division of labor, with men predominantly the hunters and women the gatherers. Scholars have used data from anthropological studies of modern hunter-gatherer groups to reconstruct the usually good lives of early *Homo sapiens* as follows:

> Life lived by our prehistoric ancestors was not characterized by constant dep-rivation . . . with both men and women contributing substantially to the family, the economy, and the social world. . . . Life was rich in human warmth and aesthetic experience and offered an enviable balance of work and love, ritual and play.[1]

The **Kung San** of southern Africa, one of the most studied, late-surviving hunter-gatherer groups, are typical. A nomadic people, the Kung utilize simple tools and build temporary houses. An intricate knowledge of their environment is expressed in a language that recognizes 500 species of plants and animals, yielding a diet that consists of 105 different foods. Utter mastery of an environment shared with large predators is typical of such groups. Once scholars gained firsthand knowledge of hunter-gatherers like the Kung, they began to appreciate the highly skilled nature of this mode of life, the clear rationality of the people, and the very sophisticated languages and cultures that had evolved among them. This new and empirical understanding disproved the theories of nineteenth-century social scientists, who had speculated that religion had its origins in the fear and ignorance of humans facing a threatening and incomprehensible world

The human capacity for language to create and build culture was almost certainly present by 100,000 BCE among the Neanderthals and those who succeeded them, the *Homo sapiens*. By 30,000 BCE, humans were performing ceremonial burials, painting and carving art, keeping rudimentary records on bone and stone plaques, and crafting elaborate personal adornments.

From this time onward, the human record shows our species constantly adapting and refining their material world, and it was by this time that humans acquired the capacity to think symbolically, almost certainly as a result of their development of more complex languages. We who cannot conceive of complex thought without the medium of language can easily imagine the advantages (in hunting, warfare, etc.) that a leap ahead in linguistic capacity must have given to those early humans. Since, as we saw in the first chapter, religion is so much centered on humans establishing and expressing life's ultimate truths, scientists have posited a breakthrough in cognitive ability that changed the destiny of our species forever: "categorizing and naming objects and sensations in the outer and inner worlds, and making associations between result-ing mental symbols . . . for only once we create such symbols can we recombine them and ask such questions as 'What if . . . ?.'"[2] The simultaneous emergence of

Prehistoric cave art: the first shaman. Over fifty examples of animal–human figures like this one suggest that shamanism had its origins in the prehistoric era.

modern humans and religion indicates that many "what if" questions were aimed at explaining the unseen powers of life, the inner world of personhood, and the ultimate mystery, that of death. Artifacts of prehistoric religion have been found that reflect human engagement with each of these realms.

FERTILITY, CHILDBIRTH, AND SURVIVAL

One striking kind of object found across Eurasia in late prehistory is what scientists have called **"Venus" figurines**, small stone sculptures of females with large breasts and hips, often with their genitalia emphasized. To understand these objects, we must enter into the reality of prehistoric human life. Small tribes were doubtless greatly concerned with ensuring the regular birth of healthy children to keep their own group numerous enough for success in subsistence, hunting, and warfare. Further, since at that time all pregnancies and all childbirths were high-risk events and since it was realized that mothers' bountiful lactation helped ensure the survival of newborn children, it is likely that the figurines are related to concerns about birth and the survival of children in small community groups. Some scholars therefore interpret the Venus figurines as icons representing a protecting, nurturing "mother goddess." They have speculated that the makers of these objects recognized and revered a special female power that lay behind the mystery of conception and birth; they focused on the miracle of females producing beings from their own bodies and celebrated the ability of women to perpetuate human life.

Added to this evidence of veneration of a mother goddess is another strong archaeological find: After 15,000 BCE the dead were uniformly buried in mounds or graves in the fetal position, suggesting that people now perceived the earth as a womb from which some sort of new birth was expected. Some have gone further, to conclude that the so-called Venus icons indicate the predominance of hunter-gatherer groups that were dominated by women, who alone could bring new life and hence were expected to lead their group in harmony with nature. This presumed matriarchal period, in which women had superior status, is said to have ended with the expansion of groups dominated by aggressive warrior males (such as the Indo-Europeans), who adopted settled agriculture and came to rule the new, patriarchal, societies. With little more than figurines and burial practices as evidence, it is difficult to prove or confirm these speculations or to declare their universality.

RELIGION IN PREHISTORY: THE SECRET OF EARLY CAVE RITUALS

In the famous cave paintings of Eurasia, hunted animals such as bison, bear, and deer are rendered with grace and subtlety in a variety of styles. Humans are also shown, some in poses that are still puzzling, challenging us to understand who created the images and the meaning of their context.

Again, we must use our imagination to understand the context and to surmise the place of religion. Caves could be dangerous places, and groups of individuals taking the trouble to go several hundred yards under the earth, traversing narrow, damp, and dark passageways, seem to engage in no ordinary task. Archaeologists surmise that these sites were related to the hunts undertaken by bands of able-bodied men. Hunter-gatherers needed animals for their survival. They hunted to secure the meat essential for their diet, the skins for clothing, and the bones and sinew used for tools and adornment. Some painted cave scenes also indicate that the prehistoric hunt was often dangerous: Wild bison, cave bears, and large cats are shown inflicting lethal injuries on humans.

The hunt required group coordination for success, since tracking, stalking, encircling, and using spears or stones to make kills at close range could not be achieved without coordinated action, individual bravery, and strong group loyalty. A hunting expedition could fail if a single member broke ranks and failed at his station, endangering not only himself and others in the group, but the entire tribe, which was depending on the hunters. Having documented similar rites among modern hunting tribes, scholars view the prehistoric caves as ritual theaters for initiating adolescent boys into the ranks of hunters, sites of instruction in hunting lore, killing practices, and ritual. Perhaps it was to these remote sites that elders brought frightened initiates and dramatically staged rituals that revealed the prey the men pursued and established the youths' new identity as adult hunters. Through hunting ritual, young men bonded with the other adult males with whom they would risk their lives.

Scholars believe that prehistoric hunting group initiation ceremonies were held in undergound sanctuaries decorated with carefully rendered images of animals like this early masterpiece of cave art.

Such practices in the service of human survival formed the basis of the first religions according to the definitions set forth in Chapter 1: They helped *bind* a group critical to the society's success, and they reinforced the human need to *be careful* with regard to the unseen powers surrounding them. The second point is especially important if we assume that the elders taught that each animal, like every human being, has an inner spirit or soul, one that must be respected in death and returned to the world or sent on its way back to the animal spirit world or afterlife. We now turn to this topic and trace its presence in a variety of modern indigenous groups.

Indigenous Religious Traditions: Soul Belief and Afterlife

Today thousands of separate native peoples still exist, testimony to the resilience of the human spirit and the power of strong social and cultural bonds. Their religions have been an integral part of their survival, in each case somehow reflecting the group's connection with its lands, identity, modes of subsistence, and historical memory. There are indigenous peoples today who subsist primarily as hunter-gatherers, shifting slash-and-burn agriculturalists, or settled agricultural cultivators, as well as those who have assimilated in various ways into the world's modern states and economies. The traditions of these indigenous groups relating to the sacred, though uniquely grounded in each group's separate historical existence, remain an important part of the story of the world's religions today.

The host of religious practices evident in indigenous peoples' lives across the planet represent a legacy of extraordinary human diversity, imagination, and wisdom. The myths passed down from person to person through oral narratives recount what is sacred to the group: the origins of life, its relations with animals, its connections to landforms, and the norms governing the members of the group as human beings. Indigenous religions are rich in imagination and complexity, conveying the breadth of human spiritual experience across earth's diverse natural settings. They reveal in total humanity's seemingly universal inclination for reverence. The religious experiences cultivated among these groups show how extensive humanity's experimentation with altered states of consciousness and extremes of bodily endurance has been, while the range of carefully choreographed rituals performed to heal, revere, and express group solidarity details the multitude of ways our species has conceptualized and faced the dual mysteries of birth and death.

The presence of a human belief in some sort of afterlife emerges from the earliest archaeological records of ceremonial burials. In hundreds of excavations, burial clearly was done to preserve the body and provide it with decoration (colors, jewelry, flowers, animal skulls, or antlers), foods (meat, grain), and tools (spears, sticks). These arrangements suggest that early humans felt that there was a nonmaterial component of the self, an essence that "lived on" after the physical body had perished and decayed. Thus

Awakening the Spirits: A Bullroarer

Bullroarers are powerful ritual tools that convey the bond between living and dead members of scattered aboriginal groups, from those in prehistory up to those still used among native peoples in Australia. A bullroarer is a sphere that has a hole at one end, and when the device is swung around on a string, air passes through, resulting in a booming-whirring sound. The sound waves vibrate at a frequency that affects the human viscera, evoking a strange feeling, one that conveys the presence of the totemic spirit.

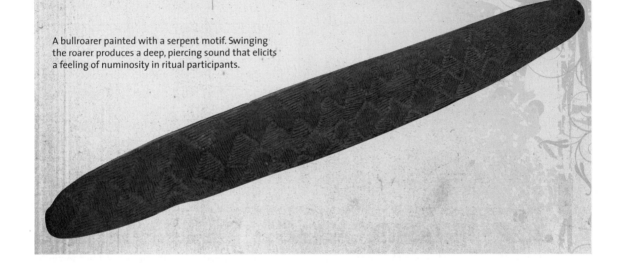

A bullroarer painted with a serpent motif. Swinging the roarer produces a deep, piercing sound that elicits a feeling of numinosity in ritual participants.

the disposal of human corpses is clearly more than merely functional: Death seems to be likened to sleep, not mere dissolution, and the function of burial seems to be to open a gateway to an afterlife.

We have noted the common belief that living beings and some inanimate objects possess a special life force was first labeled by scholars as *animism*. An early and still widely popular articulation of **soul belief** was made in 1871 by **E. B. Tylor** [1831–1917], who argued that religion originated in the universal human perception that there is an invisible soul or intangible spirit inside our visible, tangible bodies. He argued that in all "primitive societies," such a soul belief shaped similar belief systems, positing further that this formed the basis of humans sharing a spiritual bond with each other and with animals, plants, and the dead.

More recent studies of contemporary surviving indigenous religions focus less on belief in vaguely defined souls or spirits and more on the phenomenon of how indigenous peoples actually perceive and establish relations with a range of others, human and nonhuman, through their sensory experience. For indigenous societies today, being religious is not about creeds or texts that need interpreting; instead, people experience an embodied engagement with the environment around them, one in which certain stones, animals, trees, and the dead may "speak" through cultivated human mediation

"The first thing when we wake up in the morning is to be thankful to the Great Spirit for the Mother Earth: how we live, what it produces, what keeps everything alive."

—Joshua Wetsit, an Assiniboine from Montana

Source: *The Sacred: Ways of Knowledge, Sources of Life.*

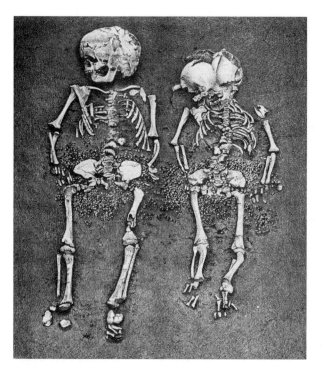

Burial of children from 20,000 BCE: With the remains are perforated shells and remnants of decorated clothing.

and in which emotions, memory, direct experiences, and altered states of consciousness play a part. *First people* typically establish a very physical human relationship with the world, one in which the ecosystem is deeply sensed as alive, as fertile, and in the flow of a larger, ordered cosmos.

In surviving hunter-gatherer societies, human life is more bound up with the recurring rhythms of nature and group interconnections than is the case today in urban industrial societies. The people live by the rising and the setting of the sun, the phases of the moon, and the seasons of the year. Time is circular. This **circular time** follows the pattern of the celestial and natural world. Human lives, too, revolve like the seasons: from life to death, as from spring to summer, fall to winter and then spring and the returning of new life, ever and again in a circle. In myth and ritual and in contact with their sacred centers of revelation, indigenous peoples feel themselves to be part of the largest rhythms of life. There is flow and equilibrium with the environment; finding the good life has always meant learning to live with the plants, animals, and spirits that share the indigenous peoples' own world, discerning their motivations and intentions, their love and anger.

This assertion of the practical and integral relatedness with the natural home world of hunted animals, essential plants, and surrounding landforms is realized through the indigenous peoples' engagement of all their five senses, guided by myth, mind, and emotions. Resident spirit beings that have souls also have personalities and the faculty of hearing, and many command the ability to speak; the myriad indigenous traditions vary, in fact, by the languages these spirit beings speak, their personalities, and the landscapes they occupy. The human community's attuning of its senses to this reality through ritual ensures their harmonious passage of time through the seasons by their finding food, avoiding illness, sustaining group harmony, creating healthy children.

All known indigenous peoples have imagined their universe populated by a multitude of supernatural beings that interact with them in life. Many groups believe these ties extend into an afterlife; some assume that souls of the dead reincarnate as humans or other life forms. Relating with these spirit beings (or souls) entails making ongoing, reliable connections with them; accordingly, indigenous religions tend to be very orthoprax in performing their communal rituals due to their emphasis on adherence to the established rules of human conduct as a religious obligation.

Among most indigenous peoples today, ancestors are in some way still connected with the living; their dreams or visions support the idea that the dead can "return" in nonmaterial form. As we will see, this belief is supported by spirit mediums who serve

The Problem with *Animism*

The term *animism*, though still in widespread use, is rooted in an invidious distinction. In religious history, an *animist* was said to see the world as inhabited by a host of souls (*anima*) that are embodied in a variety of life forms. By applying the term to indigenous peoples who usually worship a polytheistic pantheon, early scholars tried to create the basis for a distinction between them and peoples adhering to the major monotheistic religions. (Tylor and others saw monotheism as a superior form of religion that emerged among animist peoples, in conformity to the accounts of the Jews in the Hebrew Bible.) But does belief in souls truly separate humanity's religious belief systems and its thousands of believers? All three Abrahamic faiths hold that human beings possess souls (*anima*), as do traditional Indian and Chinese religions. In that sense, most world religions are animist. Furthermore, even the monotheistic religions hold that a multitude of non-human "souls" inhabit the world alongside human beings: angels, ghosts, *jinn*, demons, etc. *Animism* as a blanket term also masks the large array of very different conceptions of "soul" recorded in human religious history, including peoples (e.g., the Chinese) who believe that human bodies are inhabited by two or more souls. Further consideration of *animism* as an intercultural term finds it too problematic for use: pejorative against non-Western adherents and masking a host of important analytical differences.

as communicators with the dead, who enable a departed soul to speak to the living "from the other side." Although many in the contemporary Euro-American world do not take the content of dreams or trance state pronouncements as seriously as facts derived from "normal waking reality," like most humans before the modern era, indigenous peoples today regard dreams and visions as very significant sources for understanding the ultimate meanings and purposes of human life.

Death is not an ultimate, irrevocable end, nor does it imply a final disconnection between the living and the dead in most indigenous societies. On the contrary, death is an elevation of one's status to that of sacred ancestor. Ancestors, in turn, are venerated as spirits who can help the living by guiding them to the hunting grounds and bringing prey animals their way or by invigorating the wild foods or cultivated crops. By the same token, misfortune in a community may be the fault of the living, who have incited the ancestors' anger and punishment by breaking a moral law or neglecting a ritual. In such situations, harmony between the living, the dead, and all of nature needs to be restored.

Ancestral spirits are seen as ambivalent forces and as custodians of the traditions. Thus the spirits may harm those who flout custom and bless those who are faithful to it. Some scholars, following Tylor, believe that later religions evolved from early animist views of the world and efforts to manage the activities of supernatural spirit-beings. Recent archaeological evidence suggests that the most elaborate burials in late prehistory were conducted to protect the living from the power of malevolent souls. Perhaps powerful ancestral spirits became the world's first gods.

Among the **Dani**, a simple agricultural group in highland New Guinea, belief that the soul survives into an afterlife profoundly shapes the ways of the living. In their death rituals, the Dani try to direct the soul of a person who has just died to a distant ghost hamlet. Yet many ghosts are thought to return to cause problems, especially if their last rites were not done properly or their death is not avenged in timely fashion. Thus Dani elders take great care when performing funerals, and they erect small guest houses in each hamlet to accommodate, and pacify, ghost visitors.

Further, rival Dani villages engage continually in lethal warfare, whose main purpose is for the men to satisfy a newly departed kinsman's spirit by killing someone on the enemy's side. The Dani moral code includes the precept of "a life for a life." Moreover, since losing a kinsman inevitably weakens the collective community and each individual's soul, avenging the loss of the deceased by killing an enemy tribesman is the only means to restore the vitality of the survivors' souls. In fact, Dani kinship and food production is organized around the central need for supplying the feasts that must be held to mark deaths and celebrate revenge killings. Appeasing ancestral ghosts is always in mind.

The Dani, like the Blackfoot tribe of the Northern Plains of North America, are representative of the many indigenous groups in which shamans are absent or marginal. Lacking a class of priests, every adult learns to perform the most common rituals. But there are in both societies wise religious leaders who are very much regular members of the social group who are looked to for leading major communal festivals based on their ready knowledge of the intricate rites and the success of rituals under their leadership. Dani religious leaders are thoughtful in hosting the regular visits of ancestral ghosts; the Blackfoot wise men and women religious leaders show care in treating spirits as honored guests, feeding them, making lovely home altars, and assembling the finest medicine bundles for offerings.

Religious tradition pervades the lives of indigenous peoples. If they live in the prescribed ways, which always requires them to show respect for the beings around them (human and nonhuman), members of the group will lead successful lives.

Aboriginal men from Arnhemland, Australia, painting their bodies to show their identification with a totemic ancestor.

TOTEMISM: AUSTRALIAN ABORIGINAL RELIGION

Across the world, anthropologists have noted that many indigenous people use a group symbol, or **totem**, to establish fundamental group identity, identify proper marriage partners, promote collective solidarity, and regulate relations with outsiders. A totem is an animal, reptile, insect, or plant that is emblematic of the community and is treated as sacred. The relationship between totems and humans reveals a special circle of kinship and connection between humans and the rest of nature.

Totemism is still found among some Native Americans and is common among the various **aboriginal peoples of Australia**. To understand this belief system, we can take an example from the latter: Members of the aboriginal kangaroo clan believe that their origins occurred in the **Dreamtime**, when the world as we know it was being created. Their myths inform them that their clan consists of the descendants of their totemic progenitor, the first kangaroo, who created them from her own body and essence, established their existence as humans, and then led them to their current home territory, making landforms, including rivers and mountains, and other creatures. Accordingly, the group members ritually decorate their bodies with kangaroo drawings; and before children are considered to be adults, they must learn the distinctive dances and songs recounting the group's totemic story. Elder men pass down these secrets to the young men through initiation; they are most protective of the sacred symbols, the polished wood or stone *churinga* that symbolize the totem and are inscribed with the most sacred maps or tales of the founder and other heroes. The group is also protective of its own "songlines," the myths that are sung to trace in detail the progenitor's trail of creation over the land, an oral record giving the group claims to shared identity and territory.

The art of contemporary Australian Aborigines depicts totemic beings and their role in creation during the "Dreamtime."

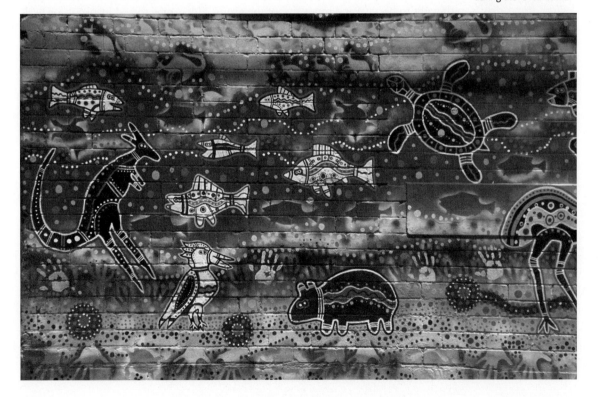

Teachings of Religious Wisdom

Aboriginal Dreamtime

Death is not to be feared, for there is no heaven or hell. At death, people return to where they came from. Life is thus a transition from coming into being from *kar-nannunnge*, or Dreamtime, to going out of being, back to Dreamtime. This living world is only a shadow of the reality of Dreamtime. In the Dreamtime, the humans and animals were one . . . but because of a split in time, the world we live in became partially separated from the Dreamworld and as a result human beings became separated from other animals. Humans learned to make fire, speak language, follow the incest taboo and to have kin. Although this differentiates humans from animals in this world, it does not make humans better than animals.

Adapted from: David McKnight, *Lardil: Keepers of the Dreamtime* (San Francisco: Chronicle Books, 1995).

Harming or eating a kangaroo is almost always forbidden, or **taboo**, to members of the kangaroo clan. The totemic kangaroo spirit that dwells in the home territory is thought to be alive and protective of the group. Elders pray to and invoke it for healing and guidance. Women of the kangaroo clan who want to become pregnant visit the places where the totemic spirits reside, for they believe that conception—via spirit/soul acquisition—cannot occur without exposure to the totem's life force.

There is also a unique and regularly performed ritual that unifies the totemic group. In addition to singing and acting out their myth of origins, all the "kangaroos" in the group, on this one annual occasion, gather to renew their primordial identity and "become one flesh" again. How? By hunting down a kangaroo and ingesting its flesh. These rites are performed to increase the totemic species and give spiritual strength to individuals in the group. Here, again, in the totemic belief system, humans and nature form a spiritual totality: Although the design of the world was fixed once and for all in the Dreamtime, it is the task of humans, through their totemic rites, to maintain and renew this creation.

The French sociologist **Émile Durkheim** argued that totemism points to a key feature in all religious life. It is the sacred totem (in our example, the kangaroo) that gives the group a singular focus and in so doing really stands for the group itself. For Durkheim, religion is at root a cultural means by which members of a society, however small or large, hold their own group's identity, survival, and worth as sacred. In other words, through their collective focus on, and identification with, a common symbol and to explain the unseen but deeply felt cohesive force of their own social group, humans instituted religion. Durkheim's influential theory is that whatever else has come to define religious beliefs across the world's human groups, religion's power to bind us together is what established it and keeps it central to human life.

Shamans: "Technicians of the Sacred"

What happens if the group's band of skilled hunters come home empty-handed after a month? How to respond when debilitating illness marked by fever, chills, and physical weakness afflicts a growing number of villagers? Who can halt or reverse the series of misfortunes befalling a family that has let its ancestral shrine fall into ruins? Only a **spirit medium,** or **shaman**, referred to variously as *medicine man, folk healer, witch doctor*," and so on, can intervene with the unseen powers. These terms taken together designate some of the usual traits attributed to shamans.

Among the many fascinating scenes shown in prehistoric cave art are over fifty images of humans that suggest the depiction of no ordinary person. Two are famous: a bison hovering over a man, with a pole surmounted by a bird, and a human seeming to morph into a composite animal who walks hidden among a large herd of deer. These two ancient paintings may be the first recorded depictions of the shaman, an individual with special powers, whose roles, even 30,000 years ago, may have included healing the souls and bodies of others, dealing with death, and venturing into the realm of the dead. The Kung healers in recent decades have embellished rock walls with shamanic paintings, and records of similar practices have been found in ancient caves in Europe and Asia. Scholars have posited that the prehistoric shamans are shown discerning the movements of animal herds, guiding the hunters to success, and perhaps recalling the errant souls of the living.

The term *shaman* identifies a religious specialist who mediates between the human community and the usually unseen supernatural beings also populating our world. The role varies across the world: In some indigenous societies they dominate in the group's religious life; in others, the medium remains a marginal, often-distrusted figure resorted to only in dire circumstances, where chiefs, priests, or healers perform the group's ritual and healing functions. And some indigenous societies have no tradition of spirit mediums at all. The most common shaman's role worldwide is the ability to heal (both literally and metaphorically) through **spirit flight** achieved in trance or an altered state of consciousness; in some indigenous groups, shamans utilize psychotropic drugs to achieve or aid their otherworldly journey. Shaman healers usually cooperate with spiritual beings and in some places are distinct from **sorcerers,** mediums who manipulate the spirit world and coerce the supernaturals without their consent, often for their own benefit and against community values.

Where found, shamans are universally ritual specialists, intermediaries who attempt to connect this world to another realm of being impinging on humanity. By these acts, they knit together the community in the face of the chaos of disease, death, and discord. Many shamans through their spirit flights return to teach their communities, and through trance rituals they demonstrate that the daily, ordinary world is not all there is. A deeper spiritual order enfolds the known, everyday world. In most indigenous societies, the living and the dead, the community and its sacred ancestors, form one

Shamans Across the World

The shaman remains the key religious specialist in many societies today. The term *shaman* (alternatively pronounced "SHAY-man" or "shah-MAN") comes from the Evenk, a group of hunters and reindeer herders in Siberia. The term was adopted for all similar practitioners, however, because early scholars thought that the Siberian shaman tradition had spread across Eurasia and into the Americas, a theory that is increasingly doubted today. Four religious figures are central to an understanding of the world's religions: the shaman, the prophet, the sage, and the priest. The first is our concern in this chapter, for the shaman is still found among peoples on every inhabited continent and in the earliest records of our direct forebears.

Though differing in details of clothing and techniques, shamans are found across the world today: left, a Yanomani shaman in the Amazon; right, a Korean shaman in Seoul.

community. Binding the community together, the shaman uses his or her body as a bridge to connect these two worlds. If harmony in an indigenous community has been shattered by troubling ancestral ghosts, only the shaman, who is able to visit both worlds and communicate the needs of one to the other, can restore balance.

Shamans have been found in over a thousand indigenous societies, and their practices vary widely. A commonly held conception in the indigenous religions is that sickness can be due to the loss of an individual's soul, by accident or by theft. In some indigenous societies, people believe that illness can be induced by an enemy's inserting a foreign object such as a piece of bone or an insect into a victim's body. The common characteristic of the shaman's intervention is to discover this, locate the object, and remove it to cure the afflicted party.

The trance state can be reached by drumming and singing alone, but in global perspective shamans have also discovered a long list of psychotropic agents for altering consciousness to their purposes. Fasting is common, but practices may also involve the inhaling of incense, snuffs, or smoke from psychoactive herbs or the ingesting of mushrooms or potent plant concoctions. The shaman's trance may be marked by loud breathing, protruding eyes, insensitivity to temperature or pain, convulsions, or trembling. In many traditions, the shaman's soul is thought to leave the physical body, free to fly to the heavens, beneath the earth, or under the sea. On these *spirit flights,* or *soul journeys*, shamans attempt to locate another person's soul, perhaps because it has wandered off in this world or passed on to the afterlife and become lost. A common belief is that the dead need a shaman's assistance to reach the afterlife dwelling place of the clan's ancestors.

Shamans through initiation find connection with a protective spirit, or **tutelary spirit**. This is a supernatural agent, often an ancestral spirit, whose help is required to perform the difficult soul journeys, negotiate with evil spirits, compel a soul to return, or increase the individual's healing powers. In many tribes, shamans have human helpers who watch over their unconscious bodies during trance states, for they can remain stuck as spirits if their souls cannot return to their bodies.

The shamanic world is one in which spirits coexist with humans in a layered cosmos, with humans occupying the earth between an upper and a lower world. The spirits are particularly accessible to humans around sacred physical objects or unusual places. As we saw in Chapter 1, each culture regards these locations as being connected to the "center of the world" (*axis mundi*). Most commonly, such sites are actual or symbolic sacred mountains or sacred trees, revered as places of original revelations, intensely alive with spiritual power, or **numinous** presence. Several examples show how shamanic traditions from around the world today share common traits.

❖ *Case Study in Healing Trance: Kung San Healers*

The Kung San of southern Africa believe that the dead go to an afterlife, a "next world," populated by ancestors, one that is similar to this world and is linked closely to the living. Souls that miss the living return to earth as ghosts and try to sicken friends and family members in an effort to hasten their arrival in the next world. The most accomplished Kung shamans (**n/um kausi**) have the ability to enter into a trance during night-long dances, in which everyone joins in ceremonies of rhythmic drumming and singing around a fire. With this group support and social purpose, anthropologists suggest, the Kung shamans activate a natural force within their bodies, the *n/um,* a power that "boils" in and moves up the spine. The body shakes and sweats, and inhalations grow forced and deeper as the shaman slips into a trance state. Thus empowered, the shaman begins to touch the bodies of others to transfer into them the healing force of the boiling *n/um*. Expert healers can also identify and suck out poisons from the

"You dance, dance, dance, dance. Then *n/um* lifts you up in your belly and lifts up in your back, and you start to shiver. In trance, you see everything, because you see what's troubling everybody. . . . Then *n/um* enters every part of your body, right to your feet and even your hair. . . . Then *n/um* makes your thoughts nothing in your head."

—Kinachau, a Kung San healer

Source: Richard Katz, *Boiling Energy: Community Healing Among the Kalahari Kung* (Cambridge, MA: Harvard University Press, 1982).

bodies of the sick; some may massage the patient with a mixture of the shaman's own sweat and blood. Healers who perceive the ghosts of troublesome ancestors watching the dance outside the community circle may hurl stones at the uninvited spectators or at deities in the shadows who are identified as causing difficulties. The most effective Kung shamans are honored, but they are otherwise typical members of the tribe; most are men.

The most skilled Kung shamans enter into a deep trance state (*kia*) so that their souls can leave the body and journey to the "next world." There they confirm the fate of the dead, investigate causes of sickness, or convey messages between the dead and the living. The spirit flight is a practice attributed to shamans in nearly all indigenous societies, past and present.

The shaman's role is universally regarded as mortally dangerous. The Kung call entering trance "being half-dead" and with great care guard a shaman's physical body while the healer's soul journeys to "the other world." Like many indigenous peoples, the Kung are also careful not to startle sleeping individuals, for fear that souls wandering during sleep will not have time to return to a person who has been awakened suddenly.

Men and women who become shamans in the Kung or other cultures must train through long apprenticeships. But in most groups it is common for shamans to feel that they were chosen for the role by a tutelary spirit, often in spite of their own resistance. Novice shamans must prove their ability by surviving an initiation ordeal that may require fasting and acts of extraordinary physical endurance as well as demonstrating the capacity for trance, the grace of a tutelary spirit, and evidence of supernormal powers. Many shamans feel that they wear out their bodies by repeatedly undergoing near-death experiences in the course of soul journeys or the ingestion of spirit-infused herbs.

Modern Native American art depicting the flight of the shaman.

A Kung healing ceremony. The trancing and healing performed by Kung shamans depends on the community's participating in drumming, singing, and dancing.

FINDING A SPIRIT ALLY: MAGAR SHAMANS OF NEPAL

Among the Magar peoples who live in the Himalayan foothills in west central Nepal, young men study the healing arts as apprentices under a master shaman. Some come because they are his relative, but others take the training after having an acute illness or a visionary dream or feel drawn to healing as a "calling." For a Magar to become a shaman, he must master songs and chants and develop physical fortitude and determination. Each candidate must also show the ability to command a personal tutelary deity by speaking in the esoteric and ordinary languages to which the spirits respond, both to ensure their healing presence and as the means to communicate with the shaman when he is in trance. Training concludes in a ceremonial trial in which each apprentice must slowly ascend a tall, delimbed pine tree trunk placed in the village square, at the top of which a living piglet has been bound. The tree's roots are said to "remain in hell" and its branches are "in heaven." Imitating spirit flight, the fasting initiate climbs up, holding his drum and drumstick, chanting his spirit songs as he enters an altered state of consciousness. Ascending to the top after several hours, the initiate suddenly drives his drumstick into the pig's neck, sucks its blood, and utters a chain of prophecies, sustained by his spirit allies, who are summoned through songs to help in the ordeal. When successful, the candidates fully adorn their bodies with multiple belts and necklaces made of assorted bells and cowry shells worn over traditional Magar dress; they also can don a special headdress made of the bundled tail feathers of mountain pheasants. Their initiation concludes with a blood offering that is now due to and

Tales of Spiritual Transformation

The Peyote Ceremony: Divine Communion

From that time, whenever they held peyote meetings, we all attended and . . . one time something happened to me. . . . I was sitting with bowed head, . . . we prayed, . . . then I saw Jesus standing there. . . . I will pray to him, I thought. I stood up and raised my arm. I prayed. I asked for a good life—thanking God who gave me my life. And as the drum was beating, my body shook to the beat. I was unaware of it. I was just very contented. I never knew such pleasure as this. There was a sensation of great joyousness. Now I was an angel. That is how I saw myself. Because I had wings I was supposed to fly but I could not quite get my feet off the ground. . . . I knew when I ate peyote that they were using something holy. That way is directed toward God. Nothing else on earth is holy, . . . and if someone sees something holy at a peyote meeting, that is really true. I understood that this religion is holy.

—Shirley Etsitty, Native American Church

Source: *The Sacred: Ways of Knowledge, Sources of Life* (Tsaile, AZ: Navajo Community College Press, 1996).

expected by the helping spirits. The master and new shaman conclude the rite by jointly chanting their primary healing text:

> For my patient, I have provided complete protection,
> I have provided safety, I have provided protection,
> I've distanced the crises, distanced the obstructions,
> life joined to life, breath joined to breath,
> blood joined to blood, flesh joined to flesh,
> body joined to body, breath joined to breath.[3]

"The greatest peril in life lies in the fact that human food consists entirely of souls. All these creatures that we have to kill and eat, all we have to strike down to make clothes for ourselves, have souls, souls that do not perish and which must be pacified lest they revenge themselves on us for taking away their bodies."

—Ivaluardjuk, an Inuit healer

Source: *The Sacred: Ways of Knowledge, Sources of Life*, p. 12.

BEAR SACRIFICE: A WIDESPREAD ARCTIC AND PACIFIC RIM TRADITION

We have noted how Shamans can serve as mediums who bring the spirits down to earth for "ritual negotiations." An example of this practice is the bear sacrifice, once one of the most widespread rituals in the world and common across the upper Pacific Rim and the circumpolar region from northern Japan to North America. As observed in modern times, shamans carefully manage the sacrificial rituals, offering gifts from humans in exchange for an animal's life. A common belief in hunter–gatherer societies is that animals are actually spirits in disguise who assume animal bodies to interact with humans. This may have been the earliest example of humanity conceptualizing divine incarnation, the embodiment in earthly form of a supernatural being.

A bear raised from infancy is exercised in preparation for a community sacrifice by Ainu tribesmen in northern Japan.

Among the **Ainu** people on Hokkaido Island in northern Japan, spirits that incarnate themselves as animals are called *kamui*. They dwell in an "other world" mostly but can contact humans by coming to earth and assuming life in a bear's body. The Ainu conception is that humans and *kamui* are of equal status. Although the latter (when unencumbered by a body) can fly and have magical powers, only humans can give them what they really need and want: precious wine and *inau*, the earth's fragrant willow sticks. In the Ainu understanding, the spirits don animal bodies to acquire their fur as "clothes" to trade, for they can get *inau* and wine in exchange. This transaction requires that they be ritually hunted and have their bodies killed to complete the exchange that benefits both parties.

The Ainu shaman performs special rituals to attract a spirit in its bear incarnation. A young animal, knowing that an exchange has been requested and consenting to it if humans have kept up their part in earlier exchanges, leaves trail signs that allow hunters to track and capture it. Villages then raise the specially chosen animal until it becomes fully grown. Afterwards, the shaman addresses the bear respectfully, makes the proper offerings, performs a ritual execution, and releases the *kamui* spirit to return to the other world, happy with its gifts. The Ainu believe that if the sacred conventions of the exchange are duly observed, the *kamui* just released and other spirits will continue to assume animal form. Thus the shaman ensures that the people will have a continuous supply of meat and shelter.

Similar traditions are found from Siberia, across the Bering Strait, throughout the polar circumpolar region, and south into the western temperate zone, presumably carried by the earliest migrants as they dispersed into the "new world" over 10,000 years ago.

A Séance: Shaman Combs the Hair of the Goddess on the Ocean Floor

When there is an incurable sickness or a famine or after an unsuccessful hunt, the Inuit shaman is employed to descend to the seafloor. He sits behind a curtain and says again and again, "The way is made ready for me!" after which the audience responds, "Let it be so." Finally from behind the curtain, the shaman cries, "Halala-he-he-he halala-he-he!" Then he drops down a tube, which is believed to lead straight to the bottom of the sea. The shaman's voice can be heard receding further in the depths, and finally it disappears. During the shaman's absence, the audience sits in the darkened house and can hear the faint sighing and groaning of the dead. As soon as the shaman reaches the seabed, he has to dodge three deadly stones that churn around and hardly leave room to pass. He also has to get past the father of the goddess, Takanakapsaluk, and a fierce guard dog. Approaching the goddess, the shaman finds her angry, with hair uncombed, filthy, and hanging over her eyes. The creatures of the ocean sit in a pool beside her. The shaman gently turns the goddess toward the animals and a nearby lamp, combing and washing her hair. He then asks why the animals are not coming, and she replies that they are being withheld because the people have eaten forbidden boiled meat and because the women have kept their miscarriages secret, failing to purify their homes afterward. Mollified by praises and promises to make amends, Takanakapsaluk releases the animals and they are swept back into the ocean. The shaman's return is marked by a distant, then louder call of "Plu-a-he-he!" as he finally shakes in his place, gasping for breath. After a silence, he says, "Words will arise," and then the audience members begin to confess their misdeeds. By the end of the séance, there is a mood of optimism.

Source: Summarized from Piers Vitebsky, *The Shaman* (New York: Macmillan, 1995), p. 125.

SHAMANS WHO "REPAIR THE WORLD"

Shamanistic healing processes elicit community support, meeting needs for belonging, comfort, and bonding with others. Shamanistic healing practices in Asia heal emotional problems by eliciting repressed memories and restructuring them, by providing opportunities for social confession and forgiveness, resolving social conflicts, and occasioning expressions of unconscious concerns. A shaman's expertise can also be effective when a human group fails to act properly. The practices of the Inuit (who dwell around the arctic region) illustrate the shaman's role in "repairing the world." The Inuit believe that the great goddess Takanakapsaluk, Mistress of Sea Animals, lives on the ocean floor and releases the whales, seals, fish, and other marine creatures that humans may kill for their subsistence. But the Inuit believe that when their community performs the ritual improperly or someone breaks a moral taboo, the goddess's hair "becomes soiled" and she burns in anger, holding back all creatures in her domain. Their legends explain that polar bear spirits often aid in the Inuit shaman's perilous journey. The nearby box shows how Takanakapsaluk can be mollified by a shaman who goes into trance.

The wish to heal the world in Asia today often brings shamanic traditions into conflict with one of the world religions. Shamans in Indonesia are viewed by conservative

Muslims as in conflict with Muslim orthodoxy; sacrifices by shamans in India can cause conflicts with high-caste Hindus. Similarly, in some regions of Tibet today, rivalry between Buddhist monks and shamans exists over how to define acceptable ritual practices. While Buddhist and shaman traditions overlap in promoting social harmony, fostering healing, and respecting local deities, they fundamentally disagree over the consequences of killing living beings. Most Tibetans in the southern Himalayas have adopted Buddhist teachings about karma, rebirth, and morality, but many remain unwilling to abandon their ancestral practice of having shamans perform the "guiding the soul" rites after death. They also continue to offer annual thank offerings to their local deities, this consisting of a deer sacrifice in which the shaman extracts the still-beating heart from the animal. From the Buddhist perspective (as we will see in Chapter 6), killing an animal leads to bad karma and future punishment; from the shamanic perspective, if the mountain guardian deities do not receive their shaman-led annual "red offering," the rains will not fall, children will fall ill, and life will become impossible.

Indigenous Religions Today

THE CATACLYSMS OF COLONIALISM

A theme that runs throughout this book is the traumatic disruptions to life and religious traditions caused by modern European colonialism. For the indigenous societies of the planet, this coercive expansion of invading outsiders and the political dominance they imposed has been nothing less than disastrous.

This cataclysm had many facets. Native peoples of the New World and other remote regions were decimated by the diseases of Eurasia, to which they had no natural resistance. Often simultaneously, the disease-bearing outsiders plundered the native people's riches, utilizing horses and superior weapons technology to achieve their aims. In the early colonial era, millions of people in small-scale subsistence societies were killed or enslaved. In countless instances, the outsiders appropriated and transformed the native lands when natural resources were discovered there. Whole peoples were ruthlessly swept aside, and ways of life that had evolved over centuries were violently ended. Since religion is closely related to a community's way of life, the genocide and disruptions suffered by the world's indigenous peoples inevitably included the destruction and deformation of ancient religious traditions.

Over time, as the worst cruelties of colonial rule eased, the survivors and their descendants faced stark choices. Would they risk the chaos of migration by retreating into the receding natural frontiers of forests and mountains? Would they acquiesce to a nineteenth-century government's program of forced resettlement on reservations? Or would the best choice be for individuals to go their separate ways, to assimilate with the dominant society and submit to the national laws of others? Whatever the choice, the solidarity and cultural integrity of most of these displaced groups worldwide has weakened over every generation. It has inevitably been the young who have seen the limits of their minority status, rejected the old dialects and religious customs, and responded to the allure of the dominant culture by embracing assimilation.

Exposure to missionary religions and their alien exponents often contributed to the downfall of the indigenous religions. Beliefs and practices of many native peoples elicited much hostility and criticism. Governments in the Americas and Australia forced indigenous children to attend missionary schools, where Christianity was aggressively taught and in which traditional practices were ruthlessly banned, including even forbidding any utterance of native languages. Missionaries viewed shamans as obstacles to the advance of the colonizing powers and often accused the native healers of combining evil with fakery: acting as "servants of the devil" while also being imposters or religious charlatans who exploited a naive, credulous people. For the Euro-Americans, for example, shamanism represented the chaotic wilderness, the shaman a shady character and source of disruptive chaos that threatened the colonial order. Under these circumstances, native peoples in many cases had to hide their drums, medicines, and sacred images. They believed that the only way to preserve their culture was to take it underground.

Other native peoples, however, organized in attempts to restore their place in the world and give new life to their traditions. In North America, shamans rallied to attempt to revitalize native peoples in the nineteenth century through a movement called the **Ghost Dance**. After the decimation of the buffalo by white hunters, which greatly contributed to the destruction of the native way of life on the Great Plains, several elders had the same visionary revelation: Their tutelary spirits announced a way to restore the lost world by bringing back the ancestors and causing the whites to disappear. Native American religious leaders then preached that this could be accomplished if all the people performed a new dance ritual as prescribed by the spirits. Soon this Ghost Dance was practiced with fervor across the Great Plains by those whose kin had died, with the dancers falling unconscious in hopes of experiencing reunion with their deceased relatives. One leader in this movement had this vision of the Ghost Dance recorded:

> All Indians must dance, everywhere, and keep on dancing. Pretty soon in the next spring, the Great Spirit come. . . . The game be thick everywhere. All dead Indians come back and live again. . . . White can't hurt Indian then. Then big flood come like water and all white people die, get drowned. After that, water go away and then nobody but Indians everywhere and game of all kinds thick.[4]

The pain of engagement with outsiders is unmistakable in this new religious movement, one that sought to bind a vision of ecological renewal with the restoration of traditional religious consciousness. Although similar prophetic revitalization movements arose later, the U.S. Cavalry ended this nationwide movement in 1890 by massacring

"Our church is the world."

—John Emhoolah, Kiowa leader of North America

Source: *The Sacred: Ways of Knowledge, Sources of Life.*

The Kayapo of Brazil: Selective Modernity and the Survival of Tradition

Kayapo chiefs act as religious and political leaders, trying to retain control of the land that is essential to the continuation of tradition.

The Kayapo until recent decades killed all intruders on their lands, whether lumberjacks, gold miners, or rubber-tree tappers, and were regarded as the most dangerous natives of the Amazon rain forest. Outsiders made every effort to exterminate the Kayapo, going so far as to drop blankets that were infected with smallpox from airplanes onto their villages. But in the middle of the twentieth century, Kayapo chiefs changed their relationship with outsiders, and in 1982 they regained ownership and control of most their indigenous lands, the largest tract held by native peoples in South America. On a limited scale, their leaders have sold rights to cut timber and to allow outsiders to mine for gold, using the substantial rents and taxes collected to sustain and protect their culture.

The Kayapo consider themselves an integral part of the universe, bound to the cycles of the natural year and nature's ongoing rebirth. Returning from their hunts, men sing to the spirits of the game they killed in order for the animal or reptile spirits to remain in the forest. Each species is connected to a distinctive song that begins with the cry of the dead animal. A "center of the world" is located in each village's central plaza, where rituals and public life take place. To go back to the time of mythical origins and stimulate the energy required for life's prosperity and continuance, the Kayapo dance the myths recounting their origins and subsequent incidents, recalling their past to reaffirm their identity and innate vitality.

Kayapo shamans specialize in ritual healing. Their supernatural visions and capacity to contact tribal spirits enable them to perform rites that recall and restore the integrity of the *mekaron,* the soul double in each person's image; at death they ensure that this soul makes a successful journey to their "village of the dead," located on tribal land, near a mountain range, where it lives an afterlife similar to that in the village of the living.

Now that some of their young men have gained an education and attracted the support of international organizations upholding the rights of native peoples, the Kayapo have secured a firm legal existence in modern Brazil. Their chiefs have acted decisively and creatively to selectively modernize yet preserve their religious traditions. From their taxes on tenant miners, they brought the group into the national cash economy, even going so far as buying airplanes and hiring Brazilian pilots to police their territory. They invested in radios and video equipment for recording group rituals and communicating with other Kayapo across their large territory, all to cultivate their identity, ritual celebrations, and cultural survival. Traditional lip plugs and body painting remain common in village life, and group hunts keep male and female jungle survival skills honed; yet these have been integrated alongside the adoption of Western medicine, canned foods, and business connections in the global economy (such as supplying Brazilian nut oil to the corporation The Body Shoppe). As material wealth has increased, Kayapo chiefs, by adapting to the possibilities of modern life, have been outspoken in having their group maintain their jungle traditions and resist compromising their sociocultural integrity.

the men, women, and children gathered for Ghost Dance at Wounded Knee, South Dakota.

In 2008, no indigenous societies remain that have not been exposed to the world of outsiders, with their missionaries, armies, nation-states, and corporations. Some have even been the targets of genocidal persecution. Most of the Kung people have been relocated onto reservations, forced to give up hunting, and directed to adopt agriculture or simple craft production. The Ainu of northern Japan have suffered land seizures and legal discrimination, with few so stigmatized willing to profess knowledge of the old traditions and shamanic practices. Native peoples of the Amazon rain forest have been displaced by land-clearing settlers and threatened by multinational mining projects. The history of Native Americans since 1500 is a shameful story of genocide and land taking, made worse by legal discrimination against Native American religious practices. In every decade, hundreds of indigenous languages and religious traditions are declining in use and disappearing forever. It is hard for those centered in the dominant world civilization to absorb vicariously the shattering impact of the past centuries on the earth's "first peoples." Many groups today are involved with land ownership disputes with the federal government, and they call for the return of human remains of their ancestors collected by museum curators of previous generations.

Some indigenous groups that have survived with their cultures most intact live far from resources the modernizing world has sought: in the trans-Arctic zone, deep in the rain forests, high in the remotest mountains, or on isolated islands far from the continental landmasses. Others have found successful means of assimilating, with members gaining education and employment outside the group and then integrating modern economic life with indigenous tradition. Those groups that have retained autonomy, resisted assimilation, and worked to revitalize their identity show both the near-boundless adaptability of human culture and the resilience of the human spirit. Using the Internet, groups like the Kayapo in Brazil have now shared their antiexpropriation strategies and principles of cultural revitalization with other groups across the globe; their example emphasizes the role of the young as bicultural actors who negotiate with the world outside the indigenous group. They have also harnessed the power of modern video to document infringements on their lands by outsiders and as an effective medium to communicate about group issues and share cultural teachings between Kayapo in separate regions.

Shamans in some indigenous groups were pivotal figures who led groups in facing the crises of modernity. Because traditionally they were entrusted with mediating between spirits and humans, shamans have been the natural choices to act on behalf of the group when the outside world intruded. In the face of repression, many shamans saw confrontation as the only hope for their group, led rebellions, and died in vain defense. Siberian and Mongolian shamans under Soviet rule, for example, retreated to the deep wilderness and continued to practice there.

Religious leaders found other creative responses. Some were inspired to weave together alien and indigenous religious beliefs and practices, a practice called **syncretism**. In present-day Mexico, for example, shamans have integrated Catholic saints and sacramental theology into healing rites that utilize peyote. Another example of

Shamanic Traditions: Forming Modern Organizations

Until recent decades, shamanic traditions remained isolated from each other among the typically rural and disconnected indigenous communities scattered across Asia. Using communication media and benefiting from global contacts that include the Internet,

Asian shamans today are organizing to ensure their traditions' survival. In Korea, contemporary government policies fostering cultural preservation have encouraged the institutionalization of shamanistic traditions, emphasizing the practitioners' professionalization and formal training. Across South Korea today, shamans register and can even attract new patrons through the Musok Pojonhoe Preservation Association, founded in 1988. Similarly, the Geser Fund was started in Siberia in 1993 to promote the celebration of the shamanist epic "Geser" in the republic of Buryatia. This group was responding to over a half century of repression by the Soviet Union that greatly weakened traditional culture and shamanic religion. In addition to spreading knowledge of Siberian ecology, shamanism, and traditional culture throughout the world, it now seeks to include related peoples and shamanic traditions among Mongolians, Tuvans, Yakut, Altai, and all other Siberian peoples.

combining elements from different traditions to create a new religion is **Bwiti,** a West Central African religion. Organized in the early twentieth century among the forest-dwelling Babongo and Mitsogo people of Gabon and the Fang people of Gabon and Cameroon, Bwiti incorporates animism, ancestor worship and Christianity into its belief system. As with the Native American Church, a mild hallucinogen plays a role, in this case the root bark of the *Tabernanthe iboga* plant, which is now specially cultivated for its religious purpose. Individuals joining the Bwiti community are taught that iboga induces a rich spiritual experience, one that allows the disciple to be healed and solve family problems.

Many indigenous peoples, especially those decimated by disease, forced immigration, or land loss, have been attracted to missionaries of the major world religions seeking to convert them. Governments often cooperated with this goal. In many colonized lands, rituals of the indigenous religions were banned. It was also common that marriage was only recognized under national laws if conducted by a Christian priest. Possessing neither wealth, institutional power, nor prestige among the colonial rulers, indigenous peoples in the early contact periods who persisted in their practices were subjected to discrimination, and some states, such as the Soviet Union, imprisoned shamans in psychiatric hospitals. Many studies have found that even after an indigenous people's successful accommodation to a dominant colonial culture, what often

"The Catholic church is a beautiful theory for Sunday, the iboga on the contrary is the practice of everyday living. In church, they speak of God, with iboga, you live God"

—Nengue Me Ndjoung Isidore, Bwiti religious leader in Africa

Swiderski S., 1990-1991. La religion Bouiti, VOl. 1, page 628.

Religious leaders in the Bwiti movement creatively combine regional and Christian traditions.

survives as its "shamanic tradition" is only fragmentary, reduced to practical applications such as healing services.

In a world turned upside down, one in which the ancestral spirits clearly failed to protect the group or safeguard its territory, radical change was inevitable. Over generations, many shamanic traditions themselves have been diminished or reformulated to match the new life circumstances. Under colonial conditions and until today, cultures that were thriving only a few centuries ago exist only in dimming memory. What has proven the most enduring of these indigenous traditions, even in regions that came to be dominated by one or more world religion, is shamanism.

SHAMANISM IN MODERN ASIA: DIVISION OF LABOR WITHIN THE WORLD RELIGIONS

Shamanism continues to exist as an integral part of the pluralistic religious cultures of Asia. In most settlements across the region, there is a shaman who can enter into the trance state, if called on to heal or to solve practical problems. Such shamanic practice today has been harmonized with the doctrines of the dominant religions and is toler-

Protest against modern states is a regular fact of life among indigenous peoples in the world today. Struggles to retain control of the land, secure their legal rights, and insure the education of the young are central to the survival of indigenous religious traditions today.

ated by the Hindu, Buddhist, or Islamic religious establishments that are also by now deeply rooted in these areas.

This pattern of coexistence also includes East Asia, where shamans augment popular Confucian beliefs and ancestral rituals, a tradition of pluralistic accommodation going back to the beginnings of recorded history, a relationship that will be discussed in Chapter 8. Here we can say that given the widespread belief in deities inhabiting this earth and in the soul's afterlife destiny, it is not surprising that East Asians still recognize the utility of spirit mediums who attempt to communicate with the dead. Divination has provided answers to such problems as where grandmother's soul might be residing, whether the ghost of a dead child is causing family troubles, and what might be done to gain the favor of a god who could help end a drought. Unhappy spirits (*kuei*) are also thought to cause distress to the living, so here, too, shamans have had an important role in healing the sick.

Typically, a client approaches a spirit medium today because of the suspicion that an illness is due to ghost possession. The medium goes into trance in the sick one's presence and speaks or acts (sometimes writing on a slate or sand-covered board) after having made contact with one or more spirits. The medium's communications are usually interpreted by an assistant, who acts as the intermediary for the family and community members present. For example, contemporary mediums in Taiwan, called *dangki*, become possessed and rapidly write divinely inspired characters in red ink on yellow papers. Sometimes the objects become amulets for their patients; alternatively, they may be burned, whereupon their ashes are mixed with water that is then drunk as medicine. The role of these spirit mediums has, if anything, *increased* with the modernization and

"Look around. . . . So much of nature has been ruined. Spirits of trees and rocks are displaced and haunt humans because they have nowhere else to go. No wonder the country is a mess."

—Kim Myung, a Korean shaman

Source: *New York Times*, July 7, 2007.

rising prosperity of Taiwan. The same phenomenon has been reported in modern Korea as well.

In most urban communities of China and Japan, shamans are typically regarded as marginal figures of low status, but in South Korea their practices are uniquely honored and sought by people of all faiths. Korean shamans called **mudang** tend to be predominantly women, drawn into the role from one of two backgrounds: troubling personal experiences that led them to initiation or inheritance of the role through kinship lines. An estimated hundred thousand Korean shamans practice their healing arts today, dealing with life's pragmatic problems. Their séances, called *kut,* are usually held to contact a deity to request economic blessings, healing, restoration of good marital relations, or help in becoming pregnant. The mudang enters a trance and then begins to speak with voices attributed to deities. Typically the first statements are complaints of deficiencies in the offerings laid out or about impurity, which Korean supernaturals particularly dislike. When sponsors apologize and promise to do better next time, the divinities usually entertain the sponsor's request(s). A second type of ritual has the mudang go to the next world with the soul of someone who has recently died or to check the status of a newly departed soul.

GLOBAL NEO-SHAMANISM: EXPROPRIATION BY "WHITE SHAMANS"

Traditional shamanistic practices now appeal to those in the dominant societies who are drawn to the mysteries of life and want to discover them outside the practices and normative worldviews of the major world religions. With their esoteric and primordial qualities, shamanic practices are seen by some in the West as "uncontaminated," the last remaining spiritual frontier on earth. Now growing numbers of adventurers, romantics, and spiritual explorers from urban civilizations across the world seek out shamanic experience as the representative of nearly lost worlds, hoping to recover something of value. Thousands of Euro-Americans each year sign up for tours to Siberia, the Amazon, or the Himalayas to observe and even be initiated by local shamans. A number of Westerners (hence "**white shamans**") have created global organizations propagating a purported "universal" shamanic tradition, charging high fees for tours, courses, initiations, and healing services, some pledging to use some of the proceeds to assist indigenous shamans.

In indigenous societies, the shaman has a social rather than a personal reason for entering into trance and contacting the spirits, with a primary concern for the community and its well being. This is an orientation that contrasts sharply with the neo-shamans, whose primary interest is in personal development and a self-healing disconnected from any wider community.

Some native peoples regard this development as an attempt by the conquerors to take the last of their possessions, their culture. Well aware of how much their peoples have lost and ever zealous to guard their traditional secrets, many shamans today dis-

THE FOUNDATION FOR SHAMANIC STUDIES

The Berkeley-trained anthropologist Michael Harner founded the nonprofit Foundation for Shamanic Studies in 1985 " to foster shamanism worldwide . . . [so that] people everywhere can benefit from his groundbreaking work in shamanic journeying and the practices of shamanism not bound to any specific cultural group or perspective." The group also seeks to foster "greater respect for the knowledge of indigenous peoples and ultimately help to preserve and dignify this wisdom for future generations." Extending its influences to every continent, the foundation states that it has sought to preserve shamanic traditions in many countries, including the Republic of Tuva, Siberia, Somaliland, Australia, Canada, Nepal, Siberia, China, Central Asia, and the Amazon. A Living Treasures Program provides an annual lifetime stipend to exceptionally distinguished indigenous shamans where their tradition of shamanic healing practices is in danger of extinction. As trademarked by the founder, trained leaders certified by the Foundation for Shamanic Studies conduct fee-based workshops, introduce participants to a variety of advanced shamanic methods, including "extraction healing, soul retrieval, . . . divination, and work with the spirits of nature." There were over 200 workshops held in 2007, taken by several thousand individuals.

Source: http://www.shamanism.org/

trust the outsiders and doubt their sincerity. Responding to these postmodern possibilities, the shaman is again mediating between worlds in creative ways. As David Chidester has noted:

> Acting on behalf of a community, even when that community was displaced and dispossessed, shamans developed new religious strategies, not only for preserving archaic techniques of ecstasy, but also for exercising new capacities for memory, concealment, performance, translation, and transformation in negotiating indigenous religious survival under difficult . . . conditions.[5]

In the last chapter, we will trace further this now-global arc of interaction between indigenous religions, their leaders, shamanism, and "white shamans." We will also see how the shamanic experience of trance, communication with other worlds, and spirit flight have found their way into the syncretistic practices of many of the "new religions" that have arisen across the world.

SUMMARY

Evidence of religion in prehistory reflects the major concerns of our species as hunter-gatherers. Fertility was important for group survival, the need to hunt for prey was a constant and central fact, and there was ongoing concern to maintain group and gender

boundaries. Indigenous religions among early and later hunter-gatherers and early settled cultivators aided group survival.

We can also discern the emergence of the first religious specialist, the shaman, who
cultivates the universal human capacity for entering altered states of consciousness.
Both serving and leading the people, the shaman has given peoples confidence and
direction in dealing with the world's unseen forces. Shamanism is still widespread in
the world today. Even where one or more of the great world religions has been adopted
by a population, shamanic traditions continue to find patrons. In some cases, shamans
express concepts associated with one of the now-dominant world religions (e.g., the
soul, hell, the force of karma). In other instances, a shamanic cosmos exists side by side
with that of a world religion. Today, shamanism is practiced "underground" if there is
reason to fear persecution. In most places, however, it is tolerated, perhaps even integrated with the dominant world religion.

In the next chapters, we can find repeatedly the imprint of indigenous religions, especially soul belief and trance. Soul beliefs remain nearly universal in the great religions, with
East Asia's widespread ancestor veneration an important example of archaic practices that
still remain compelling and satisfying. Death rites continue to be powerful expressions of
religious tradition, and states of altered consciousness are still an important means for
heightening spiritual growth. The metaphor of human life existing on a plane between
heaven above and a netherworld below is found in all major world religions. Finally, sacred
places that are believed to be at the center of the world (the *axis mundi*) in the early indigenous traditions continue to be revered in the great world religions: Divine revelations occur
on mountains (as to Abraham, Moses, Muhammad, and the Daoist sages), and trees connect
humans to life's sacred cosmic mysteries (Buddha was enlightened under a tree; Jesus was
crucified on a wooden cross). As for the connection with shamans, when examining the
lives of the founders of the world religions, prophets as well as sages, we can notice the performance of miracles such as healing the sick and ascending to the heavens on magical
flights, in every case demonstrating the mastery of what began as a shamanic art.

Assimilating indigenous animistic and shamanistic traditions into urban-based civilizations goes back to the very beginnings of recorded human history, as we saw in
Chapter 1. We will see in subsequent chapters how world religions from antiquity
onward were central factors in the absorption of tribal peoples into states by "converting them" away from their indigenous religions. It will also be seen in the final
chapter that the "civil religions" of modern nations have been focused on legitimating
the violent and often-genocidal work of assimilating indigenous peoples.

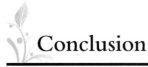

Conclusion

For at least the last 30,000 years, humans have evolved primarily through their cultures,
not anatomy. Art, religious practices, and complex symbols were all present among
modern *Homo sapiens* from the beginning. And all three emerged simultaneously. What

should we understand from this circumstance? Religion is an essential element in our species' evolution: It has helped humanity bond more tightly, face the unknown, hunt more effectively, and reconcile with death. Cultural historians see all these factors helping human groups maximize the quality of their diet, which in turn enabled them to better organize and to better understand and adapt to their environment as well as to each other. With more free time, there were greater possibilities for individuals to specialize and so introduce cultural innovations.

To the extent a group adopted religious beliefs and practices that abetted its survival, that group obtained advantages vis-à-vis other groups. As a force binding communities, as a means of "being careful" about the unseen, and as a decisive factor in helping human groups adapt to their environment, the world's indigenous religions point out the central issues we face in understanding the continuing role of religion in later human life.

Discussion Questions

1. What are the problems inherent in knowing and understanding the religions that existed before the development of written language?

2. How might the history of religions be written by a member of an indigenous people?

3. In many hunter-gatherer groups, the people often refer to themselves as "the true people." How would sudden awareness of the existence of other people in itself undermine the cosmos posited in such indigenous religious traditions?

4. Do you think that it is valid to generalize from modern hunter-gatherers back into the past to reconstruct the origins of religion? Why or why not?

5. How might a modern shaman explain the endurance of her tradition and the attraction of shamanic practices by those living in modern industrial societies?

6. Interpret the tradition of rock and roll festivals in the West and the range of behaviors displayed in them from the standpoint of a historian of indigenous religions.

7. Scholars who have studied tribal peoples now counsel sympathetically imagining indigenous religions as "lived through the body" and involving the entire spectrum of human perception. Explain why this approach has value, given the practices of Kung shamanism.

8. The scholar of comparative religions Joseph Campbell once suggested that the dominant world religions all differed from the indigenous religions by their requiring followers to distance themselves from the powerful personal religious experiences that were routine in many indigenous societies. While you are invited to test this assertion in the following chapters, can you see any problems with traditions that invite everyone to have regular immersions into the sacred as described in this chapter?

Key Terms

aboriginal peoples of Australia

Ainu

animism

Bwiti

circular time

cosmogony

Dani

Dreamtime

E. B. Tylor

Émile Durkheim

Ghost Dance

Homo religiosus

Kung San

Lakota

mudang

n/um kausi

Native American Church

numinous

shaman

sorcerers

soul belief

spirit flight

spirit medium

syncretism

taboo

totem

tutelary spirit

"Venus" figurines

"white shamans"

Suggested Readings

Beck, Peggy, Anna Lee Walters, and Nia Francisco. *The Sacred: Ways of Knowledge, Sources of Life.* (Tsaile, Arizona: Navajo Community College Press, 1996).

Eliade, Mircea. *Shamanism: Archaic Techniques of Ecstasy* (Princeton, NJ: Princeton University Press, 1964).

Gardner, Robert. *Gardens of War. Life and Death in the New Guinea Stone Age* (New York: Random House, 1969).

Grim, John. *The Shaman: Patterns of Religious Healing Among the Ojibway Indians* (Norman: University of Oklahoma Press, 1983).

Harris, Marvin. *Our Kind* (New York: Harper & Row, 1989).

Hayden, Brian. *Shamans, Sorcerers and Saints: A Prehistory of Religion* (Washington DC: Smithsonian Institution Press, 2004).

Katz, Richard. *Boiling Energy: Community Healing Among the Kalahari Kung* (Cambridge, MA: Harvard University Press, 1982).

Kendall, Laurel. *Shamans, Housewives, and Other Restless Spirits* (Honolulu: University of Hawaii Press, 1988).

———. *The Life and Times of a Korean Shaman* (Honolulu: University of Hawaii Press, 1988).

Lame, Deer, and R. Erdoes. *Lame Deer: Seeker of Visions* (New York: Simon & Schuster, 1972).

Lawson, E. Thomas. *Religions of Africa: Traditions in Transformation.* (San Francisco: Harper and Row, 1984.)

Mumford, Stan. *Himalayan Dialogue: Tibetan Lamas and Gurung Shamans* (Madison: University of Wisconsin Press, 1989).

Pfeiffer, J. E. *The Creative Explosion* (New York: Harper & Row, 1982).

Ritchie, Mark. *Spirit of the Rainforest: A Yanomamo Shaman's Story* (New York: Island Lake Press, 1996).

Shostack, Marjorie. *Nisa: Autobiography of a Kung Woman* (New York: Random House, 1982).

Taylor, Timothy. *The Buried Soul: How Humans Invented Death* (Boston: Beacon, 2002).

Vitebsky, Piers. *The Shaman* (New York: Macmillan, 1995).

Notes

1. Marjorie Shostack, *Nisa: Autobiography of a Kung Woman* (New York: Random House 1982), p. 16.

2. Ian Tattersall, "Once We Were Not Alone," *Scientific American,* January 2000, p. 62.

3. Gregory G. Maskarinec, "Healing," in Mariko Walter and Eva Friedman, eds., *Shamanism: An Encyclopedia of World Beliefs, Practices, and Culture* (Santa Barbara, CA: ABC Clio, 2004), p. 141.

4. Quoted in Sherman Alexie, *The Lone Ranger and Tonto Fight in Heaven* (New York: Atlantic Monthly Press, 1993), p. 104.

5. David Chidester, "Colonialism and Shamanism," in Mariko Walter and Eva Fridman, eds. *Shamanism: An Encyclopedia of World Beliefs, Practices, and Culture* (Santa Barbara, CA: ABC Clio, 2004), p. 48.

3

Hinduism

MYRIAD PATHS TO SALVATION

⁓❁⁓ Overview

"*Namaskar.*" Millions of Hindus every day extend this ancient Sanskrit greeting to holy seekers and other respected individuals as well as to their gods. But
then, in a suburb of Calcutta, devotees lead a goat toward the small temple where
a priest sprinkles pure water on its head; after seeing it "consent" to its fate by shiv-
ering, the priest skillfully wields a sharp knife to slit the animal's throat, severs the
head, and pours the spurting blood from it on the icon of goddess Kali, saying, "*Om
namaskar Kali-Ma*" ("*Om* homage to Mother Kali"). Elsewhere, in a desert oasis
town in western India, a sadhu who has renounced all family ties in quest of salvation walks slowly down a narrow byway, wearing a humble robe and carrying an
alms bowl; a white cotton cloth covers his nose and mouth, indicating the sadhu's
vow of nonviolence (which precludes even the unintentional inhaling of insects).
A housewife offers some fruit, bows, and says, "*Namaskar baba-ji*" ("Homage to
respected father"). Despite the apparent contradiction, no one would dispute that
animal sacrifices to Kali and absolutely nonviolent ascetics are following ancient
and legitimate Hindu traditions. Nor can we ignore the fact that other venerable
Hindu traditions empower holy men to take up weapons to defend their faith or
that in countless temples across the Hindu world today priests accept only the
purest vegetarian offerings designed to nourish and please the deities.

From this bewildering set of examples, we can see that Hinduism is unlike the
monotheistic world religions surveyed already. In addition, it lacks both a single
canonical text accepted by all followers and an elite who exert control over the
development of its fundamental beliefs and practices.

Ancient Hindu traditions continue to thrive today amid all the changes brought by colonial rule, independence, and the advent of science. In India and across the Hindu diaspora, there are newly built monasteries for study (**mathas**) in the traditional way, at the feet of recognized masters, or **gurus**. And there are also yoga centers in the major urban centers, catering to India's new middle class, which resemble those found in London or Chicago. New Hindu sects have arisen, usually around charismatic teachers, who combine classic doctrines with ideas from other Asian traditions or the West, using video and Internet media to extend their outreach. Yet in India today there are also communities in which very conservative

Hinduism Timeline

CA. 3500–1800 BCE	Indus Valley civilization in northwestern South Asia
1500 BCE	Decline of major Indus cities; populations migrate east to Gangetic plain
1500–500 BCE	Formative period of Vedic civilization
900–400 BCE	Shramana period of wandering ascetics and composition of the Upanishads
300–100 BCE	Texts of brahmanical orthodoxy formulated (e.g., *Laws of Manu*)
100 BCE–400 BCE	Composition of devotional texts and epics *Ramayana* and *Mahabharata*
50 BCE–300 BCE	Composition of the *Bhagavad Gita* and Patanjali's *Yoga Sutras*
100 CE–700 CE	Hinduism established along rim of Indian Ocean in Southeast Asia
320–647	Classical temple Hinduism established
500–FF	Development of Advaita Vedanta school; textual expressions of Hindu tantrism as counterculture
788–820	Life of Shankara, Vedanta school exponent of Advaita Vedanta and creator of Hindu-monasticism
800–1200	Six brahmanical schools established as divisions in elite philosophical Hinduism
1025–1137	Life of Ramanuja, philosophical defender of *bhakti* faith
1200–1757	Muslim rule of North India; Buddhism virtually extinguished in South Asia
1420–1550	Era of great devotional saints (e.g., Mirabai, Ravidas, Kabir, Chaitanya, Surdas)
1469–1539	Life of Nanak, the founder of the Sikh faith
1526–1707	Mughal dynasty; Muslim rulers alternate between anti-Hindu and ecumenical policies
1708	Death of tenth guru, Gobind Singh; Sikh text *Adi Granth* declared guru of the community
1757–1857	British East India Company dominates Indian political life
1815	Christian missionaries present in most cities and towns of British India
1828	Founding of the Brahmo Sabha (later Brahmo Samaj) by Rammohan Roy
1834–1886	Life of Ramakrishna, charismatic guru with ecumenical teaching

priests memorize, recite, and pass down orally and in secrecy to their sons the earliest hymns and rituals, some dating back 3,000 years.

In the great centers, such as Varanasi and Hardwar, pilgrims come by the hundred thousands each year to make offerings and see the deities enshrined in their
magnificent temples, while musicians and dancers in traditional training studios
nearby continue to perfect their dramatic renditions of religious themes. In many
villages across the Indian subcontinent, where 60 percent of the population still
lives, ritual practices within families and in local temples remain vigorous. What
we label "Hinduism" ranges from monotheism to polytheism to atheism; from

1858–1947	After uprising, British crown assumes direct rule over India; South Asian ethnic groups recruited for government service across British Empire spread Hinduism globally
1863–1902	Life of Swami Vivekananda, Ramakrishna's disciple, who led global Ramakrishna Mission
1875	Foundation of the Arya Samaj by Swami Dayananda Saraswati
1893	Speeches by Swami Vivekananda inspire interest at Parliament of World Religions in Chicago
1920–1948	M. K. Gandhi (1869–1948) leads civil disobedience campaigns, articulating ecumenical Hindu reformism influenced by Western culture
1923	Founding of the Rashtriya Svayamsevak Sangh (RSS), Hindu nationalist group
1940	Ashram established by Sathya Sai Baba, beginning of large global movement
1947	Independence of India from Britain; prime minister, J. Nehru, declares India a secular state
1948	Gandhi assassinated by Hindu extremist
1964	Vishva Hindu Parishad (VHP) founded to unite Hindu leaders and devotees worldwide
1964	International Society for Krishna Consciousness (ISKON) established by Bhaktivedanta (1896–1977)
1984	Sikh extremists occupy Golden Temple in Amritsar; armed removal by Indian army; assassination of the prime minister, Indira Gandhi
1987	Weekly Indian television series *Ramayana* inspires rising sentiments of Hindu nationalism
1992	Hindu agitation in Ayodhya culminates in destruction of Babri Mosque; Hindu–Muslim riots across South Asia
1998	The Bharatiya Janata party (BJP), a Hindu nationalist political party, wins parliamentary majority for the first time; rules until 2004
2002	Hindu hooligans riot in BJP-led Gujarat state, killing 2,500 Muslims, looting Muslim businesses, and displacing 200,000
2004	BJP loses national parliamentary elections but retains control of ten states across India

nonviolent ethics to moral systems that see as imperative blood sacrifices to sustain the world; from critical, scholastic philosophical discussion to the cultivation of sublime, mystical, wordless inner experiences.

"Hinduism" is the term used to indicate the amalgam of spiritual traditions originating in South Asia that comprises the third-largest world religion today. The term owes its origins to *Sindhus,* the Persian word for the great Indus River. Conquering Muslims used *Hindu* to designate people who lived east of the Indus, and later the British applied the term to the non-Muslim natives of the region.

A singular term for "Hinduism" was never in vogue in premodern South Asia, and it never stood for a single way of being religious. Some South Asian intellectuals and politicians in the last two centuries did adopt it to stand amid the apparent singularities of the Muslim and Christian. What is meant, or what should be meant, by "true Hinduism" has remained contested throughout history, especially in the modern and postcolonial eras.

Religion in South Asia has been the most pluralistic and least centrally organized in the world, a characteristic dating back at least a millennium, when the Arab geographer Alberuni identified forty-two discrete "religions" in South Asia. While conservative religious ideology still is used to justify the caste system and social inequality, other ancient traditions argue forcefully—in ways similar to those in the Western prophetic faiths—for the reform of society and for "God-given" egalitarianism. Hinduism itself thus incorporates differences at least as fundamental as those between Judaism, Islam, and Christianity. Therefore, it is only by distinguishing the various "Hindu" traditions from the more general and monolithic term "Hinduism" that we can compare this tradition with other world religions.

Though the great majority of Hindus live on the South Asian subcontinent, an important postcolonial development has been the global diaspora of South Asians. Their migration to other parts of the world has made Hinduism a global faith today. The estimated number of Hindus had surpassed 800 million by the turn of the millennium; after Islam, it is the second-fastest-growing world religion.

Among the contemporary nation-states, India remains the heartland of Hinduism (see Map 6.1). The modern state of India has been a secular democracy since its inception in 1947. It has over eighteen major culture regions, whose ethnic groups speak over a thousand distinct languages. Every region in South Asia has its distinctive religious history as well. The most profound differences are seen between the traditions of North and South India.

Among the other South Asian states, Nepal was until 2006 the world's only Hindu nation, with a majority of its 23 million people identifying themselves as Hindu. Two Muslim nations, Pakistan and Bangladesh, contain Hindu minorities (3 percent and 16 percent, respectively), most of whom remained despite the chaos and bloodshed occasioned by partition of British India in 1947. Fifteen percent of Buddhist Sri Lanka's population of 25 million is Hindu. Five to 10 percent of Malaysia's large population is Hindu. Small communities of Hindus are also found in Myanmar (Burma), Indonesia, Fiji, and the Caribbean.

Map 6.1 India, with major ancient and holy places.

In North America there are over a million Hindus, with immigrants far out-numbering converts. In the United States, as across Europe, Hindu temples serve as centers of religious teaching and ritual practice. The yoga traditions that involve training the body for flexibility and mental peace have been the most influential vehicle for spreading Hinduism among non-Indian peoples. The most well-known Hindu tradition that has attracted Euro-American converts since the 1960s has been the so-called Hare Krishna movement (ISKON) and **Transcendental Meditation (TM)**.

In this chapter, we will survey this broad spiritual tradition, one that spans almost every conceivable religious orientation—in belief and practice—that has ever been recorded in human history. Beginning with the earliest records of urban civilization in South Asia, the chapter describes the earliest form of religious life shaped by the Vedas, texts that are among the oldest (3,000 years old) in human history. Building on them and citing later revelations, we move through a succession of religious beliefs and practices that have found expression since then, without a priestly hierarchy or any institutional authority stifling the religious imagination. We finally focus on how these loosely connected traditions were affected by Islamic rule (1200–1780) and then, more severely, the impact of British colonial rule (1800–1947). A final goal of this chapter is to convey a sense of modern and postcolonial change amidst what still are extraordinary continuities in religious life today, some of which date back three millennia. In addition to an array of traditions that can be described as falling within the circle of "orthodox Hinduism," so vibrant has religious life in South Asia been that it also spawned three major heterodox religions that have themselves become global in scope today: Buddhism and Jainism, which began 2,500 years (the former the subject of the next chapter, where the latter is also discussed); and the Sikh tradition, which began about 500 years ago (and is covered in the latter portions of this chapter).[1]

Encounter with Modernity: Hindu Challenges to India as a Secular State

Religion in South Asia has undergone a continuous, additive development process throughout its history, one that has tended to preserve the past, even amid striking innovations. Hindu traditions have thrived and multiplied without any single priestly group, theologian, or institution ever imposing a universal or reductive definition of the core beliefs. Hindus have since antiquity respected the remote past as a more refined era of spiritual awareness. There have been no heresy trials or inquisitions in South Asia's long history; in fact, debating spiritual truths, often with great subtlety, was a regular feature of premodern court life and in society at large.

This pattern continues to the present, with the result that Hinduism's multiplicities are continuously extended: Very ancient traditions are preserved alongside those originating in the medieval era, and these threads exist in interaction with the traditions introduced by nineteenth- and twentieth-century reformers.

Although in many respects South Asia preserves elements of premodern religious culture with a vigor matched in few other places across the globe, there is no "unchanging East" in South Asia—or anywhere else! Religions have changed as the circumstances of individuals and societies have changed: The scientific ideas associated with the Enlightenment have affected nearly everyone through education, technology, and medicine; the views and practices of Christian missionaries as well as the political practices of the modern state impacted most regions as well. Most important, the pattern of reform and synthesis that has kept this religion so flexible and fluid has continued as leading Hindus have entered the global religious arena and adopted mass media to serve the faith. Classical and reformed Hinduism alike as well as political movements emphasizing religious identity have proven extremely successful at attracting the loyalty of believers of every sort, from highly educated intellectuals to illiterate villagers.

Visionaries such as M. K. Gandhi and Jawaharlal Nehru, who led South Asia to independence, subscribed to the prevailing norm in Western political thought, insisting that for India to be modern it should be a secular democracy, formally favoring no religion. In the last decades of the twentieth century, however, this stance was questioned by an increasing number of Hindu citizens.

In reacting to perceived threats from modern secularism and non-Hindus, Hindu revivalist groups have created new organizations styled on Western prototypes. Among the many responses to British colonial rule and the changes it brought to South Asia, one of the most enduring has come from institutions calling for thoroughgoing reform of "Hindu-ness" (*Hindutva*) in national life and the reconstitution of India as a Hindu state. With roots among nineteenth-century reformers, this ideology began to be forcefully articulated in 1923 across the nation by the **Rashtriya Svayamsevak Sangh** ("National Union of [Hindu] Volunteers"). This group, known as the **RSS**, proposed a nativist definition of "Hinduism" as devotion to "Mother India." Members have worked in the political arena to promote candidates wishing to repeal the secular rule of law India instituted in 1947, when the country gained independence from Great Britain. By 2000, RSS membership had grown to an estimated 4.1 million.

It was only with the most recent incarnation of an RSS-allied political party, the **Bharatiya Janata Party (BJP)**, that Hindu nationalists finally found success in electoral politics across the nation. In the elections of 1995, the BJP won more seats than any other party in the national parliament, defeating the Congress Party, which had dominated Indian politics since independence. In the 1998 elections, the BJP became India's ruling party, a position it held until 2004.

The BJP is led mostly by high-caste politicians and appeals primarily to middle-class urbanites. It rose in prominence as its leaders sought to symbolize the unity of a militant and revived Hindu India through a series of motorized "chariot festivals" across the nation, culminating in reworked traditional rituals in which the waters from all the country's sacred rivers were brought together and merged. The BJP and its allies also stoked popular resentment over government-sponsored affirmative action initiatives that set quotas for civil service hiring and admission to state colleges for the most disadvantaged, or "scheduled caste," members, a move aimed to break high-caste control over the nation's and educational institutions.

The most strident and hard-line BJP policy is to foment confrontations with South Asian Muslims by accusing the secular government of favoring them in its civil laws and of protecting medieval-era mosques that were purportedly built on North Indian sites sacred to Hindus. The BJP today seeks to have the Hindu majority strike back to undo acts of centuries past and repress Islamic activism. The first and most violent focus was on Ayodhya, where in 1528 the Mughal ruler Babar built a Muslim house of worship known as the Babri Mosque. Modern BJP partisans claim that the site was the birthplace of Rama, a human incarnation of the god Vishnu. Responding to the call made by many Hindu groups, one that was dramatized in a widely distributed video production suggesting that the activists had been miraculously given Rama's blessing for this "service," thousands of volunteers converged on the site in December 1992. They attacked and subdued government troops protecting the site and then broke up the Babri Mosque with hammers, steel rods, and crowbars. In the aftermath, rioting broke out between Muslims and Hindus in other Indian towns and in Pakistan. Over 2,000 people perished.

The RSS- and BJP-led movements, labeled as "fundamentalist-nationalist," advocate paths to religious modernization found elsewhere in the world: They adopt the latest technological media yet reject the Enlightenment-inspired critiques of religious belief and insist that the secular political systems established in the colonial and postcolonial eras give way to a religious state. They have used the ancient idea of Mother India to express symbolically their sense of the "rape" of the Mother Goddess during years of Muslim, colonial, and postcolonial secular rule. Guru Golwalkara, the RSS chief between 1940 and 1973, put it this way:

> When we say this is a Hindu nation, there are some who immediately come up with the question "What about the Muslims and Christians?" But the crucial question is whether or not they remember that they are children of this soil. . . . Together with the change in their faith, gone is the spirit of love and devotion for the nation. They look to some distant holy land as their holy place. It is not merely a change of faith, but a change even in national identity.[2]

Beyond declaring loyalty to the land and the Hindu state, however, fundamentalist-nationalist literature remains elusive and necessarily vague on what exactly "Hinduness" means, and for good reason: Hindus have remained divided on this question since antiquity and certainly throughout the era of colonial rule and up to the present.

In 2007, the BJP leaders in Madhya Pradesh passed laws requiring the public school curriculum to include the elementary yoga practice of sun worship (*surya asana*), a series of movements that are accompanied by devotional chanting. A state court soon after struck down the legislation, concluding that yoga is a religious practice and that the law contradicted India's secular constitution. The outcome is not surprising, but controversy that India is a secular state again served to roil the Hindu majority across the country.

Despite these setbacks, the appeal of the Hindu-India movement has grown stronger. Hindu nationalists have provided a focal point for political action by those involved in guru-oriented sects, with their emphasis on personal devotional enthusiasm (discussed later in this chapter), and for those middle-class Hindus now drawn to yoga centers of today (also discussed later), both of which offer different versions of "Hinduism." Nationalist politicians thus appeal to the simplest level of religious identity and, despite recent electoral setbacks, attract a growing number of middle-class Hindus across the nation. As the American scholar Daniel Gold has concluded, "If personal religion entails among other things the identification of the individual with some larger whole, then the Hindu Nation may appear as a whole more immediately visible and attainable than the ritual cosmos of traditional Hinduism."[3] To understand better the significance of Hindu nationalism's challenge to modern secular India, we must go back to the beginning and trace the historical development of Hinduism.

Premodern Hinduism: The Formative Era

THE ARYANS AND RELIGION IN THE VEDIC ERA

The recounting of South Asian history until recently included legends of an invasion of the subcontinent by an aggressive, light-skinned people who called themselves *Aryans* and spoke an Indo-European language. These warriors, in their horse-drawn chariots, were imagined destroying cities of the Indus Valley nearly as ancient as those of Egypt and Mesopotamia, subduing the darker-skinned speakers of Dravidian languages that presently inhabit the southern subcontinent. This rendition of history was used to explain the modern distribution of "north" and "south" India as separate linguistic and racial zones. The Aryans, supposedly culturally superior, allegedly forced the invaded people to migrate southward over the Vindhya Mountains to settle in the lower peninsula.

Built on very forced readings of thin textual evidence, this view of history contained a racial assumption welcomed by early European scholars and by high-caste Hindus in the modern and postcolonial era. Then, when Sanskrit, the language of Hinduism's Vedic hymns, was discovered to be related to most languages of Europe, it was also concluded that the ancestors of the modern Hindu elite were distantly kin to the British. Western archaeologists and the

Bull seal, Harappa, c. 1800 BCE. Although the meaning of the zebu bull symbol here is uncertain, this animal was later regarded as the vehicle of the great god Shiva.

British colonial government supported such research and found this imagined history attractive. British imperial apologists, in particular, welcomed support for their view of modern Indians as superstitious and modern Hindu priests as corrupt, thereby justifying their presence.

Although migration in prehistory is accepted by objective historians as explaining the linguistic geography of Eurasia, scholars now find no justification for understanding *Aryan* as a racial term, and they reject utterly any suggestion that the ancient Aryans or their descendants were or are culturally superior to darker-skinned people. The Indus Valley cities likewise are now thought to have declined not through conquest but owing to regional climatic changes. There are also signs that the Indus Valley culture in fact shared many continuities with subsequent "Aryan" culture. Indeed, "Aryan" in social terms really had no meaning beyond designating participants in early Vedic sacrifices and festivals. By 700 BCE, "Aryan culture" had been adopted by most politically dominant groups across the Indo-Gangetic plains, but most of the religious beliefs and ritual practices of Hindus today are those recorded in texts that were composed *after* the original four Vedas, to which we now turn.

VEDIC RELIGION

Knowledge of early Indic religion comes from the four **Vedas**, a collection of over a thousand hymns of praise and supplication addressed to the gods, the oldest of which is the *Rig Veda*. Composed in archaic language and set in poetical form, these hymns show no systematic development, ordering, or single mythological framework. It is likely that the Vedic hymns were collected and appreciated by only the most elite social groups of that earlier millennium (1500–500 BCE).

Early Vedic religion was centered on the fire sacrifices (*yajna* or *homa*). The sacrifice depended on the knowledge of a special, hereditary group of priests called **brahmins**, who chanted the Vedic hymns and orchestrated highly intricate and time-consuming rituals intended to gratify the numerous Aryan deities. Accompanied by carefully cadenced chants, the brahmins placed grain, animal flesh, and clarified butter in a blazing fire, thereby transforming the offerings into fragrant smoke to nourish and please the gods. The entire universe was thought to be maintained by this sacrifice: If kept happy, well fed, and strengthened through the offerings, the deities would sustain creation and ensure the prosperity of the sacrificers.

The language of the Vedic hymns, called *Sanskrit*, was thought to be divine in origin. The hymns were memorized by brahmin priests and taught to men in succeeding generations. The Vedas existed for over two millennia in oral form; The earliest extant written manuscripts, which date back only to the eleventh century of the common era, include annotations showing proper accents and supplying ritual contexts. This very archaic tradition still is followed in scattered communities across India today.

The major deities of the Vedic world, all male, were those connected to sacrifice, martial conquest, mystical experience, and maintenance of moral order. Agni, the fire

A brahmin priest in Nepal prepares a sacrificial fire pit for his patrons.

god whose flaming tongue licks the offerings, was essential for the successful ritual. The Aryan warrior deity par excellence was Indra, and he has the greatest number of hymns dedicated to him. It was Indra who subdued alien deities, and it was Indra who was called on to lead the Aryan men into battle. Soma was conceived to be a divine presence dwelling within a psychoactive substance of the same name, which was drunk by humans and deities before battle and at the end of major rituals. Another strong deity, Varuna, was thought to enforce the moral order of the universe and to mete out punishment or reward. The hymns indicate that humans can approach Varuna with personal petitions for forgiveness.

Death and afterlife in the early Vedic era were envisioned as alternative destinies. There was the possibility of becoming an ancestor (*pitri*) and reaching a heavenly afterlife if one lived morally, but only if one's family, in the first after-death year, performed special memorial rituals (*shraddha*). These were designed to embody the initially disembodied spirit in its arduous journey to become, as several hymns poetically describe it, one of the twinkling evening stars. Some Vedic texts imply that the essence of a father is also born in his sons, resulting in the continuation of his life. Alternatively, those whose deeds were immoral or whose families failed to do the proper shraddha rituals lost their individual identity and merely dissolved back into the earth.

Vedic religion was marked by faith in the power of the gods, ritual acts to influence them, and the spiritual resonance of Sanskrit words. The Aryans believed with absolute certainty in the primacy of their deities. In later eras, however, the dominant devotional tradition placed all the central deities of the earliest pantheon into minor roles: Indra is the king of the minor heavenly hosts, Agni is confined to be a guardian

"In your offspring you are born again; That, O Mortal, is your immortality."

—*Taittiriya Brahmana*

Source: Quoted in Patrick Olivelle, *Samnyasa Upanishads* (New York, Oxford University Press, 1992), p. v.

of ritual, Soma is seen as the deity residing in the moon, and Varuna becomes the lord of the ocean. Similarly, the Vedic concept of *rita,* the natural human order that the gods enforced, is replaced by three dominant themes in subsequent Hinduism: reincarnation, the law of karma, and the concept of **dharma** (duty).

KARMA, YOGA, AND THE QUEST FOR LIBERATION

Scattered references in later Vedic hymns indicate that a very different spiritual orientation had entered the Aryan world. The practice of asceticism—involving retreat into the forest, silent introspection, and the cultivation of trance states—was likely the first indigenous spiritual tradition absorbed into the dominant religion. Such practices found a receptive community in certain circles, and their synthesis of this spirituality emerges clearly in the **Upanishads**, the remarkable tracts that began to be appended to the Vedic hymns after 1000 BCE. The dialogs themselves and the name they are given—*upanishad* means "sitting near devotedly"—convey a context of disciples learning at the feet of masters who have gone beyond the Vedic sacrificial framework to adopt ascetic practices. These gurus developed new teachings and practices aimed at realizing the more fundamental realities underlying all existence.

The central idea they introduced is that of **samsara**, "the world," in which all phenomena are really only secondary appearances. But blinded by illusion (*maya*), humans act foolishly and thereby suffer from samsara's "fire," its pains and privations. These last until the realization dawns that the underlying reality is everywhere the same, and it is the unchanging spirit (**Brahman**). The individual soul (**atman**) wanders from birth to death again and again until it finds release from the cycle by realizing that it is nothing other than Brahman.

An individual's destiny in samsara is determined by actions (deeds and thoughts) the person performs. Good deeds eventually bear good consequences, while bad deeds ripen into evil consequences. This natural law, which operates throughout samsara and affects the destiny of the atman, is called **karma**, a complex term whose meaning is often oversimplified. It is important to note that all the world religions that emerged in India accept the samsara paradigm: the "orthodox" traditions that accept the authority of the Vedas as well as the "heterodox" religions, primarily Buddhism, Jainism, and Sikhism, that do not. Although all three hold different doctrines about the precise nature of the soul and the mechanisms of karma, each advocates specific yoga practices designed to realize the highest truth and achieve **moksha**, release from further reincarnation.

The teachers in the Upanishads argue that the ultimate reality of the world is the universal spirit called *Brahman.*[4] Through a cosmic process that is inexplicable, this unitary ultimate reality in the world's creation became subdivided into myriad atmans. Flesh-and-blood individual human beings are ultimately illusory. Atmans are the truly real entities in the world, however subtle and difficult to perceive they may be. All

"By austerity a man achieves goodness, and through goodness he takes hold of the mind. Through the mind he reaches the self, and reaching the self he comes to rest."

—Maitreya Upanishad

Source: Patrick Olivelle, *Samnyasa Upanishads* (New York, Oxford University Press, 1992), p. 160.

beings, then, have a spiritual center, sharing with one another and the forces that move the universe a common essence. This truth is stated concisely in the Chandogya Upanishad when the teacher simply states literally, "That [i.e., Brahman] thou art," or more directly, "You are divine." As we will see, it is not enough simply to know intellectually that Brahman equals atman: One must realize this truth in one's own life through yoga.

YOGA

Yoga refers to the disciplined practices by which human beings can unify and focus their bodily powers for the purpose of realizing their true spiritual essence, the atman within. First surfacing clearly in the late Upanishads, these practices were codified in a text, the *Yoga Sutras*, attributed to a sage named *Patanjali*. The yoga meditation tradition

Seeking to discern Brahman within themselves, ancient Hindu holy men practiced many forms of austerity, as shown in this Punjabi painting of yoga positions.

Sadhus have been a part of the Hindu tradition for three thousand years. Wandering Hindu ascetics today adhere to a variety of paths, from the bhakti devotional devotees to yogins seeking the divine without form.

is for the highly advanced spiritual elite, for those attempting to escape *samsara* by ending, or "burning up," all past karma.

The *Yoga Sutras* assume that yoga can be performed properly only by individuals of high moral character, who have renounced most material possessions, live in simplicity (including vegetarianism), and study the teachings regarding the "inner reality." Advanced practice then turns first to postures (*asana*) designed to make the body flexible and to free its energies and breath control (*pranayama*) to harness and direct the body's primal energy. Then, after focusing on a single object for long periods, the person experiences a series of increasingly refined states of consciousness as the mind is withdrawn from external sensation. These experiences culminate in a trance state (*samadhi*). It is in samadhi that the *yogin*, or adept practitioner, develops a direct and unbroken awareness of the luminous origin of consciousness itself: the life-giving, pure, and blissful atman.

The *Yoga Sutras* assume that the progressive practice of yoga opens up an inner vision of the commanding reality of the soul within, thereby weakening the power of ignorance and egotistic desire to distort human consciousness. The ultimate goal in yoga meditation is to dwell for extended periods in trance, reaching the highest state, *kaivalya,* an awareness that is perfectly at one with and centered in the atman. The yoga practitioner who reaches this state is said to put an end to all past karma and to experience moksha. This adept, freed from desire and ignorance, is thought to be omniscient and capable of supernormal feats, such as telepathy, clairvoyance, and extraordinary travel. This *enlightenment* experience and the capacity to know others' tendencies and thoughts makes the yogic sage an ideal spiritual guide for other religious seekers.

The great majority of Hindus from the formative period onward have oriented their religious lives around the reality of karma. Although subject to various interpretations, Hindu karma doctrine asserts that all actions performed by an individual set into motion a cause that will lead to a moral effect in the present and/or future lifetimes. This belief holds that a natural mechanism functions to make the cosmos orderly and just. One Sanskrit name for the Indian subcontinent—*karmabhumi,* "realm of karma"—reflects the doctrine's centrality in Hindu life. This has meant that inclinations to do good and avoid evil were backed up by the belief in karmic retribution for one's actions. Since old karma is coming to fruition constantly and new karma is being made continuously, it is—in most explications—incorrect to see karma doctrine as instilling an irresistible fatalism. Further, not all events in life are due to karmic accounting; Indic religious philosophies and medical theory have also recognized natural causalities as part of the human condition.

What is implicit in karma theory for typical human beings is that one's karma in daily life is in fact unknown. In practice, this uncertainty principle (similar to the belief of some Protestant Christians that no one can be certain about his or her salvation) has sustained a strong tendency for Hindus to resort to astrology for guidance at times of important decisions, such as when first to plant the fields, the choice of marriage partner, or when to set off on a journey. As Indian society developed, other ideas were tied to karma, weaving tighter the socioreligious fabric of classical Hinduism.

"This is the entire aim of yoga: rendering in personal experience of the Truth which universal nature has hidden in herself. . . . It is the conversion of the human soul into the divine soul and of natural life into divine living."

—Aurobindo Ghose

Source: Stephen Hay, ed., *Sources of Indian Tradition,* 2nd ed., Vol. 2 (New York: Columbia University Press, 1988), p. 155.

First appearing in the Upanishads, where it is described as the "seed sound" of all other sounds, **OM** (also written in full phonetic rendition as AUM) is one of the most prominent symbols of Hinduism. Repeated as part of almost every mantra for offerings and meditation as well as written calligraphically on icons and other symbols, OM has become an ever-present and multivalent symbol, often reflecting sectarian differences. Upandishadic interpretations were carried on and developed in, for example, yoga, where OM is seen as a symbol of cosmic origination and dissolution, and past-present-future-dissolution (A/U/M/ silence) in its one resonating sound. OM's components also include all four states of consciousness in yoga theory, with A as waking, U as dreaming, M as dreamless sleep, and the syllable as a whole "the fourth." OM is the sound-form of *atman-Brahman*. Repeating OM is thus the key to meditation that leads to *moksha*. The theological schools discussed in the text have suggested yet further meanings: The three letters AUM represent Brahma, Vishnu, and Shiva; Vaishnavites identify OM with Vishnu; Shaivites see Shiva as Lord of the Dance creating from OM all the sounds for musical notes from his drum. The written OM, shown in the title bar to this box, adorns all the major deities as represented in the popular art forms.

Premodern Hinduism: The Classical Era (180 BCE–900 CE)

There were very few periods in South Asian history when expansive empires unified the subcontinent. The first great empire was that of the Mauryas (300–180 BCE), whose emperors helped to spread Buddhism and its ideal of compassion as a principle of just rule. As Buddhism expanded and thrived, it competed with early brahmin-led traditions.

Classical Hinduism, the product of response to Buddhism by the orthodox brahmin priests and spiritual teachers, absorbed and synthesized aspects of this missionary faith while also embracing pre-Aryan deities and other indigenous Indic traditions. As a result, nonviolence and vegetarianism became ideals of high-caste religiosity, Hindu monasteries for training and meditation were begun, and a distinctive theistic dimension of Hinduism (not part of early Buddhism) found vast elaboration and increasingly popular acceptance. Classical Hinduism in North India reaches a high point in the Gupta dynasty (320–647 CE), when wealth and the cultural expressions of devotional Hinduism flowered in all the fine arts. This tradition was so compelling that in 1200 CE, by which time Hinduism had slowly absorbed the Buddha within its panoply of gods, Buddhism had virtually disappeared from South Asia except for the Himalayan (Nepal) and Sri Lankan peripheries. The brahmins in the classical age composed Sanskrit literature that codified and disseminated expressions of this new synthesis in the realms of philosophy, theology, and law. These texts and leaders gave the subcontinent a source of unity through one fundamental paradigm: An individual's place in society is defined in terms of karma.

THE REALITY OF KARMA AND CASTE

As we have seen, the idea of karma provided a way of explaining the destiny of a being according to its moral past. Evil deeds lead to evil destiny, and vice versa; people get what they deserve, although not necessarily in a single lifetime. This idea of karmic retribution had become widely accepted by the classical era, and brahmin social thinkers built on it to formulate the basis of the ideal Hindu society in a series of texts called the *Dharmashastras* (*Treatises on Dharma*). These texts, the most famous of which is known by the English title *The Laws of Manu,* make a series of arguments about karma while also charting practices and social policies designed to keep the world in order.

The *Dharmashastras* assume that one's birth location is the most telling indication of one's karma. They also argue that high-status birth gives one a higher spiritual nature, reflecting one's good karma past. Rebirth, then, is assumed to fall into regular patterns, and this cyclicity justifies seeing society, like the animal kingdom, as broken down into groups with very separate natures and capacities. These groups have come to be called *castes* in English; one Sanskrit word for them is *jati.*

Hindu law codes became the basis of Indian law in the early classical period. They prescribed that those born into a caste should marry within that group. Such individuals were believed to have closely matching karma so that if they segregated themselves to bear and raise children, reincarnation patterns should be maintained consistently and clearly. Those born into a caste were also expected to perform the traditional tasks of that group. The four main groups were called *varnas,* or classes: *brahmins,* who were to master the Vedic and ritual practice; *kshatriyas,* who were to rule justly and protect society, especially the brahmins; *vaishyas,* who were to specialize in artisanship and trade, multiplying the wealth of the society; and *shudras,* the workers needed to perform laborious and menial tasks for those in the upper jatis.

The *Dharmashastras* also identify the top three classes as *dvija,* or twice born, meaning "born again" through a Vedic initiation. Groups despised by the higher castes, such as *chandalas,* were assigned to perform polluting tasks, such as street sweeping and carrying dead bodies. Under each varna, hundreds of caste subgroups were arrayed, and to this day these vary regionally in their surnames and specific social functions. It is also important to note that in antiquity (as in real life today), intercaste marriages, political events, and local history resulted in much more social flexibility than is prescribed in the brahmanical texts.

Each caste was thought to have a singular proper duty to perform in life; the term for this, *dharma,* is central throughout the subsequent history of Hinduism. The *Dharmashastra* texts argue that one must live in accordance with one's place in the world, which has been assigned from all earlier lives. Only by doing so does one make the good karma needed to move "upward" in samsara. As one famous passage in *The Laws of Manu* [10:97] warns, "Better to do one's own dharma badly than another caste's dharma well."

Hindu religious law, therefore, does not see all human beings as having the same social and religious status or as being subject to the same legal standards. While religious views underlie this system of social inequality, Hindu social theorists argued that

A sadhu Hindu ascetic, coated in ash, consults a ritual text.

in the fullness of time—beyond a single-lifetime frame-work—samsara and its law of karmic retribution allow for certain, inescapable cosmic justice, matching karmic past to social function. In the end, every soul will move upward through samsara to be reborn as a brahmin male and reach salvation. Individual freedom is sacrificed for harmony and for society's ultimate and eventual collective liberation.

Thus, in theory, the religious underpinning of the caste system has served to legitimate the social hierarchy beyond Vedic times. It preserves the purity and privileges of the highest castes and argues that society depends on brahmins: If they live in purity and use their ritual mastery to worship the gods properly, they ensure that divine grace will sustain a fruitful society and a nonthreatening environment.

Consistent with this belief system, Hindus—like Jews, Christians, and Muslims—came to regard themselves as "chosen people," but, in their case, whose actions in previous lives justified their superior status. The highest castes used religious doctrine and caste ideology to justify their efforts to convert and subjugate other groups in their midst. As we shall see, this sanctioning of high-caste privilege had early critics among Buddhists and Jains and, later, Hindus as well. Some modern reformers from the lowest social groups point out that these Hindu doctrines were and are an intellectual justification for the high-caste minority to rule over the low-caste majority. As Bhimrao Ambedkar, one of the legal reformers of the early twentieth century, stated,

To the Untouchables, Hinduism is a veritable chamber of horrors. The sanctity and infallibility of the *Vedas, Smritis,* and *Shastras,* the iron law of caste, the heartless law of *karma,* and the senseless law of status by birth are to the Untouchables veritable instruments of torture which Hinduism has forged against the Untouchables.[5]

The classical Hindu writers also prescribed other endeavors to realize the ideal Hindu life. To explain the extraordinarily precise attention shown to detail and to the ideal human lifetime, we must consider the individual's quest to fulfill his or her dharma fully.

THE FOUR STAGES OF LIFE

The twice-born man becomes a full person only after he has passed through the first of four stages, known as the student; the prescribed life then proceeds to that of the householder, the forest dweller, and the homeless wanderer (*sadhu*). A student studies in the house of his teacher, learning to the extent appropriate to his caste and individual aptitude a curriculum that formerly included memorizing major portions of Vedas as well as acquiring proficiency in archery, medicine, astrology, and music. Upon completing the student phase, a man returns to be married; as a householder, his duty is to perform the traditional rites and raise children in the proper manner to continue the father's lineage. The *Dharmashastras* require women to subordinate themselves to men, although husbands are supposed to respect their wives and maintain happiness within the household. Marriage is treated as a sacrament, and divorce is not allowed.

Once a couple notices their hair turning white, "sees their son's sons," and finds the household well handled by their male descendants, they are directed to become forest dwellers. In this stage, they focus on spiritual matters by retreating to the forest, living only on wild foods and with bare necessities; they renounce sensuality and sex, with rituals and meditation becoming their chief concern. The fourth portion of life, the homeless wanderer, builds on the third, on the supposition that knowledge and discipline have led the forest dweller to the gateway of moksha realization. Persons now wander alone; no rituals need be done, and they renounce all but what can be carried, as the remaining days are devoted to pilgrimages to holy sites and to yoga practice. From the classical era onward, the widespread dissemination of teachings about caste and stages in life, called *varnashrama Dharma*, has given "Hindu doctrine" its area of strongest consensus.

THE FOUR AIMS OF LIFE

Since individuals differ in their karma-determined capabilities according to caste and stage of life, the classical Hindu theorists in the *Dharmashastras* also identified four legitimate aims or ends that could be the focus of human striving. The first, *artha,* can be translated as material gain or worldly success. South Asian folk literature of animal stories and human parables imparts instructions toward this goal in life, an indication that belief in karma has never stifled pious Hindus' interest in "getting ahead."

The second aim, *kama* ("sensory pleasure"), was seen as an acceptable goal for embodied beings, especially householders seeking to fulfill the duty of propagating the family line. Many in the west have seen the *Kama Sutra,* a text that treats the cultivation of sexual pleasure explicitly, but many chapters are devoted to achieving "the good life" in many other spheres as well. The third aim, *dharma,* fulfilling the duty prescribed by one's caste, we have already discussed; the other ends of life are justly pursued only if they remain consistent with one's caste and gender-appropriate duties. The last of the four goals, *moksha*—release from the cycle of future rebirth and redeath—is adopted by few, but the texts counsel that true ascetics pursuing this goal should receive everyone's respect and support through almsgiving. Hindus still venerate the sadhu saints, who follow this path of spiritual wandering.

EPICS AND THE DEVELOPMENT OF CLASSICAL HINDUISM

For the majority of Hindus, the ideals of the law books, the theologies of classical Hinduism, and the models for religious life are conveyed in the plots and characters of the great epics. By the classical era, the two great Hindu epics had been composed from oral sources that doubtless originated in heroic accounts of early battles fought by warriors in the Aryan clans. The longer of the two, the *Mahabharata,* records an escalating and ultimately devastating feud between rival sides of a family as they vied for control of the northern plains, each one aided by supernatural allies. The moral element of this story—one side has usurped power from the other, but the rightful heir has no desire to shed the blood of his kin to take it back—is explored with great subtlety. The *Mahabharata* conveys the existential dilemmas of Hindu life, its characters encountering moral issues in family relations, gender conflicts, caste duty versus individual wishes, etc. Through textual recitations, dance dramas, art, and now comic books, Hindus have "dwelled in these stories" and subplots. This rivalry ended in a war of immense carnage that in theological interpretation marks the onset of the current age, the **Kali Yuga.** The *Mahabharata* and its most famous portion, called the ***Bhagavad Gita***, allowed for diverse and nuanced evaluations of dharma, especially that pertaining to warriors, kin, and women and regarding the role of divinity in human affairs. The epic reveals the many difficulties, paradoxes, and ambiguities that face those who wish to apply the lofty religious ideals of the *Dharmashastra* to often-gritty and ambiguous real-life circumstances.

The same quality of "speaking with many voices" is true of the second great epic, the *Ramayana*. Here, the underlying historical circumstance is the rivalry between one Aryan clan—symbolized by the hero Rama—and the non-Aryans of the south, portrayed as powerful demons subject to unbridled lust, immorality, and disrespect for Vedic sacrifices. Invoking the forces of nature and his animal allies, Rama does succeed in defeating the demon Ravana and establishing a unified Hindu kingdom. The tale has proven very malleable in giving groups across South (and Southeast) Asia a narrative to express their own views on ethnic relations, the good king, gender relations, and the relationship between northerners and southerners. In fact, there is no one *Ramayana* today, for through its tellings and retellings hundreds of groups have claimed their particular version as sacred and central to their own Hindu ideal.

MAINSTREAM HINDUISM AND THE RISE OF DEVOTION TO THE GREAT DEITIES

The deities who dominated Hindu life by the classical age differed in name and conception from those of the earliest Vedic hymns. An entirely new collection of Sanskrit texts, called **puranas,** was composed to extol the glories of these great gods, specify their forms of worship, and celebrate the early saints who cultivated divine love for

Tales of Spiritual Transformation

Swami Satchidananda's Moksha

"My highest experience . . . of Advaita Oneness was in 1949, a few months after my *sannyas* initiation [as a celibate ascetic]. It was in mid-winter, when I visited Vasishta Cave, where the sage Vasishta performed austerities. I went into the cave, . . . where I reached a large room with a seat. As I sat there and meditated, I had the experience of transcending my body and mind, realizing myself as the Omnipresent. I forgot my individuality. It is impossible to explain exactly what this is. I must have spent several hours in that state. Then I heard a humming sound, OM chanting, coming from a long distance away. Slowly, slowly, it became louder. As it neared I became aware of my mind and body. . . . For some time, I couldn't see anything in the normal way. All over I saw light, light, light. The whole world appeared as a mass of light. There was only peace and peace was everywhere. The state persisted the whole day. I have had this experience very often, mostly when I visit a holy place."

Swami Satchidananda went on to become a guru whose teaching was centered in North America, founding an ecumenical movement called *Integral Yoga* in 1966. Since 1986, Integral Yoga has been centered in Yogaville, a thousand-acre ashram in rural Virginia, and has spread to twenty-eight countries and nearly 400 centers across North America.

Source: From Sita Wiener, *Swami Satchidananda*. (New York: Bantam, 1970), p. 88.

The bow asana, as demonstrated by the yoga master and guru Swami Satchitananda (1914-2002).

Cyclic Time in Hindu Thought: *Cosmic Eras*

The Hindu view of time defines the universe as binding beings together in an eternal dance of life, death, and rebirth. The Vedic texts contain a multitude of creation accounts, and later texts combine them in a more circular vision of successive eras of cosmic dissolution followed by equally long eras when the created world undergoes a regular series of transformations. Once primal creation has begun, our world evolves through four eras called *yugas*.

The first and longest era, the *Krita Yuga*, is a golden age without suffering or wants: Meditation and virtue come naturally to all beings. In the second and third *yugas*, people are strongly inclined to proper duty (*dharma*); yet the inclination to virtue slowly wanes, and eventually there is the need for castes to be formed to keep order and the *Vedas* to be composed to aid those striving for truth and goodness. But

in the *Kali Yuga*, which in the current cycle began in 3102 BCE, human life moves from bad to much worse: Brahmins become unworthy, the Vedas are forgotten, castes mix unlawfully, and life spans decrease as a result of war and famine. The Kali Yuga ends with the destruction of the earth after a series of natural disasters culminating in a great flood, when Vishnu will again sleep on the waters. Some texts recount that after 1,000 of these four-era cycles, a greater destruction will take place, one in which all matter will be consumed in fire, reducing all reality to pure spirit. As an instance of Hinduism's diversity, we must also note that later sectarian groups proclaimed a dissenting, triumphal alternative to this pessimistic scenario, avowing that the grip of evil on the Kali Yuga has been (or will be) ended through the devotional practices of true believers.

them. The purana stories recount examples of human incarnation, instances of divine omniscience, and episodes of grace. Heroes in these stories become models of exemplary devotional faith, or **bhakti**. Just as Hanuman the monkey king serves Rama and Radha the consort loves Krishna without limit, so should one devote the full commitment of heart and mind to one's own bhakti practice.

All the puranas—which many Hindus revere today as the "fifth Veda"—share an important assumption about humanity living in the Kali Yuga, the post-Vedic age: This era, said to have begun in 3102 BCE, is defined as the period of degeneration, in which human spiritual potential is declining. The puranas declare that the deities have extended their grace to humanity in ever-increasing measure in return for their devotees' unselfish devotion to them: While the ascetic practices of yoga do not end (and not all Hindus accepted Kali Yuga theory), this ideal of bhakti became the predominant one for Hinduism from the classical era until the present day.

Hinduism's shift toward bhakti follows its characteristic "add-on pattern" in merging a new theology with the fundamental ideas of the formative era: samsara, karma, and moksha. The devotional tradition accepts the early cosmic model but builds on it by asserting that the great deities, such as Shiva, Vishnu, and Durga, have the power to reward devotion by altering the karma of the *bhakta* (devotee). Though these deities are omnipotent and omniscient, they are usually seen as augmenting the earlier tradition, not challenging it. By absorbing human karma, they can bring their grace to persons seeking liberation from worldly suffering and ultimately from samsara. This view is most dramatically expressed in the *Bhagavad Gita,* where the deity Krishna argues that desireless action is possible only through egoless bhakti faith and that the true suspension of all action (which produces additional karma) is impossible.

By the classical era, purana texts asserted the existence of 330 million deities. How could the theologians account for such mind-numbing diversity? The bhakti gurus argued that polytheism reflected the grace of the divine, since the diverse needs of a humanity comprising innumerable individual karmas could only be met be a diverse set of gods. The crucial goal facing each Hindu is to find and focus on the one deity whose form is most appropriate to his or her level of spiritual maturity.

The common principle of simplification in later Hinduism was that each devotee should choose a personal deity (*ista deva*) to be at the center of his or her religious life, a focus for personal communion through an emotional relationship. Although most teachers (and families) believed that "good Hindus" should respect all the great deities as well as the lesser spirits thought to dwell in each locality, it was nonetheless essential for each person to establish a single divinity to meditate on and to venerate as a channel for grace. Among theologians, the terms and mechanisms of salvation vary; in many of the puranas, rebirth in one's chosen deity's heaven—not exit from samsara—is proclaimed as the highest human goal.

A linga, the image commonly used to worship Shiva.

The concept of "chosen deity" entailed commitment to knowing extensively and loving selflessly that particular god. This meant making offerings (*puja,* to be discussed later), meditating, and studying the purana stories to be able to discern as completely as possible the divine personality. One formula for the stages of bhakti progress described the stages of devotion, moving from listening, singing, and worshiping to self-surrender.

Each of the great deities of Hinduism has come to be known through the purana texts, and theologians provide different explanations for how and why the divine beings have manifested themselves to save humanity from mundane dangers and to bestow ultimate salvation.

❖ Ganesh

Judged by the number of shrines and the universality of his image, the elephant-headed Ganesh is the tradition's most popular divinity. Most Hindus worship Ganesh not as a divinity who will help them achieve salvation but more to secure his aid in worldly life. With a potbelly and love of sweets signaling his sensual orientation, Ganesh, who is commonly honored

The Dance of Shiva

One of the most lyrical and evocative symbols of Hinduism, especially in the sweeping design of South Indian artisans, is that of Nataraja, Shiva as Lord of the Dance. The upper right hand holds the twin-sided drum, from which sacred sound emerges, counting time and originating sound's creative resonance. The opposite hand shows on it a flame so that in Shiva's holding a fire, he points to his being a refuge in the fires of *samsara*. Fire also alludes to this deity's role as destroyer at the end of a great world era. Both hands move together in Shiva's great dance, ceaselessly integrating cosmic creation and destruction, including all the gods. Another hand shows the "fear-not" gesture, and the fourth points to his upraised foot, the place Hindu devotees touch most often in ritual. Shiva dances while treading on a demon who symbolizes heedlessness. Thus, to enter into the Dance of Shiva means to brave the circle of rebirth, transcend the limitations of time and apparent opposites, and join with the divine powers of the great deity whose grace and eternal energy can remove spiritual obstacles. Because the cosmos has become a manifestation of Shiva's power, a dance done simply for the purpose of his own entertainment, wherever individuals can cultivate artistic pleasure, they can find union with Shiva.

Shiva Nataraja, Lord of the Dance: twelfth-century bronze image from southern India.

with offerings at the start of most rituals and journeys, is regarded as the kind, "fix it" god in the pantheon.

✤ Shiva

The **Shaivite**, or one whose chosen deity is Shiva, focuses on two beliefs: that Shiva's essence is found in all creative energies that saturate this world, and that one can find one's own divine nature by dedicating bhakti practice to this lord. Shiva's identity in the puranas merges opposing sides of Hindu life: He is the ideal ascetic revered by yogins, the god who in the Himalayas underwent long penances while dwelling with cobras, clad in deer skin, and covered in ash. He is also conceived of as a divine householder who marries the goddess of the snow mountains (Parvati) and fathers divine sons Ganesh and Kumar.

In Hindu legend, Shiva saves the world repeatedly and requites devotion with his grace. However, Shiva also has a wrathful side and will punish humans as well. The puranas attribute to Shiva the periodic cosmic upheavals that return the universe to a formless, empty resting state. The sectarian Shaivite theologians see the linking of world creation, fertility, and destruction as signifying Shiva's omnipresence, making him the supreme "Great God."

❖ Vishnu and His Avataras

Although they may respect Shiva, Vishnu devotees (**Vaishnavites**) believe that their chosen deity is the one who truly underlies all reality. Vishnu alone sleeps atop the cosmic ocean in the universe's eras of dissolution, and he alone begets the god Brahma, who then begins another cycle of creation.

The great theme of Vishnu theology is that of incarnation. The puranas dedicated to him recount many episodes in the earth's history when demons or evil threatened creation. At these times, Vishnu assumed the form of whatever was needed to smash the threat. Some of these incarnations, or **avataras**, were animals and most were local heroes.

Vishnu remains alive and connected to the human community of devotees through temple icons and rituals and through the singing of songs recounting his greatness. The texts also sense his being poised for humanity's future salvation, and one avatara, Kalki, is expected to come riding on a white horse to guide humanity as the Kali Yuga turns darker.

Avatara theory thus provides the most systematic example of Hinduism's theological pattern that spawned a profusion of sects, moving readily from the acceptance of multiple particular deities to arrange them in ordered hierarchies. But most Hindus, whether intellectuals or commoners, will assent to the same theological understanding, namely, that "ultimately all the gods are one." There is also a long history of Hindus (and Buddhists) refraining from staking out one final dogmatic position, since many traditions hold that Ultimate Reality is beyond all human naming or philosophical comprehension. Accepting this limitation has given Hinduism its flexible strength and its adherents an openness to ongoing revelation.

❖ Rama

We have already encountered Rama, hero of the *Ramayana,* who slays the demon Ravana and reveals the ideal of proper filial obedience to parents, loyalty to brothers, and the exemplary conduct of Hindu kings. His alliance with the monkey leader Hanuman also signals the ideal of harmonizing the divine with the natural world. A second form of Rama is one dedicated to destroying any evil kings who would molest brahmins or their rituals.

Bearing a mace, a discus, and a conch, Vishnu is represented as Lord of the universe.

✤ Krishna

The most complex and multifaceted of the Vishnu avataras, Krishna is revered in many forms: the infant trickster god, whose every prank and every gesture reveal his underlying divinity; the child who as "the butter thief" also steals the hearts of the world's mothers and fathers; the brave youth who rescues villagers from the poison of evil serpent deities (*nagas*) and from the cruel rains sent by the Vedic god Indra; and the divine paramour and consort of the female cowherds (*gopis*). Finally, Krishna is the mature guru who offers counsel about the necessity of serving the world according to one's dharma, clarifying choices among the many spiritual practices. Many of his sectarian devotees believe that Krishna is in fact the reality from which all the gods originate.

✤ Devis

The consolidating pattern in Hindu theology is readily apparent in the development of the myths of the goddess. Hindu goddesses are born of the earth and can bestow its wealth. Rivers are all goddesses. Early Indian art depicts the fertile, creative power of the universe in scenes where a young woman touches a tree, her innate energy (*shakti*) causing it to burst into bloom. Those who predominantly worship goddesses are thereby called *shaktas,* and theirs is the third general group among Hindu deity worshipers, alongside Vaishnavites and Shaivites.

The earth goddess may be addressed as Ambika ("Mother"), Sita ("[born of the] tilled furrow), or Sati ("the Virtuous"). All these forms draw on the creative, mothering female force. Another widespread and primordial sense of female divinity is that associated with destruction; this has been primarily in the form of the smallpox goddess, called in the north Shitala or Ajima (so vibrant is this devi theology today that with the disappearance of this disease, Shitala has become the deity to appeal to against the rising scourge of HIV/AIDS).

Yet other related female forms are the goddesses who destroy demons, Durga and Kali. Those needing to confront death to arrive at mature spirituality can make Kali their "chosen deity": To visualize the dance of Kali means seeing that life inevitably becomes encircled by death and so always keeping in mind that the gift of human life should not be frittered away. Devotional communion with Durga and Kali requires bhaktas to offer them life blood through animal sacrifice to secure their blessings.

Hindu theology also views the pantheon as balancing the distinct powers that are uniquely those of male and female. The cosmos, like the human species, is seen as created and sustained by the same combination of gender energies: the male shakta and the female shakti. Each is incomplete and even dangerous without the balancing influence of the other. Thus, most all of the Hindu deities are married. Shiva is married to Parvati, or Uma, Vishnu to Lakshmi (important as the wealth god-

---

"O Mother! Thou art present in every form;

Thou art the universe and in its tiniest and most trifling things.

Wherever I go and wherever I look,

I see Thee, Mother, present in thy cosmic form.

The whole earth— earth, water, fire, air—

Are all thy forms, O Mother, the whole world of birth and death."

Source: David Kinsley, *The Sword and the Flute* (Berkeley: University of California Press, 1975), p. 116.

Durga, riding her vehicle, the tiger, carries the weapons of the male gods.

dess), Brahma to Saraswati (goddess of learning), Krishna to Radha, Rama to Sita, and so on. We shall see later how tantric Hinduism carries the implications of this theology into individual yoga practice.

Premodern Hinduism: The Postclassical Era (900 CE–1500 CE)

THE FORMATION OF MAJOR HINDU SCHOOLS OF THOUGHT

During the late classical era, the brahmin elite concerned with philosophical views (called *darshana*) consolidated their positions in systematic expositions, which became and have remained authoritative for the tradition. Every school's texts sought to explain the nature of the physical world, the boundaries of individuality, the basis for establishing human knowledge, and the means to salvation. All told, these texts and the epics comprise an extraordinarily large sacred literary tradition.

The orthodox schools formed in response to the heterodox, or nonstandard, schools of Buddhism and Jainism. Some of them were confined to small circles of high-caste scholastics, but the others, discussed here, came to dominate the Hindu intellectual tradition.

❖ *Sankhya*

One of the oldest systematic philosophy schools to appear, and closely aligned to the yoga classical school, the Sankhya school's ideas were especially important in subsequent Hindu thought. The Sankhya school (literally, "analysis") posits a dualistic universe of matter (*prakriti*) bonded in various combinations with spirit (*purusha*). Both matter and spirit are eternal, with an infinite number of purushas eternally distinct from one another.

Sankhya admits the reality of gods but denies the existence of a transcendent God. The purpose of spiritual life is isolating purusha from prakriti. Although its goal is to go beyond the material world, the Sankhya nonetheless developed a powerful analysis of material formations, specifying twenty-five *gunas,* the individual qualities by which matter can be clearly understood. Sankhya's differentiation of spirit-matter combinations, which has informed Hindu culture to the present, is applied to the analysis of human personality, gender, species, the seasons, aesthetics, and even foods.

One typical use of Sankhya theory is to assess the spiritual status of human beings. All beings are combinations of three primary material qualities or "strands" that bind spirit to the material world: *sattva* (associated with purity, goodness, subtlety), *rajas* (passion, raw energy), and *tamas* (darkness, inertia, grossness). In the Sankhya view, too, even the gods are qualitatively similar to humans, different only by having more sattva. This school thereby sees the incarnation of divinities in human form as part of the universe's natural processes.

❖ Advaita Vedanta

The Advaita Vedanta school is monistic; that is, it regards the singular reality of the universe as impersonal spirit, a view that draws on the Upanishads' formula Brahman = atman. This school of thought began at the time of the Buddha and became the prevailing scholastic philosophy of South Asia after 500 CE, and it is most often emphasized by modern Hindu reformers. Advaita Vedanta's enduring central place among Hindu philosophies was due to the brilliance of the great religious virtuoso **Shankara** (c. 788–820). His succinct commentaries and original treatises received additional exposure through public debates with proponents of other schools (including Buddhists).

Shankara argued that the apparent difference between the material and physical worlds is pure illusion (*maya*). Only study and yoga practice can enable a seeker to gain true knowledge, reversing the "superimposition" on pure spirit of deluded perceptions of two worlds. This path the Vedantins called *jnana yoga,* "union through discriminating knowledge."

Shankara admitted that one could in elementary and intermediate stages of spiritual development relate to Brahman as a personal divinity with characteristics ["*saguna*"] such as power and grace (**saguna Brahman**). But ultimately, moksha can be achieved only by going beyond this projection of a deity in terms of human characteristics to experience Brahman by merging one's own soul with **nirguna Brahman**, that reality "without characteristics."

Shankara also organized the first great network of Hindu monasteries (*mathas*) that supported male ascetics whose rule of conduct specified vegetarianism, dress in an ochre robe, use of a walking staff, and horizontal forehead markings. At monasteries established originally at Dvaraka in the west, Puri in the east, Badrinath in the north, and Shringeri in the south, this order grew, expanded, and survives to this day.

❖ The Theology of Qualified Monism: Vishishta Advaita

While Shankara's monistic thought and practice appealed to intellectuals and ascetics, it was quite distant from the religious experience of most devotees who revered the gods. It remained for later theologians, particularly **Ramanuja** (c. 1025–1137), to link scholastic theology with popular theistic practice. Ramanuja argued that human beings could not really recognize the divine, except in the perceivable world. Why? Since Brahman pervades all reality, the religious path to moksha cannot and need not proceed beyond saguna Brahman. Like Shankara, Ramanuja wrote his own commentary on the Upanishads, but he reached a very different theistic conclusion about their ultimate spiritual truth. He emphasized Vishnu as the form of Brahman most effectively worshiped.

Ramanuja asserted that each individual is ultimately a fragment of Vishnu, wholly dependent on him, and that a perfect continuous intuition of this could be realized only through concentrated and intense devotion (*bhakti yoga*). This theology also holds that souls do not ultimately merge with Brahman, maintaining a "separate nondifference," even in moksha.

Shri Yantra, symbol of the goddess used in meditation

✤ *Tantric Hinduism*

Post–classical era Hinduism produced two major innovations: sectarian monasticism and **tantra**. Like the bhakti theology already mentioned, the tantric tradition built on earlier ideas and practices but advocated new forms of spiritual experience. The name *tantra* relates to weaving, signifying "warp and woof," in this case likely indicating the interweaving of teaching and texts. The emergence of tantra can be seen in both Hinduism and Buddhism, indicating how thoroughly these later traditions affected each other.

Tantric teachers accepted Kali Yuga theory, and their texts typically begin by underscoring how the tantric path to salvation in this lifetime is suited for the Kali Yuga age, when individuals and the world itself are in spiritual decline. The assumption is that what worked for the Vedic sages is too subtle for today. Similarly, what was then prohibited to the seeker is precisely what is needed today for spiritual breakthrough. Still, tantric teachings are not given openly or universally, but are bestowed by teachers only to those deemed capable of practicing methods that, as we shall see, contradict the dharma-based morality of the upper castes. The method of transmitting the teachings from guru to student, of course, goes back to the ancient period. However, the vows not to reveal to noninitiates the lessons of the teacher are more highly restrictive than in earlier practice.

The six centers of the tantric body, displayed in relation to a yogin.

There are many tantric schools, each deriving from an enlightened saint called a *siddha,* who discovered in an intensive personal quest a method of meditation and understanding that culminates in moksha. This personal lineage was passed down in small circles following specific beliefs and practices derived from the original master. All the tantric paths are rooted in the ancient yoga traditions we have discussed. *Tantric yoga,* too, regards the body as a microcosm of the universe; adepts believe that all bodily energies, if harnessed and focused, are capable of producing a transformative religious experience. What is distinctive in tantric yoga is that the primal energies of male and female become essential and focal. Thus, tantra incorporated the devotional worship of female deities in union with their consorts. Many tantric teachings prescribe the practice of ritualized sexual union during which both partners visualize themselves as divinities, cultivating in each other an enlightened awakening through the transformative energy that arises through their union. The goal is realization of the one blissful spirit that is beyond gender and is universal.

Most tantric traditions invite practitioners to experience this ultimate reality, one that can be found only by suspending the norms imposed by the Hindu social law and caste-determined individual conduct. Tantric yoga entails mastering complex rituals and practices that invert status and gender hierarchy norms, breaking down a person's construction of his or her identity on such conventional lines. Thus, one can select a tantric partner from a lower caste, and practitioners perform rituals designed to transform their inner being, ingesting foods such as meat, fish, and alcohol that are otherwise unacceptable for high-caste groups. Places of tantric practice include cremation grounds, the most polluted ritual sites; ritual implements include human bones and skulls. The sexual yoga and the use of gruesome items shocked orthodoxy, but they were deployed for the highly traditional goal of freeing the individual's mind to realize moksha.

Ritualized union in Hindu tantra seeks to arouse an otherwise-dissipated primal power conceived of as a serpent coiled at the base of the spine; this force, called the *kundalini,* is made to rise up the spine through a series of centers (*cakras*), visualized as wheels or lotuses. These centers are found proximate to the genitals, navel, heart, throat, eyes, forehead, and top of the skull. If the energy can be raised to this topmost center, the "thousand-petaled lotus," one's spirit is perfected and a host of supernormal powers unfold. The unorthodox practices and extraordinary experiences were thought to be dangerous for those unready for them; this made the siddha teachers wary of instructing unproven individuals and led them to prescribe dire penalties for any initiate who revealed anything about tantric practice to outsiders.

While early on tantra grew to become a "counterculture" juxtaposed against orthodox Hinduism, its influence slowly grew, even among the high castes. Later, tantric ideas shaped Hindu life-cycle rites and temple ritualism, as priests over the centuries who had delved into tantric practice revised ancient rituals to be multidimensional, keeping the older outward practices and adding meaning for the general public as well as communicating inner truths for those attuned to esoteric tantric symbolisms.

"In men of animal nature, Shakti sleeps, but for tantrics she is wide awake. He who serves shakti is the 'true worshipper.' Whoever knows the rapture of the soul's union with the ultimate is the true adept at lovemaking. All others are merely enjoyers of women."

—Kularnava Tantra V. 107–113

Source: Indra Sinha, *Tantra: The Cult of Ecstasy* (London: Hamlyn, 1993), p. 144.

THE EARLY ISLAMIC ERA: DELHI SULTANATE (1192–1525)

Soon after the conversion of central Asian and Turkic peoples to Islam in the first centuries after the death of the Prophet Muhammad (632 CE), South Asia began to absorb Islamic influences. Muslim traders entered through caravan and port towns, built mosques, and eventually brought religious scholars and clerical authorities to guide their slowly growing communities. Missionaries preaching the tolerant and mystical tradition of Sufi Islam won an especially strong reception in some quarters. The conquest of northern India by Ghuride armies from central Asia (1192) ended resistance from the Hindu ruling class, the kshatriya, and in some localities resulted in Muslim armies destroying religious monuments. The conquest was the most devastating to Buddhists, whose already-declining monasteries on the Gangetic plain were leveled and whose monks fled to bordering lands.

Over 500 years of Muslim rule followed, an era of strong, increasingly centralized government. In many areas, Muslims displaced kshatriyas as heads of regional states; in many other places, Hindu rulers continued as their vassals. The Delhi sultanate included the northern sections of modern Pakistan and India, from the Indus to the Upper Ganges. In general, authorities of the sultanate did not attempt to regulate indigenous traditions in their own regions or in kshatriya-ruled states, and Hindu traditions continued strongly. Indeed, the great bhakti saints who rose to prominence in this era have dominated the popular Hindu devotional imagination ever since. Some, called *bhaktas* (including Basavanna [1106–1168], Chaitanya [1486–1533], and Mirabai [1540–?]), taught that the highest human goal in devotion was to experience the divine in human manifestation; others, called *sants* (including Ravidas [1450], Kabir [1440–1518], and Nanak [1469–1539]), insisted that true salvation was found when seeing the divine beyond any particular form, that is, *nirguna brahman*. The devotional songs of these revered teachers are still sung across the Hindu world today.

> "Kabir says:
>
> My mind was soothed
>
> When I found boundless knowledge,
>
> And the fires that scorch the world
>
> To me is water cool."
>
> Source: Songs of the Saints of India, p. 59.

RELIGION IN THE MUGHAL ERA (1526–1707)

The great Mughal Empire that controlled northern and central India from 1526 until 1707 represented the second era of Muslim rule across much of South Asia. In its first century, Mughal rule was prosperous and peaceful, ushering in an efflorescence of Indo-Islamic culture in architecture and the fine arts. The Taj Mahal in Agra is the most famous among hundreds of magnificent buildings erected in this period. There was a significant rise in converts to Islam across North India during the Mughal dynasty.

✤ *Guru Nanak and the Rise of Sikhism*

One of the principal bhakti saints, Guru Nanak, achieved unparalleled success as founder of the last great religious tradition to originate in India, Sikhism. His disciples now number over 20 million, eclipsing the number of Buddhists in South Asia and the number of Jews globally.

Guru Nanak was born in 1469, before the beginning of the Mughal rule. A civil servant with a wife and two children, he underwent a three-day religious experience at the age of 29 that changed his life. His first pronouncement as a spiritual man was definitive and indicated the path he was about to embark on as founder of a new faith: "There is neither Hindu nor Muslim, so whose path shall I follow? I shall follow God's path. God is neither Hindu nor Muslim and the path that I follow is God's."[6]

For the next twenty years, Nanak wandered far and wide as an ascetic. Conveyed in poetry and song, his spiritual and moral teachings are set forth through encounters with animals, rulers, commoners, and holy men, Hindu sadhus and Muslim Sufis alike. Legendary accounts of Nanak's life describe his visiting Tibet and setting forth to Mecca, where his spiritual understanding and supernormal powers surpass those of all others. Sikh tradition avers that Nanak's mission was to reveal the full spiritual truth and the proper path to realize it, correcting the mistaken practices and partial truths of both Hinduism and Islam.

When he returned home from his wandering at age 50, Nanak set out to do just this. Back in the Northwest Indian region known as the Punjab, he taught all who were interested and soon attracted many disciples—"*Sikhs*"—who were drawn by the charismatic guru as well as by the community whose rules and rituals he established. Many disparate Hindu groups were drawn to this new community, which offered an indigenous monotheistic alternative to Islam. After designating a successor, Nanak died in 1539.

✢ *The Ten Gurus and the Development of the Sikh Community*

After Nanak there were nine other gurus (someone who reveals the divine), who managed the burgeoning communities being established across the region. They gathered the songs and sermons composed by Nanak, adding hymns attributed to other, like-minded saints, forming a text called the **Adi Granth.** This scripture, 1,430 pages in its final form, remains the unique focus of Sikh worship to this day. The gurus also refined the community liturgies, making the group a compelling alternative to and socially separate from similar Hindu groups. The town of Amritsar ("Pool of Ambrosia") was built and became the center of the faith up to the present day. Its Golden Temple, set in a lake, is the crown jewel of Sikh architecture. Sikh tradition holds that the site on which the Golden Temple stands was sanctified by the visit to it by Guru Nanak, who instructed succeeding gurus to develop the area into a great spiritual center that would radiate a message of love and peace to mankind. The tenth guru, Gobind Singh (1666–1708), declared that in the future, the guru of the Sikhs in spiritual matters would be the holy text itself, which thus became designated the Guru Granth Sahib. Political leadership would be the province of an elite group called the **Khalsa.**

Traditional image of Guru Nanak.

In the Gurmukhī script, *Ek Onkar* is a combination of three letters: *Ek*, *Aum*, and *Kar*, which is a line drawn over the Om, signifying continuity, timelessness, and eternity.

In the early years of Mughal rule, the Sikhs gained popularity and were welcomed at court. The emperor Akbar (1561–1605) found in the faith a tolerant monotheistic theology and regarded the followers as a disciplined moral community. Akbar's successors, however, felt distrustful about the Sikhs' growth and political influences. The fifth guru, Arjan (1581–1606), was killed on the order of one emperor, and in 1669, when another Mughal ruler ordered all Hindu temples and schools demolished, Sikhs resisted, and many were martyred. It was in response to this growing persecution that the Khalsa was formed, dedicated to struggling for the defense of the faith (*dharma yudha,* much like the doctrine of *jihad* in Islam). The Khalsa, who adopted a strict and determined lifestyle as guardians of the faith, marked themselves by their appearance: uncut hair (covered with a turban), short trousers, steel wristlet, comb, and sword. Sikhs in the Khalsa also adopted the names Singh ("lion") for men and Kaur ("princess") for women, to eliminate caste distinctions within the community.

✣ Sikh Theology and Spiritual Practices

Nanak's spiritual path contained elements of both Hindu and Muslim traditions. As in Islam, Nanak taught that there is only one "God," who never walked the earth as a man (i.e., had not had an incarnation). Nanak also set his teaching firmly in the Hindu nirguna tradition, mystically affirming that this God is entirely beyond form and human categories. To specify this god, Nanak introduced the terms **Om-kara** ("Divine One") and Sat Guru ("True Teacher").

Anticipating reformers of colonial and postcolonial Hinduism, Sikhs deny that asceticism is necessary or of value, holding that householders are perfectly capable of realizing the highest goal of salvation. Similarly, they say that ritual acts and pilgrimages have no spiritual effect. In addition, they reject the authority of the Vedas and the innate sanctity of the brahmin caste. As we have seen, the Sikhs' non-Vedic orientation has caused high-caste Hindus to regard them as heterodox.

Residing in the human heart and communicating with those who live rightly and develop their spiritual faculties, Sat Guru freely bestows grace that ends individual karma and rebirth. In Sikh spiritual understanding, the human struggle involves rejecting ego-centered living and embracing the inner life of opening to the divine Sat Guru within. Revelation occurs through the effect of divine sound on one's consciousness. The Guru Granth is the center of their rituals and ceremonies. Therefore, Sikh religiosity is centered on listening to, and congregationally singing, the hymns composed

Omkar
True name
Being who creates
Beyond fear and opposition
A form beyond time
Unborn, self-born
The guru's grace.

—Nanak

Source: Songs of the Saints of India, p. 78.

by Nanak and other saints and sitting in the presence of the Guru Granth, whose very words both reflect and impart this grace. Consciously rejecting the norms of caste society while living among a Hindu majority, Sikhs affirm the social equality of all humanity, regardless of caste, race, creed, or gender.

There is no priesthood or ordained ministry; men and women pray together. Sikhs have had to make accommodations yet establish separate boundaries through their rituals. To become a Sikh requires making a profession of belief, affirming the essentials of nirguna theology and the need for each individual to earn salvation:

> There is one God, his name is truth eternal
> He is the creator of all things, the all-pervading spirit
> Fearless and without hatred, timeless and formless.
> Beyond birth and death, he is self-enlightened.
> He is known by the Guru's grace.[7]

Festivals mark the birth or death of the Ten Gurus, but Sikhs join Hindus in observing the major Hindu festivals. Instead of Vedic or brahmanical texts, passages from the *Adi Granth* are used in community life-cycle rites for naming, marriage, and death.

Sikhs find their salvation in combining public and private worship with social action, earning an honest living, giving alms, and doing community service. The community meal and kitchen reflect many of the teachings and morality of Sikhism: the centrality of community, its egalitarian nature, and social action. Within India's Hindu caste society, it was revolutionary, bringing all together, regardless of caste and station in life. Today, it is a central practice seen everyday at the Golden Temple in Amritsar and in Sikh communities globally, where Sikhs and non-Sikhs, men and women gather together for community meals. Its spirit is reflected in the aphorism "Where there are Sikhs, there is no hunger." These activities are centered in Sikh temples, called **gurudwaras**.

The Golden Temple in Amritsar, Punjab. This great landmark for Sikhs worldwide, and the faith's chief pilgrimage center, was occupied in the early 1980s by militants seeking Punjab's secession from India.

Hinduism and Modernity

HINDUISM UNDER BRITISH COLONIALISM

The first Europeans known to have settled in South Asia in Mughal times were Roman Catholic missionaries, initially the Dominicans in the Portuguese colony of Goa by 1510 and, after 1540, the Jesuits, led by Francis Xavier. Early merchants also arrived by sea to trade for spices, silks, indigo, and cotton goods. Although they had competitors among early Dutch, Portuguese, and French traders, the British under the East India Company eventually were the most successful at establishing themselves permanently. As the Mughal Empire over its last fifty years slowly disintegrated and the region's "Hindu states" asserted their independence, civil disorder increased, causing trade and tax revenues to decline. In this unstable atmosphere, the British augmented their trade missions with garrisoned fortresses, and by 1730 military detachments were integral to the British mercantile presence. From these centers, the British leaders were drawn into conflicts; when they defeated local rulers in battle, they made alliances and extended their command and control inward. South Asia soon became a patchwork of British territory and "princely states" that submitted to the British but were still ruled in their internal affairs by Hindu royalty or Muslim sultans.

British rule produced both crisis and opportunity for reform among Hindu leaders.

Modern scholarship on India and Hinduism originated in this context of Europeans seeking to learn about native peoples in order to tighten imperial control. British officials believed that it was their duty as white Europeans to spread enlightened civilization to the "primitive peoples" of South Asia. This message was, in turn, repeated back in Europe to justify the expanding colonial enterprise that had begun with merchants.

British schools were established in South Asia to train young Indians to serve in the lower echelons of the colonial bureaucracy. In large part, it was this new class of Indians that made first in-depth contact with modern ideas from Europe, especially in political thought, the natural sciences, and Christianity. This process unfolded in the colonial urban centers, the first of which was Calcutta. English quickly became the lingua franca of the subcontinent; knowing the English language and culture became the necessary path for any ambitious Indian subject in the British domain.

By 1813 missionaries had arrived from every major Christian denomination, challenging Hinduism on every front, from theology and ritual practices to morality and caste norms. Many ministers suggested that the British triumph in India represented God's judging Hinduism to be an idolatrous and demoniac heresy. Many South Asians came to regard the missionaries as in league with the colonialists. Crude depictions of Hindus and Indian culture fomented resentments.

In 1857 widespread civil disturbances swept across British-held territories. During this period, called "the mutiny" by the British and regarded by many Indians as "the first war of independence," Indian troops and peasants gave vent to resentments over

Considered the "first war of independence" by Indian nationalists, the uprising in 1857 was fomented by alleged disrespect of Muslim and Hindu troops under British rule.

colonial law and administrative insensitivities, executing some British officers and murdering their families. Colonial troops and loyal mercenaries put down the rebellion and
exacted brutal reprisals against Indian citizens. When order had been restored, in 1858,
the British parliament dissolved the company that had held the royal charter for trade
with Asia and declared the Queen's direct rule. India became "the jewel in the crown"
of the British Empire for the next ninety years.

CHALLENGES AND RESPONSES TO COLONIALISM

The early modern era thus presented individual Hindus and Hindu institutions with a
series of challenges that they shared with other colonized peoples across the globe.
Powerful outsiders were arriving in significant numbers, proclaiming new truths and
boldly denouncing Hindu beliefs. This ideological challenge appeared simultaneously
in several forms: the scientific worldview of the European Enlightenment, humanistic
critiques of religion, racial theories of European superiority, and the triumphalist
Gospel teachings of outspoken Christian missionaries.

   The early Christian missionaries from Britain were largely Protestant. As a result,
the ideas of nineteenth-century Protestantism had a distinct impact on Hindus, who
sought to reform their own traditions. Protestant emphases that were significant among
Hindu reformers included the use of historical and scientific methods in the search for
core scriptures and doctrines, and criticism of ritual that was not consistent with these
doctrines. Other Protestant perspectives were distrust of traditional priests as purveyors
of "blind superstition" and the promotion of spiritual individualism, whereby each person is responsible for his or her own spiritual destiny. Hindu reformers were further influenced by the Protestant reliance on new lay-run institutions to organize new religious

Missionaries challenged
Hindu beliefs, while also
diffusing the knowledge
of the development
of modern religious
instituions.

movements, the linking of social uplift initiatives with religious reforms, and the prestige of monotheism. (With the exception of monotheism, the same ideas had an impact in the colonial Buddhist territories of Asia, as we will see in the next chapter.) In colonial India, too, "Protestant Hinduism" mobilized the colonized to protest against British imperialism.

Although most South Asians did not convert to Islam or Christianity, many regions in which Hindus lived were ruled by non-Hindus (Muslims and the European successors). This state of affairs was distressing because conquest by outsiders suggested that the power and grace of the Hindu deities had been eclipsed. Further, the economic dislocations due to imperialism in many instances undermined the traditional channels of financial support for Hindu scholars, activists, and temples.

The colonial government's political practice was to use religious identity as the basis for official dealings with "native constituencies." Thus, "Muslim," "Hindu," and "Sikh" became politically defined identities. This created a problematic postcolonial legacy, although it gave the British a convenient manner in which they could divide and conquer groups that arose to oppose their policies or (eventually) their very presence as overlords of South Asia. As a result, too, Hindus, Muslims, and Sikhs competed against one another for favorable treatment at the hands of the colonial government. Communal divides opened where none had existed. Since 1947, tensions between these groups defined by religion have resurfaced, sometimes tragically.

The nineteenth century saw a variety of Hindu responses to colonialism, making it an era of tremendous cultural vitality and synthesis. The early influential leaders were mainly brahmins, the traditional priestly caste that had long emphasized literacy and education and whose rank-and-file caste members supported old-fashioned, change-resistant orthodoxy. Yet among this elite group, especially those in areas of most intense contact (Bombay and Calcutta), the initial reaction to the British shifted from indifference to more engaged positions: either hostility or curiosity. Scattered terrorist groups, some led by militant sadhus, formed to attack British officers and institutions. These were mostly thwarted and went underground. Other Indians developed a genuine interest in European civilization, and increasing numbers traveled to Europe for education. We turn now to examine prominent examples among these Hindu responses.

⚜ The First Reformist Generation: Rammohan Roy, Brahmo Samaj, and the Tattvabodhini Sabha

The widespread issue that Hindus were forced to confront, one shared elsewhere by Muslims and Buddhists, centered on a question: How could it be that the world-preserving great deities have allowed non-Hindus to overshadow Hindus so utterly and to defame Hindu society? Some Hindus gave an answer similar to that heard from time to time in Islam and in other faiths struggling under colonialism: Revelation has not failed, but the community has lost true belief and practice. Therefore, the community needs to be reformed. The first to articulate this position for Hinduism was **Rammohan Roy** (1772–1833), who is regarded by many as "the father of modern India." Roy called for the reform of certain Hindu beliefs and practices prevalent across India, including superstition, caste discrimination, and the practice of widow immolation (*sati*).He argued for universal education in English so that Indians could study modern math, science, and medicine. Roy was equally outspoken in defending Hinduism against missionary attacks, drawing on his study of the Bible and rational analysis to critique Christian dogmas.

In 1828 Roy founded Brahmo Sabha, an organization to further his reformist views. In 1841 the name was changed to the **Brahmo Samaj**, whose official English title—Fellowship of Believers in the One True God—expresses its goal of uniting Hindus of all castes to proclaim a reformist, monotheistic ideology. The Brahmo Samaj's importance lies in its strong influence on subsequent generations of Hindu reformers and revivalists.

The **Tattvabodhini Sabha** ("Truth-Propagating Society") was an especially influential group in Calcutta associated with Roy's teachings. Aimed at exploring and propagating the teachings of Vedantic Hinduism in light of enlightenment rationality, the group was funded by leading members of the rising middle class that was prospering under British rule. Its meetings attracted leading Hindu teachers and philosophers; their addresses were published in vernacular languages and circulated widely among the colonial-era native class called the *bhadralok:* entrepreneurs, landed gentry, school teachers, journalists, a mixture of high castes and newly rich businessmen. Most in this influential class were schooled in England, and some were themselves involved in the colonial education system.

The Tattvabodhini Sabha's revivalism was colored by their commitment to promote the "modern Hindu's" adaptation to India's new economic and political realities. The Sabha publications merged these values—working hard, living honestly, saving rationally, and promoting altruism—with their view of Vedanta's message of the individual controlling personal desires. Along with Roy, they saw reformed Hinduism now being led by the "godly householder," not the premodern elite of world-renouncing ascetics. Instead of seeking to extirpate all human desire, Hindus should accept desire's power but guide it "according to *dharma*" (here, "justice") and for society's overall betterment: "respect for your father and mother, love your neighbors, work for the welfare of the government, rescue people from the torment of suffering, provide religious instruction to your sons and students, and give knowledge to the ignorant."[8]

Like the ethos underlying the successful Protestant businessmen then leading the global spread of capitalism, this influential Hindu elite articulated a congruent view of human mission, though they built this on a very different metaphysical foundation. For the principled, hard-working, frugal, philanthropic, middle-class householder to become a "saint" (*mahatma,* a term applied later to Gandhi), their journal set forth the path thusly:

> They always exert themselves with care, whether by keeping good company, providing counsel, quelling sorrow, treating illness, or bestowing knowledge. Such great-souled men are indeed wealthy and they alone are the true votaries of the Supreme Lord . . . they alone are able to set aside their own interests and work for the welfare of all."[9]

❖ More Strident and Sectarian: Dayananda and the Arya Samaj

Similar in many respects to the Brahmo Samaj but centered in Bombay and Lahore, the **Arya Samaj** was founded in 1875 by the brahmin teacher Swami Dayananda (1824–1883). Dayananda held the fundamentalist view that only the four Vedas were valid sources for true Hinduism and that they were in fact "infallible," containing all knowledge, even the root ideas of modern science. India, he famously proclaimed, "needed nothing from the West." For him, as for Roy, the essential Hindu theological idea was monotheism. Accordingly, he rejected post-Vedic scripture and saw later polytheism as the reason for Hinduism's decline. Dayananda tirelessly denounced practices such as child marriage, untouchability, and the subjugation of women. He composed his own simplified list of ethical norms and a description of properly reformed Vedic rituals.

Dayananda's successors made the Arya Samaj especially influential once the organization developed village institutions and schools. Numerous Dayananda Anglo-Vedic colleges and high schools continue the Arya Samaj revivalist tradition to the present day. Many of the current Bharatiya Janata party members and leaders have been influenced by the Arya Samaj. Its work was spread globally by émigrés from South Asia.

❖ Sikh Reform and Resurgence

Through their resistance to the Mughals, the Sikhs eventually carved out their own kingdom in western India that lasted from 1799 until 1849, when it was absorbed into British India. After this, Sikh men were recruited into the colonial army from 1870 to 1947, becoming renowned for their disciplined character and martial abilities. Sikhs also entered into many of the new colonial educational institutions, finding success as

Teachings of Religious Wisdom

Same Water, Different Names

The following parable by Ramakrishna was found in a pamphlet from the Ramakrishna Mission in Calcutta, dated 1976.

God is one only, and not two. Different people call on Him by different names: some as Allah, some as God, others as Krishna, Shiva, and Brahman. It is like the water in a lake. Some drink it at one place and call it "jal," others at another place and call it "*pani*," and still others at a third place and call it "water." The Hindus call it "jal," the Christians "water," and the Muslims "pani." But it is one and the same thing. Opinions are but paths. Each religion is only a path leading to God, as rivers come from different directions and ultimately become one in the ocean.

civil servants, educators, and businessmen. Soon, Sikhs were serving across the British Empire, and on retirement many settled outside India, from Singapore and Hong Kong to England. These migrants brought their faith with them, making Sikhism a large global faith today.

Sikhs also responded to the religious challenges posed by South Asia's colonial situation and the aggressive Christian missionaries who appeared in the Punjab. A Sikh reformist organization, the Singh Sabha (Lion Society), was formed in 1879 to implement socioeducational uplift programs and defend the faith. The Singh Sabha sought to vitalize Sikhism through educational and literary activities as well as political agitation; it founded a college in Amritsar and sponsored magazines and newspapers that encouraged religious pride among the Sikh communities that were spreading across India and abroad.

✤ Ramakrishna and Vivekananda: The First Global Hindu Mission

A brahmin like Roy and Dayananda but with a much more humble educational background, Ramakrishna (1834–1886) was a charismatic guru who attracted reform-minded Hindus. In Ramakrishna's revivalism, however, the teacher emphasized mystical experience and ecumenical monistic or nirguna theology. His spiritual experiences included long periods of trance in which he reported being possessed in turn by Kali, Sita, Rama, Krishna, Muhammad, and Jesus. Ramakrishna's teaching emphasized that the entire universe is permeated by the paramount divine spirit, a reality that is called different names by the world's different people, but whose essence is one. In articulating this view, Ramakrishna was updating to a global scale the interfaith ecumenical teaching of the classical Hindu school we have already discussed, that of Vedantic Hinduism.

It was **Swami Vivekananda** (1863–1902), Ramakrishna's foremost disciple, who became a guru in his own right and presented this theology in a forceful and systematic manner. Vivekananda was the first great missionary representative of Hinduism on the global stage. His popularity grew through lectures on Hinduism across America and Europe. Most Westerners' first acquaintance with Hinduism is largely a product of the teachings of Vivekananda and his later followers.

Vivekananda organized the **Ramakrishna Mission**, whose institutions spread across India. The mission advocated reformist traditions and embraced a global ecumenical awareness. Its highly organized order of monks cultivated inner spiritual development through yoga, taught "the Gospel of Ramakrishna," and established educational institutions, hospitals, and hospices open to all. Some monks trained as doctors. In 2004 there were 18 mission hospitals, 120 dispensaries, and 6,500 educational centers in India.

The Ramakrishna Mission became the first great global Hindu organization with a vision of ecumenical Hinduism as the savior of the world, not merely of India. The mission's disciples in the West now support its global reach. By 2004 it had published many books and built retreat centers, libraries, and sanctuaries in major cities in seventeen countries.

"Calling God Mother is a higher idea than calling Him Father, to call him Friend is still higher, but the highest is to regard Him as the Beloved. The highest point of all is to see no difference between lover and beloved."

—Vivekananda

Source: Stephen Hay, ed., *Sources of Indian Tradition*, 2nd ed., Vol. 2 (New York: Columbia University Press, 1988), p. 73.

THE WORK OF GANDHI: HINDU ELEMENTS IN INDIAN NATIONALISM

By the turn of the twentieth century, Britain's command over the subcontinent had grown, with its building of a vast modern infrastructure (roads, railroads, telegraph) that supported increasing trade. The presence of Christian missions and the colonial government's bureaucracy had also expanded as Europeans visited the region by the thousands yearly. Indian leaders and organizations seeking to strengthen and reform Hinduism were also multiplying through this period, however, and religious reformism and political activism frequently converged.

The growing independence movement often drew on religious identity and pride. An important player in the independence movement was the Indian National Congress, founded in 1880 in Bombay. Although dominated by brahmins and a few Muslims, who were mostly urban, English-educated lawyers, the Congress sought to speak for all Indians. While it proclaimed loyalty to the Raj, as the British colonial government was called, the Congress increasingly agitated nonviolently for greater economic development and the incremental growth of self-rule. Thus, it gained acceptance as the party to articulate an Indian voice vis-à-vis the colonial government.

The spiritual background motivating many of the Congress leaders was that of the reformists who sought to regenerate Indian culture (both Hindu and Islamic). Indeed, many were convinced that India had a spiritual message for the future of humanity. Such a sentiment was heightened, of course, by the great world wars, whose devastation

Mohandas K. Gandhi. A great political leader who merged European ideas with reformist Hindu teachings to lead India to independence.

Gandhi

M. K. Gandhi was born in a merchant family in the western region of Gujarat. As a young man he was interested in secular subjects, and he traveled to London to study law. While there he encountered for the first time the classical Hindu texts, all in English translations. He was introduced to them not by an Indian *guru* but through meetings at the Theosophical Society, a group of European mystics interested in the secret doctrines they felt were at the root of all world religions. While in England, Gandhi also read the Bible avidly as well as books by European intellectuals like Tolstoy and Ruskin and the American Thoreau.

After becoming a lawyer, Gandhi settled in South Africa, then a British colony with a large Indian minority. He was soon drawn into political activism in opposition to the racist and discriminatory imperial practices directed toward South Asians as "coloreds." From experiences with protests and community organization, Gandhi developed his central principle, one that guided his future life. He called it **satyagraha** ("grasping the truth"). This concept has roots in the Hindu and Jain doctrine of nonviolence (**ahimsa**) and in

Christianity's injunctions to love one's enemy and turn the other cheek (as a reaction to being struck in the face). Gandhi required those opposing the government to confine their protests to nonviolent acts, accept suffering for the cause, to love the opponent, and to be disciplined in personal life. Gandhi's work in South Africa among Indian immigrants transformed him and drew attention to his teachings back in India, where Congress leaders urged him to return. He did so in 1915.

Although Gandhi always retained respect for British law and the moral ideals articulated in Western religions, back in India he abandoned the dress of the Western barrister for the humble *dhoti* (loincloth) of the Indian peasant. Gandhi's greatness as a political leader was likewise built on his connection with the Indian masses, a relationship that developed through his wide-ranging tours of the countryside, his involvement with a series of peasant protests, his self-imposed poverty, and an effective organization (including a daily newspaper) that he developed with those who lived in his *ashram*.

suggested that neither science, European political systems, nor Christianity was to be triumphant in global history.

It was **Mohandas K. Gandhi** (1869–1948) who became the most significant leader to guide South Asia to independence. Gandhi himself embodies the changes and syntheses affecting South Asia as the era of globalism under colonialism was brought to an end. As a paradigmatic reformist Hindu who merged European and Indian cultures, Gandhi became one of the greatest world figures of the twentieth century.

On the national stage, Gandhi linked the Congress elite with the masses. Although some disagreed with his stands, he was a nationally venerated guru, an activist who creatively reinterpreted Hinduism in an ethical, this-worldly manner. Gandhi went on hunger strikes to move British officials (or, at times, other Indian leaders) to reconsider their positions. The honorific *Mahatma* applied to his name, meaning "great-souled [one]," expresses the profound spiritual respect he garnered in his lifetime.

Carrying on the work of earlier reformers, Gandhi decried high-caste discrimination toward others, and he especially highlighted untouchability as a blight on Hinduism. He also extended the Hindu and Jain notion of *ahimsa* (nonviolence) to articulate an entire way of life guided by this ideal. Through following ahimsa in all spheres, Gandhi argued that the modern Hindu could find the truth in humble daily work. It was a principle that could transform the individual and society, imbuing each with a spiritual center.

Gandhi's life work was crowned in 1947, when India finally gained its independence. However, celebration of this long-anticipated moment was shattered by the violence that accompanied it. The British allowed no time for the orderly implementation of their partition, which divided India, a new secular nation, from the new Muslim state of Pakistan. A civil war broke out in which an estimated 4 million people perished. Nearing the age of 80, Gandhi traveled to many of these areas in an attempt to quell the chaos, but largely in vain. He was murdered in 1948 by a member of a fundamentalist Hindu group that had opposed partition and accused Gandhi of "concessions" to Muslims and the lowest castes.

India in many respects abandoned Gandhi's concept of spiritually centered development. Only in civil law has India continued to embrace Gandhi's vision, albeit haltingly, in its rhetorical commitment to eradicate caste discrimination and by holding fast to India's fundamental identity as a secular—not Hindu—nation. Even this last legacy of Gandhism has been under attack by the high-caste-dominated Hindu parties that enjoyed increasing success during the last decade of the twentieth century, as witnessed by the rise of the BJP.

Hinduism and Postmodern Trends in a Postcolonial World

THE PERSISTENCE OF TRADITIONAL RELIGIOUS UNDERSTANDINGS

Despite the modernization of India that daily reaches ever farther into the rural regions, there has been a remarkable persistence of traditional beliefs and practices in postcolonial India. While no single school or theology is representative of "Hinduism" in all its many forms, it is possible to trace broadly shared understandings and central ideas among the traditions that have remained influential to the present.

❖ The Presence of the Divine

Whatever specific doctrines or practices an individual Hindu follows, what gives the tradition a measure of unity is the widely held conviction that there is something underlying the material world seen by our ordinary consciousness. For humans, therefore, life entails more than satisfying the needs dictated by survival. A divine reality enfolds human reality, interpenetrating the material world and human experience; this occurs primarily through the soul (atman), which animates an embryo in the womb and energizes human life.

If we were traveling to a typical village in South Asia today, we would readily notice that Hindu society is unique in its extraordinary veneration of the sacred in the daily rhythms of life. We might observe rituals honoring the rising and setting sun, see offerings being made at humble temples erected at unusual or aged natural features (stones and trees), and see the inhabitants showing reverent respect at rivers and local mountains as well as to animals such as elephants, snakes, monkeys, and, of course, cows. Devotees might invite us into shrines for the divine protectors of houses, families, artisans, and castes; farmers could take us to the guardian deities of the settlement and of their fields. The local brahmin priest could explain how everyone visits the temple to the goddesses when there are outbreaks of disease. He might direct us to speak with the local spirit medium, who could describe recent episodes of persons in the village possessed by ghosts or demons and how he intervened to cure them through offerings and trance. And then we might drop in to consult with the astrologer, who sits before a long line of patrons wishing to know how the distant deities who appear in the night sky can best be propitiated. Our brahmin host could also point out how at every key moment in a person's life—birth, coming of age, marriage, and death—he is called on to perform rituals to strengthen a family's collective spirit by seeking divine blessings.

In urban areas where some of the older traditions are less prominent, brahmins can be still found performing such rites and also adapting Hindu practices to changing times. For example, since 2004, a regular service offered to all customers of Maruti Udyog cars, the most popular automotive brand in modern India, is to have a brahmin priest perform a puja for the vehicle's good fortune; Maruti Udyog showrooms also feature a line of automotive accessories that include dashboard statues of the Hindu gods.

This excursion into Hinduism as lived tradition makes clear that there is no Hindu view that matches the Western deist notion, made popular in post-Enlightenment Western theology, that God set up creation as a mechanism and then, like a detached watchmaker, retreated to let it tick away. Across Hindu South Asia, the immanence of spirit is respected and the gods live next door. It is the human task to find harmony with them and eventually to seek salvation from rebirth by finding the spirit in whatever guise one is most suited to discover. Even in modern cities and among individuals who are highly educated, the wish to connect with and worship the divine remains strong today.

✤ Hindu Inclusivity Accommodates Wide-Ranging Sectarianism

Another distinctive and enduring characteristic of Hinduism today is the broad range of ideas about the sacred and the widespread tendency for individuals to accept alternative, opposing views. The coexistence of so many competing theologies and religious practices and even the toleration of nonbelievers have been based on two notions. First is the belief that a human understanding of the highest truth, whatever that is held to be, is never complete or perfect. Second is the expectation that as individuals learn and practice more deeply, they will see reality more clearly. From these twin perspectives, persons thought to hold false views are simply located on a lower rank in a hierarchy, not rejected. A wrongheaded person may be ignorant, immature, or incomplete but not evil. Beginning with Islam and extending into the modern era with other "Western" religions, Hinduism's acceptance of pluralism has certainly endured.

Muslim–Hindu relations continue to be important and contentious in modern India. Communal enmity on religious lines was rare after Islam won acceptance in South Asia (1000 CE), mainly because group identity developed predominantly according to caste, region, and political loyalties. It was an acceptance of coexistence, as historian Ainslie Embree has pointed out, that characterized this relationship:

> Two great cultures and religious systems, the Hindu and the Islamic, while borrowing much from each other along the margins of their existence, retained their separate, core identities for 1,000 years. Coexistence, not assimilation, was the characteristic behavior of both communities, and it was made possible by the nature of Hindu society as well as the political policies of the Muslim rulers.[10]

Hindu priest offers *tika* powder, an essential part of the daily worship service for every god. The powder will later be retrieved and used to mark the foreheads of devotees.

Religious enmity is not an eternal, inevitable standpoint in South Asia or elsewhere; in the past, as today, it is the product of a specific historical context, shaped by human actions and political policies.

Though Hindu nationalists have rejected an accommodationalist stance, even questioning the loyalty to India of Muslims and Christians, the inclusivist religious attitude is still shared by many. It has encouraged ever new spiritual searches and the appearance of new religious sects that combine beliefs and practices from various traditions, including astrology, Buddhism, and "secular" traditions such as psychology.

The fact that Hindu groups accept others, Hindu and non-Hindu, and acknowledge their value should not cloud the recognition that many Hindus are indeed sectarian in their religious orientation. While the view "all the gods are one" is widely expressed, it is not a view shared by everyone. Adherence to the ecumenical strategy of inclusivity, of accepting the legitimacy of competing religious standpoints, does not oblige one to abandon one's own sect's truth claims. Inclusivity is ultimately a means of subordinating other truth claims, be they Vaishnava theism, Vedanta monism, or Christian trinitarianism. Thus Hindu worldviews have held their primacy throughout modern times and into the postcolonial era; it has mainly been in reforming and modernizing their social institutions that Hindus have adopted non-Hindu ideas.

CONTEMPORARY HINDU PRACTICES

✤ *The Guru-Disciple Relationship*

Dating from the time of the Upanishads, one central Hindu tradition has been the relationship connecting gurus and disciples. Just as Hindus perceive the divine in their natural and settled environments, they find spirit alive in its realization by those who reach moksha, achieve spiritual powers, and share their experiences for the benefit of humanity. Charismatic saintly **gurus** still hold a central place in both traditional and reformist Hinduism. There is even a festival day each year for honoring one's spiritual guide. *Guru Purnima,* or teacher's full moon, is a day for disciples to make the year's largest material donation to the guru and, ideally, to pay a visit to the teacher.

We have noted the lasting forms of organized Hinduism that emerged in the postclassical era. Then, as now, numerous spiritual teachers emerged in the traditional manner of undergoing long periods of training with independent gurus and then attracting their own disciples. Guru residences called *ashrams* sustain the community that performs rituals, meditates, and learns together under the guru's direction. Many Hindu guru-centered institutions tend to be short-lived, and the "school" that emerges lasts only as long as the charismatic teacher lives or only through his first generation of designated successors. Others continue, and in these cases we see the central Hindu notion of *parampara,* meaning "lineage, tradition, pedigree," that is, the belief that today's teachers are connected to earlier gurus, back to the first enlightened sage in the line.

The circle of intimate disciples must master the guru's instructions on the key spiritual practices (meditation, worship, etc.), most often memorizing them through intensive repetition. They may also collect their guru's teachings, sometimes only in memory, sometimes through writing, or, today, on video! Eventually, the tested and trusted disciples are also designated as gurus by the teacher, usually once they have reached an advanced age, and so the *parampara,* the succession, continues.

Accepting a guru entails assuming a new identity, which is symbolized in the widespread practice of receiving a new name. For example, Western university researcher Richard Alpert took on the name Ram Dass when he became the disciple of the guru Maharaj-ji. The true guru is one's soul mate, but the disciple can expect the guru's full grace and loving guidance only through the complete abandonment of ego.

Given the many material and psychological rewards bestowed on gurus, the possibility of clever charlatans, too, has long been recognized by the Hindu community. Yet

Tales of Spiritual Transformation

Meeting the Guru

In the postcolonial era, Americans and Europeans who have sought Hindu teachers have left rich accounts of their first encounters. In this excerpt, Richard Alpert, the former Harvard researcher who became a popular Western interpreter of Hinduism as Ram Dass, describes his initial meeting with his guru, Maharaj-ji.

Some time later we were back with the Maharaj-ji and he said to me, "Come here. Sit." So I sat down and he looked at me and said, "You were out under the stars last night."

"Um-hum."

"You were thinking about your mother."

"Yes." ('Wow,' I thought, 'that's pretty good. I never mentioned that to anybody.')

"She died last year."

"Um-hum." . . .

"Spleen. She died of spleen."

Well, what happened to me at that moment, I can't really put into words. He looked at me in a certain way at that moment, and two things happened—it seemed simultaneous. The first thing that happened was that my mind raced faster and faster to try

and get leverage—to get a hold on what he had just done. . . . And at the same moment, I felt this extremely violent pain in my chest and a tremendous wrenching feeling and I started to cry. I cried and cried and cried. And I wasn't happy and I wasn't sad. . . . The only thing I could say was it felt like I was home.

Ram Dass with his guru, Maharaj-ji.

Source: *Be Here Now* (Kingsport, TN: Hanuman Foundation, 1978), p.55.

even up to the present, most will show respect for all who conform to the role, acknowledging that, as one proverb goes, "Only Lord Shiva can say who is the true ascetic." New gurus continue to emerge and gather followers, a source of vitality and innovation that gives Hinduism today the impression of being "a sea of ever-shifting eddies and vortices that catch up individual believers in various aspects of their devotional lives."[11]

❖ Living with Karma: Rituals, Astrology, and Rebirth

The classical doctrines associated with karma, reincarnation, and salvation are the center of Hindu (and Buddhist) belief, regardless of the school one follows or one's focus on a particular chosen deity. Karma is thus the most important spiritual force in the universe, determining one's place in the cosmos (as an animal, member of a human caste, etc.). What one does in a particular incarnation, however, then influences future destiny, so, properly speaking, Hindu belief does not posit a closed, fatalistic worldview. Nonkarmic causalities (natural forces, biological reactions, chance) also shape human life, so Hindus can say, like many Americans, "It was meant to be" as well as "Things just happen." Only enlightened saints are thought to be capable of knowing their karmic past and future; everyone else remains uncertain. For this reason, a steady menu of meritorious ritual is a sensible approach to living with karma, as is consultation with astrologers (again, a practice some Americans incline to).

Karma doctrine assumes that a natural causal mechanism conditions individual destiny; but a person's destiny can be shaped by group actions, too. Husbands and wives worship together and act together in many ways. Marriage ritual ties couples for life

A Hindu astrologer. Astrology provides suggestions about when to act in the world, in harmony with the gods and one's own karma.

Teachings of Religious Wisdom

A Maid Teaches a Holy Man How to Discern Rebirth Destiny

A certain holy man, well skilled in Brahmanical lore and who had spent his whole life in the study of the *Vedas* and other religious works, went on a journey. At the first town he entered he, . . . while resting himself [near a domicile], saw a funeral pass, . . . when, to his astonishment, he heard the mistress from within the house inquire from the maidservant as to whether the deceased had gone to heaven. Commanded to do so, the girl went out, and in a short time returned, giving an answer in the affirmative. A similar occurrence took place, but in this instance the maidservant's reply was in the negative. Lost in amazement, the sage demanded how she was able to make known the decrees of the almighty which were to him, notwithstanding all his learning, inscrutable. The maid replied that it was an extremely easy task to ascertain the destination of departed souls . . . as it was only necessary to attend at the . . . place of cremation and listen to the opinion expressed regarding them by their neighbors. If ten of them concurred in speaking in praise of the deceased, it was almost certain that he had gone to the gardens of eternal bliss; if, on the contrary, they agreed in asserting that he was an evildoer, it was equally sure that he was consigned to perdition.

Source: A .K. Ramanujan, *Folktales from India* (New Delhi: Penguin Books India, 1993), p. 55.

and can include a vow to be reborn together in future incarnations (a popular motif in South Asian folklore). Entire families are thought to be shaped by the actions of elders.

Hindus today may explain their individual and collective destiny in terms of karma causality, but as the Maid's story in the nearby box indicates, understandings about the workings of next-life destiny are anything but certain. For example, stretches in life may seem to be inexplicable except in terms of karma accumulated in the past, and some individuals do indeed see everything in life as fated from earlier lifetimes. But most Hindus believe that their destiny today and in future lifetimes is also determined in significant part by their future moral actions and ritual acts. The puranas and guru parables often state that being human and being Hindu are rare incarnations in samsara and should not be wasted. People may be reborn as other beings inhabiting this world, into purgatories (*naraka*) that receive evil human beings, or into heavenly realms (*svarga*) created by each great deity as dwelling places reserved for good and devout devotees. Indeed, many Hindus today regard being born in heaven, not in the disembodied realm of moksha, as the highest destiny.

❖ *Gestures of Respect for the Divine*

Despite the attraction of many middle-class Hindus today to the neotraditionalist movement, which we shall discuss later, respectful gestures and puja are the means by

Namaskara or namaste. The gesture of respectful greeting directed to the gods and humans

which Hindus relate to the divine wherever and in whatever form they find it. Stylized, formal greetings, prostrations, and a circumambulation are among the best-known ritual gestures.

Hindus greet each other by raising the joined palms to shoulder level and repeating "*Namaskara*"/"*Namaste*" ("salutation"/"greetings"), sometimes bowing. Some gurus teach that saluting other humans in this way is a theological statement: "I center my physical self in the atman located in my heart and salute your same holy center."

The core gesture of namaskara can be multiplied into any number of prostrations (*pranam*), principally either with the knees touching the ground or fully prone. This gesture, too, is one humans may do to other humans by, for example, grasping the feet of the one honored, such as a guru, a priest, an elder in the family, a mother-in-law (for a daughter-in-law), a husband (for a wife), or parents (for children).

Another Hindu perception of the body involves the differentiation between its two sides: The right side is the pure side and one eats with the right hand; the left hand is used to wash after calls of nature and is regarded as impure. As an extension of this, *pradakshina,* the circumambulation of an icon or temple, should be performed in a clockwise manner, keeping one's right side closest to the sacred object.

❖ *Puja*

The concept of **puja**, or homage, is also built on the assumption that humanity and the divine must maintain an intimate connection, one marked by respectful hierarchy. For

Hindu puja. Ritual is the means of expressing individual devotion and soliciting divine grace.

humans, the great deities (such as Shiva, Durga, and Vishnu) are superiors. Puja involves all the expressions by which an inferior can welcome, show respect for, and entertain a distinguished guest. Ideally, all ritual acts express a faithful bhakta's submissive, adoring, and self-negating service to the divine.

One doing puja seeks to please the deity as if the divine personage were human, that is, possessed five senses. All that Hindus offer as puja can be classified accordingly: Incense pleases the sense of smell; flowers please the senses of sight and smell; foods gratify the taste; mantras and music please the hearing; cloth and pastes please the deity's tactile sense.

The inseparability of otherworldly and mundane blessings is seen in the full process involved in making a puja offering and then receiving back the remains, **prasad**. These substances, having been proximate to the image, carry a subtle infusion of divine blessing, turning all prasad into "medicine." Food can be eaten, flowers worn in the hair, incense smoke wafted around the body, and holy water (*jal*) sipped. Colored powders that decorate an icon are carefully collected, mixed with water, and used to mark the forehead with a *tilak,* a spot in the center of the forehead above the eyes.

While the norms of different dharmas and of following one's own chosen deity have led Hindus to accept differences in religious orientation even among close family members, this "spiritual individualism" is balanced in most instances by the widespread and daily custom of families sharing from the same plate the prasad returned from the common family puja.

A good Hindu today, like a good Muslim, need never worship in public and may make all puja offerings to icons in a home shrine. In temples with priestly attendants, devotees usually place on the puja tray coins or uncooked rice to be taken by the priests, a meritorious service donation. It is through the medium of puja therefore that Hindu householders contribute to the subsistence of their priests and temples.

It is literally true that all the fine arts of South Asia developed as offerings made to the gods: instrumental and vocal music, dance, sculpture, and painting are all connected to temple rituals. Hindu temples are simply homes for ritually empowered icons that have been given "life" by brahmins chanting their heart mantras and by ritual painters who carefully paint in their eyes. They can be humble thatched buildings sheltering crude stones with no resident priests or magnificent palaces built to house jeweled images attended by hosts of priests and other temple servants. Great temples may be surrounded by monasteries, music pavilions, pilgrim hostels, and sacred ponds; these are the preeminent centers of Hindu culture, and to visit them is to see all these cultural forms directed toward serving the gods with beauty, grace, and dedication.

❖ Hindu Samskaras: Life-Cycle Rites

Being Hindu means following the proper path in life, determined by the dharma codes set forth by the ancient sages. An individual's life—like society's groups—should be properly organized. The *Dharmashastra* lists over forty life-cycle rituals, *samskaras;* they are most observed today by families at the top of the caste hierarchy. We summarize the most popular contemporary practices briefly here, using terms and culture of northern India as representative.

Birth Rituals Pregnant women are given empowered charms to protect the fetus and are made to stay within the family, isolated from demons and from sources of pollution. Despite the spilling of the mother's blood and bodily fluids, birth is a time of "happy pollution"; and for the period of the mother's recovery (up to ten days), the family abstains from puja and does not eat with outsiders. A special "release from birth pollution" ritual must be done in which the house is cleaned and purified, mother and family bathe, the father shaves, and the family holds a feast.

Early Childhood Rituals The ritual called *namkaran* serves to give an infant its formal name. Naming children after the deities is a common practice, and this can be done according to a parent's chosen deity, for the day on which the child is born, or simply for auspiciousness. The carefully noted birth time must be used to construct a horoscope, which will be kept for lifelong consultation. Before the first birthday, the final early childhood rite of first rice feeding introduces the baby to solid food.

Coming of Age Boys and girls are led on different ritual paths emphasizing male dominance and female fertility. The rites marking adulthood for both sexes establish expectations and responsibilities of full Hindu personhood; most significant is the assumption of accountability for actions, for these now "count" in karmic retribution. Since the *Dharmashastra* forbids teaching Vedic verses to women, adult females are not assigned brahmanical rites but participate in their husbands' rituals. Women's ritual customs have nonetheless developed.

Girls are initiated as women when they have their first menstruation, usually by going through a week of strict isolation, in which they are prohibited from seeing the sun or males. During this time, elder females in the family tell stories of the deities and instruct the girls on aspects of adult religious practice and the duties of Hindu women.

Boys of the top three castes are ceremonially given a sacred thread, after which they receive the first teachings from the family guru, including the rituals associated with the wearing of a multistranded thread (*janai*) over the left shoulder and right hip, a burden taken on from this day until death. (In modern times, this "wearing the thread" is maintained most consistently among brahmin families only.) Boys are also given their first mantra to memorize, the Rig Vedic Gayatri (3.62.10), to be repeated daily at the rising and setting of the sun:

> We meditate on that excellent light of the divine sun
> May he illumine our minds.

In adult initiation, boys become "twice-born" through this second birth into the knowledge of the Veda and Vedic ritual.

Householder Marriage is usually arranged by the couple's families, although many young people today can veto a choice proposed for them. The relatives setting up the match must be satisfied that the individuals' horoscopes match harmoniously, to ensure that their characters and karmas are compatible. This is a judgment usually requested of an astrologer.

Upon marriage, a Hindu woman leaves her home, often with a dowry, to live with her mother-in-law, shifting forever her ritual center to the husband's family line. (This pattern is breaking down today in the urban middle classes, where employment patterns require transfers; also, among the rural population that is drawn to migrate to cities in search of jobs and education, nuclear families are common.)

Death Death produces a crisis in the family and a state of corporate pollution that for immediate kin endures for an entire year. When someone dies, the family, out of love, wishes to perform all the rites carefully to ensure that the soul will go to its best possible rebirth. However, the death of a loved one also produces fear that the soul might be reincarnated as a dangerous ghost. This concern has given rise to the custom of cremating a corpse as soon as possible after death and before sundown. Carrying the body to the cremation site, the *ghat,* is men's work, with the eldest son lighting the pyre for the father and the youngest doing so for the mother. Hindus believe that when the heat of the cremation fire causes the skull to burst, the soul has been released to go to its next birth. The women, who stay at home during the cremation, must remove their ornaments and sweep the house, beginning to repurify the house polluted by death. The men who cremate must collect the burned remains so that the family can immerse them in a holy river.

After-Death Rites Before the family may reestablish purity in their homes and resume social life, they must perform the first rites of feeding the departed soul, who is thought to wander as a ghost (*preta*) from twelve days up to one year. Here, Hindu tradition is preserved in the performance of the ancient Vedic rites: The mourners offer *pinda* puja, ritual rice ball offerings, to feed the soul and build up its intermediate-state body to be a preta and continue on its afterlife journey. Shraddha rites for parents and especially fathers are done yearly on the death anniversary.

Hindu Festival Practice

Many Hindus today carry a small pocket almanac that organizes the Western, lunar, and solar succession of days. Why are these so popular? Since the year is punctuated by a succession of great and small festivals, or *utsavas,* some lasting only a day, others stretching over ten days, Hindus must harmonize personal, family, and business affairs with the religious celebrations. Being a Hindu today entails celebrating this yearly cycle of festival observance: doing special rituals, recalling acts of divine grace, and feasting with family.

Part of the reason for this elaborate festival agenda is that across South Asia, it is customary for each important deity to have a special day and procession (*jatra*) that is the occasion for extraordinary acts of devotion. At these times, the god or goddess is felt to be more accessible to devotees and more inclined to extend grace to those who demonstrate their faith. The Hindu utsavas offer the chance to live in a profoundly different and sacred time, when the great salvific deeds known from legend and myth are retold by religious scholars (*pandits*) or enacted through live cultural performances. In many of the utsavas, special foods, drinks, and decorations are made that appear at no other time. Some festivals are reserved for fasting, ascetic acts, or other penances.

The greatest festivals celebrated in the notable religious cities of India are immense spectacles, and arranging for the myriad cultural performances and sideshows requires the participation of thousands. Arrays of electric lights, clouds of incense, and blaring loudspeakers (what one Hindu writer has called "the most important instrument of contemporary spirituality") overload the devotees' senses. The gatherings can create a marvelous sense of community among *bhaktas,* drawing pilgrims from afar to witness and to seek blessings. The time chosen to visit the great pilgrimage sites often coincides with the major festival celebrations.

❖ Diwali

In India, the new year begins around the vernal equinox, a date also marking for Hindus the moment when creation in each world era begins anew. But across the north, the year begins with *Diwali,* the festival around the autumnal equinox that focuses on Lakshmi, goddess of wealth. On the main day families wear new clothes, sweep their houses clean, arrange a special altar with puja laid out for the goddess, and set up lamps (now, most are "Christmas lights") to guide her. On a subsequent day, brothers and sisters honor their kin ties, and individuals may do other special pujas to strengthen their health for the year ahead. Middle-class families now send "Diwali cards," akin to Christmas cards.

❖ Sri Panchami

The festival of Sri Panchami is dedicated to Saraswati, the goddess of learning and the fine arts. Students, scholars, and artists all will flock to her temples. Some temples set

Hindus associated with large temples take out the images of the great gods yearly. The most dramatic of these outings is a large chariot that is pulled by devotees to earn merit.

Sacred Cows and Hinduism

One of the striking first impressions of South Asia is the free-ranging movement of cows in villages and on city streets. Up through the 1960s, when India suffered its last major famine, many in the West said, "If only Hindus would eat beef, all their food needs could be met." What is certainly true is that cows are integral to Hinduism in many respects: One *purana* text suggests that all the divinities exist in the cow, and another sees the cow as an incarnation of the goddess Devi. Killing a cow is thus unthinkable. The cow's centrality is further seen in ritual practice: To mark and purify any space and make it suitable for *puja*, cow dung is a necessary ground coating; in addition, ingestion of any of the five products of the cow (milk, curds, butter, urine, dung) is one of the most potent sources for the inner purification for humans.

Anthropologists have also sought to link the logic of "mother cow" veneration with its crucial contributions to South Asia's subsistence agriculture. Dried cow dung is an essential cooking fuel; composted cow dung is irreplaceable in the reinvigoration of the soil for intensive growing of rice and wheat crops. Cows are also capable of eating nearly everything and recycling chaff, odd roadside vegetation, even garbage. Finally, oxen, the gelded offspring of cows, are the most reliable beasts of burden for plowing deep enough to turn over the soil. Thus, for a subsistence farming family to harvest its (typically) sole cow at times of food shortage risks its long-term survival. Here, argues the cultural ecologist Marvin Harris, lies the reason for the cow's sacredness: It is holy because it promotes survival. And besides, the initial supposition is in fact false: Tanner castes (ranked as untouchables because they collect dead cows) do eat beef. Modern fundamentalist groups have chosen the cow to symbolize "Mother India" and agitate for a ban on cow slaughter to define their nationalist goals.

up a whitewashed wall on which young children are to write their first letters, for traditional Hindu parents wait until this day to begin to teach their offspring to read and write.

❖ Shiva Ratri

Shiva's Night, Shiva Ratri, is the end-of-winter festival, one of two festivals each year dedicated to Shiva. This festival emphasizes fasting and grand offerings to Shiva's phallic icon, the *linga*. Shiva Ratri also in some localities connects with the god's identity that imagines him controlling the myriad ghosts and goblins that occupy the lower portions of the Hindu pantheon. It is also the time for ascetics to make offerings at Shiva's great temples, which accordingly fill with thousands of sadhus and yogins who meditate, instruct devotees, receive donations, and demonstrate their powers.

❖ Holi

Hinduism's "feast of love," or holi, is the year's primary festival honoring Krishna in his guise as the playful trickster god. In harmony with the theology called *lila* (divine play), devotees establish a set period for honoring the youthful Krishna. For the primary three or so days, all of society is at play, and normal caste and gender rules are suspended.

Children enjoying holi, the festival when humans join Krishna in living life as a divine sport.

In imitation of Krishna and to find harmony with his spirit, which transcends the mundane, all society should join in the lila, inverting established hierarchies and expectations. Women may sing lewdly in public or douse male passersby with buckets of water, and public officials such as policemen suffer usually playful insubordinations; in villages, an untouchable may be declared "headman" for the duration of the festival. On the last day, bonfires are lit to consume evil, commemorating Krishna's defeat of a female demon who sought his demise.

✤ Tij

Tij is the festival for women, who can act in imitation of Parvati, one incarnation of Devi, who fasted, meditated, and underwent purification in the hopes of winning the husband she deserved. In her case, this was Shiva; for unmarried women, the hope is for a good human husband; for those already married, it is for the long life of one's spouse. For Tij, some women join to spend the night at a temple, ideally one situated beside a river or having a large bathing tank, where they sing devotional songs and dance to secure divine blessings. As they pass the night, they also fast, listen to stories associated with Parvati and other exemplary women, and then immerse themselves in the sacred waters to repurify themselves before sealing their vows.

✤ Dashara

In many places the largest yearly Hindu celebration, Dashara usually falls just before the first rice harvest. It has become the occasion for marking two separate divine events. For Rama bhaktas, this festival is *Rama Navami* (Rama's Ninth) the time for celebrating both Rama's birth and his victory over the demon Ravana, when he rescued his consort Sita and instituted an era of proper Hindu rule. *Durga Puja* similarly enfolds the community in Durga's "Nine Nights" of struggle against Mahisha, the demon who could not be killed by a man and so threatened the gods and all creation. The "Victory Tenth Day" commemorates Durga's slaying of Mahisha, who had taken the form of a buffalo demon. To imitate the goddess in her moment of triumph and to bathe her images in the blood offerings that she most loves, devotees perform animal sacrifices at her temples, beheading primarily goats, fowl, and water buffalo. Durga Puja ends the festival year at the time of the rice harvest: Tradition evolved so that divine and human feasting on animal meat coincides with the time that farmers need to cull their herds, especially of old and young males, who can wreak havoc in the luxuriant rice paddies if they escape the confinement imposed by humans.

PILGRIMAGE FESTIVALS

From earliest times, Hindus believed the land bounded by the Himalaya mountains and the oceans to be holy. Thus the mountains and rivers of this region were imagined to be abodes of the deities and the places where sages have realized the highest truths. From then until now, devotees have gone on pilgrimage to see these sacred persons and places (for **darshan**, viewing the divine) and to dwell in the precincts blessed with spiritual powers. On their journeys today, Hindus do the rituals described for temples, make elaborate offerings and countless expressions of respect, and bring home treasured prasad. Modern transport has facilitated the expansion of pilgrimage in modern times.

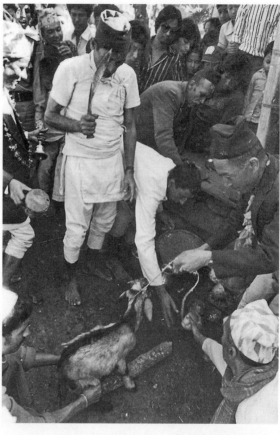

A middle-caste priest in Nepal prepares to sacrifice a goat to the goddess Durga.

✤ Himalayas

The most dramatic and famous among the myriad Hindu sacred sites are located in the Himalayas, the world's highest mountain chain, where the very names of the snow-clad peaks reflect the perception of divine residence. According to one passage in the *Skanda Purana,* seeing any of the Himalayan peaks will transform one's karma: "As the dew is dried up by the morning sun, so are the sins of mankind by the sight of Himalayas."

✤ Ganges

Rivers are also focal areas for pilgrimage. The Ganges and its tributaries that flow down from the Himalayan glaciers all are associated with divinity: The Ganges itself, conceived as a goddess, was sent by the gods to succor humanity in the midst of a horrific drought. The Ganges is thus a divine entity; and as such, many bathing rites are done along its banks, where devotees hope to draw on her capacity to "wash away" bad karma. Ganges water is seen as the best source for purifying a ritual space, so pilgrims collect it and store it for future ritual use.

All rivers in South Asia are identified with the Ganges. A common legend known across the continent states that each river shares a subterranean connection with it. The points on the river best suited for human pilgrimage and ritualism are tributary confluences called *tirthas*. The literal translation of the word (ford, or river crossing) also indicates metaphorically that it is easier to cross the great river of samsara to reach heaven or moksha at a tirtha. Many of the great religious cities of South Asia are located along rivers.

✤ The Kumbha Mela

The largest single religious gathering on earth in the early twenty-first century is not Muslims assembling in Mecca for the hajj but Hindus congregating at a holy tirtha for the Kumbha Mela. In 2007, at least 80 million Hindus gathered to bathe at Prayag ("place of sacrifice"), on a riverside near modern Allahabad, where the Ganges, Yamuna, and invisible Saraswati rivers meet. The pilgrims entered the water at the exact

Pilgrims at the Amarnath Cave. Devotees worship the ice lingam of the great god Shiva found within this Himalayan hillside.

Temples like this in the Himalayas attract pilgrims and local devotees.

Ritual bathers in Varanasi, also known as Kashi or Benares. Located on the western bank of the Ganges and with its riverside *ghats* dominating the urban settlement, Kashi is the sacred city where pilgrims congregate.

auspicious moment connected with a story in the puranas in which the gods battled the demons over possession of a pitcher (*kumbha*) containing an immortality-giving elixir. After a long struggle, the gods won and became immortal; during the course of the battle, however, four drops of the elixir fell to earth at four places, and the site of the Kumbha Mela, which occurs every twelve years, rotates among them in a prescribed order. The Kumbha Mela draws hundreds of thousands of sadhus from their retreats to immerse themselves in the hyperdivinized river waters, where they are joined by millions of householders on pilgrimage, who bathe, offer puja, and sip the ambrosial river water, seeking an infusion of grace.

Pilgrimage in Hinduism is not a requirement of the faith as in Islam, but the benefits are elaborately outlined in the later Hindu texts: healing, good karma, personal transformation. Pilgrims can go alone on foot or in highly organized groups traveling on airplanes and buses. The goal may be to perform a ritual, such as a mortuary rite for a kin member. The more typical goal, however, is to seek general benefit through darshan and puja.

Ganges water purifies the Hindu devotee before puja.

The Religious Institutions of Contemporary Hinduism

Although there is no single formal institution that unifies all Hindus, there are standard relationships that support the regular practice of ritual and the transmission of religious ideas. Most families have a relationship with a brahmin family priest whom they call on when there is the need for a life-cycle rite or when someone wishes to perform a special puja.

The predominant religious institution of Hinduism, however, is the temple, and it is thought highly meritorious to build one that houses an empowered icon. Hindus from all classes, alone or collectively, have done so, but the temples built by the great kings enable the most complete expressions of Hindu religious culture. Yet the major temples are more than shrines: They include lands given to the deity and are supported by endowment funds that are continually augmented by the cash offered with puja.

The millions of Hindus who gather along the Ganges for a moment of grace at the Kumbha Mela form the largest religious gathering on earth today.

Temple lands are usually rented out to tenant farmers, with part of the harvest going to the temple; other properties adjacent to the temple are often rented to merchants or artisans. Both rentals provide income for the upkeep of the temple buildings and payment for the priests. Through these relationships, Hindu temples have been integral to the local economies of South Asia, sometimes as the major landowners. Modern land reform has cut back on many of these holdings, forcing temples to find other means of support.

The more organized sects and sadhu orders rely on the *matha*, or monastery, to serve as a venue for schooling and training for ritual service under an abbot (*mahant*). Some modern groups, such as the Ramakrishna Mission, have built their panregional reform movement through a network of mathas. Another familiar institution is the *ashram*, a retreat dedicated to supporting gurus and their disciples, thereby maintaining the relationship that is one of the central lifelines of Hindu culture.

CHANGING CONTINUITIES: EXAMPLES OF POSTCOLONIAL HINDUISM

Across the Hindu world each day, brahmins memorize, recite, and pass on to their sons the millennia-old Vedic rituals and hymns as well as devotional songs composed cen-

A Typical Temple

One place of worship that can be found widely in upper-caste communities across the subcontinent is a Smarta temple, attended by a brahmin priest. In it, the major gods of the pantheon we have mentioned are enshrined, with the addition of the sun god, who presides over the astrological deities. Shiva usually is the central god, most often worshipped in his linga icon.

The typical Smarta temple has the following standard layout:

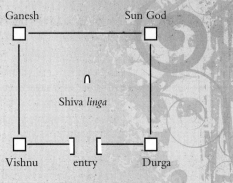

turies ago. Ancient rituals are vigorously practiced in millions of households. Certain gurus are regarded by thousands as divine incarnations. Increasing numbers of pilgrims flock to the great temples, consulting the institutions' websites for guidance. Ascetic communities in ashrams train in yoga and engage in silent meditative retreats. Religious innovations among Hindus multiplied further through the colonial period and after independence, with recent teachers and globalization adding yet newer strands to the fabric of Hinduism. A 1986 gathering of nearly a thousand abbots of Hindu monasteries, one of the first ever held, assembled teachers representing 165 different organized spiritual traditions.

Yet modern medicine, mass media, and expanding transportation technology have changed how millions of Hindus understand and encounter Hindu doctrines and myths and even how they perform the puja rituals. Within major Indian cities today, a middle class is emerging whose lifestyle and experience have been highly influenced by Euro-American media culture, education, and connections. Institutions and "yoga centers" among this middle-class elite are developing newly synthesized approaches to Hindu spiritual practices, in forms similar to those found in European and American cities. The global spread of Hinduism now impacts the faith in South Asia. Digital CDs and videos with sermons by gurus in India reach the global Hindu middle class, affording traditional doctrinal teachings far wider exposure than was ever possible by word of mouth.

Thus, Hinduism has assumed more forms today than ever in its history, and the linkage of religion to politics is growing. Since there is no one version or center of Hinduism that can stand alone, we will draw on a series of representative case studies to suggest the broad sweep of Hinduism in the postcolonial era. We will discuss first the modernizers, then those who have *not* been influenced by science, and finally those proponents of Hindu nationalism who object to India's postindependence character as a secular state.

Some teachers and movements begun in the modern era (such as the Ramakrishna Mission) make strong assertions about the compatibility between scientific thought and venerable Hindu doctrines. The "big bang" hypothesis of creation, relativity theory, and the cosmological theories of multiple universes are referred to by these modernizers as compatible with—even anticipated in—the ancient scriptures. Hindu exponents have also proposed scientific explanations for rebirth and karma doctrines. Even the Vedas have been interpreted to credit the seers with awareness of contemporary technological possibilities (e.g., airplanes, genetics, brain waves). Hindu confidence that the traditional teachings will stand up to whatever science discovers is striking among modernists. Just as many scientists around the world (including many in India) refrain from suggesting that their discoveries are ever likely to disprove the existence of God or the reality of

Temple in Madras. Large temples are complex institutions with landholdings, charities, and resident priests.

spirit, many highly educated Hindus have found no reason to abandon the essentials of their faith. Those with technological savvy have energetically expressed their faith on the World Wide Web, and by 2008 almost 20,000 websites were dedicated to the many sides of Hinduism. A sample of recent events and developments indicates how Hinduism has endured so strongly among such modernists.

❖ Ganesh's Milk Miracle

A deity who attracts the devotion of nearly all Hindus is elephant-headed Ganesh, divine son of Shiva and Parvati. Ganesh is beloved for his earthy character, his potbellied

Elephant-headed Ganesh, Hindu god of success, is found in every Hindu community. He is always worshiped first and before any major undertaking.

silhouette, and his reputation as a remover of life's obstacles. Ganesh temples are found in nearly every locale where Hindus live. On September 21, 1995, at temples across North India, priests and devotees reported that icons of Ganesh had begun to drink the cows' milk that was being offered to them as part of the daily puja. The stories soon spread across the subcontinent by telephone and in press accounts, so thousands of Hindus from all walks of life rushed off to visit their local temples to offer milk, hoping to witness the phenomenon. Telephone and the Internet just as quickly spread the news across the globe, and Hindus in London, Jersey City, Los Angeles, and Toronto began to report similar experiences.

For believers, this was merely the latest in a long-running series of demonstrations that the divine is alive, connected to humanity and capable of conferring grace on those who serve the gods. From uneducated peasants to brahmin priests, people were citing the reports of disappearing milk as ample proof of the existence of a Supreme Being who accepts the offerings of his disciples. Whatever else this incident reveals about the role of the media and the Hindu diaspora, it also demonstrates that modern believers hold the conviction that the divine is immanent, a traditional view that has shifted little amid all the changes of the modern era.

The reaction was interesting, too: The "miracle" gave rise to widespread public debate and rallies organized by Hindu societies (such as New Delhi's "Guru Busters") whose purpose is to expose charlatans and promote rational faith. Predecessors for these modern skeptics and atheists can be traced as far back as the time of the Buddha (fifth century BCE). Although the popular Western imagination about India and Hinduism has been informed by romantic accounts highlighting mysticism and exotic theistic spirituality, it is important to note that there is an equally long-established South Asian tradition of hard-nosed skepticism.

✤ Comic Books and Televised Epics

The modern printing press gave early Hindu reformers a means to reach a mass audience across the subcontinent more quickly than ever before. Ritual manuals, vernacular translations of texts, tracts on saints, inter-religious debates, or even reformers' reductive definitions of "true Hinduism" (such as that proposed by the Arya Samaj or modern fundamentalists) reach the literate masses through such publications. South Asia's religious environment during the modern era has also been unified by the lithography of religious poster art, which has spread common inexpensive images of the deities.

An important mass media format appearing well after the end of colonialism is the religious comic book. Adopting reformist doctrines and linking far-flung Hindu communities is the Amar Citra Katha series of over 250 titles, in which newly standardized versions of the great stories of Hindu scripture are offered in colorful illustrated formats; the text is written in English and in various vernaculars. Under the editorship of Anant Pai, more than 350 million copies of Amar Citra Katha texts have been sold. These have emphasized for middle-class readers that "true Hinduism" is rational,

In India, there are countless comic books devoted to describing the stories of the Hindu gods and human saints. Most are printed in the vernacular languages of the subcontinent, as well as in English. Here, a scene from the great epic, the *Ramayana*.

opposed to violence and superstition, upheld by heroic devotees, and based on the respectful accommodation of other spiritualities (Hindu and non-Hindu) in the interest of national integration.

Television broadcasts of religious epics have also been pivotal cultural events. In 1987 India's national broadcasting system, Doordarshan, began showing in weekly installments its Hindi version of the *Ramayana,* one of the two great religious epics that date back to the early classical era. Although most Indians do not own television sets, groups crowded into tea stalls or banded together to rent TVs and view the series. Many treated the experience of viewing the transmitted image like a visit to a temple. Bathing beforehand, they arrived carrying incense and garlanded the television sets. Some watched with their hands joined together, using the namaste gesture directed to the divinities on screen, and some muttered prayers as the sacred scenes unfolded, weekly for over a year.

An estimated audience of 80 million watched the one-hour Sunday morning program, and the pace of life on India's streets visibly slowed. The media's *Ramayana* gave the nation its first "national version" of the epic, one that celebrates the glories of the legendary Hindu king Rama and his struggle to establish a just and prosperous Hindu nation. Doordarshan had to extend the series to meet popular demand. It has subsequently produced and broadcast an even longer series on Hinduism's second great epic, the *Mahabharata,* as well as dramatizations of other devotional stories centered on the great deities, such as Krishna and Shiva.

The accessibility of lavishly produced TV productions of religious epics, complete with special effects, has in places undercut the relation between priest, teacher, and laity. Many argue, however, that Hindu nationalism has been strengthened by the common experience of viewing these sacred scenes.

❖ *The Dilemmas of Reform: A Young Bride Commits Sati*

Following the norms of her caste and the Hindu law books, Roop Kanwar, an 18-year-old bride, went to live with her husband's family in Deorala, in the western Indian state of Rajasthan. But seven months later, on September 4, 1987, her husband, Mal Singh, died suddenly. Following ancient custom, the young man's kin prepared to cremate him on a pyre outside the town boundaries immediately before sunset. What happened next shocked India: Roop Kanwar was also burnt alive atop her husband's funeral pyre, becoming a *sati* ("virtuous [one]"), one of forty-two known cases since 1947. Five hundred people reportedly witnessed the act. What remains unclear were the widow's motivations and how freely she went to this death.

Rajasthan state officials were called to act on the basis of India's National Penal Code that holds widow immolation under any circumstances to be illegal. Reformers argued that those connected with Roop Kanwar's death should be prosecuted as murderers. Eventually, under pressure from national politicians and women's groups, members of Mal Singh's immediate family were arrested and an investigation ensued. Several months later the family members were released on bail, but no charges were ever filed. Few witnesses could be found who were willing to testify.

Sati is one Hindu practice that the British actively sought to end through explicit legal prohibition. The immolation of widows was held up for ridicule by many Hindu modernizers as evidence of how Indian society needed to break with blindly followed traditions and to reform its ways. Yet in 1987, over 50,000 devotees gathered for a commemorative ceremony for Roop Kanwar held thirteen days after her death. The site of the burning pyre has been transformed into a shrine, outside of which artisans sell ritual photos of the site and other mementos. Since 1987, the Singh family has received many thousands of rupees from donations. Throughout the town, the young widow is now celebrated by drummers and chanting youth as a brave *Sati-ma*, a divine figure who was blessed by and merged with the mother goddess, Devi.

All India became caught up in the debate about whether Roop Kanwar's death was truly voluntary, as the Singh family maintains, or whether murder was being concealed under the veil of religion. Should the role of the secular state be to regulate this religious practice? Should the state enforce its legal code that defines sati as barbaric and prohibits the custom, as reformers urged? Or as Hindu traditionalists insisted—and many in this camp were local citizens and state politicians—should the state respect freedom of religion and allow Hindus to follow whatever path they choose to seek salvation?

❖ The Spiritual Marketplace for Neotraditionalism: Popular Guru-Based Movements

Most conspicuous over the last decades has been the rise of cults and sects catering to the urban middle class. What is it like to live in the urban middle class today in South Asia? It involves confronting conflicting claims on one's identity and loyalty, as loyalty to one's "primordial" allegiances (caste, kin, home, region) clashes with the cosmopolitan and socially fluid urban culture that aspires to "be modern" and join the global culture of CNN, the Internet, and designer clothing. Traditional ties are to be honored at some level, but they no longer can fully contain the individual's deepest feelings of belonging.

Focused on sadhus and drawing inspiration from the reformists and revivalists of the nineteenth century, most of the new sects that have attracted the support of this new middle-class elite have proclaimed their own view of "essential Hinduism" as more belief oriented and less ritualistic. Just as modern technology has undercut to some extent the roles of priest and guru, the new sects have diminished the relevance of caste and regional social identity to spiritual seeking. Several utilize mass media to promote the teacher's message and link distant adherents. A number of the new sects have quickly built an international membership. In some cases they have benefited from praise and support for Hindu gurus active abroad, which has whetted an appetite for their teachings back home in South Asia. Most also emphasize women's participation. All engage their society and include community development, medical service, and educational initiatives, combining various traditional Hindu doctrines and practices with certain tactics adopted from Protestant missionaries.

Sathya Sai Baba No modern Hindu saint has drawn devotees from as far and wide across India's urban middle classes as Sathya Sai Baba, a teacher known as much for the miraculous feats credited to him as for his instruction. A vigorous opponent of Western cultural influences on Hindu civilization and individual Hindus, Sai Baba advocates an active life informed by scriptural study and charitable giving; he teaches a form of classical silent meditation involving fixing one's gaze on a flame.

Sai Baba's trusts have established a vast network of service organizations: There are junior and senior Service Corps whose members feed the poor, act when disaster strikes, visit the sick, and so on. There are at present four Sai Baba colleges (three for women, one for men) that include educational outreach programs aimed to help small children. The ashram he established in 1923 marked the beginning of a large global movement toward neotraditionalism.

Sai Baba's fame and stature are based on accounts of his supernormal feats of multiple presence, miracle cures, and materializing out of the air items, including sacred ash, food, books, and even Swiss watches. Devotees see these powers of the traditional yogin saint as evidence that Sai Baba is an avatara of a divinity. Indeed, he has said that he is Shiva and his consort in a single body. Through Sai Baba, disciples can see one of the perennial themes nurtured in the myriad South Asian traditions: that the divine is alive and appears in human form and that this world is still enchanted with grace.

Brahma Kumaris In India today, the most ardent sectarian proselytizers (especially across the northern states) are from the group called Brahma Kumari. Their Raja Yoga centers, also called "spiritual museums," are the organizing points around which each local chapter draws interested individuals and publicity, primarily among urban dwellers. The museums display doctrine-oriented pictures, with a member providing commentary; visitors who show interest are invited to attend meditation sessions and classes. In 2007 these institutions were being maintained by 10,000 full-time religious teachers.

This is another group that stems from a charismatic teacher. The visions and spiritual experiences of the founding guru, Lekhraj (1876–1969), a jeweler from Hyderabad, inspired an early following. In 1936 Lekhraj established the Brahma Kumari sect and turned his entire wealth over to the first community.

Lekhraj attributed his vibrant visions portending the end of the world cycle to the grace of Shiva, the deity who commands the group's ritual attention. He also insisted that individuals must engage in radical purifications to survive and to inherit paradise. Such cleansing could come only through celibacy, vegetarianism, abstinence from tobacco and alcohol, and specific yoga practices. These traditional disciplines became the core practices of the Brahma Kumaris. The vow of celibacy, long an ideal for Hindu ascetics, is here extended to all householders. As a result, married couples who become disciples have to transform their marital relations to be expressions of "pure, noncarnal spiritual love." This teaching created serious domestic strife in the early community, forcing Lekhraj and his initially small circle of devotees to move to Karachi and later, after partition (1947), to Mount Abu in western India. Once there, the movement was transformed from a reclusive sect to an aggressively outgoing one.

Soon missionaries had established centers across the major North Indian cities. Here is their mission statement:

> We teach a practical method of meditation that helps individuals understand their inner strengths and values. A worldwide family of individuals from all walks of life, we are committed to spiritual growth and personal transformation, believing them essential in creating a peaceful and just world. Acknowledging the challenges of rapid global change, we nurture the well-being of the entire human family by promoting spiritual understanding, leadership with integrity, and elevated actions towards a better world.[12]

Although its bhakti doctrines and cosmology could be characterized as drawn from premodern Hinduism and its silent meditation practices are drawn from traditional yoga, Brahma Kumari social practices are reformist and focused on women. Brahma Kumaris challenge Hindu society's patriarchal doctrines and ethical norms; the sect invites women to awaken to their divinity through connecting devotionally with the powers of traditional Hindu goddesses. Women leaders in the group also

Indian schoolchildren performing yoga exercises sponsored by the state government in Bhopal Madhya Pradesh.

include members who serve as mediums, going into trance states to bring back messages from the gods as well as deceased teachers such as the founder, Lekhraj.

In recent years, the Brahma Kumaris have won recognition from India's leading politicians for supporting the establishment of a "value-based society," as members work with U.N. agencies on educational projects across South Asia. In the last decade, the Brahma Kumaris have claimed status as an independent religion, rejecting the label of "Hindu." In 2007 the group counted membership at 825,000. Over 8,000 Brahma Kumari centers exist, most in India, but also now found in over 100 other countries.

RELIGIOUS NATIONALISM: SECULAR INDIA AND ITS DISCONTENTS

As we noted earlier, many of India's anticolonial nationalist leaders were educated in England, and more than a few were unalterably committed to creating modern India as a secular democracy. They knew that religious strife in Europe had led to the formation of most modern Western nations, and they wanted to avoid the problems among the complex and competing religious communities in India that would inevitably result if any sectarian favoritism were shown. Indeed, most of the early political leaders, who were high-caste Hindus, feared what civil and partisan strife the Hindu majority might bring to the subcontinent. In the end, they succeeded, with British help, in marginalizing groups such as the RSS that wanted to establish India as a Hindu nation.

Poster at a political rally suggests that veneration of the cow provides the basis for unity among Indians of every religious group.

In practice, however, the democratic and secular Indian state has proved to be an ally of the high castes, particularly brahmins, in comparison with its British predecessor. This has led to the suggestion that in fact India's "secular state" really amounts to a form of "neo-Brahminism." Under British rule, brahmins held 3 percent of government jobs, a figure almost exactly equal to their proportion in the population. In 2000, however, their hold on civil service positions was as high as 70 percent, while their representation in the general population remained much the same as in 1947.

Yet in a curious and paradoxical development, and despite the state's administration's being heavily skewed toward their interests, high-caste politicians have convinced growing numbers of citizens that Hindus have been discriminated against by the laws and policies of secular India. Thus, throughout the 1990s, the BJP, the party controlled by members of the upper castes,

Violence between communities in India, especially on Hindi-Muslim and Hindu-Christian lines, has increased in recent decades.

campaigned on the basis of promises to establish a strong Hindu nation. Victories in state and national elections came in 1998.

The first year-long national BJP government (1998–1999) decided to explode India's first atomic bomb and encouraged rhetoric by Hindu leaders questioning the patriotism of Indian Christians. There have been incidents across the nation in which Hindu terrorists have burned down churches and murdered Christians.

The BJP and its high-caste supporters also want to reverse the secular state's efforts to uplift Muslims and others equally impoverished among the lowest castes. In regions where dominant and rich landholding, high-caste elites control most local politics, lower castes have mobilized to contest new elections in India's 700,000 villages; using their great demographic plurality, many among these humble groups, including many women, have been elected as village council leaders. As we have seen, this is an inversion of ancient Hindu caste law norms and traditional karma theory. During the first months of BJP rule, massacres in lower-caste settlements were reported across North India; in most cases investigated, the killings were found to represent efforts to intimidate groups that had voted against high-caste candidates or had sought state intervention to enforce lower-caste rights.

Then, in 2002, anti-Muslim riots in the state of Gujarat, abetted by its BJP government, left over 2,000 Muslim dead, with 35,000 homeless and still residing in refugee camps five years later. A group of outside, independent judges collected testimony and summarized these horrific events:

> Hindutva barbarians came out into the streets . . . and in all flaming fury, targeted innocent and helpless Muslims. They were brutalized by miscreants uninhibited by police; their women were unblushingly molested; and Muslim men,

women, and children, in a travesty of justice, were burnt alive. The chief minister, oath-bound to defend law and order, variously connived at the inhuman violence and some of his ministers even commanded the macabre acts of horror."[13]

International human rights investigators joined in blaming this pogrom on the VHP (see below) and its youth wing, the Bajrang Dal, for planning these events. Yet in the five years since then, no arrests have been made in Gujarat. Not surprisingly, Muslim resentments, calls for revenge, and terrorist reprisals directed against the Hindu majority have increased across India. Did the BJP's national defeat in the 2004 elections signal that the allure of strident Hindu nationalism has begun to wane?

✤ *The VHP: Hindu Leaders in Search of a Religious Nation*

Linked to the RSS and the Bharatiya Janata party, the **Vishva Hindu Parishad (VHP)** (Council of All Hindus) was founded in 1964 as an organization of religious leaders who, while retaining their own disciples and spiritual agendas, wished to promote the interests of Hindus and a general kind of spiritual Hinduism. In agreement with earlier reformers and actually internalizing some of the criticisms made by European colonialists, the VHP views Hinduism as in decline, seeks the roots of the faith in the earliest texts, and considers the *Bhagavad Gita* to be Hinduism's preeminent scripture.

A Call for Unity Among Hindu Gurus

An excerpt from an article published by a modern reformist.

The greatest curse of Hinduism throughout the ages has been its disunity—and more than that—its betraying each other. The British did not conquer India, it was given to them by its warring Hindu princes, jealous of each other. I know there is something mysterious and unfathomable in the manifestation of the Divine upon earth, and that each guru has a defined task to fulfill and that the combined task of all the gurus may be to solve the great puzzle that is this ignorant and suffering earth. Thus, it may not be necessary for each guru to communicate with each other. But nevertheless, it is of the greatest urgency today that Hindu leaders unite to save Hinduism, rather than "each one for his own" that we see today.

The Catholics have their Pope and his word is binding on all Catholics. Muslims have Prophet Mohammed's words and that binds all of Islam together. Indian Communists have the words of Marx and Lenin. . . . But the poor Hindus have nobody to refer to, so as to defend themselves. Yet, if you take the combined people power of Sai Baba [and other popular modern teachers . . .] it runs in hundreds of millions. I propose that a Supreme Spiritual Council, composed of at least seven of the most popular Hindu leaders of India, be constituted. . . . It should be a nonpolitical body, and each group would keep its independence. But nevertheless it could meet two or three times a year and issue edicts, which would be binding on 850 million Hindus in India and 1 billion over the world.

Source: Quoted in Francois Gautier, "Hindu Convert," in *India Abroad Weekly*, January 9, 2006.

Although we have spoken of the lack of a central institution as a characteristic of Hinduism, one measure of the VHP's rise is its increasing success at securing unity among hitherto fiercely independent spiritual leaders. It has also spread to twenty-five countries. Projects undertaken in common include religiopolitical festivals, missionary projects in tribal areas (including campaigns to "reconvert" some Indians from Christianity or Islam), and uplift initiatives among the "untouchable" castes. Critics have noted that such VHP efforts serve to add to the number the group can count as members of the "Hindu majority" in the state of India. But VHP supporters point out that uplift projects among the "untouchables" act on Gandhi's exhortation of Hindus to work to end the "evils of caste society."

The VHP argues that the era before Muslim rule (1200 CE) was a golden age for Hinduism, a time of social egalitarianism, prosperity, just rulers, and a wealth of enlightened seers. But with the Muslim conquest and such actions as the razing of temples to build mosques, Hindu culture declined; subsequent British domination of India made matters worse, causing further stagnation and division among all groups. The VHP views the secular state of India created in 1947 as a further means of dividing Hindus and thwarting the establishment of a great civilization centered on "Vedic spirituality." It further argues that if this secularism can be overthrown, and with it a mindset of inferiority induced during the colonial period, another golden age can begin. Accordingly, the VHP has voiced support for dismantling any mosques that were (in the party's historical determination) built over Hindu temples in centuries past. The destruction of the mosque in Ayodhya in 1992 attracted attention to the group and support from ultranationalists, as did the VHP's marketing scheme to raise funds by selling bricks for the construction of the new Hindu temple planned for the site. The VHP leaders still express their wish to see other Muslim shrines removed from Benares and Mathura, and many defend the 2002 massacres against Muslims in Gujarat as being brought on by Muslims themselves.

With greater recognition of the religious pluralism of diverse global communities, differences in ritual beliefs and practices are becoming more widely known. Sikh cartoonist Dalbir points out difficulties of following religious law. Although many Sikhs are vegetarian, Sikh dietary rules allow the consumption of all meats if the animal was slaughtered compassionately. Some cartoons have also created inter- and intra-community conflicts.

✤ Sikh Separatism and Globalization

Because the British invested heavily in irrigation and infrastructure in the Punjab, by the postcolonial era the Sikh home territory had become one of the most productive agricultural regions of India. But partition forced many Sikhs to flee to India and abandon holy sites; subsequently, Indian politicians divided Punjab politically and in development initiatives that were regarded as discriminatory against the Sikh majority. Although Sikhs became one of the wealthiest ethnic groups in postcolonial India, there were many who were left out and felt aggrieved by these events.

Following up on agitations dating back to 1925 aimed to win British support for allowing Sikhs

(not brahmins) to administer their own temples, the community had established a reformist modern organization, the Shiromani Gurudwara Pradandhak Committee. This body acted in consort with the Akal Takht, a group whose leaders manage the Golden Temple (Harmandir Sahib, the abode of God) in Amritsar, the crown jewel of Sikh culture.

Despite Sikh prosperity, radical leaders in the 1980s revived a preindependence demand for a Sikh homeland in Punjab, following the logic that had led to the creation of Pakistan as the homeland for South Asian Muslims. Guerrillas tried to transform this region into a de facto separate state they called Khalistan, extorting contributions they identified as "taxes" from Sikh farmers and merchants while randomly murdering Hindus living there. The movement had support in the Akal Takht and was funded as well by contributions from Sikhs abroad.

In 1984, after armed secessionist leaders occupied the Golden Temple in Amritsar, the Indian government sent troops to invade this shrine to arrest a separatist militant named Jarnail Singh Bhindranwale, who sought to establish an independent Sikh state in the Punjab province, killing many and declaring martial law in Punjab. In this operation, code-named Operation Blue Star, Bhindranwale was killed, along with casualties on both sides. The Golden Temple complex also suffered a great deal of damage due to the fighting. Many Sikhs regarded the attack as a desecration of their holiest shrine.

Later in the year, the prime minister, Indira Gandhi, was assassinated by two Sikh bodyguards, who had been outraged by the sacrilege. The murder triggered waves of violence: In 1987 and 1988, over 2,700 Sikhs were murdered in anti-Sikh rioting, and antistate terrorist attacks in Delhi and other large cities resulted in the death of over 3,000 Hindus. By the turn of the millennium, the separatist agitation had largely dissipated as moderate Sikhs came back into power in national politics and international support for an independent state declined.

Through the last decades of the twentieth century, the Sikh global migration continued, and now almost 10 percent of Sikhs live outside India. With over 20 million followers worldwide, including a growing number of Western converts, Sikhism is slowly being recognized for its distinctive spiritual development and as the youngest of the three great heterodox faiths that originated in India, the other two being Buddhism and Jainism.

A GROWING GLOBAL TRADITION

Hinduism has entered into Western awareness strongly. As we will also see in the case of Buddhism, this interest is selective, centered on yoga and meditation, with much less focus on ritual or law. Many Westerners have been trained as yoga teachers by Indian masters, and nearly every major American city and college town has centers where one can go to practice. For many, of course, this interest is confined to the athletic or health benefits, with the religious beliefs underlying the practices often downplayed or tailored to

Contrasting Religious Visions

Peacemaker: Pandurang Shastri Athavale and the Swadhyaya ("Truth Seekers")

Pandurang Athavale, born in 1920, grew up in a family that was active in movements sponsored by M. K. Gandhi, the Mahatma. In 1956 he began organizing social uplift programs for the poorest low-caste groups, drawing as well upon a modernist reading of Hinduism's great spiritual classic, the *Bhagavad Gita*. Living modestly as a householder, Athavale prefers to be called *Dadaji* ("Elder Brother"), resisting the usual trappings of the title *guru*. His social programs have reached an estimated 20 million people living in 100,000 villages. The scope of this movement is due to the practice of *bhaktipheri*, or devotional visits, in which he or his followers spread the message of human service to new communities. His message is simple:

> It is my experience that awareness of the nearness of God and reverence for that power creates reverence for self, reverence for the other, reverence for nature, and reverence for the entire creation. And devotion as an expression of gratitude for God can turn into a social force to bring about transformative changes at all levels in the society.[a]

Acting on this conviction, members of Athavale's organization, called Swadhyaya, help build new temples that are ecumenical, open to all, and community centers for cooperative activities. Swadhyaya has become a worldwide movement, with 350 centers in the United States alone. The magnitude of the work and the authentic spirituality of the movement were the reason Athavale was awarded the 1997 Templeton Prize, the "Nobel Prize" for excellence in religious pursuits.

Confrontationalist: Voices from the Vishva Hindu Parishad

As the following contrasting visions indicate, every religious tradition is capable of generating both visions that encourage peace and understanding and visions that encourage conflict and violence. Arguing that Hindus have suffered from disunity, mindless pacifism, and Muslim predations over the last millennium, leaders associated with the "Council of all Hindus" have argued for revival by means of changing these old and decadent religious habits. An official inquiry on the Hindu-Muslim rioting in Bombay in 1993 reported that the responsibility lay in gangs of Hindus led by the Shiva Sena ("Shiva's Army"), a VHP ally. Members of this group went on a rampage, setting gasoline fires that burned Muslim businesses and homes. In the end, at least 1,200 Muslims died. A Shiva Sena leader commented several years afterward, "Who are these Muslims? If the Shiva Sena comes to power, everybody will take an initiation of the Hindu religion [to become Hindu]."[b] Similar uncompromising sentiments were expressed by the woman ascetic Uma Bharati, who proclaimed in 1991:

> Declare without hesitation that this is a Hindu country, a nation of Hindus. We have come to strengthen the immense Hindu shakti [force] into a fist. Do not display any love for your enemies. . . . The Qur'an teaches them to lie in wait for idol worshipers. . . . But we cannot teach them with words, now let us teach them with kicks. . . . Tie up your religiosity and kindness in a bundle and throw it in the Jamuna. . . . Any non-Hindu who lives here does so at our mercy."[c]

[a] *Hinduism Today*, June 1997, p. 35.
[b] *India Today*, January 15, 1996, p. 25.
[c] Thomas Hansen, *The Saffron Wave: Democracy and Hindu Nationalism in Modern India* (Princeton, NJ: Princeton University Press, 1999), p. 180.

Across Europe and North America, increasingly affluent immigrant communities are building magnificent, traditional Hindu temples. This temple in Omaha, Nebraska, opened in 2004.

fit into the customers' existing belief system. To see the panoply of traditions and applications of yoga in the West, one need only pick up a copy of *Yoga Journal,* a magazine that in 2007 reported over 350,000 subscribers and reached over 1 million readers monthly. It has been calculated that 10 million Americans now practice yoga.

The ubiquitous Indian diaspora is increasingly important in the process of Hindu globalization. First and second generations of Indians settled in the United States are the nation's richest ethnic group in terms of per capita income, and the majority, who are Hindu, has supported the internationalization of the faith. For example, the Hindus of the Greater Boston area have organized and collected several million dollars to build a large South Indian–style temple in Ashland, Massachusetts. Temple leaders hired artisans from Madras and had the chief icons made to order; they also created an endowment that pays for the lodging and full-time employment of two brahmin priests, who are recruited for long-term assignments to serve patrons of the temple. Similar institutions exist in Austin, Texas, Los Angeles, and elsewhere.

Temples also are the natural centers for cultural awareness and revitalization movements among immigrant Hindus. For example, the Arya Samaj of North America regularly sponsors conferences in Hindu temples that seek to "empower the next generation with Vedic values" by having youth "practice those values in daily life, maintain a linguistic link to Sanskrit, inculcate a spirit of humility, give back to the community," and live by the founding motto, *Krivanto vishvam arya* ("Make this world noble").[14] Hindu nationalists have also spread their activism in America through temple institutions and summer camps for youth. The VHP has raised funds for causes back in India, and its members have sought to have public school textbooks in California rewritten to conform to their ideological interpretations of Indian history and Hinduism.

All immigrant Hindus today must submerge many of their regional traditions in joining with coreligionists from all over India to provide a homogenized working definition of "Hinduism." As with other immigrant groups that assimilated in America, parents express some dismay and nostalgia for the traditions they followed back in Kerala or Bengal; their children are taught a simplified and essentialized version of "Hinduism": to chant "OM," do simple yoga, and interpret the *Bhagavad Gita* as a text lauding "caring and sharing."[15]

Converts and immigrant groups also have supported the global extensions of religious centers founded by modern gurus. In the West there are now hundreds of Hindu teachers who travel to the West to give teachings. Several dozen have shifted to ashrams and yoga centers outside India to dedicate their lives to their Western converts and South Asian immigrants. Perhaps the most successful of all the global Hindu gurus is the sadhu **Maharishi Mahesh Yogi**, who in the 1960s came to prominence by giving spiritual instruction to the Beatles. His movement, Transcendental Meditation (TM), has taken Hindu tradition across the globe and inspired a long agenda for utopian initiatives. (See the nearby box.)

As India has become an important player in the global computer and software business, older Hindu institutions and new movements have adopted the Internet technology. For example, a famous Ganesh temple in Bombay has set up a website in which viewers can have live darshan of the main icons, hear hymns being sung, and, with a few additional mouse clicks, make credit card contributions to sponsor pujas. The website of a Vishnu shrine in the northern state of Jammu offers similar scenes and services, adding maps, regularly updated weather reports, and hostel bookings to aid the estimated 4 million pilgrims who visit the temple annually in person.

Like immigrant communities across the world today, Hindu parents create programs that instill traditional religious beliefs and practices.

Global Hinduism: Transcendental Meditation (TM)

For the past fifty years until his death in 2008, Maharishi Mahesh Yogi brought mystical Hindu teachings to the West. Having introduced mantra-centered meditation to over 6 million seekers across the world, each of whom paid for the initiation (in 2006: $2,500), Maharishi's TM has established yoga centers around the world and founded a Vedic University in Fairfield, Iowa. TM now seeks to implement the guru's vision of rebuilding the world's spirituality and healing humanity according to his interpretation of Vedic principles combined with the principles of quantum physics. With assets of $300 million in the United States, the group focuses on (i) training advanced yogis in forty countries whose levitations can "produce quantum shifts to heal humanity's overstressed minds"; (ii) coordinating sessions across the globe in which meditators numbering the square root of the world's population (8,000, according to Maharishi's theory) will positively alter the planet's atmosphere and so the planet's humane consciousness; and (iii) building 3,000 "marble peace palaces" in major cities to offset the disharmonious locations. Having turned eighty-nine in 2006 and living in an ashram in the Netherlands, Maharishi expressed his aim: "My coherence-creating groups are going to put out all this mischief-mongering in the world. The world is going to come out to be a neat and clean world. All these countries will fade away."

Source: Lily Koppel, "Outer Peace," *New York Times Magazine*, October 8, 2006, p. 24.

Maharishi Mahesh Yogi (1918–2008)

As Indian workers and entrepreneurs have become important in the global marketplace, especially in the computer and software industry, observers have discerned the rise of "karma capitalism." Here we can recognize Hindu teachings exerting a new and powerful influence in the global marketplace. Indian philosophies have been integrated in elite business schools in a variety of ways: "self-mastery" courses that now help to

The blessings of the Hindu gods are sought today by new car owners and, as shown here, by auto rickshaw owners. Hindu devotees today regularly perform pujas to avert accidents in cars, trains, and airplanes.

train managers "to boost their leadership skills and find inner peace in lives dominated by work"; Hindu "business gurus" such as C. K. Prahalad who now teach that executives should conceive of companies in more holistic ways, to redefine success as larger than monetary profit, including the well-being of employees, customers, and the environment. Classical Hindu teachings have now become a creative influence on the culture of modern business, with many now explicitly managing their enterprises to generate "good karma."[16]

Conclusion

Recalling the initial caution about taking any religious tradition as standing for all of "Hinduism," we can only generalize about the broad patterns of change affecting the religion in South Asia. There is no doubt that India is changing, just as other parts of postcolonial Asia are. Newly built roads, transport systems, education, mass media, and industrialization are contributing to the rapid development of the economic system of the country, drawing migrants from rural settlements to burgeoning urban areas and transforming the life experiences of individuals. In these settings, the Hindu traditions of the premodern world are in decline as new institutions and teachers arise to meet the needs of those living under the new circumstances.

But even with so much change, the belief in the spiritual presence of the gods, in yoga, and in the guru-centered spiritual life remains strikingly strong. It is easy to misinterpret surface changes as modifications to the religion: Do cement buildings replacing cut stone temples or electric lights replacing the butter lamps set out in the Diwali festival represent Westernization and the decline of traditional values, or simply the transposition of new technologies in the service of the centuries-old wish to please the deities with artful decoration?

In the cities, among the rapidly expanding middle class as well as among slum dwellers, there are numerous new incarnations of "organized Hinduisms." Hitherto-independent groups such as sadhus from different regions are forming new organizations to work for common interests. Likewise, laity and priests associated with major temples have pressed for the establishment of management committees to orchestrate rituals and festivals as well as for supervising temple accounts.

Thus, what in rural India was a largely preordained relationship with a family priest and local guru, in urban settings has become a matter of individual choice. Hindus in ever-increasing numbers, then, are faced with the "heretical imperative" (as discussed in Chapter 1) of making their own choices about their own religious paths. Media-savvy gurus appear on television, use video recordings and websites to link far-flung communities, and draw on a global network of disciples to build their movements. One of the most popular English-language magazines dedicated to promoting reformist Hinduism in India and abroad (*Hinduism Today*) is published not in Benares, but in . . . Hawaii.

THE CONNECTION OF RELIGION WITH SOCIAL REFORM

The impact of Christianity on Hinduism, as we noted earlier, was not primarily doctrinal but more in the arena of modeling the role of modern religious institutions and the scope of religious service in society. Just as Christian missionaries had shown that churches could be linked with schools and hospitals, Hindu reformers (e.g., the Ramakrishna Mission and Sai Baba) who have begun spiritual movements almost without exception include social welfare initiatives to address the nation's undeniable needs. Initially, perhaps, this was done in competition with the Western missionaries; but the idea also found support from many Hindu teachers promoting the spiritual power of selfless, compassionate service and extolling individuals to engage in humanitarian merit-making.

As a result, most Hindu mathas have started educational institutions, and many, such as the Ramakrishna Mission, continue to expand networks of clinics and hospitals staffed by their own trained monks. Hindu gurus cite a variety of reasons for the motivation that mathas now display for social work. A swami influential in the early VHP remarked long ago that the Indian people required inspiration from leaders who do not merely retreat to caves and meditate. Likewise, the sadhu leader of one of India's largest monasteries described his work in education as necessary to make democracy a success. Another prominent swami, while acknowledging a desire to serve the people

International organizations like the Boy Scouts have adjusted their programs to include other religious traditions.

Where in the world has the power of religious views on the environment successfully resisted the force of economic interests? Not, as yet, in India, where the Ganges is one of the world's largest sacred rivers.

and foster humanitarianism, admits that his monastic order engages in social work primarily to dispel the impression that only other religions do it. Those Hindu organizations that are growing in size and influence are all heavily engaged in addressing the poverty and suffering still endemic in modern South Asia.

One might propose, then, examining what Hindu reformers collectively are *doing*. One case study would be the Ganges River, which flows from the high slopes of the Himalayas into the highlands through sites associated with all the great gods. The Ganges has a central place in the Hindu religious imagination, and every confluence with a tributary is considered a sacred site. Texts describe the Ganges as a gift from the gods to humanity and symbolize it by a goddess; in practice, its holy waters remove bad karma and receive the ashes of one's dead kin. In addition, this great river flows through the most densely populated states of India, from which countless farmers draw water directly to irrigate their fields and grow the food that feeds several hundred million people.

But, as elsewhere in the industrial world, municipal governments have used the sacred river as a sewer and private companies have dumped in it their untreated factory wastes. The Ganges has been increasingly polluted over the last several decades, with dangerous water toxicity and pollutant levels recorded in many sections. In 1985 a coalition of religious and political leaders announced with great fanfare a campaign to restore the purity of the Ganges, with a multimillion-dollar budget and international support. Here ostensibly was a powerful convergence of spiritual need and ecological necessity, with the moral goal of protecting the health of millions.

Yet over twenty years later, few of the planned water filtration plants have been completed, funds have been misspent, and raw sewage and untreated wastes still flow directly into the river from most cities. If anything, the Ganges has gotten worse as new industries and burgeoning cities have added their discharges to the flow, creating islands of floating garbage and making its waters a vector for mass illnesses such as dysentery and hepatitis So pernicious has this problem become that at the end of the great Kumbha Mela in 2007, thousands of Hindu holy men staged two days of protest and filed a lawsuit, threatening to lead others to boycott the next festival unless the government immediately began corrective actions to clean up the river. To pose a question that environmental crises have raised across the world: Are religious convictions really an effective counterbalance to the power of business interests or the practice of political corruption?

As middle-class South Asians have raised their educational level, experienced rising prosperity, and encountered religions and societies elsewhere, they have been inevitably forced to consider "Hinduism" in comparison to these other belief systems and cultures. This process was very poignant in the summer of 2007, when the Indian elite was drawn into thinking about where their nation had traveled in the sixty years since independence and how the country now measured up both against earlier expectations and in comparison to the other great nation founded at roughly the same time, China.

The widespread opinion expressed in the popular press was that while democracy was treasured and never to be surrendered and India's meteoric rise since 1990 in the global marketplace grows promisingly, there was also the hard truth pointed to that Hindu culture and religion have failed to transform Indian society in many of the positive ways evident in contemporary China. How could caste discrimination endure? How could India's extreme poverty be tolerated among the masses while the rich get richer? How could the nation's leaders, drawn largely from the high castes, not have done more to change these realities? While no uniform answer emerged, and while not only religion was blamed, the frequent and often intense debates that swirled throughout that year signaled support for the view that Hinduism is part of the problem and needs reform. One representative example of this self-scrutiny, by the Nepali social critic Dipak Gyawali, incorporates many of the issues we have discussed, perhaps foreshadowing the direction of future change:

> In the social field, several things need to be done. The first is that modern Hindus need to rediscover the origins and rationale of Hinduism and its rituals because they are as ignorant as anyone. This is probably easier to do for a modernist Hindu because Hindu literature is now more readily available in English than in native languages or in incomprehensible Sanskrit. The second is that modern Hindus need to reject the archaic, the irrational, and the inefficient to make living a Hindu life less full of contradictions. The third is that they need to redefine the religion's core in a manner that is not exclusive but allows non-Hindu neighbors to participate as well. Finally, and most important, there is a need to reassert moral outrage rather than escape into flaccid tolerance whenever justice is being denied.[17]

Among the many voices of Hinduism today, those speaking against secularism and for reform have garnered unprecedented political power. Their daunting task in India is to demonstrate how Hindu values, beliefs, and conscience can serve the needs of all its citizens, who now number over 1 billion.

Discussion Questions

1. What reasons might be suggested for the transformation of the polytheism of the early Vedic peoples into the monism and theism of later Hinduism?

2. Compare and contrast the spiritual practice of the shaman (Chapter 2) with that of the yoga practitioner. Is it possible to know exactly how different their experiences are?

3. Why would the lowest castes regard the doctrines of karma, caste, and duty as a system designed to subjugate them?

4. What reasons would a woman have for abiding by her dharma?

5. To what extent can karma theory be considered to be a doctrine of fatalism? Do humans still have freedom of action?

6. If you were an Islamic judge in medieval India, how would you advise the local sultan who asks if his subjects who follow Krishna (as depicted in the *Bhagavad Gita*) are in fact monotheists?

7. No Hindu religious group has ever acquired the power to define what was true doctrine and what was heresy. In this context, what are the strengths and weaknesses of the Hindu tradition?

8. How does ritualism relate to the ideals of bhakti Hinduism?

9. Why was the influence of colonialism on the religions of India powerfully conveyed by the term *Protestant Hinduism*?

10. What reasons are Hindu nationalists giving to support their view that secularism is the perpetuation of colonialism and a betrayal of the great modern Hindu reformers?

11. Explain why M. K. Gandhi's biography contains a paradigmatic study of the factors shaping modern Hindu reform.

12. Critique the following statement, from an ecumenical Hindu organization: "We can follow Jesus without contradiction, for he is none other than another *avatara* of Lord Vishnu."

13. What does it say about the power of ideas regarding the sacred versus the power of profane modern economic interests that Hindu leaders and politicians have been unable to prevent their most sacred river, the Ganges, from becoming a nearly dead and toxic waterway?

Key Terms

Adi Granth
ahimsa
Arya Samaj
atman
avatara
Bhagavad Gita
bhakti
BJP (Bharatiya Janata Party)
Brahman
brahmin
Brahmo Samaj
darshan
dharma
Gandhi
guru
gurudwaras
Hindutva
Kali Yuga
karma
Khalsa
Maharishi Mahesh Yogi
matha
moksha
nirguna Brahman

OM
Om-kara
prasad
puja
puranas
Ramakrishna Mission
Ramanuja
Rammohan Roy
RSS (*Rashtriya Svayamsevak Sangh*)
saguna Brahman
samsara
satyagraha
Shaivite
Shankara
tantra
Tattvabodhini Sabha
TM (Transcendental Meditation)
Upanishads
Vaishnavite
Vedas
Vishva Hindu Parishad (VHP)
Vivekananda
yoga
Yoga Sutras

Suggested Readings

Babb, Lawrence. *The Divine Hierarchy* (New York: Columbia University Press, 1975).

———. *Redemptive Encounters: Three Modern Styles in the Hindu Tradition* (Berkeley: University of California Press, 1986).

Dass, Ram. *Be Here Now* (Kingsport, TN: Hanuman Foundation, 1978).

de Bary, William Theodore, ed. *Sources of Indian Tradition,* 2nd ed., 2 vols. (New York: Columbia University Press, 1988).

Dimmitt, Cornelia, and J. A. B. van Buitenen. *Classical Hindu Anthology: A Reader in the Sanskrit Puranas* (Philadelphia: Temple University Press, 1978).

Hawley, John, and Mark Juergensmeyer. *Songs of the Saints of India* (New York: Oxford University Press, 1988).

Hopkins, Thomas. *The Hindu Religious Tradition* (Belmont, CA: Wadsworth, 1982).

Jaffrelot, Christophe. *The Hindu Nationalist Movement in India* (New York: Columbia University Press, 1996).

Jones, Kenneth W. *Socio-Religious Reform Movements in British India* (Cambridge: Cambridge University Press, 1994).

Larson, Gerald James. *India's Agony over Religion* (Albany: State University of New York Press, 1995).

Narayan, Kirin. *Storytellers, Saints, and Scoundrels: Folk Narrative in Hindu Religious Teaching* (Philadelphia: University of Pennsylvania Press, 1989).

Zimmer, Heinrich. *Myths and Symbols of Indian Art and Civilization* (Princeton, NJ: Princeton University Press, 1970).

Notes

1. Most Sikhs regard their faith as constituting a separate faith that rejects the authority of the Veda, the legitimacy of brahmin priesthood, and the associated ideology of caste. While we will point out how these and other contrasts came to define a very successful and distinctive tradition, we cover this tradition within this chapter for thematic consistency with other chapters treating similar patterns of diversity (Christianity and Islam).

2. *India Today,* January 15, 1996, p. 22.

3. Daniel Gold, "Organized Hinduisms: From Vedic Truth to Hindu Nation," in M. E. Marty and R. Scott Appleby, eds., *Fundamentalisms Observed* (Chicago: University of Chicago Press, 1991), p. 581.

4. For the sake of simplicity, in this text we use *brahmin* to indicate the priestly caste and *Brahman* to indicate the "world spirit," although in fact they are similar Sanskrit words: *brahman* and *brahmana,* respectively.

5. Bhimrao Ambedkar, *What Congress and Gandhi Have Done to the Untouchables* (Bombay: Thacker and Company, 1934), pp. 307–308.

6. W. Owen Cole, "Sikhism," in John R. Hinnells, ed., *A Handbook of Living Religions* (New York: Penguin, 1984), p. 240.

7. Patwant Singh, *The Sikhs.* (New York: Doubleday, 1999), p. 23.

8. Brian Hatcher, "Bourgeois Vedanta: The Colonial Roots of Middle-Class Hinduism," *Journal of the American Academy of Religion* 75, 2007, p. 313.

9. *Ibid.* p. 315.

10. "Hinduism," in Sumit Ganguly and Neil DeVotta, eds., *Understanding Contemporary India* (Boulder, CO: Lynne Reiner, 2003), p. 204.

11. John Stratton Hawley and Mark Juergensmeyer, *Songs of the Saints of India.* (New York: Oxford University Press, 1988), pp. 44–45.

12. http://www.bkwsu.com/index_html

13. Quoted in the "Financial Times of London," March 31, 2007, Section FT, p. 1.

14. *India Abroad Weekly,* August 4, 2006.

15. "Camp Joins Summer Fun with Teaching the Hindu Faith," *New York Times,* February 11, 2007.

16. "Business Filter," *Boston Globe,* October 30, 2006, E-2.

17. Dipak Gyawali, "Challenged by the Future, Shackled by the Past," *Himal South Asia,* May 1997, p. 19.

4

Buddhism

WAYS TO NIRVANA

Overview

For over 2,000 years, a simple recitation of "going for refuge" (the **Three Refuges**) has been used to mark conversion to Buddhism, to affirm one's devotion, and to start Buddhist rituals:

- *Buddham Saranam Gacchami* — I go for refuge in the Buddha
- *Dharmam Saranam Gacchami* — I go for refuge in the teachings
- *Sangham Saranam Gacchami* — I go for refuge in the community

Today these three phrases are repeated across Asia and increasingly beyond, in Japan and Nepal, from Mongolia to Thailand, by immigrants and converts from Moscow to San Francisco. But for the student first encountering Buddhism, how different those who "go for refuge" appear. High in the Himalayas, a Tibetan monk wearing a humble red woolen robe seals himself into a cave retreat for three years and three months of meditative solitude. In the heart of urban Seoul, Korea, a layman wearing a stylish three-piece suit declares the opening of a 24-hour Buddhist cable TV channel at a press conference in the ultramodern headquarters of a major Buddhist reform organization. In tropical Singapore, as householders gather to view 2,500-year-old bone relics of the Buddha, monks in yellow robes chant and extol the blessings of worshiping these mortal remains.

For Mrs. Wang of Taiwan, being a Buddhist means chanting set phrases in hopes of rebirth in the heaven of a Buddha. For Mr. Khatt of Cambodia, being a Buddhist means bestowing charity and doing good in order to achieve a better life in his next rebirth. For Mr. Vajracarya of Nepal, being a Buddhist means performing

Buddhism Timeline

563 BCE	Birth of Siddhartha [some traditions give 463 BCE]
528	Enlightenment of Shakyamuni, the Buddha; creation of the *sangha*, the monastic order
c. 510	Establishment of nuns' order
483	Death of the Buddha [some traditions give 383 BCE]
482	First Council collects and organizes oral accounts
383	Council of Vaishali leads to the first split in the sangha
273–232	Reign of Ashoka, convert to Buddhism, who spread Buddhism throughout India and beyond (Afghanistan, Burma, Sri Lanka)
250	Council of Pataliputra leads to division into "18 schools"
240	Sanchi stupa and other stupas built across India; relic cult at stupas central to community
c. 100	Origins of the Mahayana school, beginning with *Prajnaparamita* literature
80	First collections of written canon begun, beginning with the Vinaya, the monastic code; Pali Canon collection begun in Sri Lanka
c. 85 CE	Composition of the *Lotus Sutra*
50–180	Spread of Buddhism into central Asia via the Silk Road
124	Buddhist monks in western China
c. 200	Writings of Nagarjuna, the most influential Mahayana philosopher; Madhyamaka school formed
220–589	Buddhist missions reach Southeast Asia, Java, Sumatra, Korea, Japan, Vietnam; Buddhist monasteries established throughout China in era of weak central state
c. 300	Rituals and visualization meditations dedicated to bodhisattvas developed by Mahayana monks
c. 300	Origins of Pure Land school in India
320ff	Development of Yogacara school, led by monastic brothers Asanga and Vasubandhu
c. 425	Writings of a monk who shaped the Theravada school, Buddhaghosa, in Sri Lanka
c. 500	Rise of the Vajrayana Thunderbolt school in India, which eventually dominates Buddhist communities in northeastern India, Nepal, and Tibet
c. 600	Formation of the Ch'an school in China inspired by teachings of the Indian monk Bodhidharma
700–1270	Buddhism dominates Sri Vijaya kingdom on Sumatra-Java; rulers build Borobodur stupa
749	First Buddhist monastery in Tibet
760–1142	Pala Dynasty rules North India, patronizes Buddhist monasteries, and promotes Mahayana traditions; tradition in decline elsewhere in India
841–845	Extensive destruction of monasteries in China and defrocking of Buddhist monks and nuns

900ff	Restoration of Chinese Buddhism, principally the Pure Land and Ch'an schools
c. 1000	Second introduction of monastic Mahayana Buddhism into Tibet from India
1192	Muslim rule established across northern India; final destruction of Indian monasteries and decline of Bodh Gaya as center of Buddhist pilgrimage
1193–1227	In Japan, formation of new schools: Zen brought from China by Eisei (1141–1215) and Dogen (1200–1253); Pure Land by Honen (1133–1212) and Shinran (1173–1262), and school founded by Nichiren (1222–1282)
1000–1400	Era of Pagan Kingdom in Burma, establishing one of the great centers of Buddhism
1642–1959	Tibet dominated by Gelugpa monastic school under the Dalai and Panchen lamas
1815–1948	Era of British colonial rule. Conflicts in Sri Lanka lead to reformist movement styled "Protestant Buddhism" that influences Buddhists across Asia.
1851–1868	Rule of King Monghut in Siam, who revived the sangha and placed it under state control
1864–1933	Anagarika Dharmapala, Sri Lankaese reformist, founder of the Mahabodhi Society, who spread reformism across Asia
1871–1876	Heavy Meiji persecution of Buddhism; 70 percent of monasteries lost as 75 percent of monks defrocked
1871	Fifth Buddhist Council held in Burma
1877–1945	Buddhist establishment in Japan supports nationalism, militarism, and seizures of Korea, Taiwan, and northern China
1893	Parliament of World Religions in Chicago; speeches by Zen monk and Dharmapala stir interest
1944	Buddhist Churches of America, a Pure Land organization, founded in California
1945	Soka Gakkai established in Japan, a branch of Nichiren school until 1991
1949–1976	Chinese Communist government persecutes Buddhists and seizes 250,000 monasteries and temples, with the Cultural Revolution (1966–1969) a period of intense destruction
1954–1956	Sixth Buddhist Council in Rangoon, Burma, culminating in the marking of the 2,500-year anniversary of Shakyamuni's death
1956	Foundation of the Mahasangha Sahayaka Gana in central India, a Buddhist organization
1959–present	Exile of the fourteenth Dalai Lama from Tibet and the era of the globalization of Tibetan Buddhism
1976–present	Slow restoration of Buddhist institutions in China
1982–present	Civil war against Tamil minority in Sri Lanka polarizes Buddhist community
1987	Founding of Shakyaditya, a worldwide organization of Buddhist women
1989	Foundation of the International Network of Engaged Buddhists by Thai activist Sulak Sivaraksa
1990	Revival of Buddhism in Mongolia after 88 years of suppression
1991	Founding of *Tricycle*, a Buddhist mass market magazine in America
1998–present	Full ordination taken by Theravada nuns in Chinese monasteries, reviving a lost tradition
2007	Monks lead democracy protests in Burma, resulting in fierce government repression of sangha

intricate rituals to honor the gods and Buddhas who out of their boundless compassion can bless his community. For forest monks in Thailand and American disciples of a Japanese Zen master practicing in his monastery in the Catskills, being a Buddhist means reaching enlightenment by meditation alone. It is true that each of these Buddhists reveres an image of the Buddha, who is seated in meditation, serene and exemplary, but one cannot help but wonder what the historical Buddha might say if he heard how differently these disciples now construe his teachings. The oldest of the world's missionary religions and perhaps the most accommodating in adapting to its widely varying communities in its global diaspora, Buddhism is in modest revival in most areas of the world today after having suffered debilitating setbacks throughout the modern era. Understanding Buddhism thus entails knowing about most of the peoples and cultures of Eurasia: from the homeland on the Ganges in South Asia into the high Himalayas, across the tropical states of Southeast Asia and over the central Asian deserts, and throughout the imperial domains of China, Korea, and Japan.

This chapter will examine how Buddhism in its creative diversity has sought to direct devotees to secure these goals. We will sketch the life of the Buddha, another of humanity's great and most significant religious teachers. We will then explore his basic teachings and chart the various interpretations as the tradition spread by monks and nuns reached from northern India to East Asia, Southeast Asia, and in the last two centuries to Europe and the West.

Rough estimates place the number of Buddhists at 350 million, making it the fourth-largest among world religions. Over 98 percent live in Asia. Globally, there are as many Buddhists as there are Protestant Christians. Buddhists today are divided into two factions, those following the **Mahayana**, or "Great Vehicle," and those following the **Theravada**, or "Teachings of the Elders." Roughly 62 percent of people today are adherents of the Mahayana and 38 percent are Theravada followers. With most Mahayanists located in the countries north of the tropics, the label *Northern Buddhism* is also used for this grouping, as opposed to the *Southern Buddhism* of the Theravadins. In a half-dozen Asian states (Sri Lanka, Myanmar, Thailand, Laos, Cambodia, Japan), Buddhists comprise the overwhelming majority of the population. They are significant minorities in Nepal, China, South Korea, and Singapore, while their presence in Malaysia (10 percent), Indonesia (3 percent), and India is less marked. (It should be noted that specific percentages, figures taken from Western almanac sources, are at best rough estimates, with wide margins for error.)

Buddhists today are becoming ever more aware of the diversity of Buddhist paths. Although modern activists and intellectuals may contest exactly "what the Buddha taught," Buddhism's basic teachings about life, mortality, and spiritual development continue to inspire adherents amid the often-traumatic changes of recent centuries. In every land, venerable institutions and reformist groups alike are seeking to adapt the faith to the changing world and to revive the essential practices that lead to Buddhism's perennial threefold goals: establishing moral community, securing worldly blessings, and realizing nirvana.

Encounter with Modernity: Socially "Engaged Buddhism"

With the end of World War II and, soon after, the demise of colonialism, most Asian nations faced the need to reinvent their societies politically and culturally. Those who sought the rebuilding and renewal of Buddhism in postwar China, Mongolia, Vietnam, and North Korea faced crippling hostility from communist rulers who regarded Buddhist doctrine as superstition and Buddhist institutions as parasitic on society. These nations engaged in "revolutionary campaigns" aimed at disbanding the communities of monks, nuns, and householders, destroying their buildings and images, and discrediting all forms of Buddhist belief and practice. There were other pressures as well, many of which have ultimately exerted more benign effects.

As Asia's rapid industrialization and urbanization created new forms of social dislocation and wealth, for example, there were dramatic increases in the numbers of landless, wage-dependent workers and an unprecedented rash of ecological crises. At the same time, Asia saw an expansion of higher education and the rise of educated classes alongside new commercial elites. As a result of these changes, Buddhism was transplanted and drawn into entirely new social contexts, political struggles, and global dialogs.

One image of modern Buddhism came in the aftermath of the December tsunami that struck the Indian Ocean on December 26, 2004. Myriad press accounts of the first humanitarian responses reported that small groups of Buddhist householders immediately gathered what medicines, bandages, clothes, and food they could and headed

A statue of Buddha is all that survived the 2004 tsunami in Galle, Sri Lanka.

directly to the coastal area to render compassionate assistance. Those interviewed in Sri Lanka and Thailand typically explained in a self-effacing way that they were strengthened and motivated by their Buddhist tradition's teachings—that suffering is sad but inevitable in life and that acting compassionately is a central duty. This unprecedented tragedy showed how strong that adherence to basic Buddhist doctrines still is today—"at the grassroots level"—as they are applied to modern situations of human suffering.

Another image of modern Buddhism is that of a Vietnamese monk sitting cross-legged, engulfed in flames. This and other monk suicides in 1963 protested the South Vietnamese government's failure to respect Buddhism and to adopt a policy of national reconciliation. Among the many Buddhist monks who challenged the corrupt South Vietnamese state was Thich Nhat Hanh, who argued that when faced with immense suffering, Buddhists must take action and engage their society. While Buddhism's ascetic traditions advocate renunciation of the household life and forest dwelling for nirvana-seeking meditation, Nhat Hanh drew on other sides of the tradition to urge Buddhist monks and nuns to defer solitary individualistic practice in favor of staging nonviolent confrontations with the governments and other agencies responsible for profound suffering.

Inspired by the monks of Vietnam, contemporary Buddhist activists in Asia and now in the West are responding to crises posed by environmental despoliation, political corruption, and global hunger. Accordingly, they are identified as "engaged Buddhists," and they refuse to turn away from suffering, counseling instead "mundane

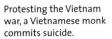

Protesting the Vietnam war, a Vietnamese monk commits suicide.

awakening." In this way, engaged Buddhists hope to elicit compassion on the part of individuals, villages, countries, and eventually all people, arguing that it is as ancient and as fundamental to Buddhism as the ascetic and solitary practices of the spiritual elite.

Buddhists engaging with society in political arenas now span the world, offering examples of revival from India to Japan: the Trailokya Bauddha Mahasangha Sahayaka Gana of India, which has worked since 1956 to convert from Hinduism low-ranked castes in India and help raise them out of poverty; the Sarvodaya Shramadana movement in Sri Lanka seeks to promote rural development through harnessing the service commitments of lay volunteers; various postwar Japanese Buddhist groups such as the Soka Gakkai work to transform society through political activism informed by Mahayana Buddhist ideals. On the ecumenical front, monk reformers such as Buddhadasa of Thailand and the Tibetan Dalai Lama have connected with those of other faiths to mobilize mutual seeking of the common good. In the late twentieth century, Sulak Sivaraksa, a Thai lay activist, formed the International Network of Engaged Buddhists to foster connections and develop this latest interpretation of the Buddha's teachings.

Zen Buddhist leader Thich Nhat Hanh in 2007, at the opening of a three-day requiem for those killed on both sides of the Vietnam War.

Another major development in Buddhism since World War II has been the global diffusion of the tradition on a scale unprecedented in world history. Buddhist social activism has made the tradition more attractive to many in the West. In Asia, engaged Buddhists have no shortage of traumatic provocations, given the region's rapid industrialization, the explosion of urban slum settlements, the alarming degradation of forests and watersheds, the predations of corrupt politicians, and the bloodshed from ethnic conflicts and civil wars. These profound changes and crises have disrupted the regions' rural societies, including many of the communities that have long sustained Buddhist monastic institutions.

The engaged Buddhists, predominantly in the urban centers, now promote new understandings of Buddhism and Buddhist action, often confronting politicians and corporations. Can this movement revitalize the tradition from the capitals to the rural hinterlands and mitigate suffering without reducing or compromising its principal values? To discover the "engagement" this movement advocates, to understand its importance, we must start with the founder and trace the historical development of his teachings.

Socially Engaged Buddhism: Some Examples

Thai activist Sulak Sivaraksa puts the ancient Buddhist concept of suffering into the framework of today's world: In Buddhist terminology, the world is full of *dukkha* ["suffering"], i.e., the dangers of impending world destruction through nuclear weapons, atomic fallout, air, land, and sea pollution, population explosion, exploitation of fellow human beings, denial of basic human rights, and devastating famine. . . . World dukkha is too immense for any country, people, or religion to solve. We can only save ourselves when all humanity recognizes that every problem on earth is our own personal problem and our own personal responsibility. . . . The language of Buddhism must offer answers which fit our situation. Only then will Buddhism survive, today and tomorrow, as it has in the past, influencing humankind positively and generating love, peace, and nonviolence. [a]

An even more forceful exhortation is provided by the Vietnamese monk Thich Nhat Hanh: The word *Buddha* comes from the root *budh*, which means "awake." A Buddha is one who is awake. Are we really awake in our daily lives? That is a question. . . . Society makes it difficult to be awake. We know that 40,000 children in the Third World die every day of hunger, but we keep forgetting. The kind of society we live in makes us forgetful. That is why we need exercises in mindfulness. . . . Our earth is like a small boat. Compared with the rest of the cosmos, it is a very small boat, and it is in danger of sinking. We need a person to inspire us with calm confidence, to tell us what to do. Who is that person? The Mahayana texts tell us that you are that person. [b]

[a] Sulak Sivaraksa, "Buddhism in a World of Change," in Fred Eppsteiner, ed., *The Path of Compassion: Writings on Socially Engaged Buddhism* (Berkeley, CA: Parallax Press, 1988), pp. 16–17.
[b] Thich Nhat Hanh, "Call Me by My True Name," in Fred Eppsteiner, ed., *The Path of Compassion: Writings on Socially Engaged Buddhism* (Berkeley, CA: Parallax Press, 1988), pp. 34–37.

Premodern Buddhism: The Formative Era

THE BUDDHA: CONTEXT AND BIOGRAPHY

We saw in Chapter 6 that North India during the Buddha's lifetime (563–483 BCE) was a place of spiritual questioning and ascetic searching unmatched in the history of religions. The dominant Aryan society was evolving from small pastoral settlements to city-states and a more diverse economy. In the context of this transformation, the old sacrifice-centered Vedic religion controlled by members of the brahmin caste was becoming for some much less plausible as an explanation of humanity's deepest connection to the universe. In remote retreats and near to the emerging urban centers, there were many seekers called **shramanas** who pursued ascetic practices (yoga) to realize the true essence of human consciousness, life, and reality. The society in which the Buddha was born was ordered by caste and brahmin ritualism. In addition, however,

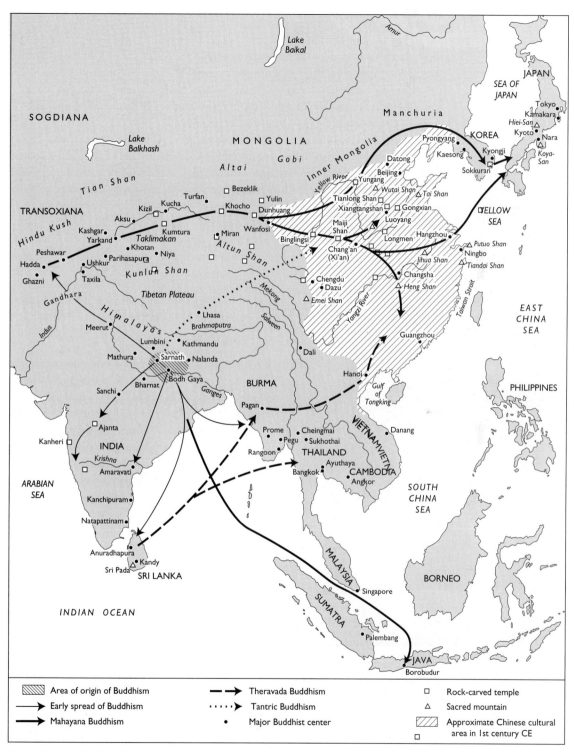

Map 7.1 The spread of Buddhism.

Legend:

- ▨ Area of origin of Buddhism
- → Early spread of Buddhism
- ⟶ Mahayana Buddhism
- ⤍ Theravada Buddhism
- ⋯► Tantric Buddhism
- • Major Buddhist center
- □ Rock-carved temple
- △ Sacred mountain
- ▨ Approximate Chinese cultural area in 1st century CE
- □

Map labels:

SOGDIANA, Lake Baikal, Lake Balkhash, MONGOLIA, Gobi, Altai, Tian Shan, Manchuria, Amur, JAPAN, SEA OF JAPAN, Tokyo, Kamakara, Hiei-San, Kyoto, Nara, Koya-San, KOREA, Pyongyang, Kaesong, Kyongji, Sokkuran, Inner Mongolia, Yellow River, Datong, Beijing, Yungang, Wutai Shan, Tai Shan, Tianlong Shan, Xiangtangshan, Gongxian, Luoyang, Longmen, Hangzhou, YELLOW SEA, Putuo Shan, Ningbo, Tiandai Shan, TRANSOXIANA, Hindu Kush, Kashgar, Yarkand, Aksu, Kizil, Kucha, Kumtura, Turfan, Bezeklik, Yulin, Khocho, Dunhuang, Wanfosi, Miran, Niya, Khotan, Taklimakan, Altun Shan, Binglingsi, Maiji Shan, Chang'an (Xi'an), Jihua Shan, Changsha, Heng Shan, Peshawar, Hadda, Ghazni, Ushkur, Parihasapura, Taxila, Kunlun Shan, Gandhara, Indus, Tibetan Plateau, Mekong, Salween, Chengdu, Dazu, Emei Shan, Meerut, Himalayas, Lhasa, Brahmaputra, Lumbini, Kathmandu, Mathura, Sarnath, Nalanda, Dali, Hanoi, EAST CHINA SEA, Guangzhou, PHILIPPINES, Sanchi, Bharhat, Bodh Gaya, Ganges, BURMA, Pagan, Gulf of Tongking, Ajanta, INDIA, Kanheri, Krishna, Amaravati, Prome, Pegu, Rangoon, Cheingmai, Sukhothai, THAILAND, Bangkok, Ayuthaya, Danang, VIETNAM, CAMBODIA, Angkor, SOUTH CHINA SEA, Kanchipuram, ARABIAN SEA, Natapattinam, Anuradhapura, Sri Pada, Kandy, SRI LANKA, INDIAN OCEAN, MALAYSIA, Singapore, SUMATRA, Palembang, BORNEO, JAVA, Borobudur, Yangzi River, Taiwan Strait there were ardent, nonconformist shramana seekers who questioned almost everything the old Vedic tradition asserted about spirit, morality, and social hierarchy. Some lived naked, in silent retreat, or even sealed in clay pots; most explored various trance states and adopted renunciatory lifestyles. Still other ascetics advocated materialism, nihilism, agnosticism, or fatalism.

Like the Upanishadic seers, most shramanas believed that life consists of a countless series of rebirths, that these are determined by an individual's karma, a natural and moral causal force that accrues from one's deeds, and that rebirths continue until through moral perfection and yoga practices one "burns off" one's karma to reach a state of liberation, which in Buddhism is termed **nirvana** or *sambodhi*. Shramanas differed widely on the exact means of reaching this goal, and they debated the details of personhood and universe. They contrasted themselves with the priestly brahmins as cobra versus mongoose, two mortal enemies from the animal world.

The Buddha's birth, depicted in a Chinese sculpture.

✦ Siddhartha's Early Life

The most famous man ever to become an ascetic was born the son of warrior-caste parents who ruled a small state in the Himalayan foothills. According to legendary accounts, Siddhartha's birth was accompanied by auspicious celestial signs and a wise man's prediction that the child would be successful as either a universal monarch or a great ascetic. Thus the infant was named Siddhartha, which means "the one who attains the goal." The young prince, whose mother died a week after giving birth, grew up in a palace where his father did everything in his power to ensure the first destiny. The son trained in the martial arts and was pampered with all the pleasures of rule, including marriage, a harem of concubines, and every form of pleasant artistic distraction.

Siddhartha's life changed when he followed an inclination to go with his faithful chariot driver to see the world beyond the palace walls. All the textual legends describe the profound impact of seeing a sick man, an old man, a dead man, and a shramana. These "four passing sights" overturned Siddhartha's rosy assumptions about life and also offered a vision of the ascetic path he could take to escape the spiritual emptiness he now felt in his sheltered existence. Within days, Siddhartha slipped away, abandoning his palace and family, including a newborn son. He began at that moment his search for a teacher among the forest-dwelling ascetics. The legends state that he was 29 years old.

✤ Siddhartha Begins His Quest

Siddhartha found a shramana guru, Arada Kalama, whose way of meditation allowed one to achieve a "state of nothingness." Siddhartha soon mastered this technique, but he also recognized that the accomplishment was limited in value. His quest led to a second teacher, Udraka Ramaputra, who taught a method of attaining trances that brought an experience of "neither perception nor nonperception." But again Siddhartha found that his fast-won mastery of this yoga still left him short of the highest goal.

The Buddha encountering the "four passing sights" that inspired his religious quest and eventual awakening.

He set forth alone again and soon joined five other men, who vowed to explore together a rigorous ascetic practice involving fanatical fasting (down to a few rice grains daily), breath control, and long periods seated in unmoving meditation. He adopted this lifestyle for about five years but finally rejected it, also, as too extreme, much to the dismay of his fellow seekers, who then ridiculed and abandoned him. Through this experiment, Siddhartha came to understand that the spiritual life is best undertaken as a middle path between the extremes of sense indulgence (the life in the palace) and asceticism so zealous that it weakens the body. One name for Buddhism, "the Middle Way," stems from this insight.

Although physically weakened and spiritually dismayed, Siddhartha did not quit. He was buoyed by a gift of rice and barley gruel from a village woman, and he came to sit beneath a great ficus tree by a river outside the town of Gaya. He vowed to find either success or death. The legends relate that his revitalized meditations were disturbed by Mara, a supernatural being regarded by Buddhists as the personification of death, delusion, and temptation. Mara summoned

his demons, who appeared as armed soldiers to elicit fear and as alluring females to provoke lust, but Siddhartha touched his right hand to the earth, asking it to bear witness to his merit and eventual success. This earth-touching gesture, seen often in depictions of the Buddha in art, brought forth earthquakes and a cooling stream that washed away Mara and his hordes.

✤ *The Bodhi Tree and the Deer Park*

Later that night, after resuming his meditations, Siddhartha reached more subtle and blissful perceptions and then the attainment of superfaculties, such as memory of former lives and psychic vision, that allowed him to survey the destinies of all beings according to their karma as well as the powers of levitation, telepathy, supervision, and superhearing. Finally he completely extinguished all desire and ignorance by fully realizing his capacity for insight (**prajna**). This "awakening" to the nature of reality under the *bo* (for *bodhi*, "enlightenment") tree, poetically recounted as occurring just as the

Buddha in earth-touching gesture, a frequently encountered icon that alludes to his calling upon the earth to bear witness to his fitness for enlightenment.

dawn broke, provides the root meaning of the term *Buddha* that from this moment onward we can properly apply to Siddhartha. He is also referred to as *Gautama Buddha*, using his family surname, and *Shakyamuni*, "the sage," or *Muni*, from Gautama's clan, the Shakyas.

For seven weeks the Buddha remained in the vicinity of the bodhi tree, enjoying the bliss of nirvana. The texts recount a story that his very first disciples were house-holders, merchants who made offerings and received his benediction for their contin-ued worldly success. He also received the veneration of *nagas*, the snake deities, whose submission symbolized Buddhism's claim of "spiritual conquest" over all deities in every locality. Then Mara returned to tempt the Buddha to remain isolated, enjoying his solitary nirvana. In his attempt to prevent the Buddha from continuing to teach, the evil one cited humanity's hopeless stupidity. But the high gods also intervened to request that the Buddha live on to share his doctrine because, they assured him, there were people everywhere capable of realizing **enlightenment** by means of his teach-ings, or **Dharma**. This request inspired the Buddha's compassion, and he vowed to stay in the world, thus providing the ultimate model of the engaged Buddhist.

He then walked for days to reach distant Sarnath, a deer park outside the city of Varanasi, where he found his former ascetic colleagues. Their disdain turned to awe, however, after the now radiantly charismatic Buddha sat among them and taught for the first time the Four Noble Truths, which culminate in the Eightfold Path. The five ascetics became the first members of the **sangha**, and they were instructed to travel to different places in the four directions for the purpose of sharing the Dharma with all people of the world.

> "Compared with the man who conquers thousands in battle, the greatest warrior is the man who conquers himself. . . . If a man is strenuous, thought-ful, self-controlled, and morally disciplined, he grows immensely."
>
> Source: *Dhammapada*

❖ The Buddha's Life Work

For the next forty or so years, the Buddha empowered his enlightened disciples, called **arhats,** to act on his behalf, admit qualified seekers into the sangha, guide those who wished to meditate, and teach the Dharma to any who would hear it. Shakyamuni con-verted other ascetics, sometimes whole assemblies of them, as well as solitary shra-manas, householders, and rulers. Buddha's faculty of psychic knowledge allowed him to preach according to the exact capacity of his audience.

As the Buddhist movement grew, new situations arose that required adaptation, so, in addition to his skill at teaching, the Buddha succeeded in creating an entirely new religious institution in ancient India: the sangha of monks (*bhikkhu*). It was established on the basis of formal ordination and vows to follow the extensive set of rules that he adapted to the many environments where Buddhist monks came to live.

After much urging (at least according to some legends), Shakyamuni also gave per-mission, around 510 BCE, for the creation of a sangha for female renunciants. He also bequeathed a mixed message by emphasizing, on the one hand, that women are capa-ble of realizing enlightenment but also, on the other, specifying rules forcing the nuns, or *bhikkhunis,* to subordinate themselves to the monks in personal power and in matters of social etiquette. When admitting nuns, the Buddha also predicted that the tradition would decline. In subsequently allowing the sangha to receive lands, buildings, and other donated communal resources, the Buddha established a framework in which the sangha shifted its focus over time, from wandering to settled cooperative communal existence. This development, which also gave householder disciples a fixed focus for their patronage, in turn strengthened the sangha.

Late in life the Buddha began to suffer from various ailments, and he died in Kushinagar, a rural site, at the age of 80. His body was cremated and the remains, divided into eight portions, were enshrined in relic mound shrines (**stupas**) that became the focus of Buddhist ritual and the visible architectural structure of the Buddha's presence across the world.

Shakyamuni's life story became for Buddhists a paradigmatic example of an individual's quest for enlightenment, and his exemplary role for subsequent generations was elaborated in hundreds of stories that describe incidents from this life as well as from his previous incarnations, in which he was reborn as a human, animal, or spirit. These narratives, called *jatakas*, along with stories of his path to Buddhahood, inspired arts and literatures across Asia that conveyed the essential doctrines in explicit, personified form. The Buddha, thus, embodies the Dharma, which, as in Hindu practice, is understood as the ultimate truth, as well as the teachings that lead to it.

BUDDHISM AS THE PATH TO NIRVANA

The spiritual tradition we refer to as *Buddhism* arose from the Buddha's wish to help others realize the transformative experience of nirvana. The Buddha emphasized the

The Sanchi stupa with gateway and pathway for ritual circumambulation. This shrine, in Madhya Prodesh state, in central India, was a major Buddhist pilgrimage site in ancient India.

practical, goal-directed orientation of his way and urged his disciples not to engage in idle speculation or mere intellectualism. He taught that humanity comprises persons of very different kinds who bear different forms of karma. According to whether they are "ordinary persons," "learners," or "adepts," each is to be instructed differently. Regardless of an individual's level, to be born as a human at all, instead of as an animal or divinity, is a rare opportunity. A human life is not to be wasted; rather, people should live with purpose and an awareness of the reality of karma. Unlike the other world religions, Buddhism has but a few universally accepted doctrines. Beyond the three refuges cited at the beginning of the chapter, Buddhists have adopted varying subsets of the Buddha's teachings and many rituals, always keeping the monastic community (the sangha) as its central institution. How could a world religion accommodate such pluralism in the course of establishing its essential doctrines?

First, Buddhists (like Hindus) assume that since humanity contains persons of many sorts, many different spiritual avenues are needed to reach everyone. Teachers, therefore, formulated myriad practices, and philosophers offered multiple interpretations of the truth the Buddha had revealed.

The second reason for Buddhism's pluralism lies in an instruction from the Buddha himself: After his death, no one person or institution was to be allowed to fix a single canon or set a single norm of orthodoxy in doctrinal interpretations (the opposite extreme of premodern Christianity). As a result, by 600 years after the death of Shakyamuni Buddha, several different canons of collected teachings were made and the sangha aligned under two main divisions: the "elder traditionalists" and the Great Vehicle. The elders, or **Sthaviravadins**, were less numerous, and their sole surviving school is called *Theravada*. Since about 100 CE, the Theravadins have taught that humanity should aspire to become an enlightened arhats. *Mahayana* is the name given to the Great Vehicle division, and many schools survive today, including Pure Land and Zen, each with a great diversity of subgroups. Thus, in many respects it is quite artificial to posit a single "Buddhism" based on a common code or single text. Buddhism in popular practice among the laity, however, does show many continuities, as we will see. The first topic is the highest ideal.

❖ Nirvana

The word *nirvana* is based on the Sanskrit verb meaning "to cool by blowing" and refers to one who has "cooled" the feverish *kleshas* ("hindrances," "poisons") of greed, hatred, and delusion. It is the kleshas that inflame desire, create karma, and bind the individual into *samsara,* the world of rebirth and suffering. Buddhists often present the concept of nirvana realization by likening it to the extinction of a fire, for as this phenomenon was understood in ancient India, the flames of an extinguished fire had been released to return to a diffuse, unagitated, and eternal state. The state of nirvana thus carries similar associations: freedom and existence in an eternal state beyond all material description. Both men and women, by moral living and mastering meditation, can realize nirvana through the cultivation of *prajna*, the direct "insight" into the nature of existence.

> The Buddha declares the Law with a single voice,
> While sentient beings, each in their own way, construe the meaning.
>
> —*Vimalakirti Nirdesha Sutra*

✤ The Four Noble Truths

The earliest formulation of the Buddha's teaching, the **Four Noble Truths**, provide a central analysis of the human condition as well as a diagnosis: the path toward nirvana. The biographies recount that through the realization of these truths in his own experience, Shakyamuni reached final enlightenment.

The first Noble Truth, "All life entails suffering," instructs the Buddhist not to deny the inevitable experience of mortal existence: physical and mental disease, loss of loved ones, the bodily degeneration of old age, and the inescapability of death. The intention of this first truth is not to induce pessimism but to encourage clear, realistic observation. Even pleasure and good times, however enjoyable, have a fundamental inadequacy because they are only temporary. The appropriate response to this truth is to make the most of the spiritual opportunities of human birth and to show compassion (**karuna**) and loving kindness (**maitri**) to alleviate the suffering affecting all other beings.

The second Noble Truth states, "The cause of suffering is desire." The term for "desire" (*trishna*) literally means "thirst," a term that covers possessions, power, sex, and all that human beings "thirst after," far beyond mere food and drink. (At the advanced stages of Buddhist practice, desire for doctrinal learning and even the wish for one's own enlightenment must also be rejected to reach the final goal.) The emphasis on desire in the second truth makes plain the need for renunciation, detachment, and asceticism.

The third Noble Truth, "Removing desire removes suffering," is rooted in the central Buddhist idea of spiritual causation: The same pattern of cyclical cause and effect by which desire leads to further suffering can also be reversed and eventually extinguished in nirvana. The emphasis on renunciation also signals the importance of the sangha as a refuge for individuals who wish to remove themselves from the world of desire.

The fourth Noble Truth, "The way for removing desire is to follow the Eightfold Path," specifies the Buddha's treatment that will "cure" the human condition, with its continuous cycle of rebirth, suffering, and redeath. As the Buddhist progresses toward enlightenment, moving through moral practice, meditation, and the cultivation of the prajna, an understanding of the Four Noble Truths deepens. There are eight specific elements in the progressive path to nirvana

✤ The Eightfold Path

Among the many doctrinal lists compiled to describe Buddhist practices, The **Eightfold Path** has been the most widely disseminated. It outlines the necessary means for achieving the realization of nirvana. The usual order is as follows:

1. *Right Views,* especially of the Noble Truths
2. *Right Thought,* or thought shaped by detachment from hatred and cruelty
3. *Right Speech,* which refrains from falsehood, gossip, and frivolity
4. *Right Action,* defined negatively as action free of killing, stealing, and harming

5. *Right Livelihood,* the refusal to earn a living through casting magic spells or careers that involve inflicting harm or killing
6. *Right Effort,* to clear and calm the mind
7. *Right Mindfulness,* the distinctive form of Buddhist meditation that observes clearly the mind and body and that cultivates detachment
8. *Right Concentration,* another form of advanced meditation that attains the mastery of trance states

Another important arrangement of the Eightfold Path was organized according to three central categories of Buddhist practice:

Morality (Shila) entails Speech, Action, and Livelihood
Meditation (Dhyana) entails Effort, Mindfulness, and Concentration
Insight or Wisdom (Prajna) entails Views and Thought

The Sri Lankan Theravadin commentator Buddhaghosa (fifth century CE), who refers to the two legs of Buddhism as Morality and Meditation, on which the body of Insight stands, organized his entire summary of the faith on the basis of this division. The Eightfold Path emphasizes that moral progress is the essential foundation to successful meditation and that the measure of successful meditation is the awakening and deepening of prajna. The different elements of the path underscore Buddhism's practical emphasis on effectiveness, whether in the foundational goal of improving moral standards, good conduct, and the material welfare of society or in the service of the more advanced ideal of deconditioning desire-driven behavior, restructuring cognition, and focusing consciousness on enlightenment realization.

Basic Buddhist Formula: Buddhist Spiritual Progress and the Eightfold Path

MORALITY	→	MEDITATION	→	PRAJNA	→	NIRVANA

Items in Eightfold Path

Right speech	→	Right mindfulness	→	Right views
Right action	→	Right concentration	→	Right intentions
Right livelihood	→	Right Effort		

Commentary: Buddhist life begins with the development of moral character; along with ritual participation, moral living defines being a Buddhist for most adherents. A few individuals move on to the next stage, meditation; to the extent that meditation is successful, prajna develops. When prajna is complete and perfected, one experiences nirvana.

THE FIRST COMMUNITY AND ITS DEVELOPMENT

Life in the Buddhist sangha was a true refuge for "sons and daughters of the Buddha" (as monks and nuns were called) who wished to leave behind their homes and live for spiritual purpose. The ideal was simple: Material needs were met by householders, thus allowing the renunciants to meditate and study without encumbrances.

Texts regulating the early monks and nuns, called *Vinayas,* record how the rules and institutional life developed. For example, because the Buddha was sensitive to the state laws under which he lived, he declared criminals, runaway slaves, and army deserters ineligible to join the sangha. He also specified principles to govern the community (by seniority, as reckoned from the time since ordination) and insisted that the group meet every two weeks so that each monk or nun certified his or her personal compliance. This fortnightly ritual became a central feature of life in the sangha. The Buddha's organizational genius can be seen as well in his cultivation of a householder community that provided for the needs of the sangha. It was Buddhist householders who joined the sangha, and it was the patronage of other good Buddhist householders that established the faith's monasteries and shrines across India and, over time, throughout Asia.

After the Buddha's death, in accordance with his instruction that authority over his community was not to reside in a single person or institution, the monks and nuns settled in separate colonies, which became the monastic centers that perpetuated the faith. The renunciants repeated and memorized the sets of sermons they had heard and worked out a distinctive form of communal life. Within the first three centuries there were several gatherings of all monks, councils that met to focus on the exact rules of monastic practice.

Although the early sanghas also found considerable common ground, none of the recorded councils ever achieved exact consensus on matters of discipline or doctrinal formulation. Dissenters went off to practice as they felt proper in their own monasteries, but the monastic codes in the *Vinayas* are remarkably similar. Yet disagreements that led to schisms surprisingly involved relatively minor points. This early fact of sangha autonomy and divergent understandings of the Dharma became precedents that shaped the continuation of regional pluralism found across the Buddhist world right up to the present. As Chinese pilgrim Fa-Hsien noted in 400 CE, after traveling extensively in India, "Practices of the monks are so various and have increased so that they cannot be recorded."[1]

HOW BUDDHISM BECAME A WORLD RELIGION

In the first two centuries after Shakyamuni's death, Buddhist monks and converts spread slowly across the Gangetic plain as simply another one of the many shramana groups that emphasized asceticism and rejected the brahmin caste's privileged status, its ritual system, and especially its claim to hold a monopoly on advanced spiritual practice. It was **Ashoka** (273–232 BCE), an emperor of the powerful Maurya dynasty, whose support propelled Buddhism's emergence as a broad-based religious tradition that reached beyond the ascetics. Now it was in a position to unify the social classes of Indic civilization and link the householder population with its monastic elite.

Just as the Mauryan Empire extended across most of the subcontinent, Ashoka, through his personal prestige and imperial edicts as well as the patronage of notable monks, helped spread Buddhism from Afghanistan to the Bay of Bengal, from the Himalayan foothills to the island of Sri Lanka. As a result, the first definite traces of Buddhist monuments (monasteries and stupa shrines) can be dated to this era, as can the first systematic oral collections of the teachings. Within a century after the end of the Mauryan period, Buddhist institutions dotted the major trade routes going north and south, east and west from the Buddhist holy land, with major shrines, monasteries, and pilgrimage traditions developing at sites associated with the founder's life.

The expansion northwest into the upper Indus River, in the region called Gandhara, and into the Kashmir Valley and then beyond them up the trade routes crossing the mountains north into central Asia made these areas a key Buddhist stronghold for the next millennium. It was here that the Indic world had already met the Hellenic, for hundreds of settlements across the upper Indus were populated by descendants of the troops of Alexander the Great (356–323 BCE). Indeed, the expansion of the Mauryan Empire was enabled in part because Alexander's campaign of world conquest had faltered on the Indus. Stranded far from home, veterans of Alexander's army settled in the area, where their descendants established small states and became prominent regional traders. Many converted to Buddhism.

To understand Buddhism's successful rise to popularity among kings and commoners, however, we must comprehend how the sangha became the center of Buddhism across Asia.

Buddha from Gandhara, in the upper Indus River region, where icons were made by artisans skilled in the Hellenistic style.

SANGHA AND MONASTERY: THE INSTITUTIONAL VEHICLES OF BUDDHISM'S EXPANSION

Living in community, Buddhist monks, nuns, and devout lay followers established monasteries and shrines that rooted the faith in every locality. As Buddhist monasticism spread across Asia, it introduced independent, corporate institutions that transformed local societies and regional polities. In ancient India, the early sangha admitted new members without regard to caste as a limiting spiritual or social category. In Buddhism's subsequent missionary migrations, acceptance into the sangha offered ordinary citizens an opportunity for spiritual seeking and educational advancement that was otherwise unavailable.

Buddhism could not have existed in society at large without the support of the householders, for it was the laity that ensured the viability of the monastic institution. Throughout the Buddhist world, laypeople made donations to the sangha to "earn merit" as a means of improving their karma and garnering worldly blessings for themselves, their families, and their communities. It was this central exchange, maintained between sangha and society, that kept Buddhism vibrant.

❖ Varieties of Buddhist Monasticism

The typical Buddhist community had its center in a monastery (*vihara*), where monks or nuns would take their communal vows, meditate, study. These institutions also supported monks who practiced medicine, performed rituals essential to the Buddhist lifestyle of the locality, or managed the institution as builders and groundskeepers. Over time, distinctions developed within Buddhist monasticism: There were forest monasteries, where meditation and optional ascetic practices (*dhutanga*) could be undertaken (often under the leadership of a charismatic monk teacher), and those monasteries in village and urban settlements, which offered the opportunity to blend compassionate service to the community with individual cultivation and study. A Buddhist monk or nun could move between village and urban monasteries.

In many areas, the focus and inspiration for followers was a monk whose spiritual charisma and exemplary teaching ability drew monastic disciples and donations from the laity. The common biography of such monks mirrors that of Shakyamuni (the Buddha): disillusionments, renunciation, retreat to the wilderness, nirvana realization, and then a return to society to teach.

❖ Practical Mechanisms of Expansion

Many successful monasteries expanded. The pattern was to send out monks to establish satellite institutions following the teachings of the charismatic founder, thereby perpetuating the monastic lineage. This template of Buddhist expansion created "galactic systems" that extended Buddhism into unconverted frontier zones. The resulting network of "mother–daughter" monasteries shaped alliances of all sorts, religious and otherwise, providing the pattern of new Buddhist institution building found from Afghanistan to Bali and more recently from Bangkok to Los Angeles, Dharamsala to New York. This institutional system also resulted in the tendency for aristocratic/dominant caste families to control local monastic lineages. This pattern of certain ethnic groups dominating Buddhism in certain regions occurred in Buddhist Tibet and continues in the Kathmandu Valley, in Japan, and in Sri Lanka. In other contexts, Buddhist viharas were instrumental in breaking down ethnic and class boundaries, blurring divisions between peoples, and creating transregional spiritual communities.

Rulers across Asia were drawn to support Buddhism because of its emphasis on individual morality, its rituals designed to secure prosperity for the state as well as for its head, and the powerful legitimization that respected monastics could bestow on a regime. History has also shown that states favoring Buddhism often placed controls on the sangha's development. For example, to orchestrate the early expansion of Buddhism in China and Japan, emper-

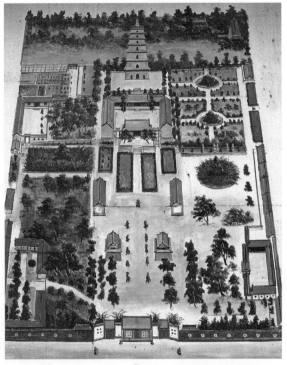

Buddhist monastery estate in China. By the end of the first Buddhist millennium, major monasteries had become complex institutions whose wealth helped popularize the tradition.

ors ordered each provincial governor to build a monastery. This command was eventually reissued to the subunits in each province as Buddhist institutions came to mirror the state's own administrative networks. Buddhist exponents, in turn, held up as a model for the ideal Buddhist ruler Ashoka, who today would be called a benevolent dictator. A fair, generous king (governor, local official, etc.) could be called a "future Buddha." The most praiseworthy title was *cakravartin,* a zealous protector and devotee. Thus leading monks in the sangha could offer those wielding political power the highest form of legitimation in the eyes of the faithful. In this manner, Buddhist doctrines, officials, and patrons permeated the secular and political lives of the societies Buddhism entered.

In places where Buddhism thrived, some monasteries in cities and villages evolved into complex institutions that were much more than refuges for ascetics. The monastery often housed the only local school, and members of the sangha served their societies by spreading literacy. Many urban monasteries also became lending institutions, appointing treasurers to see that when monies donated at shrines exceeded the sangha's requirements, the overage was reinvested (usually in trade loans) back into the local community. Interest earned through this practice was reinvested as well. On the trade routes especially, this practice, combined with profits from renting monastery-owned buildings to warehousing or retailing enterprises, garnered considerable income for the monastery treasuries. Such developments, which are attested from 200 CE onward in India and China, explain how Buddhism traveled across the Asian landscape on the basis of trade, supported by traders, and in cities along the commercial routes.

Another component in the spread of vibrant Buddhist institutions across Asia was the accumulation of lands donated by individuals and the state as perpetual endowments. Since monks were forbidden to till the soil, the sangha (as typically organized by lay managers) would rent out the cultivated lands it was acquiring. Whether its laborers grew rice and wheat or cultivated orchards, the monastery derived the food or cash needed for the sangha's upkeep. Until the twentieth century, in fact, many of the large Buddhist institutions were given indentured workers or slaves (usually entire families). Finally, shrines located within the monasteries would also earn income for the sangha in the form of offerings and from levies imposed on artisans who sold icons and votive amulets. All these elements made running a major monastery a demanding job and ensured that both donors and managers wielded considerable influence in the community.

These practices of "monastic landlordism," banking, and shrine management were also central to Buddhism's successful missions across Asia, creating the means to endow the faith with reliable income and a strong material culture. Buddhists attracted a following not only with their spiritual teachings but also with well-constructed, often-remarkable buildings, shrines, and image halls that complemented the Dharma. Tied to the productive base of society, successful Buddhist monasteries were ornamented with masterpieces of art, their libraries grew with manuscript production, and their leaders could develop an effective presentation of the Dharma. Many viharas also organized endowed charities that fed the poor and dispensed free medical care.

But there was one problem. As a practical matter, monastery autonomy and the lack of an overarching authority to regulate the monks' and nuns' obedience to the *Vinaya* norms made political leaders the arbiters of the integrity of Buddhist institutions. These officials had to "purify the sangha" periodically—that is, remove those who were acting contrary to the Vinaya norms or perhaps had not entered the vihara through the proper ordination. Thus, Buddhism's strength through concentrating wealth and human resources was also its historical weakness: Viharas were vulnerable to the vagaries of state patronage and royal protection as well as to the devastating effects of internal corruption and civil disorder.

Premodern Buddhism: The Classical Era

THE PAN-ASIAN EXPANSION OF BUDDHISM

In his first sermon after receiving enlightenment, Shakyamuni Buddha told his former companions, the five ascetic monks, to spread the new teaching universally and to use the local dialects in these communications. Thus, from its inception Buddhism has been a missionary religion, teaching a message directed to and thought suitable for all peoples.

As the first missionary religion in the world, Buddhism initially spread to places not unlike the urban and trading centers where it had begun. Within the first millennium of the common era, Buddhism was found throughout South Asia and well into central Asia on the overland routes. Monks also traveled on the maritime trade routes to Sri Lanka and across Southeast Asia. Monasteries welcomed all who would observe the rules of residence. By this time, small circles of philosopher monks had divided into more than eighteen schools of doctrinal interpretation. What gave the religion unity was a common reverence for the Three Refuges; however, Buddhism never was a unified tradition either doctrinally or institutionally.

By the year 100 CE, Buddhism had entered China through central Asia on the silk routes. As it grew more popular and spread across East Asia over the next six centuries, monks and pilgrims traveled on the land and oceanic routes between the two great ancient civilizations of Asia. The taking root of Buddhism in this region constitutes one of the greatest instances of cross-cultural transmission and conversion in world history, parallel in scope only to the transformations wrought by the world's other great missionary faiths, Christianity and Islam. Buddhism added original conceptions of space, time, psychology, and human destiny that challenged indigenous notions. It also introduced a new social institution that fostered its missionary success: the land-grant monastery, whose members could be drawn from diverse social classes.

THE CORE DOCTRINES

Textbooks always emphasize the division between traditionalists (Theravada) and adherents of the Great Vehicle (Mahayana), which grew among intellectuals in Buddhism's first millennium. For the lay majority, who focused on morality, merit, and blessings, however, such doctrinal differences were mostly irrelevant. For householders, the sangha's conformity to the Vinaya code was the major concern, because upright monks and nuns could be relied on for proper performance of rituals that benefited individuals and the community. In addition, householders would earn merit by making donations to the sangha itself.

We have suggested that an individual's beliefs and meditation practices were largely personal matters; indeed, from the earliest days, monks (or nuns) following very different interpretations of the Dharma coexisted under the same monastery roof. We first consider doctrines and ethical norms that all Buddhists shared and then move on to discuss teachings that differed from school to school.

PRAJNA *AND* REALIZING NIRVANA

Necessary for the attainment of nirvana and often translated as "wisdom," *prajna* refers to the capacity for deep spiritual discernment. The term is better rendered as "insight," however. In Buddhism it means "seeing into" reality as it truly is, characterized by

"Enlightened beings are like lotus flowers, With roots of kindness, stems of peace, Petals of wisdom, Fragrance of conduct."

Source: *The Flower Ornament Scripture*, trans. by Thomas Cleary, from *Everyday Mind*, a Tricycle book edited by Jean Smith.

Tales of Spiritual Transformation

The Enlightenment of Zen Master Sokei-an Sasaki

Although the canonical texts warn monastics not to discuss their own spiritual attainments, the following account of his enlightenment is from a respected modern Zen master.

One day I wiped out all notions from my mind. I gave up all desire. I discarded all the words with which I thought and stayed in quietude. I felt a little queer—as if I were being carried into something, or as if I were touching some power unknown to me . . . and Ztt! I lost the boundary of my physical body. I had my skin, of course, but I felt I was standing in the center of the cosmos. I spoke, but my words had lost their meaning. I saw people coming toward me, but all were the same man. All were myself! I had never known this world. I had believed that I was created, but now I must change my opinion: I was never created. I was the cosmos; no Mr. Sasaki existed.

Source: *Zen Notes*, 1(5), 1954, 17–18.

suffering, impermanence, and supporting the existence of those traits known as the **Three Marks of Existence**. Buddhist salvation is often referred to as *enlightenment* because this fullness of prajna eliminates ignorance and completely clears the mind to see reality.

The state a Buddha or an arhat, a fully enlightened follower, achieves at death is referred to as *parinirvana* ("final nirvana"), although the texts say that strictly speaking this after-death state is beyond conception. Nirvana has been described in both negative and positive terms: a deathless realm where there is neither sun nor moon, neither coming nor going, but also a state that is tranquil and pure. Most of the early scholastic treatises recognized nirvana as the only permanent reality in the cosmos. It is not, as erroneously depicted by early Western interpreters, to be seen as "annihilation," which is an extreme position rejected by the Buddha.

❖ Nonself Doctrine

The concept of **anatman** ("no-*atman*" or "nonself") is used to reject any notion of an essential, unchanging interior entity at the center of a person. The "atman" the Buddha rejected is the indestructible soul posited in the Upanishads and subsequent Hinduism, as described in Chapter 6. Buddhist philosophers argued that the universal characteristic of impermanence, one of the Three Marks of Existence, most certainly applies to human beings. As a result they regarded the human "being" in terms of the continuously changing, interdependent relationship between the five aggregates called **skandhas**.

Buddhist analysts begin with the person as a collection of the skandhas: the physical body, which is made of combinations of the four elements (earth, water, fire, air); feelings that arise from sensory contact; perceptions that attach the categories good, evil, and neutral to these sensory inputs; habitual mental dispositions (*samskaras*) that connect karma-producing will to mental action; and the consciousness that arises when mind and body come in contact with the external world.

The spiritual purpose of breaking down any apparently unchanging locus of individuality is to demonstrate that there is nothing (or "no thing") to be attached to or to direct one's desire toward. The no-self concept, however, presented exponents of Buddhist doctrine with the perpetual problem of explaining moral causality: How can the doctrine of karma, with its emphasis on compensation for one's good and bad moral decisions, operate without the mechanism of the soul, as in Hinduism or Christianity? Early texts show that this question was clearly posed to Shakyamuni Buddha: If there is no soul, how can the karmic "fruits" of any good or evil act pass into the future of this life or into a later incarnation? The standard explanation given is that karma endures in samskaras that are impressed in the fifth skandha, consciousness. Although always evolving and so impermanent, one's consciousness escapes the body at death and passes over to be reincarnated in the next life form.

While the no-self or no-soul doctrine was at the center of Buddhist thought for the philosophical elite, householders across Asia still typically conceived of themselves in terms of a body and a soul. This contradiction may indicate how peripheral some philosophical doctrines were to the mainstream of popular Buddhist understanding.

✤ Impermanence and Interdependence

Another universally accepted doctrinal formula in Buddhism is one that specifies the causal pattern of psychic and bodily states conditioning a person's bondage to suffering and rebirth. Known as **dependent**, or *conditioned*, **origination** (*pratityasamutpada*), this doctrine views reality as an ongoing, impermanent, and interdependent flux in the form of a circle divided into twelve parts. Whatever point of entry you take, the next clockwise element is the experience conditioned, and the adjacent element in the counterclockwise position is that condition directly affecting the present. Without spiritual exertion, we spin around, life after life, under these conditioning patterns. Used in this way, the twelve-fold formula reiterates the basic doctrines already cited: Craving and ignorance are the two chief causes of suffering (Noble Truths Two and Three); and the human being has no soul, only changing components of bodily life units (skandhas). This complicated formula can also be reduced to two key elements that Buddhism focuses on, the interaction of desire and ignorance that keeps humans being reborn in samsara:

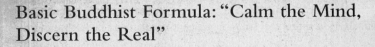

Basic Buddhist Formula: "Calm the Mind, Discern the Real"

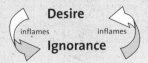

Desire   [remedy: renunciation/ detachment]

inflames   inflames

Ignorance   [remedy: meditation ⇀ prajna]

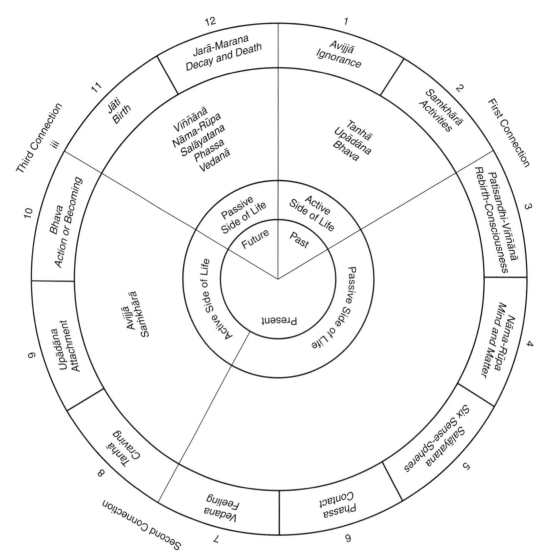

Diagram representing the formula of dependent origination, including several interpretive schemes.

❖ Buddhist Moral Precepts

The early Buddhists specified that moral practice is the first and necessary foundation for moving farther on the path toward nirvana. Buddhist ethics entails an "ideology of merit," in which making good karma and avoiding bad is the only sensible approach to life. Popular Buddhist stories focus on the reality of rebirth, covering thousands of lifetimes, which leads to the realization that all contemporary beings have been one's parents and children throughout a vast number of rebirths. Thus, acting morally toward them should be natural and logical. Buddhist doctrine also emphasizes the wisdom of cultivating detachment, discernment, and compassion (karuna).

The earliest moral rules the Buddha established consisted of five precepts. In South and Southeast Asia, they are chanted regularly in modern Theravada rituals by both monks and laity. In these communities, the precepts are regarded as general ideals applicable to everyone. Mahayana schools tended to regard the precepts more as vows, to be chanted only if one intends to follow them completely. (One can omit reciting a precept if one does not expect to be able to observe it.) The five precepts listed here are paired with corresponding positive traits that can be developed to counteract the inclination to violate a precept.

1. Not to destroy life intentionally → kindness and compassion
2. Not to steal → generosity and renunciation
3. Not to have sexual misconduct → seeking "joyous satisfaction with one's spouse"
4. Not to lie → loving the truth, seeking it, pursuing discernment and insight
5. Not to become intoxicated → mindfulness, contentment, awareness via meditation

Later in the history of Buddhism, householders began to observe eight precepts on holy days, entailing a stricter observance of the original five along with three additional renunciations:

6. Not to eat (solid) food after noon
7. Not to view shows, dancing, or singing or to wear garlands, perfumes, jewelry
8. Not to sleep on high or wide beds.

In addition to the eight precepts, there is a set of ten precepts, observed by novice monks and undertaken as a long-term commitment. They comprise the eight but split one of these into two parts and add a final prohibition against handling money. This final rule was made to ensure that begging for food would be the norm for monks and nuns, an exchange between laity and sangha that bound together the Buddhist community.

❖ Karma and Causality

One can make the case from textual sources that karma doctrine is not fatalistic because one is continually making new **punya** ("merit") or **pap** ("demerit") to change the ongoing calculus of karmic destiny. Buddhist philosophy does stress the potential for certain strong karma effects to set off mechanistic causal connections between past and future. Nevertheless, a person's karma, like all phenomena, changes every instant.

Further, the Buddhist understanding of causality is that not all contingencies in life are karma dependent. In fact, according to one Theravadin text, events are more likely than not to have had causes other than karma. Since only Buddhas can ascertain

Teachings of Religious Wisdom

Teachings on Living with Compassion

Thus as a mother with her life will guard her son, her only child, let him extend unboundedly his heart to every living being. And so with loving-kindness for all the world, let him extend unboundedly his heart, above, below, around, unchecked, with no ill will or hate.

—the Buddha[a]

In everything you do, simply work at developing love and compassion until they become a fundamental part of you. That will serve the purpose, even if you do not practice the more outward and conspicuous forms of Dharma, such as chanting, virtuous activities, and altruistic works. As a *Sutra* states, "Let those who desire Buddhahood not train in many Teachings but only one. Which one? Great Compassion. Those with great compassion possess all the Buddha's teaching as if it were in the palm of the hand."

—Tibetan monk and teacher
Patrul Rimpoche (1808–1887)[b]

[a] *Samyutta Nikāya* [1,8].
[b] *Words of My Perfect Teacher*, Transl. Padmakara Translation Group, 1998, pp. 209–210.

whether karma or other contingencies are at work in ongoing life, individuals are faced with uncertainty in evaluating events. Buddhists make a "general reading" of karma from birth station and biography. To be prepared for the future, however, the logic of the karma doctrine has motivated Buddhists everywhere to cultivate a lifelong practice of making punya and seeking guidance throughout life from astrology. Indeed, texts for householders emphasize that accumulation of wealth is the fruition of good past karma and that giving away wealth to earn merit is the best human expenditure. This giving, of benefit to all, is in a sense the social application of the Buddha's teaching about interdependence. These principles have been incorporated into Four Conditions and **Four Good Deeds**, doctrinal statements that have been as influential for the laity as the Four Noble Truths were for monks and philosophers:

> *Four Conditions* (to seek)
> Wealth gotten by lawful means
> Good renown in society
> Long life
> Birth in heaven

> *Four Good Deeds* (to use wealth for)
> Make family and friends happy
> Ensure security against worldly dangers
> Make offerings to family, friends, gods, and ghosts
> Support worthy religious people

The core doctrines we have discussed—prajna and nirvana, anatman (nonself), impermanence and interdependence, and karma causality—comprise the most common foundation for Buddhist belief. For householders, these ideas translate into fostering family ties, striving for economic success, making offerings to hungry ghosts and local gods, pursuing worldly happiness and security, nurturing faith, and seeking heaven.

Now we consider how in specific places and times individual Buddhists and Buddhist communities have focused on these teachings that affect individual life.

THE CLASSICAL IDEAL: BUDDHIST CIVILIZATION

Buddhist civilization was sustained by ritual exchanges between householders and renunciants, the monks and nuns whose advanced ascetic practices entailed abandonment of worldly comforts. Many formulations of proper Buddhist practice were made in the course of early Buddhist history to guide the faithful among the spiritual alternatives specified by the Buddha. The triad of moral practice (*shila*), meditation (*dhyana*), and insight cultivation (*prajna*) was an early organizing schema, as we noted in our discussion of the Eightfold Path.

Buddhist monasticism arose to provide refuge and support for renunciants seeking enlightenment, but the tradition survived by building multifaceted relationships with lay followers who provided for the monks' and nuns' subsistence. Eliciting the loyalty of a cross section of all classes, Buddhists articulated the foundations for a society with spiritual and moral dimensions. Buddhism adapted to myriad local traditions, yet still—when vital—its community remained focused on the Three Refuges: the Buddha, the Dharma (the teachings), and the Sangha (the monastic community).

The general ideals of Buddhist civilization were in place very early. Monks and nuns served the world through their example of renunciation and meditation, by performing rituals, and by providing medical services. As preservers, transmitters, and exemplars of the Dharma, the sangha's duty was to attract the lay community's merit-making donations by being spiritually worthy; complementing this, sangha members were to follow the *Vinaya* rules and seek out dedicated sympathizers and generous donors. Based on these guidelines, Buddhist societies came to exhibit an array of common traits: relic shrines as centers of community ritual and economy; monasteries as refuges for meditation, study, and access to material resources; and sangha members who assumed leadership of the community's spiritual instruction and ritual life.

Thus, Buddhism successfully developed a broad vision of the spiritual community and of proper practice. Texts speak of the devout layperson's duty to help others grow in faith, morality, knowledge, and charity, to live a life worthy of his or her family heritage, and to make offerings to the spirits of the dead. The Buddha also revealed several short texts (called *mantra* and *paritta*, later *dharani*) that, when chanted, help householders achieve the material blessings and protections needed for a good worldly life. All Buddhists are instructed to listen to the Dharma and try hard to resist its decline. Given the variety of possible practices, the only sound definition of a "good Buddhist" is simple: one who takes the Three Refuges and practices accordingly.

THE MAHAYANA: PHILOSOPHIES AND EAST ASIAN MONASTIC SCHOOLS

Despite their prolific writings, Mahayana philosophers and followers were in fact a minority in ancient South Asia, for monks of this persuasion lived in monasteries alongside Sthaviravadins, the predecessors of today's Theravadins. Mahayana only became the "Great Vehicle," the dominant form of Buddhism and the center of a vibrant subculture, in the last era of Buddhism in India (700 CE until its extinction) as well as for a millennium until around 1300 CE in Burma, and the Khmer, Indonesian, and Funan regions of medieval Southeast Asia.

The contrast between traditionalists (Theravadins) and Mahayanists seems to reflect a universal human tendency to divide religious communities between those inclined to a literal approach (holding to the letter within a conservative tradition) and those inclined to a more open-ended and experimental approach to spiritual matters. The Mahayana in this light might be compared to the Sufis in Islam, opposed to the strict scholars of the law (ulama); the Christian analogy would be the mystics in opposition to the official church.

On the philosophical level, there were fiercely contested disagreements between the Theravadins and Mahayanas that we know of chiefly from the Mahayana side. For the most part, the traditionalists ignored the Mahayanist polemics, dismissing proponents with the derogatory term *Illusionists* (*Vaitulika*). The pejorative label the Mahayanists applied to these opponents, the "Lesser Vehicle" (*Hinayana*), suggested diminished religious effectiveness, commitment, and vision.

We shall discuss the Madhyamaka and Consciousness Only schools of Mahayana thought as well as some minority schools that happen to be well known today and a tradition called the Thunderbolt Vehicle.

✤ The Madhyamaka

Among the earliest texts expressing Mahayana ideas are those called the *Perfection of Wisdom* (*Prajnaparamita*). In these texts of varying length, comments attributed to the Buddha or notable monks poke fun at the Theravadin arhats and seek to poke holes in their scholasticism. More importantly, however, the *Prajnaparamita* texts represent a search for the ultimate truth behind the words of the oldest scriptures. Since Mahayana thought emphasizes interdependence, its exponents saw the Theravadins' focus on an individual's pursuit of nirvana as "selfish" and so reflecting ignorance of the Buddha's highest teaching. Most Mahayana exponents held that the laity as well as monks could attain enlightenment.

Opposition to the Theravadins coalesced in the writings of the monk Nagarjuna (born c. 150 CE), one of India's greatest philosophers and founder of the **Madhyamaka** school. Nagarjuna developed a deconstructive method that reduces all assertions to arbitrary propositions and applied this analytical treatment to a wide-ranging subject matter. In one of the most courageous explorations in the history of religions, he argued that all language is conventional and that all classifications set up by it are mere constructions, including all Buddhist constructs, even *nirvana* and *samsara*. It is through understanding how humans construct reality arbitrarily from no-thing-ness (*shunyata*) that one can be fully released from all illusions and desires and from the cycle of rebirths. Nagarjuna's deconstructive philosophical effort was religious. His aim was to clear away all false assumptions and even the subtle attachment to language and scholastic categories, thus opening the way to Buddhist meditation practices that transcend words, the only viable means of finding true refuge and final enlightenment.

❖ "Consciousness Only" School

The other major school of Mahayana thought continued to develop the Great Vehicle from Nagarjuna's standpoint. The "Consciousness Only" (**Cittamatra**) school largely agreed with the Madhyamaka critique of experience as empty but asserted that the real arena of spiritual transformation can therefore be further specified within human consciousness. This school's great thinkers were the brothers Asanga and Vasubandhu (active c. 380 CE), who developed intricate theories of consciousness and causality. They described how karma works within the stream of consciousness, where past actions may block pure, passionless seeing. Further, the spiritual life must be devoted to purifying mind or consciousness, since this is all that truly exists. Again, the practical effect of such theories was to promote the traditional Buddhist practice of meditation, as indicated by another name often applied to this faction: *Yogacara*, or "yoga practice," school.

❖ Buddha-Nature School

Another Mahayana philosophy grew later from Madhyamaka roots in East Asia: the **Buddha-nature** (*tathagatagarbha*) **school**. Its proponents held that if it is true that nirvana and samsara cannot be separated in any meaningful way, then nirvana must interpenetrate all reality. And if this is so, one might say that all beings have a portion of nirvana and so possess the latent potential for its realization. Among the many metaphors developed to convey the interdependence of all reality with the Buddha nature, that of Indra's jeweled net had widespread appeal. Just as each jewel in the net

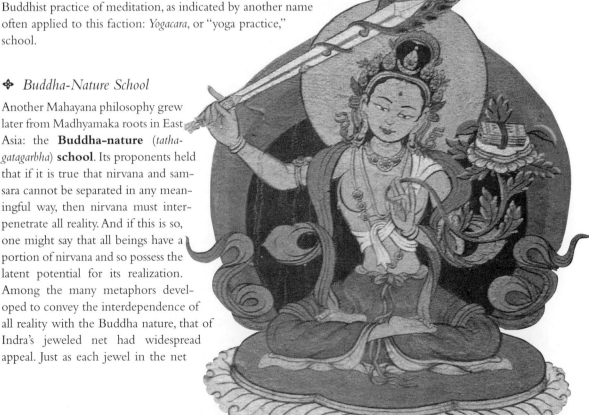

Manjushri, the bodhisattva of scholars, who cuts through ignorance and delusion with his sword of prajna.

reflects every other one, including the reflections of the reflections, even the tiniest thing contains the mystery of the universe. Although support for a school centered on this doctrine eventually declined in China, its ideas and metaphors influenced a Mahayana tradition in East Asia called *Ch'an* in China, *Sŏn* in Korea, and *Zen* in Japan. The Buddha-nature doctrine appeared to some as a reversion to belief in the soul; but it, too, reinforced the need for traditional meditation practices.

Tara, the popular female bodhisattva who is believed to have arisen from the tears of compassion from Avalokiteshvara.

✤ *The Lotus Sutra and Celestial Bodhisattvas*

One of the most popular Buddhist scriptures in East Asia was the **Lotus Sutra**. Originally written in Sanskrit by 100 CE, this work was later translated into every East Asian language spoken by Buddhists. Through parables, accounts of astounding magical display, and hammering polemics, the *Lotus* develops the Mahayana doctrine of cosmic Buddhahood. It recounts how amazed and confused the arhats became when Shakyamuni Buddha revealed that the human Buddha to whom they were so attached is in fact the embodiment of a more universal Buddha reality that can materialize in many forms simultaneously throughout the cosmos. The *Lotus* describes how the Buddha's preaching skillfully adapted the Dharma to suit the level of the audiences. Even his dying was a show, performed to encourage the active practice of devotees so that they would take seriously the shortness of mortal life. The *Lotus* asserts that the nirvana of arhats is incomplete, merely a preliminary stage in enlightenment seeking. Rather, all beings are destined for Buddhahood through eons of rebirth in samsara.

The religious ideal in the *Lotus Sutra* and in other Mahayana texts shifts from the arhat to the **bodhisattva**, or "future Buddha." Disciples following the Great Vehicle are encouraged not to be satisfied with the arhats' limited nirvana, when Buddhahood is the proper, final religious goal for all. Why? Mahayana teachers point out that given the reality of interdependence, no individual can be an enlightened "being" somehow independent of others. Bodhisattvas should therefore not imagine ending their careers until all beings are enlightened, a mind-boggling and very long-term commitment.

The *Lotus Sutra* is only one among a large class of texts that focus on bodhisattvas who have garnered the merit necessary to earn rebirth as divinities. These "celestial bodhisattvas" continue to serve humanity by offering compassionate intervention to secure worldly blessings and even the means to salvation. In the popular imagination, by the end of the faith's first millennium they had become the Buddhist parallels to Hindu or Chinese deities. The most popular and universal celestial bodhisattva was **Avalokiteshvara**, who came to be known as **Guanyin** in China, *Kannon* in Japan, *Chenrizi* in Tibet, and *Karunamaya* in Nepal. Wherever Mahayana Buddhism spread, texts recounting the local deeds of this and other heavenly beings were commonly disseminated through storytellers, art, and popular texts. For the great majority of Buddhists in East Asia, being a Mahayana devotee meant performing rituals and asking for blessings from these compassionate divinities.

❖ Pure Land Schools

Perhaps as an extension of the Buddha's injunction that the sangha should "show the householders the way to heaven," **Pure Land** Buddhism arose in India, around 300 CE, as yet another "cabin" within the Great Vehicle. This school's texts describe how certain bodhisattvas vowed to create celestial paradises on reaching Buddhahood. In these "Pure Lands," there existed all the conditions needed for the individual to be reborn and reach enlightenment. The popularity of this Buddhist orientation, which deferred enlightenment seeking from the human state until rebirth in a heaven, probably had its origins in Shakyamuni's predictions of Buddhism's decline after a thousand years. This expectation legitimated a new spirituality to match the changed times.

The most important and highly developed of the Pure Land schools was that associated with the western paradise called *Sukhavati*, skillfully created by a Buddha named **Amitabha** in Sanskrit (*Amitofo* in Chinese, **Amida** in Japanese). An ordered system of Pure Land doctrine and practice developed in China and featured the chanting of Amitabha's name (*Namo A-mi-t'o Fo*) as a meditative act and communal ritual. Exponents assured Pure Land followers that by drawing on this Buddha's distinctive cosmic power through chanting and other devotional practices, even those with bad karma could be reborn in Sukhavati. It was the Chinese monk Shan-tao (613–681) who effectively brought Pure Land teaching to its widest audience, preaching to court officials and to the masses.

In Japan, Pure Land Buddhism continued to evolve as devotees were taught that their own "self power" was insufficient to reach nirvana and only the "other power" of celestial Buddhas and bodhisattvas could be relied on. Rituals at death were dedicated to having an individual's lifetime accumulation of merit (punya) be directed to attaining rebirth in the Pure Land. Over the years these schools expanded, and hopes for Pure Land rebirth became extremely popular among the laity. Pure Land schools were also the first to deemphasize the requirement of monastic celibacy by its ordained sangha.

The Bodhisattva Vow: "May I be a protector for the unprotected A guide for wanderers A boat, a bridge, a causeway for those who desire the other shore A lamp for those who need light"

Source: Shantideva's *Bodhicaryavatara*.

Avalokiteshvara, the most popular celestial bodhisattva in the Mahayana tradition.

❖ The Meditation School

By about 600 CE, a Mahayana school called **Ch'an** had formed in China. In contrast to the Pure Land emphasis on "other power," the Ch'an took a position on the "traditionalist" end of the Mahayana spectrum, insisting that individual effort to reach nirvana was the Buddha's true teaching. Ch'an masters stressed meditation, this-life realization, and "self power." This school still bases its authority on an unbroken line of enlightened teachers from Shakyamuni onward, with each subsequent enlightened master, in turn, transmitting a "mind of enlightenment" to his key disciple wordlessly, beyond all scriptures.

Milarepa, the great tantric saint of Tibet, whose songs are beloved for conveying the struggles of solitary meditation and the joy of enlightenment.

Less concerned with a single text and formed in close association with Daoist concepts and aesthetics (covered in Chapter 8), Ch'an lineages respected the Mahayana scriptures but also compiled their own texts recounting the teachings of their own patriarchs and masters, including their approaches to unlocking the gates of nirvana realization. This school also developed the use of paradoxical word problems called **koans** ("cases") that masters forced their disciples to ponder and answer. Resolution of the koans—with words, roars, bodily gestures, or composed silence—could lead to small awakenings of prajna or even to complete nirvana realization. Ch'an masters also insisted on the necessity of mindfulness meditation.

The paradigmatic figure of this school is Bodhidharma, the patriarch who reputedly brought the mind-to-mind transmission tradition from India to China, early in the seventh century of the common era. He is depicted as a fierce meditating monk dispensing terse spiritual admonitions. Later known as **Zen** in Japan, the Ch'an school also developed in monasteries upholding strict monastic rules. Its lineages eventually split along the line of those believing in gradual versus sudden enlightenment.

> "Unless you enter the great ocean of passions, you cannot get the treasure of full knowledge."
>
> Source: Vimalakirti. Nirdesha Sutra.

❖ The Thunderbolt Vehicle

One additional branch of elite doctrine and practice that emerged among Mahayana Buddhists was the **Vajrayana**, the **Thunderbolt Vehicle**, a tradition that some scholars would consider to be distinct from the Mahayana school. Also called *tantra* and similar to the Hindu practice of that name, it developed after the faith's first millennium in South Asia. Initially the Vajrayana was the province of wandering mendicants whose spiritual seeking on the fringes of society began even before the Buddha's era. Perhaps in reaction to the complacency stemming from the mainstream view that final enlightenment would not be achieved until after many future lifetimes, the tantric traditions emphasized realizing salvation speedily and in this lifetime. It was also an esoteric tradition, meaning that it was not public or openly shared but was passed on only to those the tantric teacher thought to be capable of understanding and practicing.

> "That by which the world is bound, by that same energy its bonds are released; But the world is deluded and knows not this truth, And he who is deprived of this truth will not gain Enlightenment."
>
> Source: Hevajra Tantra.

Tantric Buddhism used Indian yoga techniques and unconventional means under the guidance of an accomplished teacher, and it drew on the Mahayana philosophy that equated samsara with nirvana. It agreed that all beings partake of the Buddha nature, the *tathagata-garbha doctrine*, and identified the essence of the Buddha's teaching as the pursuit of unshakable diamond-like insight by whatever means brought immediate success.

The central experience of tantric Buddhism is *sadhana,* communion with a celestial Buddha or bodhisattva through the experience of identification with his or her body, speech, and mind. Dozens of sadhanas emerged. The sage who discovered each path is thought to have experienced this deity as the embodiment of enlightenment. Thus an initiate is taught to place the deity in his or her mind's eye, repeat mantras that resonate with that form, and build an existential connection with it, performing *mudras* (hand gestures) and other rituals that help to solidify the identification. When complete, one's identification ultimately leads to the attainment of enlightenment equal to that of the divine form.

Some tantric traditions consciously break the norms of orthodox caste society. Men and women assume identities as divine, enlightened consorts, and their sexual union is developed as a unifying experience of the dual energies of *prajna* (the feminine, as insight) and *upaya* (the masculine, as means of practice). Sexual consort yoga was doubtless once an element in some tantric traditions. (In modern Nepal and Tibet, "consorts" are often spouses.) But as these traditions were systematized in textual form by Buddhist monks after 900 CE in North India, the requirement of literal sexual yoga practice was reinterpreted to allow its replacement by symbolic visualization.

Tantric icon showing visualization of salvific insight and skillful practice as the union of female and male siddhas.

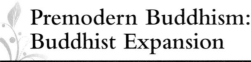

Premodern Buddhism: Buddhist Expansion

As Buddhism expanded across Asia up to the early modern era, in each cultural region monks, nuns, and disciples adapted the traditions to local cultural conditions. Across Asia, all the sanghas developed Buddhist rituals to help individuals through their lives, from birth to death. In applying the faith's resources to fulfilling the religious needs of the householders, monks and nuns from all Buddhist doctrinal schools served their lay communities in a similar manner. We now survey the wide-ranging trans-Asian pilgrimage of Buddhism by geographic region and then note the distinctive beliefs and practices that gave the faith its local appeal.

SOUTH ASIA

With the decline of the great Gupta dynasty in North India by 650 CE, small regional polities controlled the Hindu-Buddhist societies of South Asia. Buddhism survived mainly in the northeast under imperial patronage, its presence confined largely to monasteries at the major universities. Nalanda and Vikramashila, for example, fostered a vigorous articulation of Mahayana Buddhist philosophy, meditation, and popular piety. Ties to Tibet, Nepal, and centers in the Srivijaya kingdom of Sumatra-Java extended the influence of the Great Vehicle.

After Buddhism's successful transplantation in China, Sri Lanka, and Southeast Asia, monks and householders traveled to study in South Asia and to acquire texts. They also completed pilgrimage visits, venerating the "sacred traces" (cremation relics, begging bowls, etc.) of the Buddha and arhats that were entombed in the stupas. The Buddha's enlightenment tree in Gaya and the temple erected nearby were at the center of such visits. As Indic Buddhism declined, distant pious rulers from Sri Lanka and Burma sent funds and artisans to renovate the Gaya site, however. By 1296, when the last such donations were recorded, most every Buddhist monastery in the Gangetic plain had been abandoned for centuries and many shrines had been left to decay. The decline of the faith in South Asia was due partly to the successful development of popular devotional Hinduism and by the Hindu monasticism organized by the saint-scholar Shankara, whose Advaita Vedanta school we discussed in Chapter 6.

Another factor in Buddhism's decline was the arrival in South Asia of Islam, another missionary faith that slowly spread throughout the region. By 750 CE, Muslim conquests and conversions to Islam in central Asia and in northwestern India were undermining the predominance of Buddhism. As we have seen, Buddhist monasticism was strongly tied to trade and mercantile patronage; and as the trade moving along the silk routes shifted to Muslim merchants with connections westward, the monasteries lost a major source of support. In addition, an era of raids into North India culminated in 1192 in the first period of Muslim rule from Delhi. Across the northern plains, most remaining Buddhist institutions were plundered, and the destruction dispersed Indian monks into the Himalayas, to coastal urban centers, and across the seas. In the southern peninsula of the Indian subcontinent, Buddhism also declined slowly, but scattered monasteries existed there as late as the seventeenth century.

Buddhism's dominant region shifted to East Asia after its major sacred centers in India lay in ruins. Because many early versions of the first Buddhist textual collections had been lost, each school settled on surviving texts and scholastic traditions to establish its own doctrinal authority. Once **Bodh Gaya** was no longer accessible, pious donors built "replica Bodh Gaya temples," now found across Asia to accommodate regional pilgrims. In Southeast Asian states, Sri Lanka was regarded as the center of Theravada scholarship and disciplined practice. In East Asia, China became the prime center of Mahayana tradition, although after 1250 Tibetan Buddhists at times exerted strong influences within China, south into the Himalayas, and north into Mongolia.

The island of Sri Lanka embraced Buddhism, and its early kings after 100 BCE supported the sangha and built monuments to express their devotion. Although both Mahayanists and Sthaviravadins practiced there throughout the first millennium, the Theravada school eventually prevailed. The "reforms" instituted by various Southeast Asian kings in the 1300s drew on respected Sri Lankan monks, whose leadership ensured the dominance of Theravada traditions in Burma, Siam (now Thailand), and both Laos and Cambodia. Theravada has remained the dominant tradition in these countries since that time.

CHINA

In East Asia, Buddhist schools formed around charismatic teachers whose interpretations favored one or another of the many texts as the Buddha's highest teaching. Mahayana Buddhism alone flourished, translated in terms compatible with Daoist mysticism, the indigenous gods, and aspects of Confucian morality and state governance (see Chapter 8).

Under the weak regional states of the pre-T'ang era (up until 645 CE), Buddhism found widespread support. Indian and Central Asian monks had begun a determined project of translating the hundreds of Buddhist texts into Chinese. In addition, monks, merchants, and rulers had obtained many precious relics and had them enshrined in monasteries across China. Finally, Chinese Buddhists came to recognize **Wu Tai Shan,** one of China's sacred mountains, as the home of Manjushri, one of Mahayana Buddhism's chief celestial bodhisattvas (a topic discussed earlier in the chapter). This belief grew as devotees by the thousands ventured to this extraordinary site and had powerful meditative visions of this future Buddha. So strong was belief in Wu Tai Shan's Buddhist holiness that by the beginning of the T'ang dynasty, its fame spread back to India; the Chinese annals note that hundreds of Indian pilgrims traveled to China in subsequent centuries to seek Manjushri's spiritual blessings at Wu Tai Shan.

Through textual transmission, the location of relics in monastic shrines across the country, and recognition of this (and other) sacred mountains, by 600 CE all of Asia was unified by Buddhism as China itself was integrated into its sacred realm. With the consolidation of the T'ang state in Chang-an (modern Xian) and its revival of the traditional Confucian literati class, the destiny of Buddhism rose and fell according to the degree of support from the reigning emperor and his court. Despite the generosity of imperial patrons and wealthy donors who profited from trade along the legendary Silk Road, many Confucian officials who manned the permanent state bureaucracy criticized Buddhism. They argued that monks and nuns were disloyal to parents, country, and ancestors, asserting as well that the rising wealth of the monasteries weakened the overall economy.

Anti-Buddhist sentiment culminated in the great persecution of 841–845. Nearly every Buddhist monastery was dismantled, metal images were melted down for the state treasury, and renunciants were ordered to return to lay life. Buddhism eventually rebuilt and rebounded, but the faith never permeated Chinese society so thoroughly again, nor did all the early Chinese doctrinal schools truly recover. From the Sung era onward, it was the Ch'an and Pure Land schools that survived, being less dependent on official recognition or aristocratic patronage. Leading monks repositioned the faith in Chinese society by emphasizing their disinterest in politics and their insistence that renunciants maintain a disciplined lifestyle. In addition, they stressed the compatibility of Buddhism with Daoism and Confucianism.

During the short-lived Mongol conquest of China marking the Yuan dynasty (1271–1368), Tibetan Buddhism became the state religion and its distinctive Mahayana–Vajrayana traditions were granted strong support across the empire, primarily in imperial strongholds. The Mongols' conversion to Buddhism, soon after their

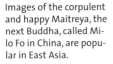

Images of the corpulent and happy Maitreya, the next Buddha, called Mi-lo Fo in China, are popular in East Asia.

thirteenth-century campaigns of violent conquest across Eurasia, marks another point at which Buddhism changed world history, in this case by undercutting Mongol martial values and expansionism.

With the return of native Chinese rule under the Ming (1392–1644), Mahayana traditions were embraced by a large sector of the population: worship of the celestial bodhisattva Guanyin; veneration of the sixteen saints designated as protectors of Buddhism until the coming of the next Buddha; and the practice of releasing animals (typically fish or birds) to earn merit. The corpulent form of the next Buddha **Maitreya** (Chi: **Mi-lo Fo**) appeared as a distinctively Chinese image. From the early Ming, too, the practice of householders keeping detailed merit account books gained in popularity. In China as elsewhere, merit-making and ritual observances dominated the religious life of most Buddhists.

SOUTHEAST ASIA

Southeast Asia after 1200 was ruled by regional states that sought their legitimacy in supporting the Theravada Buddhist monastic system introduced from Sri Lanka. Buddha relics were imported as well, and stupas in the Sri Lankan style were built across the region. The "reforms" already mentioned effectively reduced the presence of the Mahayana to a few isolated communities, and all of these eventually disappeared. The Khmer state for several periods was ruled by kings who favored Mahayana Buddhism, and they constructed magnificent temples and monasteries.

From the early eighth century, the large and prosperous Srivijaya Empire in Sumatra and Java also supported the efflorescence of both Hinduism and Mahayana Buddhism. These rulers created the colossal stupa at Borobodur, the crowning monument of this era. But with the empire's decline in the thirteenth century, the smaller states ruled by regional kings favored local religions or (later) the schools of Islam originating in India.

Yet in the majority of the Southeast Asian polities, it was Theravada Buddhism that thrived under rulers who claimed legitimacy under the cosmic law of karma, whereby they were reaping past merit to rule. Their states supported the sangha and sponsored rituals designed to have the powers of the Buddhist universe continually regenerated. In turn, they expected the people to emulate their example by following the Dharma, supporting a just Buddhist order in the territory, and accepting their place in the karma-determined social hierarchy. The many hundreds of grand stupas, image halls, and monasteries built in these prosperous states show the success of premodern Theravada Buddhism. The great Buddhist monuments legitimated the state, created spectacular sanctuaries, employed artisans and the masses, and lent prestige to the sangha. Across Theravadin Southeast Asia, this form of "state Buddhism" survived even after the kingdoms of the premodern era gave way to smaller regional states. However, this form of traditional, hierarchical Buddhism was to be challenged in the modern era as new ideas and political systems emerged.

JAPAN

Mahayana Buddhism was adopted across East Asia, originally reaching Japan in the seventh century. By 1230, Japanese monks again had traveled to China to undertake the last transplantations of Chinese schools: two forms of the Ch'an became the Soto Zen school (instituted by the monk **Dogen** [1200–1253]) and the Rinzai Zen school (under the monk **Eisai** [1141–1215]). Both vied for popularity among the aristocrats and warriors who controlled Japanese society in the post-Kamakura era (after 1350).

The Pure Land school also found widespread popular acceptance through the public preaching campaigns undertaken by charismatic monks. Since their simplification of Buddhist practice entailed only the *nembutsu,* the chant "*Namo A-mi-t'o Fo,*" the honorific repetition of Amitabha Buddha's name imported from China, householders could hope for nirvana in Pure Land rebirth. A thirteenth-century Japanese monk named Shinran continued the basic rituals and textual interpretations imported from Chinese Pure Land teachers and added emphasis on *mappo,* the so-called decadent-age doctrine, reflecting acceptance of Shakyamuni's prediction of Buddhism's decline. Shinran argued that human beings were completely dependent on the Buddha's grace to reach nirvana and had simply to acknowledge their grateful acceptance of it to enter the Pure Land. Shinran's school, the Jodo Shinshu, became a vital separate lineage, and its sangha was the first in Japan to drop the requirement of celibacy.

A third track in this era of new Japanese schools is represented by **Nichiren** (1222–1282), a prophetic and charismatic monk who taught that the *Lotus Sutra* is the only true Buddhist text. Like Shinran, Nichiren subscribed to the doctrine of mappo and argued that the instability of the turbulent times confirmed it. He also accepted the ultimate reality of an omniscient cosmic Buddha immanent in the world and in persons. Practice in the Nichiren school was simplified to three devotional acts: a short honorific repetition of the *Lotus Sutra*'s title (*Nam-Myoho Reng-e Kyo*), meditation on

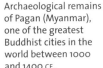

Archaeological remains of Pagan (Myanmar), one of the greatest Buddhist cities in the world between 1000 and 1400 CE.

"Nichiren confuses his enemies," a woodcut print by Utagawa Kin-uyoshi (1798–1861). Nichiren's disciples fol-lowed the teacher's example of practicing aggressive missionary exposition, a trend that has marked the school up to the present.

an image of the cosmic Buddha designed by Nichiren, and pilgrimage to the school's national shrine. Later, the monk's followers taught that Nichiren himself was a bod-hisattva. Their interpretation of Buddhism emphasized Japan's special significance in leading Buddhism through the declining stage of history, a visionary view that endured to inspire several splinter movements in the modern and postwar eras.

THE HIMALAYAN REGION

In Tibet, Mongolia, and Nepal, Mahayana schools also became supreme. Across the highland frontiers, Vajrayana traditions came to be regarded as the Buddha's highest teaching, and the monks who introduced Buddhism there taught that Buddhist belief and practice have both outer and inner levels of understanding, the highest of which was accessible only through tantric initiation and practice. In these regions, Vajrayana traditions developed in rich elaboration, and dedicated elites practiced exhaustive meditation regimens. Tibetan scholars translated a vast corpus of Sanskrit texts, com-mented on them, and composed their own interpretive tracts. Ritual masters also applied the texts and teachings to many aspects of life, designing rituals to promote health, prosperity, and the best possible rebirth. Even flags, watermills, and hand-turned wheels were adapted to broadcast the Buddha's teaching, continuously earning merit for individuals and communities.

"In short, at all times and all occasions be not separated from these three, namely devotion to your teachers, an open heart to the world and all it contains, and compassion to sentient beings."

Source: Dolpo lama's advice.

The Potala in Lhasa, Tibet, was the palace of the Dalai Lamas from 1649 until 1959, when the fourteenth Dalai Lama went into exile.

In Tibet, too, the celestial bodhisattva doctrine was made more accessible to the laity: Extraordinary monks and nuns came to be identified as their incarnations (*tulku* in Tibetan) of these divinities. Indeed, after 1250 as these "incarnate lineages" became institutions endowed with lands and households, some tulkus assumed power as both religious and political leaders of their regions. With the aid of the Mongols, leaders of the major Tibetan monasteries ascended to rule over central Tibet, a situation unprecedented in any other Buddhist society. With the triumph of the **Gelugpa** school under the Dalai and Panchen Lamas in 1642, Tibetan polity assumed its modern form, dominated by large, land-owning monasteries (joined by roughly 15 percent of the male population).

 ## Buddhism and Modernity

EARLY MODERN BUDDHIST POLITIES: MONKS, NUNS, HOUSEHOLDERS, KINGS

One decisive factor in Buddhist history has been the relation between the institutional religion and political power, a recurring source of controversy from the colonial period until the present, as we will see again shortly. Buddhists have always looked to the legend of Ashoka (273–232 BCE) to define their exemplary relationship with rulers as protectors and patrons. Only with such support can the sangha's integrity be ensured, the Buddha's monuments maintained, and the teachings passed down. In premodern Sri Lanka, the king appointed a senior monk as the *sangharaja* ("ruler of the sangha"); in every Theravada country today, leadership and jurisdiction over the sangha are found in the form of a single monk or monastic council appointed by the state.

A dramatic modern instance of this exemplary royal support was Burma's King Mindon, who convened the Fifth Buddhist Council (by Theravada reckoning) in 1871. The only complete textual canon among the early collections of the Buddha's teachings was recited and corrected at this conference. These writings, revered today as the **Pali Canon**, were then inscribed in their entirety on large marble slabs set up in the city of Mandalay. Postcolonial Buddhist governments across the world sponsored similar activities in 1956 on the occasion of the Theravadin school's determination of the 2,500-year anniversary of Shakyamuni's parinirvana.

For most of its history, the Buddhist sangha has existed in polities ruled by kings or emperors. As a result, a mutually beneficial tradition developed: the sangha adopted rules in harmony with those of states and would applaud exemplary moral leadership on the part of the monarch. In premodern times, monastic Buddhism usually served to promote social stability, accommodating itself to local traditions. The monks also chanted mantras and performed merit-making rituals on behalf of rulers, a custom that continues in modern Japan, Thailand, and Nepal.

BUDDHIST MONASTICISM

A monastery (vihara) can be of humble construction or built to imperial, aristocratic standards. Each, however, must have a place for the monks to sleep and a building in which they gather for reception into the sangha, fortnightly recitations, and other proceedings. Monasteries may also have one or more stupas, a "bodhi tree," a meditation hall, and one or more image halls.

The subsistence of the monks and nuns has remained dependent on the donations of food and shelter by the lay community. Originally, all sangha members gathered their food in morning begging rounds, and the day's solid food had to be eaten by noon. By the modern period, however, Buddhists had developed other routines: In some places members of the laity would come to the monastery on a rotating schedule with food donations; in other places, monks cooked their own foods. Many Mahayana monasteries of East Asia interpreted the moral rules to require vegetarianism of the monks and nuns, but in recent centuries the restriction against alcohol was taken by most to mean "no intoxication," not complete abstinence.

✣ *Meditation Practices*

As we have noted, meditation remained essential for all aspirants, lay and renunciant, seeking to move on the final path to nirvana. This practice by monks and nuns, even if only a few, certifies Buddhism's continuing spiritual vitality, inspiring layfolk to respect and take refuge in the sangha. Until the modern era, however, it was almost entirely the elite among monks and nuns who practiced meditation.

Buddhism inherited and extended the spiritual experiments of ancient India. The practice of trance (*samadhi*) is accepted, even encouraged, but this state does not lead to nirvana realization, hence is not given highest priority. The key practice is called *mindfulness meditation* (**vipassana meditation**): a careful attending to, or being mindful of, the three characteristics of existential reality—suffering (*dukkha*), impermanence (*anitya*), and nonself (*anatman*). The practice as taught today is simple: While remaining motionless, the practitioner seeks to focus all awareness on the breath, letting go of all intervening thoughts that arise. Attention to and comprehension of these realities opens up an awareness of the "inner life" we normally ignore. With such heightened awareness, mindfulness meditation has other critical effects: It shows how suffering and change are inevitable, it nourishes personal detachment that stills desire, and it cultivates the spiritual insight (prajna) that dispels ignorance. The development of prajna and the removal of ignorance eliminate bad karma and create good karma. Perfection eventually leads to the fullness of prajna in a breakthrough, transformative experience of an enlightened mind (*bodhi*).

Mahayana meditations elaborated on these precedents. Ch'an or Zen mindfulness meditation, like Theravada vipashyana practice, focuses first on the breath. Given the Mahayana teaching that all beings possess the Buddha nature (*tathagatagarbha*), meditation

Western nuns reciting from texts at a Tibetan center in London.

can comprise any activity practiced with mindfulness, from walking to class to sipping espresso, or (more traditionally) from engaging in martial arts to arranging flowers.

In Pure Land meditation, the fervent wish to attain nirvana in an otherworldly western paradise (*Sukhavati*) encourages devotees to visualize that extraordinary paradise as described in the texts. These practices are especially important as death nears, for individuals who can visualize this realm are promised painless passage into heavenly rebirth through the boundless grace of the Buddha Amitabha.

Schools devoted to esoteric Vajrayana innovations developed yet other forms of meditation under the heading of *sadhana*. These tantric practices are based on mind's-eye visualizations of enlightened bodhisattvas and mantra recitations to jump-start spiritual development. By controlling the appearance of mental images, one sees all experience as mind-constructed and thus empty (*shunya*) of any ultimate reality.

Again, however, it is necessary to emphasize that most Buddhists—yesterday and today—concentrated their devotional activities on rituals and on accumulating merit rather than on meditation, and so we turn to gift giving as the foundation of Buddhist practice.

✤ Punya and Dana: The Fundamental Buddhist Exchange

The Buddha set out a "graded teaching" to order the spiritual teachings to be given to disciples. This framework begins with the merit-making donations that enable a Buddhist community's diverse cultural activities. Still used as a guide for modern Buddhist teachers, the sequence counsels progression through the following stages of religious striving:

1. **Dana** ("self-less giving" to diminish desire)
2. *Shila* ("morality")
3. *Svarga* ("heaven")
4. *Dharma-deshana* ("instruction on doctrine") on the Four Noble Truths

This hierarchy of progressive practices defines a "syllabus" for advancing in spiritual attainment. Stages 1 and 2 lead to heaven birth (3), the fruit of merit; the doctrines in stage 4 are the instructions concerning reaching enlightenment, beyond good karma making.

Just as merit, or punya, has provided the chief orientation point and goal in the Buddhist layperson's worldview and ethos, dana has always been the starting practice for accumulating it. Merit making for most Buddhists, including most monks and nuns, is the central measure of spiritual advancement. Merit making remains the universal, integrating transaction in Buddhist settings through the modern era, regardless of the respective intellectual elite's orientation toward competing Theravada, Mahayana, or Vajrayana doctrinal formulations or spiritual disciplines.

The wish for merit leading to rebirth in heaven has remained the most popular and pan-Buddhist aspiration; indeed, monks from the very beginning were instructed to

Householders releasing animals earn merit by bestowing the gift of freedom and life.

"show the laity the way to heaven" by acting as a "field of merit." Householders can "plant" donations in this field, and the "harvest" in good karma they earn will be great. Punya is needed for a good rebirth, and although Buddhist doctrine holds that heaven is a temporary state, the reward of heavenly rebirth has motivated many to be "good Buddhists."

Merit making can lead one close to nirvana, but it also has practical, worldly consequences, impacting destiny both now and across future lifetimes. Therefore, Buddhists seek punya to change the karma "account" that affects them in this life as well as to modify future rebirth destiny.

To maximize punya and so enhance the course of spiritual advancement, popular texts urge all disciples, monastic and lay, to cultivate such practices as venerating images, fasting, taking extra precepts (as described at the very beginning of this chapter), organizing compassionate actions and charitable institutions, arranging public recitations of the texts, and undertaking meditation.

The most universal expression of lay Buddhist faith and punya seeking has been through dana. Making donations for spiritual purposes and setting aside time for moral observances, such as saving an animal and returning a lost object, remained the foundation for householder practice; these still comprise the most visible Buddhist activity today. Passages in the Mahayana texts also articulate the value of dana to the individual as an expression of compassion (*karuna*) and as a renunciatory practice that undercuts desire and attachment.

Another popular pan-Buddhist practice is merit transfer—an idea that philosophers have struggled to rationalize. Texts exhort persons doing something meritorious to share the good deed's karma effects with family, community, and all beings simply by announcing the intent; such sharing is believed to increase the initial merit earned by helping others.

✤ Rituals and Festivals

Buddhist monasteries developed ritual procedures and a yearly festival calendar for the purpose of imposing some uniformity on the widespread sangha network. The monk's vocation came to include priestly duties, performing rituals that linked the Buddha's spoken words with simple gestures. In the simplest (and still most popular) universal Buddhist ritual, monks pour water into a vessel as they chant words revealed by the Buddha. Now imbued with healing powers, the liquid can be drunk or sprinkled over the bodies of those needing assistance. All Buddhist schools also offer food, incense, and flowers to Buddha images, bodhi trees, and stupas.

Selections from a Chinese Buddhist Merit Account Sheet

100 Merits: Save one life; save a woman's chastity; prevent a child from drowning; continue a family lineage

50 Merits: Prevent an abortion; provide for a homeless person; prevent someone from committing a serious crime; give a speech that benefits many

30 Merits: Convert another to Buddhism; facilitate a marriage; take in an orphan; help another do something virtuous

10 Merits: Recommend a virtuous person; cure a major illness; speak virtuously; save the life of a good animal; publish the Buddha's teachings; treat servants properly

5 Merits: Prevent a lawsuit; cure a minor illness; stop someone from slandering; make an offering to a saintly person; save any animal; pray for others

3 Merits: Endure ill treatment without complaint; bury an animal; urge those making a living by killing to stop

1 Merit: Give an article to help others; chant a Buddhist scripture; provide for one monk; return a lost article; help repair a public road or bridge

100 Demerits: Cause a death; rape; end a family lineage

50 Demerits: Induce an abortion; break up a marriage; teach someone to do great evil; make a speech that harms many

30 Demerits: Create slander that dishonors another; disobey an elder; cause a family to separate; during famine, fail to share food grains

10 Demerits: Mistreat an orphan or widow; prepare a poison; kill an animal that serves humans; speak harshly to parent or teacher

5 Demerits: Slander spiritual teachings; turn away a sick person; speak harshly; kill any animal; write or speak lewdly; not clear an injustice when possible

3 Demerits: Get angry over words spoken; cheat an ignorant person; destroy another's success; be greedy

1 Demerit: Urge another to fight; help another do evil; waste food; kill insects; turn away a begging monk; take a bribe; keep a lost article

Source: Guide formulated by Liao-Fan Yuan (1550–1624), a Zen master of Jiang-su Province.
Translated in *The Key to Creating One's Destiny* (Singapore: Lapis Lazuli Press, 1988), pp. 43–46. Passages edited and in places paraphrased.

Mahayana rituals are seen as an important part of a bodhisattva's service to others, and most emphasize mastery of word chains called **mantras,** known for their spiritual powers. A mantra can be spoken to bless and protect the speaker, the sangha, and an entire settlement. Ritual chanting of the Buddha's own sayings is thought to further the foundations of spiritual practice and infuse towns and families with powerful blessings, including good karma. Ritual service thus came to dominate Mahayana Buddhism in its missionary program, especially mantra recitations that expressed the faith's spiritual ideals and activated the unseen cosmic Buddha powers promised in the Mahayana texts.

The bimonthly Buddhist holiday called **uposatha** occurs each fortnight on the new-moon and full-moon days. On uposatha, sangha members privately recite the details confirming that they are monastics in good standing according to the Vinaya rules. This recitation follows a private confession, to the renunciant's superior, of any transgressions

Theravada monk sprinkling a laywoman with water over which the sacred words of the Buddha have been chanted

of the rules during the period. Uposatha continues in the modern era to serve as the regular occasion to review, correct, and certify the proper standards of monastery discipline in Theravada societies.

Emphasizing the fundamental interdependence between sangha and lay community, householders visit the local vihara on these days to make dana offerings. On these days, too, devout layfolk take the opportunity to don white robes, camp on the monastery grounds, and observe eight of the ten monastic rules. They join with many more layfolk who have come simply to release animals or to make offerings to Buddha images and remain to hear monks preach the Dharma. Thus, the lunar fortnight rhythm dominates the festival year. The regular succession of uposathas and the two half-moon days are when Buddhists typically undertake meritorious actions, perform rituals, and engage in meditation practices. Thus, each week has a special day for Buddhist observances. Like other great world religions, Buddhism also formed the basis of distinctive cultures that organized the year with regular monthly and yearly festivals. Some orchestrate reliving classical Buddhist events "in the beginning": Celebrations of the Buddha's birth, enlightenment, and nirvana are universal, although occurring in different seasons. Other, more regional sacred events likewise mark the year. These include Shakyamuni's descent from heaven after preaching to his mother, events marking a key point in a popular bodhisattva's life, or the death anniversary of a local saint.

❖ *The Universal Buddhist Shrine*

For all Buddhist schools, the stupa (or **caitya**, a term that can also signify any Buddha shrine) became a focal point and singular landmark denoting the tradition's spiritual presence. Buddhism eventually recognized "eight great relic caityas" for pilgrimage and veneration in South Asia. Stupa worship thus became the chief focus of Buddhist ritual activity, and this has continued through the modern era to the present. The Buddhist relic cult began early, inspiring monks, nuns, and householders to circumambulate the shrines (in the clockwise direction) and to have their own cremated remains deposited in the same great stupa or in smaller votive stupas located nearby.

Throughout Buddhist history, the stupa has served as a place to go to recall the Buddha's great acts, a "power place" tapping the Buddha's (or saint's) relic presence and its healing potency, a site to earn merit through joyful, musical veneration, and a monument marking the conversion and control of local gods and spirits. In the Mahayana schools, the stupa was also thought of as a symbol of Buddhahood's omnipresence, a center of Mahayana text revelation, and a perfect form showing the unity of the natural elements (earth, fire, air, ether) with the Buddha nature.

Later, Buddhists identified stupas as the physical representations of the eternal teachings. They also expanded the possible sacred objects deposited in them to include Buddha's words in textual form. Amidst many understandings, Buddhists at every level of sophistication believe that ritually correct veneration of stupas will earn them merit. In practice, believers converge at stupas to mark events associated with the Buddhas or saints. Stupas thus remain the natural sites for Buddhist festivals of remembrance and veneration.

Buddhist stupa being whitewashed by a monk in Ladakh, in northern India near the Tibetan border. Monks, nuns, and laity have built these shrines since the Buddha's death.

❖ *Death Ritualism*

In all Buddhist countries today, despite many regional differences, death rituals are the exclusive purview of the sangha and a key time for monks to expound core teachings and receive dana. Buddhist mourners carefully dispose of the corpse, relying on ritual performed by monks to ensure that the dead person does not become a hungry ghost (*preta*) or, worse, a demon (*yaksha*). They also seek to avert bad destiny for the deceased by making punya and then transferring it to the dead person. In adopting such practices, Buddhists straddle both alternatives to the ancient Indic question of whether destiny is based strictly on an individual's own karma over a lifetime or whether the proper performance of rituals during and immediately after death can override unfavorable karma and manipulate rebirth destiny. Since Buddhism is conceptually centered on the doctrine that the cosmos is governed by karmic law, ritual traditions naturally surround death, the critical time in the operation of such causal mechanisms. Both Theravada monks and—more expansively—Mahayana ritualists apply ritual expertise to this time. The tradition's dependence on after-death ritual service for sangha donations is evident in all modern Asian traditions; even when some people are otherwise hardly observant in modern urban areas of Japan, death rituals performed by Buddhist monks are universal.

BUDDHISM UNDER COLONIALISM

The modern era was one of widespread decline for Buddhism across Asia. Medieval states either lost their autonomy or were destabilized by colonialism, first by European

Gathering of devotees at the southern shrine of the Swedagon stupa, a Burmese temple in present-day Myanmar.

powers (the British in Burma, India, Sri Lanka, Tibet, and China; the French in Indochina; the Portuguese and Dutch in Sri Lanka; the Dutch in Indonesia) and later, in the early twentieth century, by Japanese conquest and occupation. In East Asia, the imperial Chinese state was weakened by the colonial powers (primarily Britain), whose aggressive trade practices backed by military intervention disrupted the Chinese economy. The civil disorders that followed also undermined Buddhist institutions. (These events are discussed in Chapter 8.)

The impact of European colonialism on Buddhism can be summarized under two broad domains, institutional and doctrinal. Although Dutch, British, and French colonial governments had somewhat different ideologies guiding their rule in Asia, all administrations eventually declined to fulfill the traditional native king's role of patron and protector of the local religions, including Buddhism. As a result, the means of accommodation that had evolved over the centuries to perpetuate Buddhism ceased to exist, sometimes without warning, in every colonized polity. When the Portuguese and Dutch took power in Sri Lanka (1505–1658), for example, they seized the ports and lowlands, destroyed monasteries, persecuted Buddhists, forcibly converted many to Catholicism, and caused the Sinhalese king to flee to the central highlands. When all the island had become Britain's colony (1815), the British moved to end state support for the sangha and discontinued patronage dedicated to the upkeep of Buddhist buildings everywhere. Colonial administrations also typically ceased enforcement of indigenous land tenure relations and taxation, withdrew from supervision of monastic ordination, and halted ceremonies according respect to venerable monastic leaders, sacred symbols, and temples. The roots of modern crisis and Buddhism's decline across the region are easily traced to this abrupt deprivation of resources and political support.

CHALLENGES FROM COLONIALISM, COMMUNISM, AND MODERN CRITICS

In the realm of ideas, the colonial powers introduced two alien and often-contradictory systems of thought: on the one hand, the scientific notions derived from the Enlightenment, and on the other, theories of racial, cultural, and religious superiority that were used in attempts to legitimate the triumphant expansion of Euro-Christian peoples. European medicine, often effective where folk remedies and rituals had unpredictable results, presented another challenge to every local culture's worldview.

The fruits of the Enlightenment—democracy, modern science, and technology— were imported into Asia through schools built by the colonial governments. One motivation for establishing the schools was to provide trained native people who spoke the language of the colonizer. The reach of the colonial governments was broader, however, for in fact they were the official and secular extensions of the European home states. In addition, the colonial administrators were for the most part supportive of the expansion of the Christian missionary presence. (For example, in many places colonial law recognized as legitimate only marriages conducted by Christian ministers.) It was with such backing that the first modern global missions were created: Across Asia, lay and ordained Christians built churches and established educational institutions, hospitals, and charities; some proselytized aggressively through public preaching and pamphlets attacking Buddhist beliefs and practices.

After the fall of the Ching dynasty in 1912, socioeconomic conditions remained unstable under the Republic of China, only to worsen further with the rise of communism and the Japanese invasion, first in Manchuria (1931) and then southward into the Chinese heartland. Throughout the twentieth century, the traditional Buddhist schools and Buddhist thought were subject to criticism not just by the communists but also by leaders of a modernizing faction called the May 4th Movement. To respond to those who claimed that Buddhism was parasitic and corrupt due to its landholdings, China's greatest modern reformer, Taixu (1889–1947), suggested that Chinese Buddhists should follow the ancient Ch'an school's policy of combining field labor with spiritual life, developing a "Buddhist work ethic" within the monasteries. Though critiqued fiercely by the elites, the Chinese sangha endured: In 1930, there were 730,000 monks and nuns who maintained 267,000 registered monastic temples. The sustained Communist Party policy of thoroughgoing destruction, denigration, and disestablishment that began in 1949, however, had no precedent in Buddhist history.

Although at first disturbed and demoralized, Buddhists recovered from and responded to colonial-era challenges in various ways. Few converted to Christianity, however, despite such obvious inducements as access to charitable services and gaining an inside track to promotions into government service.

Although hampered by the disruption of their institutions, Buddhist intellectuals and preachers emerged to engage in the dialog with science and Christianity. In Sri Lanka, for example, early Protestant missionaries, having assessed Buddhist monks as uniformly indolent and ignorant, felt themselves on the verge of mass conversion. Yet a series of public debates ended badly for those missionaries, a reversal that restored public faith in the ongoing relevance of Buddhist doctrine.

In Sri Lanka, the dialectic between the West and Buddhism was most intense, and decisive new directions for Buddhist modernization were identified in the island nation. Reformers involved the lay society more fully in Buddhist institutions and spiritual practices (primarily meditation), motivating some among the laity to take the place of former royal patrons. The lay reformers, in turn, insisted that monks respect the sangha rules and discipline, and they supported the revival of monastic meditation practice, usually in newly created reformist monastic schools. Finally, Buddhist intellectuals carried out historical investigations, offering modern demythologized reinterpretations of the Buddha and Buddhist doctrine analogous to the scholarly "search for the historical Jesus" that was emerging within Protestant Christianity at the same time. To publicize these reforms, Buddhists adopted one aspect of Christian missionary methodology: They began by investing in printing technology and undertaking publications that defined reformist doctrines and practices. They also rediscovered the practice of public sermonizing.

Reformers in Thailand, as in Sri Lanka, also articulated new interpretations of "true Buddhism." They taught that Buddhism in its pure form was not concerned with communal rituals or harnessing the cosmic powers of Buddhism to support the secular kingdom. Rejecting the adaptive local traditions that had developed in the process of the globalization of Buddhism, reformers insisted that the only genuine center of the faith was the individual's quest for mind cultivation and salvation. Doctrines describing the interdependent and impermanent nature of existence were emphasized, while the teachings about hungry ghosts and snake gods were rejected. Most reform leaders were critical of—even hostile to—"superstitions," rituals, and other local accommodations. Meditation was now the heart of "true Buddhism," and it was no longer restricted to monks and nuns: All Buddhists could and should feel capable of seeking nirvana.

THE BUDDHIST REVIVAL GAINS STRENGTH

By the early twentieth century, reformers had created new institutions to advance the revivalist goals directly. Also supporting the revival process in Asia was the first generation of Europeans sympathetic to Buddhism, who saw in the faith a nontheistic spirituality that was a compelling alternative to dogmatic monotheism. Many Western seekers interpreted Buddhism as encouraging spiritual experimentation through meditation rather than requiring blind faith. Its philosophy was seen as ancient wisdom marvelously preserved and still accessible.

The exigencies of imperialism had resulted in easier travel for Westerners, and this development enabled sympathetic Europeans and North Americans to assist native Buddhist modernists as they argued back against Christian ministers. Westerners both educated native intellectuals on Christianity and shared with them Enlightenment critiques of Christian dogma. Members of the Theosophical Society, a European group formed to pursue the secret, mystical teachings thought to underlie all the world religions, created new institutions, including English-medium Buddhist schools and lay organizations such as Buddhist teaching programs modeled after Christian Sunday schools. Buddhist nationalists also became involved in politics, seeking more favorable relations with—and eventually independence from—the European colonial governments. This experience in Sri Lanka was eagerly shared across Asia with modernists from Japan to Burma.

Early Western scholarship also added to the awareness of modern Asian Buddhists. Indeed, sites associated with Ashoka and many long-forgotten early monuments were discovered in the course of archaeological expeditions under the auspices of the British colonial government. European scholars used modern critical methods to translate and interpret the earliest canonical texts and then disseminated them globally. In fact, it was common for the newly educated indigenous intelligentsia in Buddhist countries to read their first passages from a canonical Buddhist text in English translation. (As in medieval Europe, only the elite among monk-scholars could read the original sacred texts.)

As Buddhist literature in English became available and was assimilated, voices from outside the sangha joined the contested discussion of "what the Buddha really taught."

Thus, throughout the Buddhist world, the leaders of the old Buddhist establishments were often challenged to conform to the standards of discipline set forth in the monastic texts. In most Buddhist countries, colonial and postcolonial governments sought to eliminate sources of political dissent by imposing on the sangha regulations supposedly designed to "keep pure" the local Buddhist institutions.

BUDDHISM FOR WESTERN CONSUMPTION: MEDITATION AND ATHEISM

The efforts by the colonial powers to control Buddhism and Buddhists had a paradoxical effect. The global diaspora of Buddhism flowed "backward" on the networks of empire and through Western converts who became aware of Asian religions as a result of expanding communications and travel. For some Euro-Americans, the Enlightenment-based critiques of the Western monotheistic religions were persuasive and led to a search for religions that did not depend on belief in a personal God. By 1920, Buddhist centers in the West had been established by Euro-American converts and immigrants. As depicted in early popular and sympathetic accounts, the Buddha was a rationalist who rejected ritual and also a heroic social reformer. Buddhism was seen not as a religion but as an atheistic philosophy, compatible with science. Buddhist meditation, however, was regarded as an authentic, ancient spiritual practice, an aspect that attracted Westerners interested in the new field of psychology.

Euro-American contact with Mahayana Buddhism came strongest and earliest with Japanese Zen. Westerners were drawn to the spirit of iconoclasm and to meditation and to Zen's connection with the fine arts conveyed by early exponents, such as D. T. Suzuki (1870–1966). In the years immediately following the Second World War, Zen Buddhism particularly attracted segments of the bohemian and intellectual Western society, furthering an interest that still grows today. It was in the years leading up to World War II, however, that Japan embarked on an imperialistic course that obscured the peaceful face of Zen Buddhism for decades.

EFFECTS OF JAPANESE IMPERIALISM ON BUDDHISM AND ON ASIA

The role of Japan in twentieth-century Asia was undeniably pivotal. Once the country opened itself to the modern world with the restoration of the emperor in 1868, Japan's leaders sought to create a modern industrial state based on nationalism. Shinto was promoted as the shared national faith, and the emperor was revered as a living god. The nationalist movement also involved the deliberate diminishment of Buddhism. Despite its 1,400 years in Japan, Buddhism was criticized as "a foreign religion" inferior to Shinto. Many Buddhist monasteries and temples had their lands confiscated and state patronage withdrawn. Buddhist doctrines and practices were critiqued as "unnatural." In response to these changes, some Buddhist organizations instituted reforms that involved undertaking social work, educational initiatives, and the renewal of global missions. Some schools, such as Zen, even issued strong public pronouncements in favor of the government's nationalism and militarism, with prominent monasteries raising money for armaments. Many new Buddhist movements also began, but outside the older schools.

Japan's rapid and successful modernization effort encouraged not only nationalism but imperialism as well. Led by former samurai and others who had studied in Western countries, Japan annexed neighboring Korea (1910) and northern China (1934) and eventually invaded more distant Asian countries (Indochina, 1940; Burma, 1942). Soon after the Pacific phase of World War II began with the attack on the U.S. base at Pearl Harbor in 1941, the Japanese occupation extended from Manchuria, Korea, and China south to Micronesia and as far west as the borders of India through Southeast Asia.

Buddhism and Postmodern Trends in a Postcolonial World

By the mid-twentieth century, Asians had begun to recover from World War II, and many conquered or colonized peoples were reclaiming their independence. The place of Buddhism in these new societies is as varied as ever. Buddhist movements today make use of the same approaches seen across the globe in other faiths. Some leaders reject modernity, seeking to return to practices that had been identified as "corrupted" by modernizers in the colonial era. Others strive to move Buddhism to an entirely new plateau, seeking to adapt it to the global realities of the postcolonial world. Still others blend traditionalism and reform, "rescuing" from the past what in their view is the essence of Buddhism while employing modern technologies to propagate the Dharma. New institutions have been created to champion strict adherence to monastic norms, scholastic learning, and meditation. Most commonly, organizations led by laypersons have been the most active and effective in adapting Buddhist teachings and practices to the world today.

SOUTH ASIA

South Asia is the "holy land" where the Buddha was born, was enlightened, and died and where Buddhism has endured over 2,500 years. Among the contemporary countries of the region—India, Pakistan, Bangladesh, Sri Lanka, Bhutan, and Nepal—only in the Himalayan regions of the north and on the island of Sri Lanka to the south has Buddhism remained strong.

❖ *The Remnants of Buddhism in India: Reconstruction in the Places of Origin*

Today, Buddhism is found in India only in very small, and recently established, communities. Most important for the faith's revival in the land of its origins are the sacred sites that were unearthed during the British-led archaeological digs of the nineteenth and early twentieth centuries. Among the hundreds of sites that were abandoned or had sunk into oblivion after the Muslim conquest of South Asia (since 1200 CE), the site where the Buddha was enlightened under the bodhi tree became the most significant and controversial. Identified by British officials in the mid-1800s and "restored" through colonial excavations and constructions (in the modern city of Gaya, Bihar), the "Great Enlightenment" temple built at the site, called the Mahabodhi, has again become a focal point for Buddhists. Its reformers in the colonial era focused on reestablishing the sanctity of this temple as their first step in reviving Buddhism. In recent decades, over twenty Buddhist monasteries from around the world have erected branches in Gaya as well as libraries, study centers, and pilgrim hostels. Reformist Buddhists are also attempting to reestablish the site as Buddhism's holiest center and pilgrimage destination, a shrine that unifies all Buddhists. Despite hard work by generations of reformers, this remains an unmet goal.

Even after decades of negotiations, control over the Bodh Gaya temple has eluded the Buddhist organizations, for Hindu priests and politicians have failed to turn over ownership of the shrine. (The Hindu nationalists mentioned in Chapter 6 also had a role in this conflict.) By 1992, frustrations at unfulfilled promises peaked, and several resident monks were moved to take extreme measures. Two threatened to immolate themselves, and several others began fasts unto death. The provocation for this confrontation was severe: Hindu priests had enthroned a *lingam,* the phallic icon of Shiva, on a temple altar and performed pujas to treat the five Buddha images in the temple as if they were deities in the Hindu epic, the *Mahabharata.* This shrine was declared a "World Heritage Site" by UNESCO in 2002 and remains a focal point of regular demonstrations for reformers contesting Hindu control.

❖ *"Protestant Buddhism": An Enduring Colonial-Era Reformation of the Faith*

Anthropologist Gananath Obeyesekere has described the modern reformation of Buddhist tradition begun in colonial Sri Lanka as "**Protestant Buddhism.**" He uses the term to convey two distinct but connected historic trends. The first is intuitively obvious: the adoption of aspects of missionary Protestant Christianity into the Buddhist framework to revitalize its institutions, practices, and doctrines. The second is a deeply ironic reference to a past marked by the arrogance of missionaries and British colonial discrimination against Buddhism.

The early influential mediator of such "Protestantism" in Sri Lanka was the American convert Henry Steele Olcott (1832–1907), who came to the country and helped activist Buddhist leaders organize their efforts. Olcott emphasized the importance of the laity in revitalization and the founding of Buddhist publications and schools. He also composed a *Buddhist Catechism* (1881) and invented a five-color Buddhist flag, both of which are widely used across the world today. Modern Protestant inclinations were evident in the reformist insistence that spiritual and scientific truth be compatible and that the only true practice was meditation, not the mindless observance of ritual. Furthermore, the reformers believed—in agreement with the Protestant missionaries—that the practice of Buddhism in Sri Lanka had been corrupted by idolatry, Hindu polytheism, and an undisciplined and corrupt monastic "priesthood." The laity, however, could reestablish "true Buddhism" through adhering to the pure philosophy and meditation practices taught by the human Buddha. Popular texts and village traditions were strongly critiqued, and two new sangha schools were created with ordination lineages from Burma, both requiring the strictest adherence to Vinaya rules.

A Sri Lankan protégé, who adopted the name Anagarika Dharmapala (1864–1933), continued Olcott's initiatives and went beyond them, preaching and publishing tracts to spread his vision of revitalized Buddhism. At the age of 29, Dharmapala addressed an ecumenical conference, the Parliament of World Religions, held in Chicago in 1893. He impressed hearers from all over the world with his definition of modernist Buddhism as compatible with science, free from dogma and superstition, tolerant of other faiths, and committed to social reform.

Dharmapala also found an enthusiastic reception among the Sri Lankan laity, especially among the newly educated professional elite and the merchant middle class, who owed their rising positions in the world to the changes wrought by the colonial modernization of the country. Dharmapala energized the Buddhist reformers in Sri Lanka; his speeches and writings also contributed to the linkage between the faith and the nationalist struggles.

Dharmapala celebrated Sri Lanka as a uniquely pure Buddhist country, elevated the Sinhalese ethnic group as a "chosen Buddhist people," and harshly demonized those opposing the country's Buddhist restoration. Scholars today see these influences as having set in motion the cultural forces that have made the postindependence state, Sri Lanka, a zone of extremes where bloody conflict has taken deep root alongside uncompromising reform.

Dharmapala's founding of the Mahabodhi Society in Calcutta extended "Protestant Buddhist" reform into other countries in Asia. In recent times, "Protestant Buddhism" has fostered an individualist ethos among those whose ties to a village or traditional sangha have been broken through urban migration. Those influenced by these reformist ideas see it as their own responsibility to practice meditation and study the Dharma (usually in English translations) in the quest for nirvana. Joining the sangha or seeking spiritual guidance from an ordained monk is also not necessarily the norm for those whose view of Buddhism has been affected by "Protestantism."

❖ Buddhism in the Himalayas: Shangri-La?

Many Westerners first became aware of Buddhism through fictional works such as *Lost Horizon,* the film version of which was set in an idyllic, tropical valley amid the scenic, snow-blown Himalayan peaks. It is true that, in fact, Tibetan Buddhist communities have survived in the remote and picturesque settlements nestled among the world's highest mountains, but this region has hardly been a utopian zone for Buddhism in the post–World War II era. Along the southern Himalayan region, the isolation of the states on the Tibetan frontier (Ladakh, Sikkim, Bhutan) enabled them to retain their independence until the end of the Second World War. Since, however, religious conservatism also kept the monks and leaders of these states isolated and ignorant about the modern world, there was little impetus for reform or adaptation to the postwar international political order.

In 1949 most of the territories on the Tibetan plateau ruled by the Gelugpa school's Dalai Lama were declared part of the People's Republic of China, which sent its army to enforce this claim. The far peripheries of India and Nepal once oriented to Lhasa were isolated from the greater Buddhist centers, while central and western Tibet have been ruled by China as "the Tibetan Autonomous Region" until today. Up to the bitter end of China's Cultural Revolution (1976), all religious practices in the region were repressed and most Buddhist temples, monasteries, and shrines were destroyed. Thousands of Tibetans have died since 1949 in conflicts that set Chinese against Tibetan and Tibetan against Tibetan. The fourteenth Dalai Lama, Tenzin Gyatso, went into exile in 1959, and 10 percent of the population has left the country as well.

After 1980, official toleration of limited worship and monastic ordination returned, as did state-sponsored rebuilding of select monasteries. But increasing Tibetan protests since 1987 met with further restrictions and arrests, while increasing Chinese migration into the region has reduced Tibetans to a minority in their homeland. Buddhist tradition is slowly being restored as the Chinese government accommodates monastic training and ritual practices as long as they are not perceived as promoting Tibetan independence.

Three nations have remained free refuges of the Tibetan Buddhism. Nepal has several million Buddhists among the highland-dwelling Tibeto-Burman peoples, in its settlements of Tibetan refugees, and among the Newars of the Kathmandu Valley. Kathmandu is the modern capital of Nepal, and this valley is also Asia's largest center for international institutions connected with the major schools of Tibetan Buddhism.

Tibetan Buddhism also has survived in mountainous areas of northern India (in Ladakh, Himachal Pradesh, and Arunachal Pradesh). India has likewise accepted Tibetan refugees, for since 1959 the Dalai Lama's government in exile has been located in picturesque Dharamsala. Finally, there is Bhutan in the eastern Himalayas, a nation formed in 1907 as the royal kingdom ruled by the Wangchuck family. It is the world's only nation that has Tibetan Buddhism as its state religion.

Most regions where Tibetan Buddhism still flourishes have lost political autonomy. The central, northern, and eastern portions of Tibet were absorbed by China, while Ladakh and Sikkim were absorbed into modern India; Bhutan alone remained independent from India, but only in its internal affairs. In exile and in the isolated enclaves, Tibetan Buddhist institutions have sustained the faith, but these Buddhists struggle as refugees in poverty and as resident aliens within the larger states.

Yet amid the destruction, discrimination, and displacement that came to independent Tibet, there has also been the extensive migration of Tibetan Buddhist teachers into almost every country of the world. Now publishing houses, learned lamas, Internet websites, and charismatic meditation teachers cross the globe to spread Buddhist teachings. While their predecessors were completely out of touch with the modern world and its spiritual challenges, contemporary monk-scholars and meditation teachers are now leaders in "bringing the Dharma to the West." The Fourteenth Dalai Lama, Nobel Peace Prize winner in 1989, is well known as a world leader and is certainly the most recognized Buddhist in the world.

THERAVADA BUDDHISM TODAY IN SOUTHEAST ASIA

The first regions missionized in antiquity by Buddhist monks have remained the stronghold of Theravada Buddhism. In Sri Lanka and Burma, a new era began with the withdrawal of the British (1947). Buddhism became a pillar of the new nations' identity, and the Buddha was elevated to the status of cultural hero and ancestor.

While supportive of the respective struggles for independence, Buddhism in these states had also been enriched and enlarged by revival movements throughout the colonial period. Most of these involved the laity in the administration of its institutions and saw the establishment of new monastic schools emphasizing revival through strict discipline, meditation, and social service.

Buddhist leaders in the first decades after World War II were also at the forefront of addressing the relationship between socialism and communism, the political ideologies that had risen to popularity as alternatives to capitalism in guiding the newly independent states. Some monks were highly suspicious of communism and allied themselves with aggressive anticommunist campaigns, with one going so far as to say that "killing communists entails no demerit!" However, other, more leftist political activists and high civil servants used Buddhist rhetoric quite creatively to justify participation in communist regimes, as seen in this 1951 speech by a government minister of newly independent Burma:

> I declare that I have implicit faith in Marxism, but at the same time I assert that I am a true Buddhist. Both of these philosophies are correlated. . . . In the beginning, I was a Buddhist only by tradition. The more I study Marxism, however, the more I feel convinced in Buddhism. Thus I have become a true disciple of Lord Buddha by conviction and my faith in Buddhism has grown all the more. I now believe that for any man who has deeply studied Buddhism and correctly perceived its tenets there should be no obstacles to become a Marxist. Vexed by anxieties and fears in respect to food, clothing, and homes, human minds cannot dwell on old age, disease, and death. But with the satisfaction of men's material needs, humans can boldly face these three phenomena. Marxism cannot provide an answer to spiritual liberation. Neither can science. Only Buddhist philosophy can. It must, however, be conceded that material satisfaction in life can only be attained through Marxism.[2]

A TOOTH RELIC VISITS MYANMAR

The Buddha's cremation relics have been the most sacred and precious objects for devotees from the faith's very beginnings. Not only are they the sole remnants of the enlightened one, a "sacred trace" of his earthly existence; they are also thought to be infused with immense power, and mere proximity to them is believed to confer spiritual and worldly blessings.

In 1994 the Chinese government loaned a tooth relic to Myanmar. Placed in a jewel-embellished palanquin and conveyed from the Boeing 757 to a silk-draped float pulled by an elephant, the relic was taken to its shrine in the Maha Pasana cave in Rangoon, where over the next six weeks a half-million devotees came to venerate it and make offerings. SLORC, the country's ruling junta, who had sponsored the visit, used the state-controlled media to emphasize that its members were exemplary Buddhists. In 1995 the junta underwrote the construction of a new temple in the capital where the relic has been displayed in later visits. Displaying and respecting Buddha relics have been recognized as signs of just rulers in Buddhist states since antiquity, and the SLORC generals no doubt intend their sponsorship of tooth relic veneration to win popular approval and counter dislike of their authoritarian rule. After regaining independence from the British Empire in 1948 and undergoing a short period of experimentation with "Buddhist socialism," Myanmar's government has often dealt harshly with persons suspected of fostering dissent. After allowing elections in 1989 but not liking the results, the junta suspended democracy and put the winner, Nobel laureate Aung San Suu Kyi, under house arrest, where she remains today. Nonviolent protests for democracy led by monks in 2007 were similarly put down by government troops, who arrested monastic leaders and shot demonstrators.

The tooth relic arrangements represent ironies of a kind not uncommon today. The Communist Party of China found it politically expedient to utilize a Buddhist relic for advancing its goals in international relations. For their part, the junta ruling Myanmar has been supplying many of the images China now requires to rebuild the temples demolished by Red Guards during the most destructive years of the Cultural Revolution (1966–1969).

THREE CONTEMPORARY FACES OF THAI BUDDHISM

A constitutional monarchy since 1932 and a country never ruled by a European nation, Thailand is another predominantly Theravada country. Thai Buddhism remains one of the most dynamic faiths in the world today. The society supports traditional and reformist scholarship, the ancient spiritual practices of forest monks, and pioneering reformist initiatives. Thai reformers have assumed active roles in working for the modernization of the country through government development programs in infrastructure building, agricultural innovation, education, and health care. Several notable independent monks have opposed the state's toleration of corruption, pollution, and environmental destruction. However, mainstream Thai Buddhist monastic institutions have benefited from royal patronage and the rising wealth that accompanied the economic boom of the late twentieth century. Certain charismatic monks and a host of new lay-oriented independent Buddhist institutions are also active in offering leadership to revitalize the faith. The burgeoning urban areas, where neither old community ties nor traditional monasteries effectively meet the needs of the new city dwellers, have been fertile ground for such reformists. Three examples illustrate the sorts of Buddhist innovators active in contemporary Thailand: the Dhammakaya, Santi Asoke, and the work of two monks, Phra Boonsong and Luang Pi Daeng.

The Dhammakaya The Dhammakaya is the fastest-growing Buddhist reform group in Thailand, attracting the well-educated and newly affluent classes as well as the royal family. Founded by the charismatic monk Phra Monghon Thepmuni in 1978, Dhammakaya spreads its teachings and meditation practices through the sophisticated use of publications and mass media. The movement has established a presence in every major city and town across the country, where its very highly educated monks administer a program of rigorous training for the laity. Another binding force of Dhammakaya is Phra Thepmuni's meditation technique, one that has more in common with Mahayana practices of the Himalayas than with traditional Theravada methods. For its followers, the Dhammakaya has reduced the ritual complexity of the traditional monastery to a few simple practices. It has also emphasized that making money is compatible with Buddhism and has translated utopianism and interdependence teachings through the slogan "World Peace Through Inner Peace." As of 2007, the group numbered its supporters at over 1 million, with branches in twenty countries.

Monastics and householders of the modernist Dhammakaya school reside in individual tents of mosquito netting on a mass meditative retreat in Thailand.

Santi Asoke Santi Asoke differs in many respects from Dhammakaya: It has won a much smaller following (perhaps 100,000, as estimated in 2007) and has garnered much less wealth. Since its founding in 1976, however, movement activists have critiqued what they regard as the complacent establishment monastic schools' compromises with state and business power. Santi Asoke ("People of Ashoka") are named after the first lay ruler in Buddhist history, the Indian emperor who (in Buddhist accounts) spread the faith across India and ruled according to the Buddha's ethical norms. Accordingly, this group seeks to reform Thai Buddhism through a return to austere ethical practices such as abstaining from meat, alcohol, and tobacco as well as avoiding gambling and hedonistic entertainment. Santi Asoke grew out of the work of forest monk reformers who in the 1920s and 1930s sought to revitalize the sangha by a return to an ascetic lifestyle for monks, complemented by rigorous meditation schedules. Santi Asoke's monks wear white robes instead of the traditional yellow because their founder, the charismatic but confrontational Phra Bodhiraksa, was defrocked by the Thai government's monk-monitoring body in the 1980s. The "Protestant" influence is evident in Bodhiraksa's criticisms of traditional rituals as "superstition and magic" and his outspoken rejection of the common Thai ritual of worshiping Buddha images.

Phra Boonsong and Luang Pi Daeng Not all reformers in Thailand have been new institution builders. Phra Boonsong (1941–), the abbot of Phranon Wat in central Thailand since 1972, is a dedicated environmentalist. When he arrived in the area, the ecosystem was sick. Runoff from the Chin River, which flows by the monastery, was polluting paddy fields, and declining agriculture and fishing yields were causing men and women to seek employment in the cities. So Phra Boonsong worked to improve the region's ecological balance by appealing to the traditional Thai prohibition against killing inside a monastery. He began by declaring the river adjacent to it a "pardon zone" for all water creatures. Next, from profits made by selling fish food to local Buddhists (who in turn gave it to the fish, earning merit), he was able to add fish stock to the river. The fish multiplied in that nearby stretch of the river, slowly adding to the breeding population available for harvest by many fishermen living along the river. This success enabled Phra Boonsong to convince the National Assembly to enact laws allowing monasteries nationwide to establish similar breeding zones, and over 200 have done so. He has also begun planting fruit trees on deforested hills, with organic orchards managed to reduce the use of expensive, watershed-polluting chemicals. The expertise of the Phranon Wat monks in species use, grafting, fertilizers, and marketing is now being shared across Thailand, allowing other monks to spearhead similar efforts toward environmental awareness across the nation's rural hinterlands.

Abbot Luang Pi Daeng likewise could not ignore the world outside his monastery, Wat Hua Rin in Northern Thailand. His monastery buildings now include medical examination rooms, handicraft production outbuildings, and a meeting hall where people with HIV/AIDS come for health monitoring and support group meetings. Taking alms from households with an HIV-infected member to illustrate that the disease cannot be transmitted through casual contact, this monk has worked to end the abandonment of those who have contracted this disease and to find employment in new monastery-located handicraft industries for them. In addition to providing spiritual counseling, Luang Pi Daeng has applied the Buddhist teaching of suffering and interdependence to this crisis that has deeply affected Thai life: "I showed them that if we don't help those with AIDS, all of us suffer."[3] Luang Pi Daeng's work was instrumental in the establishment of the UNICEF-funded Sangha Metta Project that has trained over 4,000 monks in seven countries about AIDS prevention and treatment.

✤ Buddhist Revival in Postwar Indochina

By 1985, all the countries of the Indochinese peninsula had begun to liberalize their economies and relax restrictions on religious observances. As communist governments retreated from dogmatism to pragmatism and tolerated the enduring popular attachment to Buddhism and indigenous religions, civil authorities in Vietnam, Laos, and Cambodia began accepting the place of Buddhism in national culture and politics.

A French colony until 1953, Cambodia suffered through the Vietnam wars with the French and the United States and, in the aftermath (1975–1979), the genocidal conflicts under the rule of the Khmer Rouge led by Pol Pot. Under Pol Pot's communist regime, Buddhist monks and institutions were targeted for murder and destruction. While several Cambodian Buddhist centers were relocated among refugees over the border in Thailand, only after the withdrawal of the Vietnamese in 1989 did the restoration of Buddhism begin. Several prominent figures seeking national reconciliation have been Theravada monks.

Vietnam has increasingly tolerated the restoration of Buddhist monasteries and temples since north and south were reunited in 1975. Nevertheless, the government has imprisoned monks it regards as too involved in politics, and the officially sanctioned (and so-named) Vietnam Buddhist Church has won only minimum popular acceptance. Vietnam's population of 75 million resembles China in its religious orientation, with Buddhism the most widespread tradition existing alongside Chinese Daoism and Confucianism, indigenous cults, and Roman Catholic and Protestant Christianity. Vietnamese Buddhism today is predominantly Mahayana in the north, with Theravada monasteries found in the south.

The modern state of Indonesia contains the largest Muslim population in the world, though its western islands of Sumatra and Java were once at the center of an empire that supported both Hinduism and Buddhism. Under a constitution that officially protects all faiths, Indonesian Buddhists are a small minority (2 percent of 205 million), but the faith has undergone a vigorous revival since 1950. Small communities dedicated to predominantly Mahayana Buddhism likewise exist among minority ethnic Chinese communities in Malaysia and in Singapore, the city-state that separated from Malaysia in 1965.

Tales of Spiritual Transformation

Maha Ghosananda, Witness to Buddhist Peacemaking in Cambodia

Ordained as a young boy in Cambodia, Somdet Phra Ghosananda (1928–2007) through middle age pursued a virtuoso monastic life, one that led to his spending years outside of his native land meditating in Thai forest monasteries and completing a doctoral degree in Pali textual studies. In 1976, when Maha Ghosananda heard of Cambodia's political upheaval and the atrocities of Khmer Rouge rule, he resolved to return to worldly action. So he left his forest monastery to work in refugee camps along Thailand's Cambodian border, where he built modest monasteries and trained new monks who helped meet the needs of the suffering population. He especially taught the *Metta-Sutta*, the classical expression of the Buddhist ideal of forgiveness and compassion.

After the fall of the Khmer Rouge, Maha Ghosananda returned to his native land, where he was named Supreme Monk Patriarch of Cambodia. Seeking to increase international support for Cambodia's people and to promote anti-landmine activism while drawn to invitations to preach Dharma and teach meditation among Cambodian immigrants in the United States, the great monk traveled there and founded over fifty international monasteries. But his first priority was to promote peace in Cambodia and foster national reconciliation through Buddhist morality.

Seeing the constant conflicts still common then in the countryside between Khmer Rouge remnants and the new government, he informed his fellow monks, "We must find the courage to leave our temples and enter the suffering-filled temples of human experience." [a] Even though he discovered that the Khmer rouge had murdered his entire family and destroyed his native village, he never wavered from his conviction: "It is the law of the universe that retaliation, hatred, and revenge only continue the cycle." So he began the practice of *Dhammayietra* ("Pilgrimages of Truth") in 1991.

Despite often finding his group close to the falling shells and lethal firefights, Maha Ghosananda led groups of monks and growing numbers of householders, who walked with heads down and hands folded, chanting the Buddha's words from the *Metta-Sutta*:

"Hate can never be appeased by hate;
Hate can only be appeased by loving-kindness."

Recognized by the Japanese Niwano Peace Foundation and several times nominated for the Nobel Peace Prize, this beloved, self-effacing monk—called "Cambodia's Gandhi," gave up the satisfactions of scholarship and the bliss of meditation to take decisive action to heal a genocidal national conflict.

[a] *The Economist*, March 24, 2007.

EAST ASIA

❖ *Guanyin Rises Again in China*

Mahayana Buddhists have for fifteen centuries shared a common faith in Avalokitesh-vara, whose cult was found from central Asia to Japan in shrines located in almost every settlement and home. The celestial bodhisattva has come to be called Guanyin in China and Kannon in Japan. Originally depicted as a male, this divinity is now usually represented in female form. With Buddhism's missionary transplantation across East Asia, she became the refuge for all who desired rebirth in the western Buddhist paradise, for those who met dangerous life circumstances, and especially for women who wanted safe childbirth and sons. As Daoism organized and was systematized in response to Buddhism in China by the T'ang era (617–907), Guanyin was so popular (and Daoism so eclectic) that icons of Guanyin were accepted sights in Daoist temples or in clan temples otherwise dedicated to the veneration of ancestors.

The violently iconoclastic phase of Mao Zedong's Cultural Revolution (1966–1969) nearly eliminated Guanyin from public places all across China and from private shrines as well, since Red Guards who found icons in their house-to-house searches claimed them as sure indicators of "reactionary elements." When icons were discovered, householders were in danger of being declared "enemies of the people," publicly humiliated, and even killed. Since the mid-1980s, however, Guanyin has returned to favor, and state-run factories have produced a large variety of images for sale, many at newly opened temple votive stores. Pilgrimage sites have been opened for Guanyin as well. Indeed, it is evident that even party members, especially among the younger and professional generations, tend to believe in the efficacy of worshiping this Buddhist divinity. Even so, the government's acceptance of the revival of Buddhist devotionalism stands in contrast to its harsh repression of other faiths that have taken root in China, from Christianity to the popular sect Falun Gong.

Since the death of Mao Zedong and the end of the Cultural Revolution in 1976, the Communist government of China has slowly allowed many Buddhist institutions to be reopened, including monasteries that train monks and nuns in traditional ritual and meditation practices. Augmented by meritorious gifts from Chinese living outside China, Buddhist institutions have been rehabilitated across the nation as the government has ended restrictions on lay devotees' setting up home shrines and undertaking pilgrimages.

❖ *Buddhist Revival in South Korea*

The formerly unified Korean culture area, artificially split into North Korea and South Korea after World War II, was strongly influenced by Chinese cultural borrowings, including Buddhism, throughout its history. As South Korea experienced rising economic prosperity from the 1970s onward, it attracted patrons and activists who sought to build the spiritual programs of the monasteries, present the Buddha's teachings in modern media, and reverse the slide of Buddhism in the face of Christian proselytizing and government discrimination.

Despite many setbacks over the last century, the surviving Korean Buddhist institutions remain well endowed with landed income and have created an important niche in Korean society by establishing schools, universities, and lay meditation centers. As in other Buddhist countries undergoing successful economic modernization, Korean Buddhism is experiencing a renewal. Its modern institutions are upgrading monastic education, creating mass media publications, and developing an urban, middle-class Buddhist identity based on householder rituals, meditation, and youth organizations. The latest Korean innovation is the cable channel All-Buddhist Network Television, whose programs offer a mix of sermons, chants, rituals, and chefs teaching vegetarian cooking.

❖ Buddhism in Japan Recovers After World War II

Japan, like the United States, is a country of ever-broadening religious expression. Buddhism has contributed to this through its classical monastic institutions and by its doctrines providing starting points for many of Japan's "new religions." In the mid-nineteenth century, the Meiji state's ultranationalist governments deliberately weakened Buddhism through ideological campaigns and institutionally. By the 1930s, many abbots of co-opted "establishment schools" were in fact actively fanning the flames of war. World War II left monasteries in ruins and prominent clergy in disgrace. But after the war, the sanghas of the oldest schools retained their nationwide presence under a system of head and branch monasteries developed in the late Tokagawa era (1600–1857), and some communities worked to restore their spiritual integrity. Today, most Japanese families are still registered as *danka* ("parishioners") of a monastery branch of one or the other Buddhist schools for, at the very least, the performance of family death rituals.

But for many Japanese, Buddhism has remained in their lives. The great number of individuals undertaking pilgrimage circuits across the heartland of historical Japan to honor the Mahayana bodhisattva Avalokiteshvara, here called Kannon, attests to Buddhism's importance today. The Saikoku route, which is a sacred journey organized as far back as the thirteenth century, still attracts pilgrims to visit its many sites, including some of the greatest and most magnificent temples in Japan. This route has risen from postwar obscurity to host 30,000 participants in the late 1960s and over 90,000 by last count in the late 1990s. This "pilgrimage boom," as the popular religious revival has been labeled by journalists, was aided by the proliferation of modern pilgrim facilities. Moreover, the example of the Saikoku Kannon pilgrimage inspired the formation of other thirty-three-stage Kannon pilgrimage routes in at least seventy-two other regions of Japan. Scholars do debate about how much this rapidly increasing pilgrimage is due to religious dedication to Kannon and how much is due to a less pious "cultural tourism."

Examples of recent revival show the continuing relevance of Kannon in Japanese life. One is lighthearted: The Zenshoji temple northwest of Tokyo has paired the bodhisattva with the Japanese craze for golf by erecting a 6-foot Kannon who holds various golf clubs in her hands. Hundreds of golfers come daily to pray briefly for the mercy of lower scores. More serious is the recent creation of a thirty-three-stage pilgrimage route with a focus on worship of a completely new form of this bod-hisattva: *Boke Fuji Kannon* ("Senility Kannon").

A final example of a new form of Kannon devotionalism in Japan is the cult organized to seek the forgiveness of the spirits of aborted fetuses (*mizuko*). Buddhist temples throughout Japan have seen a revival in rituals on their memorial grounds as women have set up icons to which they offer food and other ritual gifts to spirits to whom they denied birth in human form. Kannon and another compassionate bod-hisattva, named Jizo, are popular in this form of worship at many temples. Japanese women typically request that the compassionate deities guard and bless these wander-ing spirits until they fulfill their destiny and continue on to another human rebirth, as in classical Buddhist teachings. The **mizuko cult** has spread widely, promulgated by many temples that not coincidentally benefit from the income derived from the spe-cial ritual services they provide.

BUDDHISM TODAY IN DIASPORA AND IN ASIA

✤ *Buddhism in the West*

The economic boom that swept Asia in the 1990s and the global migration of Asians are the most recent developments affecting Buddhism today. To a large extent, newly affluent Buddhists have done what Buddhist householders have always done with a portion of their surplus wealth: make merit through pious donations. This infusion of new wealth has been used to rebuild venerable monasteries and temples, support new reform sects, and modernize Buddhist institutions by establishing schools, starting peri-odicals, and creating mass media outlets on television and the Internet. The most afflu-ent and internationally minded, particularly those in East Asia, have shifted the tradi-tional missionary ideal from national to global outreach, building on the migration of the home ethnic group (e.g., Taiwanese, Thai, or Japanese), but often seeking a wider audience beyond. One exception to the trend of new Asian affluence pushing the international expansion of Buddhism is the Tibetan diaspora, which has depended largely on donations by affluent Euro-American supporters, including Hollywood actors and rock stars.

The global migration of Buddhist monastic institutions and ideas has been so great that a representative of every major Asian school can now be found on every conti-nent, and numerous non-Asians have by now been accepted for ordination as monks and nuns in every nation's sangha. In addition, awareness of the basic Buddhist doc-trines of karma, nirvana, and Buddhahood, formerly confined to the educated classes of the world, is now accessible to all via the global mass media. In 2008 a search for "Buddhism" on the Web elicited over 2.5 million connections.

In the Zen and Tibetan schools in North America, especially, converts now speak of the emergence of new "American schools of Tibetan (or Zen) Buddhism." An explo-sion in publications, educational programs, and meditation sessions marks the unmis-takable deeper adaptation of the faith within Western societies. Interestingly, these Euro-American Buddhist schools are selective in their adoption of Asian Buddhist traditions:

Boke Fuji ("Senility") Kannon: A New Incarnation of a Buddhist Deity

The late 1980s saw the appearance of icons that depicted the goddess Kannon holding a flower in one hand and opening the other in a gesture of mercy to two elderly people, one male and one female, who clutch at her robes in supplication. Consistent with her renown developed over one and a half millennia for compassionately "mothering" her devotees and bestowing this-worldly boons to those who call on her, this new form of the bodhisattva has arisen as senility or Alzheimer's disease has caused great emotional distress to many in Japan (as elsewhere). Both for the elderly and their families, who share a Confucian responsibility for parental care at this stage of life, old-age suffering has surfaced as a weighty problem, suggesting a creative Buddhist response. Thus temples have established social and spiritual programs, developing amulets, shrines, and pilgrimage routes for devotees to visit in search of preventive blessings. Buddhist priests, aware of physicians' counsel that the best way to keep senility at bay is for the aged to keep active, are encouraging this approach. By organizing pilgrimages, for example, they make available to the elderly enjoyable, stimulating, and hopeful activity, in which the pilgrims can both articulate their worries and acquire peace of mind.

A contemporary Boke Fuji ("Senility") Kannon amulet from Japan.

They have eschewed celibate monasticism, featured meditation, and minimized ritualism, much like the "Protestant Buddhists" of Asia. This expectation of Westerners is especially noteworthy in the Pure Land schools established in America: These centers have found the need to offer programs in meditation for the laity, even though back in Asia their monastic life is more focused on chanting.

The modern diaspora of Buddhism in some respects can be seen as the global continuation of the faith's ancient missionary spirit. In North America, Buddhist missionaries have been led by teachers of Japanese and Korean Zen, all lineages of Tibetan Buddhism, Theravadins emphasizing vipassana meditation with ties to the countries of Southeast Asia, Japan's Soka Gakkai sect, and the various Pure Land schools (in rough order of importance).

In the 1950s the perceived iconoclasm of Zen—its nonconformist appeal—attracted Americans who participated in the Beat Generation culture of jazz, poetry, and experimental literature. The lure of Zen meditation practices has drawn Western practitioners from the 1960s onward. Zen's connection with Japanese fine arts and martial arts also helped Zen-oriented teachers and their institutions across the globe to reach a wider artistic and athletic audience.

The Japanese Soka Gakkai, a modern religiocultural offshoot of the Nichiren school, has an international following eager to reinterpret Buddhism and take political action to foster the development of a more enlightened world civilization. Pure Land Buddhism has been transplanted among East Asians who have migrated to urban areas worldwide, particularly the West Coast of North America and Hawaii. Indeed, migrants from every Buddhist country in the world have contributed to the globalization of their faith by establishing temples and monasteries in their adopted homelands. The latest groups of Asian Buddhists in America have emigrated from Southeast Asia.

Outside Asia, Buddhists still remain a small minority in the census figures and usually are found in urban areas. Among today's immigrants and Western converts, as in Asia, "being a Buddhist" does not necessarily imply an exclusive identity. Thus, the census figures, which show, for example, roughly a million Buddhists in North America as a whole, do not accurately reflect the penetration of Buddhist concepts and practices in contemporary national culture.

With intellectuals worldwide, however, awareness of Buddhist thought and practice is widespread. Advertising agents now deploy Buddhist ideas and practices routinely to promote materialistic attachments: Popular advertising since 1999 found the Dalai Lama's image being used to sell Apple computers, a Nike sneaker called "Nirvana," and a designer sandal called "Buddha." The word *Zen* has been reduced to a vapid cliché because it has by now been appended to hundreds of objects, certain to elicit consumer curiosity.

"Change Your Mind Day" in Central Park

Each year in late May, the Buddhist magazine *Tricycle* sponsors a gathering in New York's Central Park that draws a variety of teachers who are active in America. Other attendees—"longtime practitioners, meditators-for-a-day, Dharma bums, and dog-walkers"—are led through a series of guided spiritual exercises in the half-day program. In 2007, following 108 gong strikes, American abbots from Zen monasteries and Westerners initiated as teachers in Tibetan lineages gave sermons, Japanese monks led chants, and an American meditation master directed the group in Theravadin-style vipassana meditation. A friend of the late Allen Ginsberg read poems by this famous convert to Buddhism. A perennial favorite followed: a spirited debate in Tibetan scholastic style punctuated by hand-slapping exclamations between a Tibetan lama and an American convert who argued about the nature of nirvana. A T'ai Chi teacher directed a group exercise using martial arts and Japanese dance movements. After a musical interlude, a Tibetan monk gave teachings on loving-kindness, a Sri Lankan abbot discoursed on discipline in Buddhist practice, and a Chinese monk talked about the centrality of compassion. Another round of gongs ended the extraordinary inter-Buddhist ecumenical event attended by 3,000 people. By 2008, Buddhists in twenty cities were planning similar "Change Your Mind" events.

Buddhism as Commodity and Buddhist Imagery as Sales Pitch

Although Zen is not mentioned in it, the ad on the left, for a truck, completely misunderstands the basic message of Buddhism, that is, that possessions and attachment undermine spiritual life. The image on the right makes the equally absurd suggestion that electronic distractions are somehow a kind of spiritual practice.

✤ *The Reshaping of Buddhism in Asia*

In the postcolonial period, then, Buddhists have had to determine how to situate their tradition in the new secular polities. The effort has entailed reconstructing sangha–state relations after colonial neglect of the religious institutions, responding to scientific thought and modern medicine, reckoning with the religious pluralism introduced by Christianity and other faiths, and revising law codes in relation to national minorities. The results have been mixed. In Bhutan and Sri Lanka, the dominant ethnic groups have promoted Buddhist nationalism at the expense of non-Buddhist minorities, while in Myanmar, members of the military have used Buddhist symbols in a manipulative way to prop up the legitimacy of their authoritarian regimes. Yet Buddhists in each of these countries have led democratic movements resisting repressive policies and violence.

Reformist monastic schools and lay movements begun in the modern era have continued to the present, with recent initiatives arising to address problems confronting the widely differing national contexts: Forest monks in Thailand respond to environmental crises, lay organizations in Japan campaign in elections to insert Buddhist values into the political culture, Mongolian leaders rebuild monuments and restore monastic education and ritual expertise, and Sri Lankan monks run for the national parliament vowing to keep their country's Buddhist identity strong.

As ethnic identity has held the loyalty of local communities, often against the demands of modern secular states, "being Buddhist" has drawn individuals to value, rediscover, and embrace Buddhism across Asia. In many cases, the postcolonial web of global interaction has shaped the process: The "Buddhism" that reformers discover has been filtered through and influenced by the thinking of Euro-American scholars and Westernized indigenous teachers.

An interesting and early example of this phenomenon occurred in Maharashtra, the modern state in central India. Since 1956, Mahar caste groups relegated to the bottom of the caste system have held mass ceremonies to convert to Buddhism, declaring their rejection of Hinduism and its institutionalization of social inequality. The Mahars' knowledge of Buddhism was informed in part by colonial scholarship; the presence in Maharashtra of ancient Buddhist sites revealed by British archaeology has obvious importance as well. The founder of this movement, Dr. Bhimrao **Ambedkar** (1891–1956), learned about Buddhism from his studies in the West, particularly at Columbia University, where Euro-American scholarship on Buddhism then held up the image of the Buddha as a social reformer. Statues of Ambedkar abound in Maharashtra villages today, monuments to the reinstatement of Buddhism tradition in the service of a twentieth-century social reform movement.

Burmese monks shout slogans during a protest in 2008 against the visit of Myanmar's Foreign Minister U Nyan Win to India.

BUDDHISM'S ELECTIVE AFFINITY FOR MODERNIZATION

At the beginning of the twentieth century, Western scholars such as Max Weber questioned whether Buddhism could prove compatible with economic modernization. Since the end of the Second World War, such skepticism has been laid to rest by the exceptional success of nations strongly influenced by Buddhism. We can now see that Weber erred in exaggerating the "otherworldliness" of mainstream Buddhism. He was not well-acquainted with the unambiguous early doctrinal emphasis on "good Buddhists" attaining worldly success, an ethos that traveled well across the trade routes of Asia and, it seems, into the twenty-first century. Modern reformers have had many canonical texts to draw on to promote the compatibility between economic development and Buddhism. As an influential reformist monk of Thailand asserted several generations ago, "Education breeds knowledge, knowledge breeds work, work breeds wealth, and wealth promotes happiness."[4]

The economic boom in Asia since World War II has clearly benefited Buddhism as newly wealthy patrons have sponsored various renewal initiatives. Moreover, many do not involve the traditional sangha's leadership. For example, Thai and Korean projects

Contrasting Religious Visions

As the following contrasting visions indicate, every religious tradition is capable of generating both visions that encourage peace and understanding and visions that encourage conflict and violence.

Peacemaker: Thich Nhat Hanh

Since his early involvement in the peace movement in his native Vietnam, the Zen monk Thich Nhat Hanh (1926–) has projected a strong and ecumenical Buddhist voice. From exile in the West, he has been a firm advocate of toleration and the necessary centrality of peacemaking when facing both personal challenges and international policy. A leading advocate of "engaged Buddhism" and author of several dozen books, Nhat Hanh has for decades argued that Buddhists must participate in social and cultural activities, with activism informed by the clarity arising from meditation. As he once affirmed, "In times like this, when people suffer so much, the bodhisattvas don't stay in the temple; they are out there." [a] His "12 Precepts of the Order of Interbeing" attempts to express universal principles of life beyond Buddhist sectarianism, rejecting absolutely killing, coercion, dogmatism, and untruthfulness while advocating a meditation-centered life.

Confrontationalist: Political Monks of Sri Lanka's Maha Sangha

Drawing on some of the nationalist pronouncements of reformists such as Anagarika Dharmapala, some monks have formed an entity called the Maha Sangha to engage in political action. These activist monks have urged their government to reply with relentless military action, not negotiated compromise, to resolve the Tamil revolt that has fueled Sri Lanka's tragic civil war since 1983. Arguing that "politics is the monks' heritage" and that Sri Lanka has special virtue as a Buddhist homeland, the Maha Sangha supports violence as the only solution. One poet has distilled their support of aggressive religious nationalism:

> My brave, brilliant soldier son
> Leaving [home] to defend the motherland
> That act of merit is enough
> To reach Nirvana in a future birth. . . .
> Country, religion, race are my triple gems. . . .
> The sangha is ever ready
> At the front
> If the race is threatened. [b]

[a] Sallie B. King, "Thich Nhat Hanh and the Unified Buddhist Church," in Christopher S. Queen and Sallie B. King, eds., *Engaged Buddhism: Buddhist Liberation Movements in Asia* (Albany: State University Press of New York, 1996), p. 351.
[b] H. L. Seneviratne, *The Work of Kings: The New Buddhism in Sri Lanka* (Chicago: University of Chicago Press, 1999), pp. 272–273.

are now under way that have transcribed the scriptures into electronic media form (CD-ROMs), a new mode of spreading the Dharma locally and globally to all with computer technology. Translation of the sacred texts into the global medium of English is another innovation. The Buddhist Publication Society, founded in Sri Lanka in 1956, has offered hundreds of vernacular (and English) translations and interpretive tracts on the Pali texts; its work overlaps with that of the Pali Text Society founded in nineteenth-century England—a group that continues to extend its English translations of canonical work from the southern Buddhist tradition, including extracanonical commentaries.

Today each of the four Tibetan monastic schools has a modern publishing house in the West that yearly prints dozens of texts promulgating explanations of Buddhist doctrine by its own teaching monks. An even larger-scale project was initiated in 1991 by the Japanese industrialist Yenan Numata. His foundation, the Bukkyo Denko Kyokai, is underwriting the scholarly translation into English of the entire Chinese canon. To do all 3,360 scriptures, the project is estimated to span the next 100 years!

STATE BUDDHISM AND THE POISON OF ETHNIC PASSION

Few areas of Asian Buddhism have been removed from the crises and changes of the modern era: Scientific thought and technology derived from the European Enlightenment challenged traditional doctrines, cosmologies, and medical theories; the impact of European colonialism forced economic transformations that undermined traditional rulers and patronage; the ideologies of Christian missionary triumphalism and racism conflicted with indigenous beliefs about the superiority of Buddhism.

With colonialism now gone, shifts in the political, socioeconomic, and intellectual spheres have changed individuals and caused Buddhists to adapt their beliefs and practices to a transformed world. Countries with Buddhist majorities now must decide how to shape society—in economic and political spheres—to best realize the Buddha's ideal of a compassionate civilization. Exponents still debate whether Buddhism should endorse military authoritarianism (on the model of the benevolent dictator Ashoka) or representative democracy (on the model of the sangha's democratic norms). Is it more compassionate to establish a "pure Buddhist state" that privileges Buddhism and Buddhists or to opt for a secular state that guarantees evenhanded tolerance of a multireligious and multiethnic society? Can Buddhist ideals be more effectively implemented in a socialist or a free-market system?

Monks across Asia face the challenge of adapting their lifestyle defined by monastic laws over 2,000 years old to the rapidly changing realities of the globalizing world.

In countries such as Myanmar and Sri Lanka, where adherence to Buddhism was a powerful force against colonialism, reform movements within the sangha weakened the older institutional lineages and led government leaders to seek ways to control "political monks." In modern China, Myanmar, and Vietnam, Buddhist monks have been called on to withdraw, study, and meditate. In India, Sri Lanka, and Thailand, on the other hand, monks have become leaders in political reform movements and in the implementation of economic development projects.

In revolutionary China and Outer Mongolia, Buddhism was identified with the old feudal order and was fiercely disestablished. Across China's Tibetan and Inner Mongolian regions, the policy of the People's Republic of China, especially during the Cultural Revolution, was to destroy Buddhist monasticism, punish believers, and repress any public expressions of devotion. Just reestablishing stupas, ordination lineages, and traditional sangha life has been a challenge over the last decades in these

Tibetan monks engaging in debate training, testing their ability to consistently expound the Buddha's teachings.

nations. It was not until 1990 that Buddhism in Outer Mongolia experienced a revival after nearly a century of suppression.

In Sri Lanka, once the nationalistic Buddhist movements had ushered in independence, they turned their efforts inward. By seeking to legislate a "purer Buddhist state" and a restoration of past glories, they created an environment in which activist monks enflamed unprecedented ethnic conflict with non–Buddhist minorities long resident on the island. Paradoxically, Buddhist universalism and the ideology of compassion have not prevented modern attempts at "ethnic cleansing" there as well as in Burma and Bhutan. Some social historians see the further weakening of Buddhist ethics in the future: As populations rise and resources grow scarcer, politicians of Buddhist Asia, as elsewhere, will be increasingly tempted to use Buddhism to unify majorities that will then repress religious minorities. Most recently in Thailand (2007), some Buddhist monks have called for declaring Buddhism the official religion of the nation, in response to Muslim terrorist acts in its southern region that murdered monks and destroyed Buddhist sanctuaries.

 Conclusion

As a refuge of intellectual freedom and spiritual imagination, Buddhist teachers nurtured and enriched the civilizations of Asia. Surveying the belief patterns of the world's Buddhist communities, one is challenged both by the sheer diversity of doctrinal expression and by the complexity of Buddhism's systematic thought. Such an out-pouring of conceptualization from a tradition that held the ultimate reality to be beyond words! Buddhism's great migration across Asia and beyond has entailed the translation of texts, ideas, and rituals into non-Indic languages and cultures. In becoming a world religion, Buddhism in practice has promoted compassionate, medically advanced, disciplined, mercantile, and literate societies. Like other great religions today, Buddhism has shown that its definition of the human condition and its prescribed ways of addressing suffering and mortality have enduring value, even in new societies and in the midst of changes that have shaken the modern and postcolonial world.

THE SANGHA: ADAPTIVE REFORMISM?

Given the repeated emphasis placed on the role of the sangha in maintaining the traditional goals of Buddhism in every society, it should not be surprising that we underline the role that spiritual exemplars, scholars, teachers, and meditators could play in determining Buddhism's future into the third millennium of the common era. A recent survey of ordained Buddhist monks and nuns estimated that there are about 700,000 worldwide. Officially, monks outnumber nuns by six to one.

Arguing that the sangha cannot keep Buddhism alive unless the monks keep pace with the educational level of the nation's population, countries such as Thailand have invested in making higher education available to individuals in the sangha. This opportunity still attracts many young men from poor rural backgrounds to take ordination. Paradoxically, becoming a monk gives many the chance to live in better material circumstances than their parents are able to achieve and to gain skills that can be, and often are, taken back into lay life. But at the same time, modern states have bureaucratized their sanghas, scrutinized the preaching and personal lives of monks, and controlled the political activities of the monasteries. In recent times, as in antiquity, the freedom accorded to one "in the robes," the refuge afforded by the monastery, and the high regard extended to charismatic monks all brought unwanted attention from political leaders. Seeing clearly the threat that the Buddhist Dharma represents to unjust or uncompassionate regimes, politicians have sought to weaken Buddhist institutions even while honoring them. In Myanmar, Vietnam, and China, monks and nuns cannot escape the fear of repression or hope to exert meaningful political influence. It is hard to imagine Buddhist monks regaining the power they once enjoyed in most Buddhist countries of Asia.

Since World War II, many developments have undermined the classical patterns and exchanges within Buddhist societies. Whereas formerly, monastic schools were an important part of the sanghas' service to local communities and a source of their recruitment, today public education has been removed from the monastery almost everywhere. If connection with and awareness of modern changes are essential to an institution meeting the needs of the lay majority, is the traditional Buddhist sangha capable of keeping Buddhist ideas and identity vibrant in the whirl of changes sweeping modern Asian societies?

Many progressive Buddhists think not. Noting that the modern sangha has a hierarchy of authority unknown in earlier times, they see little opportunity for young monks to fashion innovative applications of the Dharma in thought or action. Noting how powerful elder monks typically lack vision, purpose, or inspiration beyond the guardianship of ceremonies and tradition, many Asian householders now look to lay institutions for more promising avenues to keep Buddhism vital.

The number of men taking monastic vows across Asia has fallen far short of what population increases would predict. As a result, many village monasteries are understaffed, a trend reflecting the breakdown of rural communities that has contributed to the urbanization of Asia. While some Buddhists in Nepal, Korea, and Japan have countenanced sanghas of the "married ordained" to solve the problem of recruitment, these schools on the whole have actually shown even less inclination to revitalize or innovate. Again, it is easy to see why Buddhist reformers have almost always gone outside the boundary of the modern sangha to move ahead with their programs, at times even having to face opposition from the established monastic community.

Sri Lankan monks march in support of the Marxist party, the JVP, in May 2003.

A ROLE FOR BUDDHIST WOMEN?

Related to the issue of the sangha's adaptability and leadership is the status of Buddhist women renunciants. In 1987, at an international conference held in Bodh Gaya, 150 devout women formed a worldwide organization called **Shakyaditya.** The "Shakya Daughters" are dedicated to the restoration of the full ordination of bhikkhunis (nuns) among the Theravadins, a lineage most Buddhist monks of this school view as having died out almost a millennium ago. Throughout the Buddhist world today, there are several hundrcd thousand highly committed women who have adopted an unofficial and unheralded ascetic lifestyle involving meditation, service, or study. In every country there is also a male-dominated sangha that controls the Buddhist institutions, and the great majority of monks strongly resist changes in the gender status quo.

Yet some women who have adopted the lifestyle of the nun and donned white robes do not, in fact, even wish to take the full bhikkhuni ordination. Why? According to the *Vinaya* rules, fully ordained women admitted into the sangha must accept the formal supervision of the senior monks. Presently, in their unofficial status, these renunciants enjoy near-complete autonomy to manage their living arrangements and spiritual training. They argue that since their real loyalty is to the Dharma and their true concern is nirvana-seeking discipline, it is pointless to seek formal recognition. Yet remaining "unofficial" places severe limitations on the women's ability to build their institutions, since they are not recognized for state patronage, and householder donations to them do not yield the same prestige or merit return that comes from donations to the fully ordained monks. As a result, most of the unofficial "nuns" remain impoverished, without special honor in their societies at large, and marginal to the dominant Buddhist community.

Since 2000, over 400 women practicing in all the Theravada countries have gone to Chinese Mahayana monasteries (in mainland China or Taiwan) to receive full nun's official ordination, much to the consternation of the traditionalist monks. Can Buddhist traditions facing so many future challenges afford to relegate to the margins of their societies the energy, compassion, and merit of such women?

Members of the Thai sangha gather for chanting before a large Buddha.

GLOBALIZATION OF BUDDHISM: MONKS, MIGRANTS, AND TRANSNATIONAL CULTURE

The global migration of Asian Buddhists in the postcolonial era is another source of revival. As these groups grow and prosper in their new countries, they naturally channel a portion of their savings back to the home region. But these immigrants have also paid to sponsor monks and build storefront monasteries in the West and, in the process, internationalized the home country's institutions through a slow grassroots process of development. As Buddhist priests, monks, and expatriates move between their new and old countries, innovations and resources are being shifted as well. This immigrant-induced exchange also includes the cross-fertilization of ideas moving between Buddhist schools from distant areas of Asia and their Western exponents. It may well be that the future success—or perhaps even survival—of the modern national lineages and schools of Buddhism back in Asia will depend on an international membership, providing worldwide sources of funding and interpretive awareness. To date, only the Tibetan Buddhists in exile have been truly successful at linking the material support and ritual practice by Western converts to their traditional schools; otherwise, most Asian Buddhists and converts practice their religion completely separate from Westerners who have converted to Buddhism.

An especially promising development may be the growing presence of Buddhism in the emerging global culture. In the area of human rights, Asian Buddhist exponents have made impressive contributions. Buddhist doctrine offers many traditional ideals that have been rearticulated powerfully by reformists and activists who style themselves as "engaged Buddhists." These ideals include compassion, nonviolence, selflessness,

Buddhist monks chant during a memorial ceremony for the student victims of the 2007 shootings at Virginia Tech University.

interdependence, and detachment. There is no shortage of examples today of the existential "poisons" that Buddhists have always located at the center of their wheel of life—human greed, anger, and delusion. Yet the very compassion and selflessness that Buddhists have always embraced offer the means to lessen suffering of individuals, of communities, and of the earth itself.

An example of this determined insistence on applying Buddhist norms to modern crises is seen in the writings of the Thai activist Sulak Sivaraksa, founder (in 1989) of the International Network of Engaged Buddhists:

> When Prince Siddhartha saw an old man, a sick man, a dead man, and a wandering monk, he was moved to seek salvation, and eventually he became the Buddha, the Awakened One. The suffering of the present day, such as that brought about at Bhopal and Chernobyl, should move many of us to think together and act together to overcome such death and destruction, to bring about the awakening of humankind.[5]

Engaged Buddhism is uniting Asian Buddhists with Western converts, bringing together the energies of householders, monks, and nuns, and finding issues that connect Buddhist activists with similarly committed reformers from other faiths. It remains to be seen whether Buddhist revivalists can offer a compelling interpretation of the Dharma as Buddhists find themselves drawn into the marketplace of globalized capitalism, with its doctrines of individualism and competition and its vigorous encouragement of consumerism.

Discussion Questions

1. Buddhists past and present have looked to the incidents in Gautama Buddha's life for inspiration. Pick three major episodes in the Buddha's life and discuss what lessons they impart to a typical Buddhist householder.

2. Many modern Buddhists regard the Buddha as a reformer. What teachings can be used to support this interpretation? What historical arguments can be made against this position?

3. Which of the Buddha's teachings are shared with post-Vedic Hinduism?

4. Explain how Buddhist doctrine can argue for reincarnation but against the existence of an "immortal soul."

5. Why is compassion a human ideal that is a logical extension of core Buddhist doctrines?

6. What is the relationship between the Three Marks of Existence, prajna, and nirvana?

7. In what senses can the Buddha be called the Great Physician?

8. Why is Buddhism known as the *Middle Way*? Give at least three reasons.

9. How might the Vajrayana school be viewed merely as an application of basic Mahayana Buddhist doctrines?

10. Why is the *Lotus Sutra* so important in China and Japan?

11. How does Mahayana Buddhism resemble and differ from devotional Hinduism?

12. How is the Mahar revival of Buddhism in India indicative of the effects of "Protestant Buddhism" and the backlash from the colonial era within the Buddhist world?

13. Name five aspects of Protestant Christianity that were adopted by Buddhist reformers, shaping the nineteenth- and twentieth-century revitalization movements called "Protestant Buddhism."

14. In your opinion, how would a modern Buddhist revivalist present the Dharma and argue that it remains a religion relevant to life in the twenty-first century?

Key Terms

Ambedkar	karuna
Amitabha/Amida	koan
anatman	*Lotus Sutra*
arhat	Madhyamaka
Ashoka	Mahayana
Avalokiteshvara	Maitreya
bhikkhuni	maitri
Bodh Gaya	mantra
bodhisattva	Mi-lo Fo
Buddha	mizuko cult
Buddha-nature school	Nichiren
caitya	nirvana
Ch'an	Pali Canon
Cittamatra	pap
dana	prajna
dependent origination	Protestant Buddhism
Dharma	punya
Dogen	Pure Land
Eightfold Path	sangha
Eisai	Shakyaditya
engaged Buddhism	shramana
enlightenment	skandha
Four Good Deeds	Sthaviravadins
Four Noble Truths	stupa
Gelug-pa	Theravada
Guanyin	Three Marks of Existence

Three Refuges

Thunderbolt Vehicle

uposatha

Vajrayana

vipassana meditation

Wu Tai Shan

Zen

Suggested Readings

Bechert, Heinz, and Richard Gombrich, eds. *The World of Buddhism* (New York: Thames-Hudson, 1987).

Gombrich, Richard. *Theravada Buddhism: A Social History from Ancient Benares to Modern Colombo* (New York: Routledge, 1988).

———— and Gananath Obeyesekere. *Buddhism Transformed: Religious Change in Sri Lanka* (Princeton, NJ: Princeton University Press, 1988).

Harvey, Peter. *An Introduction to Buddhism: Teachings, History, Practices* (Cambridge, UK: Cambridge University Press, 1990).

Heine, Steven, and Charles S. Prebish, eds. *Buddhism in the Modern World* (New York: Oxford University Press, 2003).

Lopez, Donald, ed. *Buddhism in Practice* (Princeton, NJ: Princeton University Press, 1996).

Queen, Christopher, and S. King, eds. *Engaged Buddhism* (Albany: State of New York University Press, 1996).

Rahula, Walpola. *What the Buddha Taught* (New York: Publishers Resource, 1978).

Rhys-Davids, Caroline A. F., tr. *Stories of the Buddha* (New York: Dover, 1988).

Robinson, Richard, and Willard Johnson. *The Buddhist Religion: A Historical Introduction,* 4th ed. (Belmont, CA: Wadsworth, 1997).

Seager, Richard. *Buddhism in America* (New York: Columbia University Press, 1999).

Snellgrove, David. *Indo-Tibetan Buddhism* (Boulder, CO: Shambhala, 1987).

Strong, John S., ed. *The Experience of Buddhism,* 2nd ed. (Belmont, CA: Wadsworth, 2007).

Swearer, Donald. *The Buddhist World of Southeast Asia* (Albany: State University of New York Press, 1996).

Trainor, Kevin, ed. *Buddhism: An Illustrated Guide* (London: Duncan-Baird, 2001).

Wijayaratna, Mohan. *Buddhist Monastic Life* (Cambridge, UK: Cambridge University Press, 1987).

Williams, Paul. *Mahayana Buddhism: The Doctrinal Foundations* (New York: Routledge, 1989).

Notes

1. Quoted in Samuel Beal, Si-Yu-Ki, *Buddhist Records of the Western World* (New Delhi: Munshiram Manoharlal, 1983), p. xxix.
2. U Ba Swe [Defense Minister of Burma] in *The Burmese Revolution* (Rangoon: Pyida Press, 1957), pp. 14–15.
3. *Tricycle,* Winter 2004, pp. 24–25.
4. Phra Kummsaen, quoted in Kenneth Landon, *Thailand in Transition* (Chicago: University of Chicago Press, 1939), pp. 67–68.
5. Sulak Sivaraksa, *Seeds of Peace* (Berkeley, CA: Parallax Press, 1988), p. 9.

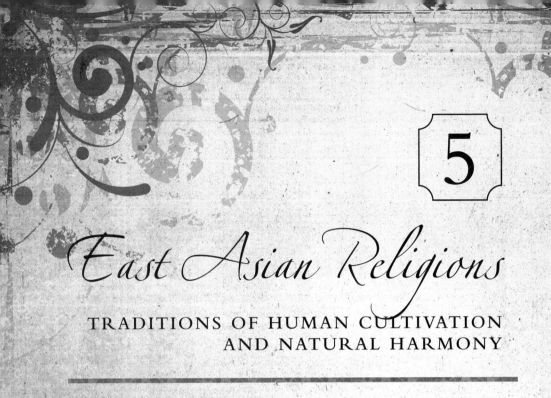

East Asian Religions

TRADITIONS OF HUMAN CULTIVATION AND NATURAL HARMONY

✦ Overview

On public holidays and lunar days traditionally deemed favorable for approaching the gods, temples in China, Japan, and Korea are packed with morning visitors, the air thick with incense smoke. In Beijing, newly married couples flock to the White Clouds Daoist temple to light candles, requesting divine aid to ensure the birth of a son; at family shrines in Seoul, honor students approach ancestral altars to report their applications to study at universities abroad; in rural Japan, farmers gather at the village Shinto shrine for the annual harvest festival, clapping their hands to punctuate their prayers of thanks—and then offering sake and purifying the sacred sumo wrestling grounds with salt. Buddhist monasteries have also attracted new patronage as economic prosperity has enriched the region: Old women hoping for medicinal cures sip water that has been blessed, executive trainees sent by corporations for "toughening up" sit in meditation, and children desperate for assistance on an upcoming exam light incense sticks.

Today, it is more difficult to find public shrines for the sage Confucius, but there is no doubt that Confucian tradition has survived the wars, political tumult, and scathing denunciations of the twentieth century. In the colonial era, every Chinese intellectual blamed Confucianism for retarding the region's development. Now its emphasis on education, strong families, individual discipline, and harmonious group relations is seen as holding the center of East Asia's stable societies and orchestrating this region's ascendancy in the global economy.

This religious pluralism sets East Asia apart. Throughout the region's history, the great majority of East Asians regarded Confucianism, Daoism, deity cults, and Buddhism as complementary, dealing with different aspects of life. Most felt that

East Asian Religion Timeline

1766–1122 BCE	Shang dynasty in China; cult of departed ancestors and oracle bone divination
1122–221	Zhou dynasty in China; yin-yang theory develops; era of intermittent civil disorder
c. 551–479	Life of Master K'ung (Confucius)
c. 520–286	Era of first Daoist sages, philosophers Lao Zi (d. 500 BCE?) and Zhuang Zi (365–290 BCE)
450–223	Era of Confucian sage scholars, Master Meng (Mencius, 371–289 BCE), Master Xun (298–238 BCE); origins of Confucian *Analects* and compilation of the *Five Classics*
221–206	Qin dynasty, the first to unify China; Great Wall completed
200 BCE–220 CE	Han dynasty in China; civil service based on Confucian teachings
220–588 CE	Period of weak central state and the growth of Daoism and Buddhism
c. 450	"Three Caves" of Daoist scriptures collected
618–907	T'ang dynasty in China; period of Confucian revival; translations of Indian Buddhist texts
668–918	Silla dynasty in Korea, centered on Buddhism as state religion
710–784	Nara period in Japan; Shinto tradition organized; Buddhism made state religion
794–1185	Heian period in Japan, ends with emperor removed from rulership
918–1392	Koryo dynasty in Korea, with ecumenical development of Mahayana Buddhism
960–1279	Song dynasty in China; period of neo-Confucianism (the "Second Epoch")
c. 1150	Goddess Mazu becomes popular in China, recognized by the state
1130–1200	Life of Zhu Xi, leading neo-Confucian exponent, who reestablished the tradition as preeminent among the Chinese literati
1185–1333	Kamakura era in Japan, era of civil disorder and the rise of new Buddhist schools
1279–1368	Yuan dynasty in China, era of Mongol rule
1336–1600	Ashikaga period in Japan; era of Shinto–Buddhist syncretism, popularity of Pure Land Buddhism; adoption of Zen among the literati and Samurai
1368–1644	Ming dynasty in China, the last era of Han Chinese rule; doctrine of harmonizing the "three faiths"
1380FF	In China, *The Canonization of the Gods* fixes folk pantheon in hierarchy mirroring state bureaucracy
1392–1910	Yi dynasty in Korea, an era marked by state-favored Confucianism
1472–1529	Life of Wang Yangming, a neo-Confucian who promoted mind cultivation and character development

1501–1570	Life of Yi T'oegye, important Korean neo-Confucian
1534–1582	Life of Nobunaga, Japanese shogun who persecuted Buddhism and gave support to Christianity
1592	Publication of *Journey the West*, written by Wu Cheng-en
1600–1867	Tokugawa era in Japan, with capital in Tokyo; Buddhism under strong state support
1644–1911	Qing (Manchu) dynasty in China; era promoting Confucianism
1815–1888	Oldest new religions in Japan: Kurozumikyo (1814), Tenrikyo (1838)
1850–1864	Taiping Rebellion in China, led by Hong Xiuquan (1814–1864)
1860	Ch'ondogyo movement founded in Korea by Ch'oe Suun (1824–1864)
1868–1945	Return of emperor's rule in Japan and the rise of state Shinto; Japan adopts Western calendar, technology, imperialist political views
1871–1945	Japanese Buddhist establishment joins Shinto nationalists and Christians in support of militarism
1880–present	Best and brightest individuals across the East Asia region studying Western learning, technology to seek rapid modernization
1889–1890	New constitution and Japanese government initiatives draw heavily on Confucian doctrines
1912	Fall of Qing dynasty in China, ending state patronage of Confucianism
1900–1945	Founding of "new religions" in prewar Japan: P. L. Kyodan in 1924; Reiyukai Kyodan in 1925, Soka Gakkai in 1930, Rissho Koseikai in 1938
1946–present	Founding of "new 'new religions'" in postwar Japan: Sukyo Mahikari in 1963, Agonshu in 1971, Aum Shinrikyo in 1989
1949–1976	People's Republic of China established; Communist Party persecutes monks, priests, institutions
1966–1976	Cultural Revolution brings renewed persecution of religions and adherents in China
1984–present	Buddhist monasteries and Daoist temples reopen, many with newly trained monks and nuns in residence; pilgrims increase rapidly and visit major sites to perform traditional rites
1994	Study of Confucianism in schools officially supported by Chinese state
1995	Aum Shinrikyo sect in Japan launches poison gas attack in Tokyo
1996–present	Return of traditional ancestor veneration to China; images of Mao Zedong and other deceased Communist Party leaders found on popular religious amulets
1999	Falun Gong, a syncretistic Buddhist–Daoist group founded by Li Hongzhi claiming 100 million followers in thirty countries, protests in Beijing; within months, Chinese government bans the group and begins persecution of practitioners
2006	Yu Dan's *Reflections on the Analects*, a book on Confucius published in China becomes a best seller in 2007, with over 10.2 million sold; Chinese government begins funding of the first of 500 "Confucius Institutes" to be established in most countries across the world to promote the study of Chinese language and culture

At a shrine atop the sacred mountain Tai Shan in southern China, devotees light incense and candles to honor the local gods.

these interrelated beliefs and practices enriched their spirituality, offering them the chance to meld the traditions harmoniously to solve personal problems and address life's questions. It was rare for individuals—elite or common folk—to feel that "being religious" meant choosing one religious tradition to the exclusion of the others. This openness stands in contrast to the common Western belief that religious conviction means signing on to an exclusive creed or seizing on one either/or alternative.

East Asia, more than South Asia, exhibits a popular and strikingly common tradition that is rooted in the **ancestor veneration** and spirit worship of earliest antiquity. Over time these practices became blended with basic elements of Daoism, Buddhism, and Confucianism, comprising what scholars call East Asia's *diffuse religion*. Given that roughly 40 percent of humanity is East Asian, no full reckoning of human religious life can be made without taking into account China, Korea, and Japan.

MODERN EAST ASIAN COUNTRIES AND THEIR RELIGIOUS ORIENTATIONS

What is today referred to as China is the People's Republic of China (PRC). With over 1.3 billion citizens, it is the country with the largest population in the world. Different dynasties up to the present have struggled to unify the dozens of minority peoples of the periphery regions with those of the core region who have called themselves Han and whose descendants speak the Chinese dialect Mandarin. Although spoken Chinese contains over twenty major dialects, the literate culture of China has used the same written language for more than 2,000 years. This has made the classical literary tradition (including all religious texts) accessible to the learned throughout the entire East Asian region (see Map 8.1). Mandarin language and Han culture effectively wielded by state officials did prove capable, at times, of unifying vast domains.

The formerly unified Korean culture area, artificially split into the separate countries of North Korea and South Korea since the end of the Second World War (1945), was most strongly influenced by Chinese cultural borrowings, including Buddhism. In the early modern period until the end of the Yi dynasty (1392–1910), Confucianism was the state religion, and the cult of ancestor worship became central in Korean society. Shamanic traditions, which are today stronger in Korea than elsewhere in East Asia, are found throughout the peninsula and are practiced by most individuals regardless of their institutional religious affiliation. Little traditional religious activity is sanctioned or reported among the 24 million people of the modern isolationist and communist state of North Korea.

China also generated wave after wave of influence over the island nation of Japan, but beginning later than in Korea. Now a constitutional monarchy headed in practical governance by a prime minister, Japan had for centuries been ruled by an emperor and a single imperial line claiming mythological origins that are distinctively Japanese. Since the end of World War II, however, Japan's 127 million people have produced the world's fourth-largest national economy. As elsewhere, this rapid transition has worked in contradictory directions, enriching devotees of every persuasion who have rebuilt institutions and created new ones while changing the society profoundly and so causing individuals to see the world in ways previously unimagined. This explains why "new religions" continue to spring up across East Asia, offering creative spiritual responses to life in today's fast-moving societies.

THE CHINESE CORE AND THE PERIPHERY OF EAST ASIA

China has been the formative center of the East Asian region from earliest antiquity. The emergence of a central state there predates the unification of Korea and Japan by at least twelve and fifteen centuries, respectively. Most modern national boundaries that demarcate the region date back to the premodern era. The two Koreas, the region of Tibet, and the republic of Taiwan are exceptions.

In very broad terms, all regions beyond China's early core can be seen as the periphery of Chinese civilization, where states and individuals selectively and creatively adapted the essential Chinese cultural forms. These forms encompass the

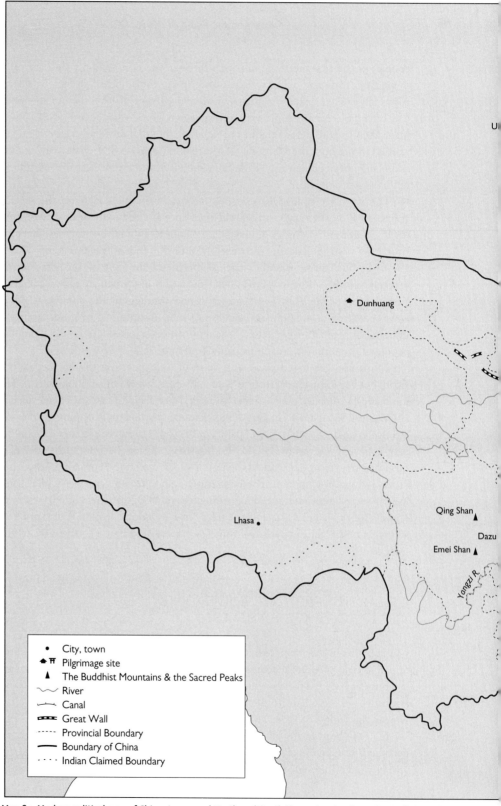

U|

● Dunhuang

Qing Shan ▲

Dazu

Emei Shan ▲

Lhasa ●

● City, town
♠ 开 Pilgrimage site
▲ The Buddhist Mountains & the Sacred Peaks
〜〜 River
—〜— Canal
▭▬▭ Great Wall
- - - - Provincial Boundary
——— Boundary of China
· · · · Indian Claimed Boundary

Map 8.1 Modern political map of China, Japan, and North and South Korea showing important religious sites.

Yellow R.

Yungang • Miaofeng • Beijing
▲ Shan
Heng Shan • Tianjin
Wutai Shan ▲

Jinan •
▲ Tai Shan
• Taian
♦ Qufu

Longmen
Layang • Kaifeng
ua Shan ▲ ▲ Song Shan
• Chang-an (Xi-an) Xionger Shan
▲ Nanwictai Shan

▲ Wudang Shan

Nanjing •
Jinhua Shan ▲ Suzhou • Shanghai
Poyue Shan ▲ Upper Tianzhu Monastery
Huang Shan ▲ Hangzhou ◄ ▲ Putuo Shan
• Ninpo
Tiantai Shan AyuWang Monastery
Lu Shan •
Shao Shan ▲ Longhu Shan ▲
Heng Shan ▲
Jinggang Shan ▲ Wuyi Shan

Nanhua Monastery ▲
▲ Caoxi Shan
Lofu Shan ▲
Guangzhou •

Hong Kong

Lao Shan •

Grand Canal

Pyongyang •
Dalian •
Seoul •
Kwangji •

Kumgangsan ▲

Tóngdo-Sa ▲

Nagasaki •

Amaterasu Jinja 鳥

SEA OF
JAPAN

Tokyo
Kamakura •
Fuji ▲
Okyoto •
Nara 鳥
Izumo • Tenri
鳥 Ise
Hiroshima •

PACIFIC
OCEAN

TAIWAN

0   500   1000 km

full range of what "culture" entails: the written Chinese characters used to record the spoken languages, the fundamental material technologies needed for subsistence (intensive rice production, the making of iron, and porcelain pottery), and the beliefs and practices of its great religious traditions. As we have seen, even Buddhism, which the Chinese themselves adopted, was transmitted to the East Asian periphery in the same pattern, through China.

Yet despite the overwhelming magnitude of Chinese culture and the nearly irresistible size and power of the Chinese states, Korean, Japanese, and Vietnamese peoples established and preserved their own separate identities. While importing and synthesizing much from China, each nonetheless developed a distinct spoken language, mythology, and spiritual connection to its geographical territory. In all these periphery states, too, the national cultures inspired people to identify with being separate culturally and politically from China, however much their elites admired Chinese culture. (In some cases, especially given the destruction and changes that have swept modern China, Chinese cultural forms of earlier eras are now best preserved in Korea or Japan.) Further, as is all too plain in the modern era, the extensive and long-standing cultural ties connecting East Asian peoples did not prevent expressions of enmity between the modern states that have ranged from colonization and warfare to genocide.

Encounter with Modernity: Postcolonial Confucian Economics

THE POSTCOLONIAL CHALLENGE OF CONFUCIANISM

By 1980 it was clear that modernity theorists who had predicted the decline of religion with the advent of science were incorrect in every instance. Nowhere have the flaws of this analysis been more striking than in East Asia, where indigenous intellectuals and reformers since the mid-nineteenth century blamed Confucianism for the region's decadence and failure to defend itself effectively against the imperialist West. The region's political despotism, social disintegration, economic retardation, scientific stagnation, poverty, and disease were all ascribed to its blind adherence to Confucian ideals and practices.

The more quickly Confucianism could be abandoned in favor of Western cultural borrowings, reformers argued, the sooner East Asia would be on the road to prosperity. For this reason, many welcomed the fall of the Chinese (1912) and Korean (1910) imperial states and with them the domination of Confucian officials and intellectuals. Yet as events transpired, not only has religion in east Asia survived, it has revived and expanded, often in surprisingly strong forms.

For example, early modernity theorists once attributed Japan's postwar prosperity solely to its successful and rapid Westernization. Although the war fomented by European-style fascism destroyed many of Japan's material accomplishments through the country's first era of modernization (1868–1945), the Japanese after World War II were still able to rebound and build what is today one of the world's strongest economies.

Scholars now see the success of Japan as the result of much more than its early and rapid Westernization: The Meiji era (1868–1912) facilitated the region's first union of Western technology and reformed Confucian social policy, one that was accomplished, too, in postwar South Korea, Taiwan, and Singapore and is now under way in post-Mao mainland China.

Thus, the socioeconomic analysis has been completely reversed. That is, we now find many scholars *attributing* the East Asians' success to the region's family-centered "bourgeois Confucianism" (as distinguished from the "high Confucianism" of the Mandarins, the former ruling elite).

The East Asian revival has also been realized in each instance by a strong post–World War II state that defines its duty in terms of providing leadership for the national economic agendas. This recent reinvention of Confucianism has produced societies marked by low crime rates, social harmony, and efficient economic behavior, which in turn has led to unprecedented success. Given the disastrous state of the region right after World War II, the overall accomplishment has been called an "economic miracle."

Now what reformers had identified as Confucianism's intractable flaws have been reanalyzed in positive terms: Family-based businesses efficiently maximize scarce capital; tightly woven kin/family relations are excellent building blocks for supply and product distribution; an education system that fosters group cooperation, memorization, and imitation has proven adept at producing individuals able to work hard and master math, science, and technology. With strong states dedicated to achieving collective economic success, it was clear by 1990 that East Asian peoples with this reformed Confucian orientation had risen to top global positions in all the major manufacturing sectors of the postmodern world and created successful twenty-first-century societies. Thus, after East Asians had acquired Western know-how, they effectively drew on Confucian elements in their cultures to mobilize indigenous social resources and create political systems that ensured the social cohesiveness needed to promote national prosperity.

Not only does this success challenge the West's historical monopoly of wealth and economic power, it disproves another former tenet of modernity theory: Is Westernization an inevitable consequence of modernization? Stated differently: Must all nations Westernize to modernize? Or is the Confucian route through strong authoritarian states an alternative for Asia, heralding what might be termed a "Third Confucian Epoch"? To understand better the significance of this encounter with modernity, we must go back to premodern times and trace the historical development of religion in East Asia.

East Asian Religions in the Premodern Era

East Asia is extraordinary among the world's regions because many beliefs and practices documented from earliest antiquity (1500 BCE) survive there in the present. To convey just how strong this conservatism has been, consider the example of deities worshipped by China's imperial court: A list of the gods receiving sacrifices from the last Qing emperor in 1907 matches *exactly* the gods mentioned in a very early record (c. 1100 BCE), with the sole exception of Confucius (who lived almost 600 years after the Shang court). Therefore, it is important to survey the emergence and early development of Chinese religions to discern religion's pivotal importance in Chinese civilization and to see how its religious beliefs and practices spread to other East Asian societies.

EARLIEST HISTORY: SHANG (1766–1122 BCE)

In the fertile valleys of the Yellow River, urban societies formed by 2000 BCE, and their settlements reveal a distinctive complex of advanced metal technologies, a pictographic writing system, and religious practices. All three of these aspects of civilization are connected in the practice of oracle bone divination, which was discovered among the northern peoples who lived within walled cities and called their rulers the *Shang*. Questions were inscribed on dried large bones of animals. A ritualist then applied a hot metal bar to the bones and discerned answers from the cracking patterns produced. Among the over 150,000 Shang oracle bones found and deciphered to date, "this-worldly" concerns predominate—questions regarding whether to undertake military action, hunts, journeys, or ceremonies as well as the interpretation of omens believed to predict weather, illness, or the sex of unborn children.

Among the Shang, too, were master metal casters who made finely decorated bronze vessels that were used in ceremonies to worship deities and ancestors. Elaborate offerings of drink and food, including animals dispatched on altars, were arrayed at early Chinese burial sites. Inscriptions on the vessels indicate that the Shang legitimated their rule by claiming the unrivaled supernatural power of their own ancestors to act on their and the society's behalf. This Shang notion of reciprocity between dead and living—food and honor bestowed by the living in return for blessings from the dead—remains to the present day a central aspect of East Asian religions.

The cult of the dead assumed vast proportions in the case of the ruling elite, for whom large tombs were dug and around whom all the essentials for life in the "next world" were buried. Among the Shang, there was the practice of interring sacrificed human servants alongside the nobles; in the case of the later emperors, similar grand tombs were built, but terracotta replicas of servants and animals replaced living beings.

Intimacy between humans and their gods, and easy access to them, is another important religious belief known from earliest antiquity. The Shang saw gods as immanent in rain, mountains, and rivers; early Chinese attributed significance to patterns and events in nature and made offerings to particular gods associated with them. Spirits were thought to affect all areas of life, from military battles and foreign relations to business fortunes, marriage, and illness. The presence of gods and ancestor spirits was most dramatically attested to by people who served as spirit mediums and were called *wu/xi* (women/men). Through their possession by the deities, the *wu/xi* made ready contact with the supernatural, and through them Chinese sought to solicit divine aid as well as to exorcise the demons blamed for causing personal sicknesses or troubles. Over time, this notion of spirit agency became a central characteristic of the popular religion.

There is an interesting Shang concept of a high deity called **Shang-di**, "the Lord Above," regarded as so powerful that only the Shang rulers could petition him. The name signifies the elevation of one Shang ancestor to supreme status, though *Shang-di* endured subsequently in popular imagination as the superior deity who monitors and provides cosmic sanction for human behavior. (Modern Chinese Protestants have used the term as a translation of *God*.)

Thus, the diffuse religion found later in East Asia stems from beliefs prevalent in early China: the organic view of an interconnected universe, one peopled by spirits including dead ancestors, and the belief that unseen forces in heaven and on earth could be influenced by the petitions of shamans, oracle readers, and divine kings.

✤ *Formative Era: Zhou, Chin, and Han Dynasties* (*1122 BCE–220 CE*)

The millennium from the Zhou dynasty (1122–221 BCE) until the fall of the Han (206 BCE–220 CE) was "formative," in the sense that during this period most of the ideas and practices inherited from the past were developed in more systematic forms and recorded for the first time in textual compilations. It is also in this era that the great sages arose whose teachings would so strongly influence not only the Chinese elite but the entire region.

The practices surrounding ancestor veneration, the worship of deities, and the important role of the spirit medium all spread as the Mandarin-speaking population of China increased and dispersed south into the Yangtze River basin and further southward. Some extensions of early concepts can be noted. There was the development of **yin-yang theory** and the five substances theory (*wu-xing*: water, fire, wood, metal, earth) to order observations of nature and natural signs. The cult of **Tu-di Gong**, the "earth ruler" who controls fertility, became widespread among the largely agricultural population. By Han times, reflecting the growing rationalization of state law in Chinese society, Tu-di was addressed in legalistic petitions.

At court and among commoners, Chinese polytheistic theology regarded the deities as neither good nor evil but as potentially both: They can be agents of illness

Defining Terms

Our treatment of multiple East Asian religions in the same chapter calls for a brief explanation of the central terms. Each topic highlighted here is developed in the chapter.

For convenience, we use **Confucianism,** a Western term originating in eighteenth-century Europe, instead of the corresponding Chinese term, *rujia*, meaning "literati tradition." The tradition of the literati (or intellectuals) is rooted in the system of moral observance and ritual performance praised in the sixth century BCE by Master K'ung (or, in English rendering, **Confucius**), whose teachings were commented on and extended by subsequent sages. The Confucian tradition was made China's state ideology over two millennia ago, and it became noted for its wisdom books, political institutions, social teachings, and attention to self-cultivation. In this cumulative form and as adapted by medieval scholars influenced by Buddhism, the *rujia* tradition became the most common shared spiritual and ethical culture of China, Korea, and Japan. The scholars who edited the foundational texts and established the expressions of this tradition are known by Westerners as neo-Confucians. A mastery of the tradition's classical texts and central doctrines was at the center of the educational system and government bureaucracy until well into the modern era (1905 in China, 1867 in Japan, 1910 in Korea). Reflecting this diversity, we use *Confucianism* without imputing to the tradition a singular creed, ritual, or institution.

Daoism can refer to loosely connected philosophical and religious traditions and so always needs further specification. **Philosophical Daoism** aims to cultivate an immediate sense of personal connection with the primal force or reality of the universe, one that its sages labeled "the **Dao**," using a character that means "way" or "path." The sages of **religious Daoism** themselves are revered as humans who had realized super-

natural physical powers or spiritual immortality and have become divine. Through meditation or alchemy, this strand of Daoism advocated the sages' path to immortality, and eventually monastic traditions (on the model of Buddhism, imported centuries later) were developed to sustain communities of seekers. Many aspects of "applied" Daoism were developed to manage worldly life in East Asia: acupuncture to adjust the flow of the life force flowing in the human body, *feng shui* to help humans live their lives in harmony with the natural energy flowing in the natural and built environment, *Yi-Jing* and other forms of prognostication to determine the proper moment to perform important tasks (marriage, travel, etc.), *wu-shu*, or the martial arts, to focus human powers in order to overcome enemies.

Deity cults in traditional East Asia were universal. Springs, rivers, remarkable geographic features—particularly mountain peaks—are still thought to have extraordinary divine inhabitants whose spiritual force, or *ling*, is immanent. The same ling is evident and personified in wind, rain, the stars, and legendary figures whose souls endured and who became deities. Each sector of the earth, in fact, is thought to have a resident deity who serves as the counterpart of the government official in charge of the village, the town, the province, and the state itself, with a hierarchy of gods mirroring the human civil service. Across East Asia, the common popular perception is that the deities exist and that they can be contacted at temples. A person will question a god and then, through ancient divination rituals, attempt to discern an answer. In the popular conception, deities, like local officials, can be paid to provide favors; the big gods may be induced to discipline lesser gods (or demons) who cause troubles. Humans out of mutual respect are obliged to show the gods thanksgiving regularly for life, health, and prosperity. Gods who fail to provide assistance are reviled and abandoned.

Diffuse religion is the useful term that indicates what for most East Asians consists of a spiritual life that is centered within the family unit and immediate locality. It has its roots in the ancestor veneration and spirit worship of earliest antiquity but incorporates general and basic elements of Confucianism, Daoism, and Buddhism. The unity of a region's diffuse religion derives from the long-established state bureaucracy practice of promulgating full expressions of the common traditions; at times, scholars were assigned to codify the myriad texts and practices to give them coherence. From medieval times until now, traditional printed almanacs have been important texts that record such teachings and orchestrate yearly practices for families and localities. Among the major elements of the diffuse religion is belief in deities and in rituals relating to them. There is also a sense that the universe has fundamental forces and powers, requiring humans to seek harmony with them to achieve health and long life. Further, the world is believed to have certain natural hierarchies that must be acknowledged and respected, in forms prescribed by the ancient traditions. This requirement of hierarchical respect extends to one's departed kin. Finally, the strength of the diffuse religions comes from the conviction that the ways of the past should be revered and studied to discern the proper path to the future. At least since Confucius, Chinese people have accorded great respect to past traditions, resulting in a very long period in which states disseminated the core elements of East Asian religion across the entire region.

The *sectarian religions* in East Asia were institutional Buddhism and Daoism and the sects that arose periodically, often with the goal of overthrowing the state. Such separate religions were meaningful primarily for the very small elites who joined an order, adopted a singular discipline within one tradition, or sought individualistic sectarian goals. But over time, many sects ceased to advocate the singularity of their approach alone.

Thus it is hard to find firm boundaries separating the spiritual traditions of East Asia. The Dao is a concept shared by all schools, for example; indeed, the Buddhists used the term to define the Buddha's teaching (Dharma) in early translations. The goal of harmony is also common in each spiritual path. We are able to treat East Asia's religions under a single heading precisely because of the commonality of this "diffuse borrowing," the nexus of the diffuse religion in the home and among kin rather than in large institutions, and the pertinent attempts by elites and commoners alike to harmonize these rich traditions. In each nation, the inclusive harmonizing trait has been expressed with only slight variation: in Japan, "Shintoist in youth, Confucian as an adult, Buddhist in old age"; in Korea, "Confucian by obligation, shamanist at heart"; in China, "Confucian in the office, Daoist outside."

Yin	Yang
Dark	Bright
Earth	Heaven
Female	Male
Autumn	Spring
Valley	Mountain
West	East
Po Soul (grave)	*Hun* Soul (heaven)

The symbolism of the *Yi-Jing* was the main system for East Asians conceptualizing the incessantly changing universe, much as math equations are used to express the essential truths underlying the discoveries of modern science. The most common *yin-yang* symbol should be viewed as ever in motion, with the circles in each sector expanding until black becomes white and white black.

Terracotta warriors, unearthed from an imperial tomb outside Xi'an, China, had been placed with the emperor to serve him in the afterlife.

and disaster or the bearers of blessings. Most of the notable deities by the late Zhou were viewed with both hope and fear, as with the Lord of the Yellow River, whose waters usually bring lush harvests but whose floods can cause widespread death and destruction. The popular Chinese view of well-disposed deities pitted against chaos-disposed demons is one that contrasts strongly with the worldview of the elite that emphasized abstract rationalism or mysticism.

Ancestor veneration developed further in the formative era, with more elaborate concepts and practices surfacing regarding the afterlife. The tomb became the key place connecting the living and the dead. Texts found in excavated tombs mention belief in a soul that survives into an afterlife, calling it a *chao-hun* ("cloud soul"). With the notable dead were buried objects that would be useful to a revived soul, including ritual vessels for consumption (such as wine flasks).

By the Han era, texts deposited in the tombs suggest the notion that a supreme overlord, called **Tian di,** keeps records on each individual soul. Tomb scrolls detail personal acts that seem intended to verify celestial records and petition that the deceased be released from blame for any evil conduct. The belief that proper tombs can facilitate beneficial exchanges between living and dead grew stronger, for rulers had texts compiled to describe the proper rites, and these practices were then widely adopted across Chinese society.

The Zhou era was marked by considerable political instability and militarism. Regional states vied endlessly for control of territory and revenues, their rulers and officials showing little regard for moral order or respect for human life. Yet individuals arose who tried to formulate the principles on which a just society could be established and by which humane leaders should be guided. These ideas would become the central pillars of East Asian life. The emergence of these visionary thinkers at roughly the same time as the Greek philosophers and Indian sages makes them part of the world's *axial age*, so-called because future history turned as a result of the teachings originating then. Those who advocated individualistic retreat, learning from the natural world, and noninterference by the state as the best way to ensure humanity's flourishing were called **Daoists**. Those who wished to cultivate their own humanity through disciplined learning, ritual practice, humility, and active social service were called *Confucians*.

❖ *Confucius and the Literati Tradition*

Although one of the most influential figures in world history, **Master K'ung** (551–479 BCE) failed to realize his own goal of securing an influential position as a state minister. He was a most gifted, inspired teacher, and because his students collected and passed down his oral teachings to their own students, his ideas took hold. Confucius developed the concepts of righteousness and of **ren,** a term that has many shades of meaning but captures the sense of "being fully human." The chief means to ren was **li**, which consisted of ethical propriety, good manners, and the cultivation of traditional ritual performances on musical instruments, in sacrifices, and in ancestor veneration. The early Confucians imagined a male-led world, and their ideal was the *jun-zi,* a cultivated gentleman who learns from his teacher in youth and then continues to study constantly, both to develop his virtue and to serve others.

The most important aspect of the li is the individual's conduct within the family. Here the central principle is filial conduct (**xiao**). The key domain for xiao is the bond between child and parent, a relationship that implies mutual obligations on both parties within a hierarchical framework. Protection and nurturing by a superior were rendered in return for selfless service and obedience. Classical Confucianism conceived of this bond as the fundamental human connection and identified four other bonds as extensions of it. These are the ties between husband and wife, between elder and younger brother, between friend and friend, and between ruler and minister. The entire set comprised the Five Hierarchical Relationships, which, properly served, were to lead the entire society toward harmony and "human flourishing." If xiao began with serving one's parents, it was to continue with serving one's ruler, thus bringing to maturity one's own character.

Image of Master K'ung, whose Western name, Confucius, was coined by early Jesuit missionaries.

In East Asia, family metaphors are likewise applied to community, state, and heaven based on this idea. Confucius' theory was that if those who ruled and ministered both followed and encouraged the society's adherence to maintaining these ideals, all would benefit and the state's harmony would be ensured. As set forth in the *Analects*, the compilation of the master's teachings, anecdotes, and sayings, Confucius became a model for emulation for subsequent generations. The cultured human should be at ease while always showing careful respect; he is firm but kindhearted, an advocate for the practice of moderation who finds a natural balance in all endeavors. In one passage, the *Analects* describes Confucius' own search for the ideal:

At 15 I set my heart on learning; at 30, I firmly took my stand; at 40 I came to be free from doubts; at 50 I understood the decree of Heaven; at 60 my ear was attuned; at 70 I follow my heart's desire without overstepping the line."[1]

Although he is described as being unsure of the reality of the spirits, Confucius was emphatic on the need for individuals to develop a deep respect for others as well as to establish harmony in the personalities of their immediate kin by their careful performance of funeral rituals and the rites of ancestor veneration.

The success of Confucius' teachings was largely due to their systematic and forceful advocacy by several great disciples, notably Master Meng (or **Mencius**, 371–289 BCE) and Master Xun (298–238 BCE). The sayings of Mencius argue that human nature

Core Confucianism: The Five Relationships and Principles According to Mencius

Relationship	Principles of the Relationship
son and father	filial piety ↔ paternal example
minister and ruler	obedience ↔ righteousness
wife and husband	obedience ↔ faithful dominance
young and old	respect ↔ precedence and example
friend and friend	mutuality and trust (*hsin*)

Core Confucianism: "The Three Bonds" (San-kang)

Ruler over the Minister
Father over the Son
Husband over the Wife

The Three Bonds emerged as principles of state administration several centuries after Mencius, who argued that if they are followed, the world will be in peace; if the three are ignored, society will be in chaos. Later Confucian reformers taught that it was wrong to use the Three Bonds as a fixed hierarchy if they lacked the notion of mutuality and reciprocity.

is essentially good, that humans are naturally compassionate, dutiful, courteous, and inclined toward learning. Mencius also developed the Confucian view that the well-being of society depends on the virtue of the rulers and that it is the state's responsibility to ensure the flourishing of its citizens. Another especially influential theory of Mencius applied Confucian thought to the destiny of a state: If a dynasty rules by virtue, then it receives the Mandate of Heaven, an authorization that can be revoked if rulers cease to be virtuous.

Master Xun, the third of the classical Confucian sages, proposed a more pessimistic, mechanistic, and hard-edged application of Master K'ung's ideas. In his view, humans are inherently antisocial and the universe turns on impersonal forces. But

Lao Zi on an ox. The sage of Daoism depicted in a Ming-era painting

since people can be trained, once shown the good, they will inherently adopt practices that lead in that direction. Hence, Xun turned Confucians toward the careful study of the past, its ancient sages, language itself, and the texts that record the history of human experience.

By the end of the formative era, the two interrelated elements of the Confucian tradition were established: *inner sagehood* and *outer nobility*. Dynasties recorded their histories, officials and the discontented argued about the Mandate of Heaven, scholars revered the past and sought to both safeguard and study its records, and all looked to the earliest sages to model their own lives. We must also note that the notion of Confucius as merely a human, this-worldly sage was not universal even in early China. By the late Han, literature had already appeared across the empire describing him as a demigod.

❖ Early Daoist Philosophy

The formative era in China saw many other teachers who proposed alternative philosophies to meet the needs of organizing society harmoniously. Yet the most important and long-enduring critique of Confucian doctrine came from those who argued that social relations would be harmonious only after humanity had synchronized itself with nature and with the Dao, the mystical reality underlying it. In today's English, the name of this school is rendered *Daoist*.

Daoist ideas were being expressed in antiquity at roughly the same time as those of Confucius, and the first great expression of Daoism is the terse and poetic *Daodejing (Tao Te Ching)*. This often-translated work, traditionally attributed to an anonymous "Old Sage," or **Lao Zi** (Lao Tzu), aims to express the nature of the Dao while paradoxically beginning with the proviso that "the true Dao" cannot be spoken or adequately defined. Various cryptic passages suggest that the Dao that pervades all reality can be truly known only through silence and through experiences that transcend words.

In this philosophical system, Dao is the prime source of creation, from which the yin and yang forces emerge in ever-shifting harmonies. Dao determines all things and flows naturally as the mysterious and spontaneous energy (**de**) of the universe, functioning without the will or purpose of a divine creator. To experience the Dao, one must let go and pursue the path of noninterference (**wu-wei**) as in Lao Zi's dictum "Do nothing and nothing will be left undone." The best teacher is (to use the example of the *Daodejing*) water that flows freely with the natural forces and in all circumstances yet can overcome all obstacles.

The Daoists felt that the Confucians harmed society through imposing rules and artificial practices that interfered with humanity's natural inclinations. Their political message was to return to primal simplicity, with the state interfering as little as possible with the lives of the people. The highest calling for humans, argued the Daoists, is not state service but retreat into the mountains, where the reality of the Dao can be felt most clearly.

The second Daoist classic, the ***Zhuang Zi***, is attributed to and named after a sage who lived several centuries later, Zhuang Zi (Chuang Tzu, 365–290 BCE). Through lively parables and mind-boggling paradoxes, his sayings explore the mysterious reality of the Dao in everyday human experiences. The most famous example perhaps is his meditation on waking from a dream of being a butterfly. He asks: Which is "real"? Was Zhuang Zi dreaming of being a butterfly, or is the human Zhuang Zi instead merely that butterfly's dream? This text also explores death and advocates accepting the changes the mysterious Dao brings, including the naturalness of death's transforming us into other life forms. Such acceptance is the necessary step toward experiencing transcendent freedom.

Daoist mysticism provided a balance against the bounded rules and regulations of strict Confucianism, offering a rich lore of parables as well as spiritual guidance to those who retreated from government service or active social life. Daoist refuge is found in nature, and the natural world inspired subsequent Chinese artists, including poets and painters.

"Standing by the deep valley makes you think deep;

Scaling the heights makes you aim high."

—*Book of Yi Xun*

Deity from a Daoist temple, where immortals are worshiped to secure blessings.

❖ "Religious Daoism" (Dao Jiao)

Daoism exists as a religious tradition as well as in the philosophical form we have just discussed. The tradition we refer to as *religious Daoism* consists of many different schools with different spiritual disciplines, all seeking a way for individuals to achieve immortality. Their texts urge the emulation of sages who now ride the clouds like dragons and reside in paradises on islands in the eastern seas. There were two main avenues to reach this goal. The first required meditation aimed at strengthening and multiplying the life force (**qi**), typically through breathing exercises, fasting, and sexual practices. This inner alchemy (*nei-tan*) creates a subtle but undying spiritual essence that can survive the gross body's death. A second path involved the study of alchemy, the art of transforming such substances as mercury and gold into an outer elixir (*wai-tan*) that can, when ingested, give birth to an "inner child" whose body and soul are invincible to decay or death. Doubtless the Daoist mystics and alchemists who lived in secluded retreats contributed to the development of Chinese science and medicine as well as to the martial arts traditions, all of which applied Daoist terms and theories to specific and more worldly endeavors. Religious Daoism also focused on temples dedicated to the divine immortals, who were requested to help in practical matters such as making the rain fall and helping with the harvest or in vanquishing troublesome spirits.

❖ Daoism Traditions: Basic Beliefs

Philosophical Daoism evolved from the *Daodejing* and through subsequent thinkers, and, indeed, certain basic ideas from this elite tradition remain important across East Asia. First, there is in Daoism the "organic" notion that humanity is interconnected in a web of interacting natural forces, some visible, some unseen, all shifting and reversing direction when they reach their apex. The opposing yet complementary yin-yang forces became the means of comprehending and analyzing the universe and its effect on human destiny. Reality is best perceived through this interconnection, for in this movement the dynamic power of the mysterious and determining Dao can be discerned from moment to moment. The classic text describing "the state of the moment" is the *Yi-Jing,* and it has helped East Asians determine the various combinations of yin and yang forces at work in a given setting. Perhaps Song-era landscape paintings influenced by Daoism best convey to outsiders this sense of human beings finding their proper place in the vast natural world: Amid the great mountains and flowing waters, humans—inevitably dwarfed by the landscape—can find transcendent harmony.

The second central Daoist notion is that some individuals can attain a state of ultimate transformation, transcending mortality via alchemical, dietary, or meditative practices that impart the power to know and control unseen forces. The human condition is thus one of great positive potential; the human body is a potentially perfectible vessel, even though those who attain immortality are few. Here, Daoists join with Confucians in seeing the world as redeemable through human agency, with

> "The mysteries of Heaven and earth are embodied in the inhalation and exhalation. . . . Your internal energy must be gathered in its three forms: generative, vital, and spiritual energy. Once soul is merged into this unified spirit, it must be nourished. Vital, it will leave the body, ascend to the heavens, and become immortal."
>
> —Daoist Sage Wang Ch'ung

A recluse in the mountains. Hermits like the one in this fourteenth-century Chinese painting looked to nature for inspiration and as a source of primal energy (qi).

nature occupying a dual role as humanity's true home and teacher. In China, then, what many other religions refer to as secular is seen as sacred.

The third Daoist conviction is that the pursuit of simplicity is essential for spiritual development as well as for the betterment of society. Only the "natural person" who "goes with the flow" (**wu-wei**), avoiding unnatural action, can find the truth, and only a society whose citizens live in a simple manner can find true peace and justice. Daoism thus, with Buddhism, provided a counterculture to the Confucian establishment, one that served those who wished to withdraw from society or to critique the excesses of those in power, and even, at times, bolstering a rebel group's intention to overthrow the regime.

Teachings of Religious Wisdom

Daoist

"A frog in a well, restricted in his environment, is unable to talk about the ocean. A summer insect, confined to its season, cannot talk about ice. A poor village scholar, restricted by his learning, cannot discuss the Dao. A person can find spiritual truth only by leav-ing his home cliffs and riverbanks and gazing upon the mighty ocean. Only then can the seeker perceive his own place and begin to understand the Great Dao."

—*Chuang Tzu*

Source: Adapted from D. Howard Smith, ed., *The Wisdom of the Taoists* (New York: New Directions, 1980), pp. 82–83.

❖ *State Religion: The First Confucian Epoch (220 BCE–200 CE)*

The first full unification of China—from central Asia to the eastern coast—was brought about by the first Qin emperor, who instituted a central bureaucracy and state religion, both designed to promote social unity by harmonizing the forces of nature with imperial rule. China's first emperor, though making good on many of his lofty ambitions, obsessively sought personal immortality through Daoist alchemy and ruthlessly suppressed viewpoints he considered deviant. His Mandate of Heaven lasted only fifteen years (221–206 BCE).

The next unification of China occurred under the Han, who established an imperial university and examination system (121 BCE) that was based exclusively on Confucian teachings and texts. By the later Han (c. 175 CE) the content of the Five Confucian Classics had been officially established for the first time. Synthesizing treatises drawing on them guided the spiritual cultivation of Chinese life thereafter. Once fixed in literary form and connected with the authority of Confucius, the **Five Classics** provided the literati of subsequent centuries with a multidisciplinary and holistic perspective on humanity. The canon comprises the *Yi-Jing* (*Book of Changes*), *Shu Jing* (*Book of Documents*), *Shi Jing* (*Book of Poetry*), *Li Jing* (*Book of Rites*), and a historical work that records events in early Chinese states for the purpose of assessing blame and praise. The classics promoted a tradition of learning from the past to guide future governance, and they supported the view that for full development, a human must integrate historical, social, political, and metaphysical awareness.

The state religion developed in the Han placed the emperor as chief priest, advised by Confucian experts on ritual performance. The integration of Daoist thought in imperial religion was done by specialists who used Daoist techniques to interpret omens in the natural world. On behalf of the kingdom, the emperor alone could sacrifice to the spirits of the departed imperial ancestors; as the Son of Heaven, he revered heaven and earth as his symbolic parents and worshipped the primary cosmic spirits. The emperor held the Confucian Mandate of Heaven as long as he acted for the well-being of the empire; earthquakes, eclipses, and unusual weather were interpreted as signs that heaven might be withdrawing its mandate.

❖ Being Human: The Individual, the Family, and the Ancestors

The Confucian worldview fostered a sense of the person as at the center of multiple relationships, the most fundamental determined by the individual's gender, generational location in the family, and status in the empire. The notion of individualism that dominates the West and has spread across the globe through modernization is quite the opposite from this East Asian understanding. According to the norms of filial piety, the young owe obedience to parents, women to men, citizens to rulers.

The Confucian vision is that society will be in maximum harmony if individuals mute their individualistic desires to conform to the dictates of the Five Hierarchical Relationships, listed earlier. The ideal was for all the family to benefit in old age from the reciprocities that required their deference earlier in life and to have their political obedience rewarded by heaven's blessings. To support this understanding, Daoism contributed the belief that since human beings are a combination of heaven (*yang*) and earth (*yin*), which in their exact balance determine gender, personality, and health, they must pursue harmony in their social relations and so respect these primary relations.

All persons are also seen as benefiting after death from the Confucian ordering of life, since the living descendants are expected to attend to all the necessary rites to ensure their best possible destiny in the afterlife. Indigenous beliefs going back to the Shang era (1500 BCE) later merged with Buddhist notions to create a composite (and not completely integrated) understanding of the individual's fate after death. What emerged in classical China (and was accepted in Korea and Japan, too) was a belief in the concept of *karma* as known from Buddhism and an understanding that after death all souls undergo processing in a netherworld. Here divine magistrates carefully calculate karma by means of rigorous bookkeeping methods and then send the soul on to its proper destiny. In this way indigenous Chinese and Buddhist ideas coexisted in harmony.

Buddhist rituals for manipulating the death passage were developed throughout East Asia; in China, institutional Daoism created these rites, as well. In Japan, the great Buddhist monasteries included within their vast estates sites for family graves where the burial remains are kept and where ritual offerings can be made for departed kin.

In conception and in practice, then, ancestors live on in the East Asian family's presence and receive ongoing ritual attention: in the grave, in an ancestral tablet (located in the home altar or clan temple), and potentially in the underworld, especially in the first years after death. The Korean and Chinese practice of burning paper replicas of items considered useful in the underworld is thought to send relief to loved ones who are waiting out an intermediate state before reincarnation.

By the end of the Han, after centuries of state support, Confucian ethics centered on hierarchy and mutual obligation had thoroughly permeated Chinese society through proverbs, storytelling, theater, and songs. The key elements of the "diffuse religion"

Modern Chinese family grave site in Singapore, sited and designed in accordance with the principles of feng shui. Here family members gather twice yearly to feast and make offerings to their ancestors.

were widely shared and had come to include the notions of yin-yang theory, geomancy (*feng shui*), the major deities of the pantheon, and the understanding of the multiple souls. The Confucian literati were also convinced that they could unite the society around a common ritual discipline, with ancestor rites the universal and civilizing norm. The early Confucian sage, Master Xun explicitly recognized that people had different views of these rites when he wrote:

> Among gentlemen, rites for the dead are taken as the way of man;
> Among the common people, they are taken as matters involving demons.[2]

DEVELOPMENT OF THE MULTIPLE TRADITIONS IN POST-HAN CHINA, KOREA, AND JAPAN

We now move into the fractured China of the post-Han centuries (220–617), a time when the Confucian tradition so tied to Han rule fell into disfavor, at just the time when Buddhist missionaries arrived and secured a permanent place in China for their faith. It is in this period, as well, that Japan and Korea enter the region's religious history.

✤ *Expansion of Buddhism*

The transplantation of Buddhism from India into East Asia is one of the greatest cultural conquests in world history, matched in importance only by the conversion to Christianity of the peoples of Europe and the Americas and the conversion to Islam by many peoples of Eurasia. Buddhist monks reached China on the Silk Road through central Asia by 120 CE and later over the sea routes. Once established in China's major urban and cultural centers, Buddhism spread to Korea by 372 and then to Japan from Korea by 552.

Mahayana Buddhism entered Asia through merchants and missionary monks but became firmly established owing to the patronage of emperors and aristocracy. Most East Asians came to believe in karma and worshiped the Buddha and celestial bodhisattvas. Many eventually accepted enlightenment as the highest spiritual goal.

Chinese literati from the beginning recognized Buddhism's deviance from Confucian values and criticized it on several grounds, including its rejection of family life and service to one's kin and the worship of deities who originated from "barbarian" peoples outside China. The Buddhist ideal of monastic retreat for personal enlighten-

With a sacred mushroom in his pocket, a Daoist immortal plays his flute in paradise.

ment was construed as an antisocial behavior. But in splintered China after the fall of the Han, the Confucian literati had no strong state backing and so little power. In Korea and Japan, the literati tradition itself was newly introduced; Buddhist monks and nuns, however, still had to win over supporters of the local gods, whose priests attributed national misfortune and natural disasters at this time to the nation's acceptance of Buddhism.

These Confucian anti-Buddhist arguments would be recycled at various times, but for almost all of its first 500 years in East Asia, Buddhism was widely and deeply incorporated into the region's religious life, finding support in the imperial courts and eventually among all segments of society, from philosophers to farmers. As time went on, Chinese, Korean, and Japanese monks would formulate their own interpretations of the many Buddhist teachings, creating distinctive East Asian schools of textual study and practice.

✤ The Institutional Development of Religious Daoism

Another effect of Buddhism's rise to prominence was to motivate the hitherto-disparate adherents of Daoism to systematize their texts and teachings and to create institutions modeled after Buddhist monasteries. The regularized meditative regimes and elaborate rituals that eventually developed in the Daoist monasteries gave individuals many avenues for being Daoist in their spiritual development and for propitiating local gods.

By 300, there were several branches of religious Daoism that had formalized early practices. Guo Hong (283–363) was the most prominent figure, known for his seeking to harmonize the tradition with Confucianism. Beginning with the notion that heaven's greatest creation is life itself, he argued that pursuing longevity and immortality must be the greatest human goal. Guo prescribed a very specific path to that goal, based on moral goodness, social service, and alchemy utilizing two metals: gold (which neither corrodes nor diminishes if buried or melted) and cinnabar (a red mercury ore that keeps changing as long as it is heated). This "inner alchemy" culminated in the practitioner's ingesting the perfectly refined substances, reversing Lao Zi's formula of creation, ending in oneness with the cosmos, as in the nearby box.

Revived Daoism competed with Buddhism for favor at the imperial courts, and devotees among the emperors spread the reformed and newly organized tradition across

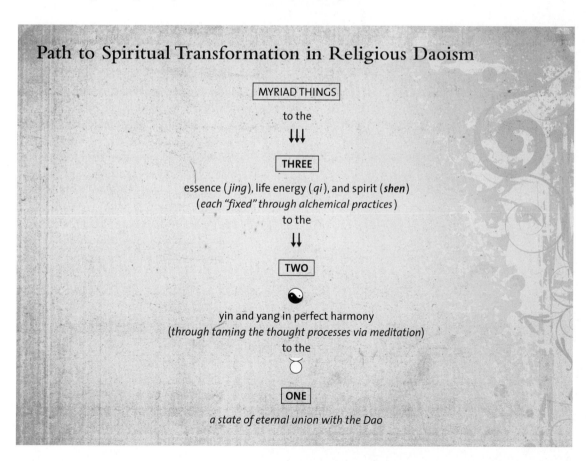

Path to Spiritual Transformation in Religious Daoism

MYRIAD THINGS

to the

↓↓↓

THREE

essence (*jing*), life energy (*qi*), and spirit (*shen*)
(*each "fixed" through alchemical practices*)

to the

↓↓

TWO

yin and yang in perfect harmony
(*through taming the thought processes via meditation*)

to the

ONE

a state of eternal union with the Dao

The eight immortals of Daoism, depicted in a Qing dynasty hanging scroll, with the Three Stars and the Queen Mother of the West. These were the chief divinities enshrined in Daoist temples from the Ming period onward.

China. The new monastic orders strengthened Daoist traditions. In 471, Master Lu Xin-jing (406–477) completed the first cataloging and organization of the Daoist scriptures. He found 1,226 texts for inclusion in this canon, which he called *The Three Caves*. Later commentaries expanded the tradition's literature by thousands of additional works. Organized Daoism never penetrated Korea or Japan through monasticism, but organized Buddhism did. We now turn to this important cultural export from China.

✤ *Early Korean Buddhism*

For the first millennium of the Korean state, Buddhism dominated the spiritual formation of the nation. Mahayana Buddhism entered the Korean peninsula through missions by Chinese monks. The Chinese monk Shundao ordained the first Korean monks in 384, and by 554 its monks and artisans had brought Buddhism to Japan along with a wave of Korean immigrants.

From roughly 700, the Korean version of the classical Buddhist formula of "state-protected Buddhism" was in place. That is, the state protected the tradition in return for monks performing rituals designed to benefit the state. Lavish patronage enabled Buddhism to flourish; all the Chinese scholastic schools were introduced, and Koreans journeyed to China, where some became influential monks. In Korea, the scholarly assimilation of the faith led not to competition but to attempts to find common ground. As a result, under the Silla dynasty, Korean Mahayana Buddhism became the most ecumenical in Asia.

RELIGION UNDER THE EARLY JAPANESE IMPERIAL STATE

In Japan, as elsewhere, Buddhism began among the elite, who saw in it a means to unite a fragmented land. Indeed, it was under the royal sponsorship of Prince Shotoku (d. 622) that Buddhism became the state religion. By 741, an edict called for officials to

Amaterasu: Kami of the Sun

In Shinto mythology, a primordial couple creates the physical world and the numerous deities who inhabit it. Most important among them were the moon goddess, a male earth god, and his sister the sun goddess, Amaterasu. In the earliest myths, distressed by her brother's impertinence and rudeness, Amaterasu hid in a cave, darkening the world. Only after the other kami gathered offerings, put on entertainments, and attracted her with a mirror did she restore light to the world. The reformed earth god and his ally, the kami of Izumo prefecture, then blessed the people of the islands of Japan. A grandson of Amaterasu, having received training from the gods and blessings from the Izumo kami, was designated the divine ruler of the nation, and he established the chief shrine for Amaterasu on the seashore at Ise, with a mirror as her symbol. Most Shinto shrines include a mirror, where devotees can honor the sun goddess.

Wood-block print of the sun goddess Amaterasu, legendary progenitor of the Japanese people.

establish a Buddhist monastery and temple in every Japanese province, enroll at least twenty monks and ten nuns, and recite texts and perform rituals for the benefit of emperor and state.

But Buddhism was not the only foreign belief system to shape the development of Japan: Confucian texts and teachers from China were also influential in the early courts. A seventh-century reform established a Confucian bureaucracy modeled after that of China. Daoist ideas of natural harmony and energy flow, both in the environment and within the person, along with yin-yang analysis, were part of this broad cultural influence. Neither a Daoist priesthood nor a monastic network, however, was ever established. Moreover, the Japanese never ceased to worship their own distinct divinities, believing the islands themselves to have been established by these native deities, the *kami,* who remain eternally present. This religious tradition is called **Shinto**.

❖ *The Shinto Pantheon of Japan*

In many respects, the Shinto tradition in Japan shares basic assumptions and practices regarding deities found throughout East Asia. **Shamanism** also developed in Japan, because its mediums gave the community access to the gods as well as to their departed ancestors. Pilgrimages to mountains thought to be divine abodes were common. However, as Shinto mythology developed, it was disseminated, systematized, and adapted by the early state. These accounts portrayed Japan as a unique spiritual territory filled with the distinctive deities called **kami.** The existence of an extensive set of legends focused on the kami enabled the Shinto priests to enshrine and relate to a unique pantheon. This helps explain why the Japanese, despite the importation of many other aspects of the country's religious life from China and Korea, were less ready to adopt Chinese deities and folk traditions.

The Shinto pantheon is headed by **Amaterasu,** the kami of the sun, credited in Japanese myth with having aided in the creation of the country and with being a progenitor of the royal family. Other kami exist in profusion. Some are associated with the natural forces of wind, thunder, lightning, and rain; some are thought to dwell in natural objects, such as mountains, rivers, trees, and rocks; some are ancestral spirits; and some dwell in certain animals, such as cows and foxes. Exponents of Shinto emphasize the "this-worldly" and positive perception of life, society, and nature that their indigenous faith has imparted. Shinto shrines often display mirrors as symbols of Amaterasu and for their symbolic meaning: Free from dust and capable of reflecting images with natural clarity, these symbolize the Shinto ideals of purity and brilliance. For this reason, too, Shinto shrines are traditionally located in bright, sunny areas. In the modern period, the state regulated and reformed Shinto for it to become, as we shall see, a vehicle for modernization.

CLASSICAL IMPERIAL CHINA (645–1271 CE)

With the era of the T'ang (618–907), when China was again unified after centuries of fragmentation that followed the fall of the Han, Buddhism reached its maximum

---

"The belief is that the new year is given to us by . . . the kami of years. What comes from the realm of the kami is inherently good, . . . so we look out upon the possibilities of the new year, and we want to purify our blunders and cast off whatever evil influences we may have accumulated in the old year."

—Shinto priest Uesugi Guji (1987)

Source: John K. Nelson, *A Year in the Life of a Shinto Shrine* (Seattle: University of Washington Press, 1996), p. 207.

development on the continent. Early on, Buddhism in northern China appealed to non-Han conquerors and in the south succeeded through popular and charismatic monastic preachers. But in the T'ang era, there developed more unified, panregional monastic networks among seven doctrinal schools; to interpret the confusing welter of texts from India, each school took as authoritative a different source of the Buddha's highest teachings.

T'ang China, with its capital in Chang'an (modern Xi'an), was the world's most advanced civilization of its time. Living within the high city walls were merchants from across the Eurasian world, distributed in communities of Nestorian Christians, Hindus, Manicheans, Zoroastrians, and Muslims. These resident aliens mixed with Buddhists and Daoists, who had their own numerous monasteries and temples. The wealth from trade, efficient taxation, and imperial patronage underwrote a golden age that found expression in all the fine arts while spreading Buddhist influences and religious practices across the empire and into both Korea and Japan. Adventurous Chinese monks, such as the renowned Xuan Zang (d. 664), even traveled to India in search of additional texts and teachers; Chinese emperors likewise lavished patronage on brahmins from India, who were reputed to be masters of longevity medicine.

However, in 845, edicts by Emperor Wu-zong abruptly and destructively halted an era of religious toleration in China. This powerful emperor was partly motivated by considerations of manpower and finances: With the success of Buddhism, more lands were being donated to the monastic community, thereby losing their taxable status; and ever more men and women were joining Buddhist orders, exempting themselves both from taxation and, in the case of the men, from military service. Wu-zong's second motivation was religious. He was an ardent Daoist and eager to advance the Daoist tradition's standing.

Within one year, Wu-zong forced 250,000 Buddhist monastics to return to lay life and confiscated all but forty-nine monasteries throughout the empire. Officials destroyed sacred texts by the tens of thousands and melted down Buddha images for the imperial mint. Although this aggressively anti-Buddhist policy was reversed by the next emperor, the damage was quite severe: Buddhism's predominance was drastically reduced, and Buddhism was never again to dominate China's religious landscape.

The later T'ang was a time marked by the resurgence of Confucianism. This tradition had continued to guide the familial life of commoners, and Confucius himself was used as a symbol of national unity. The development of classical Confucianism as the sole concern of philosophers waned, however. The literati tradition's triumph, through a selective assimilation of Buddhist and Daoist elements, lay ahead.

✦ Song Dynasty: The Second Epoch of Confucianism (960–1279)

The so-called Second Epoch of Confucianism erected for the literati a profound philosophical edifice that rivaled that of Buddhism and Daoism while supporting the older social ideology of human relatedness based on hierarchy, age, and gender. Thus, the Confucian elite again moved to the center of Chinese religious life, a development that occurred later in Korea and Japan, as well. Significantly, the Song dynasty

administrators restored mastery of Confucian learning as the basis for winning a position in its burgeoning civil service. This measure, coupled with relative neglect of Buddhism by the authorities, provided a strong inducement for a return to the Confucian
classics as a subject for study, further scholarship, and teaching. As the best minds of the
day once again were drawn into reinterpreting the indigenous tradition, private academies that instilled virtue and erudition flowered. In addition, anthologies of Confucian teachings compiled by leading Song literati were influential not only in China but
across the entire East Asian region.

The tradition's great "Second Master" was **Zhu Xi** (also written Chu Hsi) (1130–
1200). The works compiled and commented on by him, entitled *Jinsi Lu* ("Reflections
of Things at Hand"), were immensely influential. Zhu Xi gave students a curricular
order in which to study the classics and powerfully articulated long-standing polemics
against Buddhism and Daoism. Zhu Xi also added brilliant reinterpretations of Confucian doctrines, thus codifying the thoroughgoing system of thought that has been
labeled **neo-Confucianism** in Western parlance.

Despite its apparent criticism directed against Daoism and Buddhism, the neo-
Confucians in fact were strongly influenced by both. Of equal importance in securing
the success of neo-Confucianism was Zhu Xi's compilation of a ritual manual that
imparted Confucian procedures and cogent rationales for all life-cycle rites, clearly
giving non-Buddhist and non-Daoist practices around which the majority of Chinese
ordered their lives. This ritual text, like the *Jinsi Lu,* was influential across East Asia.

Neo-Confucianism's strength was that it provided both the individual and the state
with a convincing framework for understanding the world. Song thinkers argued that
Confucianism was built on the interconnected unity of humanity with the natural
world. They tried to understand perceived phenomena through a series of polarities that
associated yin-yang forces within the triad of heaven, earth, and humanity. The neo-
Confucian philosophers emphasized that education was needed to perfect human
awareness of li and that inner meditative cultivation (a borrowing from Buddhism),
which Zhu Xi called "investigating the nature of things," was needed to perfect the qi.
Almost all the neo-Confucians assumed the reality of karma as one of life's causal agents.

❖ Neo-Confucian Theories of Order, Hierarchy, and Relatedness

The established Confucian notion of the self that became reinforced in family norms
and in state law is decidedly not that of the isolated individual but of the person as "a
center of relatedness." It can be understood in terms of a series of concentric circles,
with the assumption that to reach their highest potential, persons must act harmoniously within their families, local communities, and states and with heaven beyond.
This scheme clearly implies that engagement in culture and community is necessary
for both the person and humanity overall to flourish. As the Confucian classic, the
Great Learning, states:

> The ancients who wished to bring order to their states would first regulate
> their families. Those who wished to regulate their families would first cultivate

"The ideal sage is one
who is first in worrying
about the world's trou-
bles and last in enjoy-
ing its pleasures."

—Fan-Chung-Yen
(989–1052)

Source: Arthur Wright, *Buddhism in Chinese History*
(Stanford University Press,
1959), p. 43.

their personal lives. Those who wished to cultivate their personal lives would first rectify their minds. Those who wished to rectify their minds would first make their intentions sincere.

Those who wished to make their intentions sincere would first extend their knowledge. The extension of knowledge consists of the investigation of things. . . . Only when the personal life is cultivated, the family will be regulated; when the family is regulated, the state will be in order; and when the state is in order, there will be peace throughout the world.[3]

The elaboration of meditative practices and multidisciplinary studies by the neo-Confucian masters established a rich tradition designed to develop the individual's integral relations with each circle (see the nearby illustration):

Heaven (World (Nation (Community (Family (SELF)

Such later figures as Zhang Zai (1020–1077) went on to combine this concentric conception with the Daoist ideal of finding "full humanity" by merging with the cosmos:

Heaven is my father and Earth is my mother, and even such a small creature as I finds an intimate place in their midst. Therefore that which fills the universe I regard as my body and that which directs the universe I consider as my nature. All people are my brothers and sisters, and all things are my companions.[4]

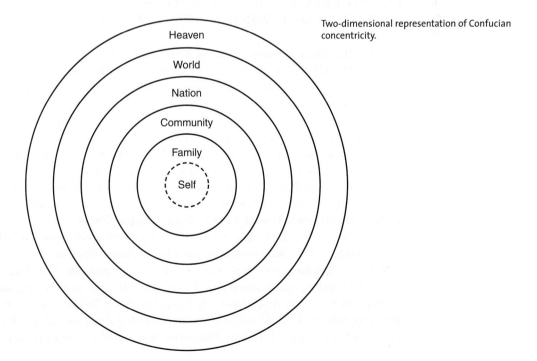

Two-dimensional representation of Confucian concentricity.

Heaven
World
Nation
Community
Family
Self

Tales of Spiritual Transformation

Confucian

Only one who is perfectly truthful can give full realization to his human nature; able to give full realization to his human nature, he is then able to give full realization to the human nature of others; able to give full realization to the human nature of others, he is then able to give full realization to the nature of other creatures; able to give this, he can then assist in the transformative and nourishing processes of heaven and earth. If he can assist in the transformative and nourishing powers of heaven and earth, he can then form a triad with heaven and earth.

Source: *Maintaining Perfect Balance*, a Neo-Confucian classic, in Daniel Gardiner, *The Four Books* (Indianapolis, IN.: Hackett, 2007), p. 124.

The popular convergence of the classical traditions in late traditional China was inspired by Zhu Xi, Zhang Zai, and other figures who sought harmony by learning from all orientations. The "diffuse religion" still extant in contemporary East Asia stems from their brilliant syntheses of ancient sources.

THE DEVELOPMENT OF BUDDHISM, DAOISM, AND CONFUCIANISM IN KOREA AND JAPAN

In Korea, Buddhism flourished under imperial support once the country had been united under the Silla dynasty (668–918). Ties to Chinese Buddhism were strong, and almost all of the Chinese schools had Korean counterparts. Korean monks were notable in China, and their commentaries on major texts were studied in both Japan and Tibet. Yet over time, Korean monks were most successful at finding harmony rather than division in their development of the tradition from the various schools and teachings.

Religion in the Koryo dynasty (918–1392) continued in this mode. Uniquely Korean was the dominance of the Chogye-chong branch of Son (Ch'an/Zen) Buddhism, which was to become the most influential in subsequent Korean Buddhist history. During this period the scholastic schools introduced from China were assimilated and merged into new entities that more closely reflected Korean culture.

The assimilation of Buddhism in Japan had ecumenical aspects as well. It had continued strongly with the movement of the capital to Kyoto by 800 CE, as various elements of Mahayana Buddhism and Daoist theories of yin-yang imported from China were effectively integrated with Shinto practices to meet the needs of an expanding state.

The later Kamakura era (1185–1333) ushered in almost 700 years of rule by military leaders who usurped the power of the emperor to establish a social system closely akin to that of European feudalism. This period was one of widespread contact with

China, as trade grew and Buddhist monks were instrumental in bringing new ordination lineages from the two schools that had survived the persecutions in post-T'ang
China: Pure Land and Ch'an/Zen. The notable monks of this era also brought exponents of neo-Confucian learning, literature, and the arts to Japan.

The disorder and suffering in the Kamakura also led to dramatic changes in Japanese religions, especially Buddhism. It was widely believed that the world had entered
into a period of **mappo,** or decline, in which human capacity for spiritual pursuit had
become degraded. This perception was used to justify new interpretations of Buddhism
appropriate for this degraded age. Thus, the Kamakura religious leaders in Japan established the framework for subsequent schools that remained relatively stable until the
early modern era.

The most popular Buddhist school was Pure Land, and in Chapter Seven we
encountered its polemical advocate, Shinran (1173–1262). Shinran and other Pure
Land exponents taught that an individual's salvation was completely in the hands of the
Buddha of the Pure Land, whom they called Amida, from the Sanskrit name Amitabha.
They emphasized the practice of repeating Amida's name and the belief that faith alone
could achieve nirvana realization in the mappo era. Shinran ended the requirement of
monastic celibacy, and Pure Land remains the largest Buddhist school in Japan today.

The second new school established during the Kamakura era was Zen, and it, too,
was brought from China, by two Japanese monks, Eisai (1141–1215) and Dogen
(1200–1253). In adopting sitting meditation, mind puzzles (koans), and unusual teaching methods, Zen masters created an innovative lineage of Buddhist practice. It also was
very traditionalist, however, in rejecting the concept of mappo and resisting the other
schools' radical simplification of Buddhism into mere ritual repetition and reliance on
faith. Zen teachers insisted that each individual had to win his or her own salvation on
the meditation mat through persistence and self-power alone.

Tales of Spiritual Transformation

Buddhist

"Late one night a female Zen adept was carrying water in an old wooden bucket when she happened to glance across the surface of the water and saw the reflection of the moon. As she walked the bucket began to come apart and the bottom of the pail broke through, with the water suddenly disappearing into the soil beneath her feet and the moon's reflection disappearing along with it. In that instant the young woman realized that the moon she had been looking at was just a reflection of the real thing . . . just as her whole life had been. She turned to look at the moon in all its silent glory, her mind was ripe, and that was it . . . Enlightenment."

Zen Master Chiyono, *No Moon, No Water*.

Another remarkable Buddhist leader of this era was **Nichiren** (1222–1282), a monk who opposed the Pure Land schools and in fact all the other Buddhist orders. He attributed the decline in Japanese life to the neglect of the *Lotus Sutra,* which he viewed as containing the supreme teaching. The Nichiren-shu advocated chanting the name of this text as the means for personal transformation as well as national renewal. (It is a practice continued to the present day in the **Soka Gakkai**, a modern Nichiren-derived school that now spans the globe.)

In the Kamakura era, ideas regarding Shinto–Buddhist accommodation were heard from both sides: Shinto exponents argued that the Buddhas and bodhisattvas were really indigenous gods, and the Buddhists built Shinto shrines in their monastic court-yards, consistent with the view that the kami were in fact protectors or bodhisattvas. This urge to harmonize the various spiritual traditions was one that Japan shared with Korea.

EAST ASIAN RELIGIONS IN THE LATE CLASSICAL ERA (1400–1800)

The four centuries preceding the modern era show few religious innovations across East Asia. It was a time when philosophies of interest to the literati were more fully commented on, printed, and disseminated, as in the case of neo-Confucianism in Japan. For Buddhism, this era is characterized by unsteadiness in both state support and spiritual vitality, with Korea the most prominent among those acting to reduce the political power of Buddhism.

Across East Asia, the diffuse religion remained central, as ancestor ritualism, local cults to important deities, and the role of the spirit mediums defined the religious field in cities and villages alike. For Ming-era China (1368–1644), the popular text *Feng Shen Yan-yi* (*"The Canonization of the Gods"*) was especially influential in promulgating the idea of an orderly pantheon of Chinese divinities in a hierarchy that included Bud-dhas, immortals, gods, and local spirits. Throughout China, a standard organization for the state's official religion was fixed in each province. There would be a Confucian temple with major disciples, a military temple featuring the war god Guan Yu and other notable heroes, and a **city god**, who supervises all the village earth gods.

✥ *"The Unity of the Three Traditions": Late Ming to Early Qing Eras in China*

The Chinese emphasis on harmony was also extended to "the unity of the **three faiths**" (*san-jiao heyi,* still a widely used phrase), meaning Confucianism, Daoism, and Buddhism. Many philosophers who were exclusively committed to one of these faiths still argued that their tradition was superior in answering the fundamental spiritual questions. But more popular were teachers such as Jiao Hong (1540–1620) who regarded all three teachings as in fact "a single teaching," stating that each merely uses separate language to articulate its truth and that all three could and should be believed. There were also other expressions of this era's delicate balance of combination and compartmentalization between these faiths:

> Use Buddhism to rule the mind, Daoism to rule the body, Confucianism to rule the world.[5]
>
> —*Emperor Xiao Zong (1163–1189)*

> Although the Three Teachings are different, in the arguments they put forward, they are One.[6]
>
> —*Liu Mi (active 1324)*

> If someone is a Confucian, give him Confucius; if he is a Daoist, give him Lao Zi; if he is a Buddhist, give him Shakyamuni; if he isn't any of them, give him their unity.[7]
>
> —*Lin Zhao'en (1517–1598)*

Among Confucians who most powerfully conveyed this ecumenical ethos was Wang Yangming (1472–1529), whose view of the "true gentleman" was based on the assumption that everyone can know the good and that "self-perfection" means knowing this goodness to the maximum. Wang argued, in language mirroring the "all beings have the Buddha nature" doctrine of Mahayana Buddhism, that all humans have the potential to achieve self-perfection, since all share a primordial awareness:

> Forming one body with Heaven, Earth, and the myriad things is not only true of the great man. Even the heart-mind of the small man is no different. . . . Therefore when he sees a child about to fall into the well, he cannot help feeling alarm and commiseration.[8]

Buddhism by the end of the Ming dynasty (1368–1644) had worked out its permanent place in Chinese civilization, as its monastic leaders taught Buddhist doctrine in ways to ensure that there would never be grounds for another imperial persecution. We thus find influential teachers such as Chu-hong (1535–1615) preaching that the essence of Buddhism was social activism as expressed through charity and moral action. He also emphasized that to be a filial child or a loyal subject was the first step in becoming a "good Buddhist." This view was expressed by many subsequent Chinese Buddhists.

The Ming dynasty also saw the beginning of regular contact with Europe, first with the Portuguese in 1514. With these traders and then with the first wave of missionaries, the Chinese found little to admire and much resented the "barbaric manners" of most of their guests. In this early era of small-scale contact, failure to institute good relations with the Europeans or to attempt to understand the world beyond China set up the problematic and confrontational geopolitical environment of the colonial era.

Teachings of Religious Wisdom

Confucian

The following is the text of a message of Emperor T'ai Tsung to a Korean ruler, returning his thank offering of two young and surpassingly beautiful women, showing his Confucian integrity, intelligence, and grace.

"Go back and say to your master that although beauty and a fair appearance are made much of by men—and truly his gifts are voluptuously beautiful—I pity them, separated from father, mother, and brothers older and younger in their own country. To detain their persons while forgetting their families—to love their fairness while wounding their hearts—this I cannot do."

The Qing dynasty (1644–1912) brought outsiders again in control of China, this time in the form of the Manchurians, who continued most traditional state administration. Confucian imperial ritual remained central to the state, and mastery of the classics was the basis for the selection of the literati who ran it.

The strengthening of Confucian ideas and practices throughout all levels of Qing society occurred through the *Sheng-zhi tu* ("*Pictures of the Sage's Traces*"), captioned accounts of Confucius' life and exemplary tales of ethical practices. The stories

Scenes from the *Sheng-zhi tu*, depicting the manner of showing filial piety (xiao).

appeared in a variety of media: on stone tablets installed in temples (Daoist as well as Buddhist), on silk paintings, and in inexpensive and widely disseminated block-printed books. Many versions of this theme appeared, offering alternative views of the great teacher. Some portrayed Confucius as a human being living an exemplary ethical life, others described miracles and magic, while still others emphasized the sage's command to make great ritual exertions. Many of these publications were also exported to Japan, where they influenced the efflorescence of Confucian studies and related arts in the Tokugawa era (1600–1868).

❖ *Japan in the Time of the Shogun (Twelfth to Nineteenth Centuries)*

In Japan during medieval and early modern times, there were no Daoist temples competing with institutional Buddhism or Shinto shrines, nor did the deities of "diffuse

Buddhism and Neo-Confucianism in a Popular Ming Tale

The *Journey to the West* (or "monkey story"), written by the Confucian scholar Wu Cheng-en (1500–1582), is a prime example of the Ming-era harmonization of the "three faiths." It recounts the journey of the great Buddhist monk Xuan Zang (d. 664) to search for texts in India. In this dangerous quest, he is assisted by the Monkey King, Sun Wukong, a figure from the Chinese folk pantheon. While ostensibly the account of a great Buddhist monk's journey, recurring incidents in the long tale (spanning four hefty volumes in English translation) are employed to teach self-discipline—a personal trait valued by both traditions—to the Monkey King and Confucian wisdom to the monk. In many episodes, the success of Xuan Zang's mission depends on the Monkey King's aid and on the monk's timely learning of the ways of the world. Translated into opera and folk ballads, the monkey story became one of China's most popular narratives, its major characters defining important personality stereotypes while conveying the pattern of Confucianism dominating the literati culture of the Ming.

The Monkey King leads the monk Xuan Zang and other companions, illustrating a scene from *Journey to the West*.

Chinese popular religion" find their way across the water. Instead, Shinto theologians presented the nation's deities in a uniquely Japanese pantheon, although the relationships between them varied by region and were not thoroughly systematized nationwide until the modern era.

Zen Buddhism, however, also exerted a strong ecumenical influence in this period. The Zen school's strong relationship with China fostered studies in both the texts of Daoism and the Confucian classics. It also promoted the acceptance of the idea that Daoist concepts and Confucian morality could be combined. Zen, the vehicle for Japan's cultural elite, adopted art forms derived from China, but Japanese masters soon took them to new levels of originality in such fields as ink painting, poetry, and tea ceremony.

Zen and the other Buddhist schools were closely tied to the ruling elites, who were a source of protection and patronage for their favorite monasteries and teachers. This relationship also led Buddhists then in Japan to vie for support among the factions at the top ranks in society, which most of them tended to view uncritically. The habit of overlooking discrepancies between Buddhist teachings and rulers' practices continued right into the modern period, when most monks were more concerned about accommodation with the elite than with reforming Japanese society or preventing war.

✤ Persecution of Buddhists and Christians

Although Buddhism enjoyed official support during most of the shogunate, Nobunaga (1534–1582) waged an anti-Buddhist campaign, going so far as to burn the great center on Mount Hiei, outside Kyoto, where Japanese Buddhism was first established. It was dislike of Buddhism that probably led Nobunaga to be receptive to the first Jesuit missionaries, giving Christianity more early support than it received anywhere else in East Asia. Much to the chagrin of the European missionaries, however, most Japanese had trouble seeing in Christianity anything but an obscure form of Buddhism. Catholic rituals appeared to be similar to certain monastic rites, and the concept of a heavenly Lord whose son became incarnate to serve humanity was not unlike Mahayana Buddhism's doctrine of the cosmic Buddha whose sons, the compassionate bodhisattvas, also served humanity.

But squabbles that developed among European Franciscans, Jesuits, and later Protestants, as well as some missionary attempts to manipulate Japanese politics in the name of their home countries, convinced Iyesu, the first Tokugawa shogun, to outlaw Christianity in 1606. When in 1616 he acted to expel all missionaries, there were already an estimated 300,000 Japanese converts. The next decades saw attempts by the Japanese state to extirpate Christianity. Some officials penned vigorous attacks against Christian doctrines that pointed out how the foreign faith clashed with the region's "commonsense" spiritual understandings and its norms of secular order. They also questioned the logic of a theology in which a reputedly omnipotent, benevolent God would allow "original sin," and they objected to biblical passages that seem to undermine loyalty to kin and ruler.

Other efforts at removing Christianity were gruesome, and many converts who would not recant their faith were tortured. A rebellion in 1637–1638 that resulted in over 37,000 deaths confirmed for its Japanese opponents the disruptive potential of Christianity. From this time onward, too, every Japanese family was required by law to be registered with a Buddhist temple, in an effort to regularize ties with Buddhism and to emphasize that in Tokugawa times being Buddhist was inherently part of being Japanese. (We will see, however, that in the post-Tokugawa era, nationalists argued the reverse, that is, that Buddhism was a "foreign religion" in Japan!)

❖ The Regional Spread of Neo-Confucianism

Confucian thought spread under the Tokugawa shoguns. Confucianism—long present among scholars, in state ritualism, and as part of Buddhist moral teachings from China—finally found its own strong supporters in a succession of prominent Japanese philosophers, many of whom were not part of the samurai elite. For some, Confucian teachings gave those of lower birth ideals to uphold against the hierarchical system instituted by Japan's hereditary nobility. Unlike in China, the ideals of Confucianism spread among both the merchant class and the samurai as Japanese intellectuals throughout the Tokugawa era studied and defended the positions of all the major neo-Confucians. There were even some Japanese exponents who came to reject the neo-Confucian system and urged return to the original classics. Efforts were also made to rationalize Shinto beliefs with Confucian doctrines.

❖ Spiritual Training for the Religious Elites

By 1600 CE, all the religious traditions of East Asia had developed institutions and courses of training for those wishing to become scholars, ritual masters, or meditative adepts. Although a very small percentage of the entire populations actually were initiated into such disciplines, it is useful to understand something of the spiritual training that the region's different religious leaders (priests, monks, and nuns) had to undertake to fulfill their roles.

Confucianism Only under the guidelines set forth by the neo-Confucian masters did the literati (*rujia*) tradition acquire its own systematic regime. The first stage of training was "disciplining the body" (*shen-jiao*) by means of the zealous study of the six arts of Confucian education: ritual, music, archery, calligraphy, horsemanship, and mathematics. All were defined very broadly. For example, *ritual* means conducting religious rites as well as mastering the proper ways of eating, walking, and asking questions. The *Analects* provides many instances of seemingly trivial events associated with Confucius, but they had their use in just this context of providing the sage's life as a model for disciplined training.

Beyond foundational training, all the neo-Confucian subschools called for the "rectification of the heart-mind" and prescribed new practices: discipline manifested by outward zeal in investigating the external world as well as the personal goal of

Tales of Spiritual Transformation

Daoist

This Daoist tale describes how Zhuang Zi learned from his wife's death and explained his spiritual realization to a friend who discovered him drumming and singing instead of maintaining the expected Confucian decorum of solemnity.

I pondered over her beginning before she was born; not merely before she was born but when there was as yet no body; not merely when there was no body but not even a vital spirit. Within an inchoate confusion there took forth a transformation and there was vital spirit. The vital spirit was transformed and there came forth form, and with the transformation there was life. Now once again there is a transformation and she died. What happened may be compared to the four seasons. . . . Now she is lying in peace in a small room. For me to follow after her weeping and wailing would be an indication that I have no thorough understanding of human destiny.

D. Howard Smith, ed. *The Wisdom of the Taoists.*, p. 88.

knowing oneself. The aim was to become a perfected person, a *sheng-ren,* who has achieved fully his or her complete human nature. A common practice to realize this is called *quiet sitting*, one that its proponents were adamant on distinguishing from forms of Buddhist or Daoist meditation. This neo-Confucian meditation was not based on stopping discursive thought but on calming the mind from the flow of events, perceiving the goodness of the in-dwelling primal human nature, and becoming aware of selfish desires.

Daoism Like the Buddhists, Daoists sought a more individualistic "ultimate transformation" through practices that originated in antiquity. For philosophers such as Zhuang Zi, only through the practice of detaching from the mind (*wai-wu*) and ceasing to distinguish separated things could one find union with the Dao. In Zhuang Zi's writings, one also finds cryptic references to a "heart-fast" (*xin-zhai*) that starved the mind of all externalities, allowing one proficient in the practice to forget his senses, ideas, feelings, and wishes and so experience only the primordial and mysterious Dao. When the spiritual adept has reached this stage, the practice of "free and easy wandering" in nature can be fully undertaken. In the traditional poetic expression, one then ascends the cloud vapors, rides the flying dragon, and travels to the infinite. Facing death involves no travail and only blissful transformation.

Shintoism Until the modern era, Shinto priests of major shrines inherited their positions and learned the rituals from their fathers; thus they were always males from aristocratic families. Over the last 150 years, priests have had to pass a state-prescribed course of training at an institution such as Kokugakuin University, founded for this purpose. The role of the *shinshoku,* as the priests are usually called, involves mastery of the daily gestures of respect offered to the kami, the annual rituals of the shrine, calligraphy, and complex forms of ritual purification. Shinto has never developed any "inner" spiritual practices. For its modern exponents, however, the artful rituals oriented to the deities throughout the seasons offer a means of achieving refined sensitivity and moral transformation.

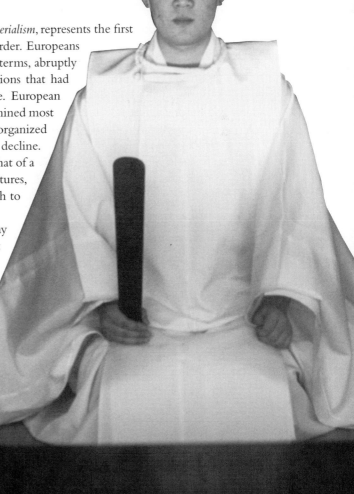

Attired in white robes that symbolize purity, a Shinto priest kneels in the Meiji temple in Tokyo.

East Asian Religions in the Early Modern Era

THE DISRUPTIONS OF IMPERIAL DOMINATION

Post-Enlightenment colonialism, also called *imperialism,* represents the first modern attempt to establish a global world order. Europeans forced Asian societies to change on European terms, abruptly imposing new ideas, technologies, and institutions that had evolved naturally over many years in Europe. European imperialism caused chaos and crises that undermined most institutions in premodern East Asia, with the organized religions especially subject to disruption and decline. Imperialism's impact in Asia can be likened to that of a strong earthquake, one that levels many structures, leaving only the strongest foundations on which to rebuild.

Understanding the world's religions today requires an awareness of this legacy, for East Asian religions and cultures were decisively altered over this period as never before. Though the effects of colonialism were overwhelmingly destructive, the fusion of older traditions with modern changes led to a number of religious innovations that were compelling and original.

By the beginning of the nineteenth century, European civilization had ascended as the supreme force on the global stage. The Renaissance had transformed Europe with powerful innovations in the intellectual, political, economic, and military spheres. The West's unprecedented sociopolitical dynamism and expansion of wealth accelerated up through the eighteenth century, when the major states (England, Netherlands, Portugal, Spain, Germany) vied, often militarily, to exert their newfound political and economic power around the globe. Internally, of course, Europe was diverse, transformed by its own class and ethnic conflicts, and facing newly arising problems; new ideologies competed with old to provide solutions to these crises. Some of these, too, were exported to Asia.

The emerging nations of Europe were above all self-assured of their superiority in every aspect of life, from morality and intellectual understanding to religion and technology. For many this included belief in the primacy of the white race, and many, too, saw in the march of colonialism a confirmation that Christianity would ultimately triumph on the world stage. Thus, some European leaders felt they were the vehicles of triumphant Christianity, and their merchants were soon dedicated to making their fortunes through overseas trade, ready to pursue often-risky ventures, and to do so quite ruthlessly.

Colonialism, like revolution (to paraphrase Lenin), was anything but a tea party. It forcibly changed every regional economy, promoted trafficking in narcotics when the opium trade was profitable, challenged East Asians' fundamental understandings regarding humanity and cosmos through science and Christian missions, and undermined the long-held view of Asia's ruling classes that their civilizations were the world's greatest.

The crisis of colonial encroachment and imperial challenge led the national elites away from their own indigenous traditions and on a forced march directed toward understanding the Western world and its technologies. From about 1850, across the region, the best minds in East Asia chose to learn about the West first and about their own traditions little, with the result that the Enlightenment mentality, with its revolutionary terms of analysis, entered powerfully into the cultural heritage of modern East Asia. Among a large portion of this Western-influenced elite, agnosticism or atheism replaced attachment to the indigenous spiritual traditions.

On the popular level as well, the era of colonialism has been perceived as a time of crisis. The common terms used to express the peoples' sense of inundation and powerlessness across East Asia were *humiliation* (*chi*) in Chinese, *bitterness* (*hahn*) in Korean, and *patient endurance* (*nin*) in Japanese. In sum, they give an overview of the modern era for East Asians as a time of trial, with each set of difficulties representative of the separate nations' slightly differing reactions to the experience of modernization.

It would be wrong, however, to see the history of East Asia as dictated solely by European actors and external forces. There were important internal dynamics at work in Korea, China, and Japan, and the different processes already under way in each shaped their emphatically different destinies under colonialism.

TRAUMATIC TRANSITIONS OF THE MODERN ERA

❖ *The Decline of Confucian Ideology and Exponents*

The crisis and rapid changes brought by the onslaught of imperialism ended the unchallenged influence of the Confucian elite in China, Korea, and Japan. The Confucian worldview and social ideology were subjected to scathing critiques by the native-born reformers of each nation, who took up the task of saving state sovereignty and attempting to match the wealth, knowledge, and power put on display by the Western imperialists. In addition, many young people abandoned the traditional curriculum to pursue "Western learning," honing their intellectual development by critiquing what they perceived as the disabilities imposed on society under the Confucian tradition. Finally, the fall of the Korean and Chinese states, whose political and economic resources supported Confucianism in many domains, made it certain that this tradition would lose its central place in the region's early modernization.

Confucianism was blamed for every ill visible in the region. The failure to develop modern trade was blamed on the classical ranking of social classes by occupation, which in the Confucian view of the good society placed at the top scholar-officials who administered the bureaucracy and taught in schools; below them were the farmers, followed by artisans, and finally the merchants. Confucius had no respect for merchants, whom he called "parasites," describing them as ever ready to take advantage of others, motivated by greed, and inclined to dishonesty.

The traditional Confucian educational system was also blamed for stifling the nation's technical development, inasmuch as it valued generalists over specialists and rewarded rote memorization and imitation, not independent thinking. Moreover, for the critics, the Confucian view of history as cyclical had made the elite prone to stagnation and disinclined to pursue innovation or progress.

The strongest terms of rejection were directed toward Confucian social norms and, at their center, family relations. The classical formula for social harmony that East Asians had incorporated from the ancient period, as we have discussed, was framed in two triads: the three bonds (between ruler and minister, father and son, and husband and wife) and the three principles (hierarchy, age, gender). Reformers found each of these principles to be an obstacle to modernization in many respects. Individuals who placed loyalty to family first, for example, were unable to extend trust to others as needed in the more impersonal workings of a modern economy. Similarly, filial deference to elders made individuals dependent on the collective family, thwarting the creative thrust toward individuality and encouraging a "Confucian personality" that either (in the young) followed authority blindly or (in the elders) gave too much power to those who were merely of senior rank. All such relationships were seen as stifling innovation. On the national level, reformers saw the "three bonds" as merely serving authoritarian political control. Both East Asian reformers and Western social scientists until the 1970s agreed that Confucianism was the key obstacle to the region's modernization.

A reconsideration of the characteristics fostered by Confucian humanism reveals that these Confucian elements also played a role in the region's ultimately successful response to the challenges of the postcolonial era. These include, for example, the high emphasis on education, the practice of carefully studying problems before taking action, the expectation that state officials will act for the good of the whole, and the intellectual elite's acceptance of responsibility for the nation's well-being. But what is certain is that the imperial system that supported the Confucian literati tradition was overthrown completely in China and Korea. By contrast, in neighboring Japan, the emperor-led state endured by melding nationalism with its own form of colonialism. Whatever Confucianism means exactly in the present day, a break with the past had irrevocably occurred. We must first turn to the important exception of Japan and its distinctive fusion of belief systems: melding modernization with Confucianism in the form of nationalist **neo-Shintoism**.

❖ State and Civil Religion in Japan: Neo-Shintoism

By 1882, a decade and a half after the demise of the shogunate and the restoration of the Japanese monarchy in the person of the Meiji emperor, the Shinto tradition was officially adopted as the state religion. To bring this about, most shrines and temples were integrated into a single system under government supervision. The emperor was revered as a divinity on earth, whose presence was a blessing to the nation. This idea was expressed at the national shrines in the capital and then in rituals regularly conducted in every local shrine as well; Japanese were directed to worship daily facing the emperor in Tokyo, just as Muslims to worship Allah face Mecca. The reformed educational system also centered its curriculum on the sanctity of the emperor, and all citizens were expected to honor him by working for the good of the nation. This was one of the Confucian elements in Japan's modernization.

A constitution adopted in 1889 limited Japanese citizens' freedom to express any opinions critical of Shinto doctrines and practices, especially the imperial ties to the indigenous deities, but it guaranteed religious freedom to followers of other religions as long as they did not undermine Shinto and were loyal to the nation. Those affected included the Buddhist schools and the Christian denominations, which were legalized again in 1863, as well as the "new religion" sects that multiplied throughout the modern era and are discussed later.

The Meiji state religion, or state-Shinto, can be labeled neo-Shintoist, for it was associated with the religious tradition of ancient origins that reveres the indigenous deities of the Japanese islands. It is also fundamental to see, however, that the "civil religion" constructed around Shintoism by the Meiji elite was thoroughly Confucian in character. It emphasized loyalty to the state, the norm of filial piety, self-sacrifice, and dedication. Moreover, it heralded the contributions of individuals that would be needed to make the modernization of Japan a success. Finally, a Confucian vocabulary was used to define the emperor's and the nation's mission, with special emphasis on the emperor's Mandate of Heaven. Thus, Meiji Japan was the first political entity in East

Asia to harness reformed Confucian values to meet the challenges of modernizing and adopting the technologies pioneered in the West.

✤ Institutional Buddhism

As we noted in Chapter Seven, institutional Buddhism took root in Asia by way of a monastic system in which monasteries became landlords reliant on lay believers to till the lands and on charitable donations from the faithful for other sustenance. At times of economic hardship or when the state could not extend customary protections, Buddhism declined. In general, the crises of the modern era across East Asia also deprived Buddhism of economic support, of donations, and of individuals who in other eras might have joined a monastic order and contributed to its vitality. Now the most gifted people wanted to learn about the West and to lead their countries in modernizing national industries, governments, and military establishments.

In nineteenth-century China, there were few signs of innovation and few Buddhists who rose to contribute to the national struggles. In Japan's long Tokugawa era (1600–1867), on the other hand, the military leaders supported Buddhism strongly, including the promotion of Buddhist pilgrimage as a means of having the Japanese acquire a sense of national integration. But the Meiji reformers felt it essential to reverse course, both to weaken pro-Buddhist foes and because they believed that Buddhist influences were inimical to Japan's Shinto-centered revitalization.

Procession bearing the local god (kami) through Kamakura, Japan during the Spring Festival.

Zealous attempts in the first Meiji years to prohibit Buddhism outright were abandoned, but the Buddhist tradition sustained considerable damage: From 1871 to 1876, the number of temples throughout Japan was reduced from an estimated 465,000 to 71,000. In 1872, the government decreed that Buddhist monks were free to marry and follow nonvegetarian diets, a move that undermined discipline and popular regard for renunciants in the sangha. The Buddhists successfully rallied support against further acts directed against them, but the Shinto-based nationalism and the state-encouraged challenges to institutional Buddhism forced followers to shift their emphases and rethink their doctrines in light of the changes under way in their society.

The Buddhist establishment after 1876 strove mightily to prove its patriotism and relevance, as a host of writers and lay organizations arose to explain why charges of disloyalty and obsolescence were unfounded. Major schools competed to implement Meiji social and national programs, and they, too, fanned the rising flame of anti-Western feelings, supported the successive war efforts (in public statements and with funds), and translated into positive doctrinal terms rationales for imperial expansion.

Compared with elsewhere in Asia, early movements led by Japanese householders to reinterpret Buddhism in terms of modern philosophy were few. Instead, religious reformers were more likely to found their own sects, drawing on doctrines as they liked, without trying to work through the Buddhist establishment.

In Korea, Confucianism was strongly supported in the nineteenth century and Buddhism was increasingly marginalized, as the government also tried to limit the economic power of monastic estates by consolidating schools and seizing lands. State decrees went so far as to prohibit Buddhist monks from setting foot in major cities. Early Western accounts of Korea describe monastic buildings as falling down and the Buddhist monks as ignorant and undisciplined.

The same remarks about Chinese monastic Buddhism in the modern era apply to Daoist monasticism as well. The institutions carried on, but they brought little to the discussion about creating the new China in the radical intellectual climate of the early twentieth century. Daoism, too, was attacked from the standpoints of science and democracy. One reformer, Liang Qichao, described this religion as "a great humiliation whose activities have not benefited the nation at all."[9]

❖ Later Christian Missions in China, Japan, Korea

The Jesuits, the first Christians to proselytize in Ming China, followed their universal strategy of focusing on converting the elite, not the masses. Unlike their counterparts in Japan, who were expelled after an era of toleration, they did succeed at winning imperial approval for their residence. Acceptance was far less ready for their religious teachings, however, than for their cogent introduction into China of European sciences, particularly astronomy, mathematics, and ballistics. The failure of early Catholic missionaries can be attributed to an inability to explain their theology in terms of traditional Chinese language or logic. For example, they never were able to find a satisfactory way of translating *God* into Chinese. No less a drag on proselytizing efforts were the very bitter controversies that broke out between the different Christian groups, particularly on the issue of whether to tolerate Confucian morality or ancestor veneration. An imperial edict proscribed Christianity in 1724, but the censure was not as extreme or as thoroughly enforced as in Japan.

The Protestant presence was significant only after 1800, as Americans and Europeans fanned out from Guangdong Province, on the South China Sea. Their missionary efforts were directed to the masses, and a Chinese translation of the complete Bible appeared in 1815. As elsewhere, the missionaries were less successful at mass proselytizing than at transmitting Western medicine, schooling, and new technologies, such as printing by means of movable type. By 1877, there were 347 missionary schools and an estimated 400,000 Chinese converts.

In addition to the earlier issues of Chinese receptivity, Christianity was associated with the bullying of colonialists and the horrific violence of the nineteenth-century **Taiping Rebellion**, which we will discuss shortly. Christianity did, however, appeal to those interested in finding a religious framework for protest against the weight of traditionalism. In addition, those needing charity or wishing to do business with Westerners often benefited by having themselves baptized.

Outlawed in Japan in 1606, its missionaries expelled in 1616, and its followers persecuted, Christianity survived there underground among remarkably faithful converts. Once granted religious freedom in 1863, Japanese Christians built churches and asserted their faith in the public domain. Soon, however, like the Buddhists, the Christians began to feel the need to prove their religion's this-worldly relevance and nationalistic credentials. They joined the jingoistic chorus supporting the war efforts launched by the state and proclaimed that Christianity strengthened Japan by supporting ethics in national life, resisting radicalism, and combating communism.

Korea remained closed to Christian missionaries until the mid-nineteenth century, when representatives primarily from American Methodist and Presbyterian denominations settled and attracted converts amidst building schools and hospitals. Korean Christians, like those in Japan, also proved their patriotism by emphasizing their independence from Western churches. Scholars are still uncertain as to why Korea embraced Christianity so much more than other Asian countries. (Latest surveys have found that 32 percent of South Koreans are converts.)

Scenes from missionary life in China: a missionary family resident in China c. 1898 shown in formal Chinese dress; a classroom in a Methodist boarding school for girls; a group of Chinese converts and Western missionaries with shipments of Bibles and evangelical publications.

THE APPEARANCE OF NEW RELIGIOUS MOVEMENTS AND RELIGIONS

From the imperial era until the present, **"new religions"** have emerged across Asia, underscoring this period as one of social dislocation, dissatisfaction, and cross-traditional synthesis. It also signals the extent to which the "established religions" of the region (Confucianism, Daoism, Buddhism) had lost their allure for some who were increasingly drawn to ideas from the West.

For the majority of peasants and artisans, the crises that resulted from foreign domination undermined many local subsistence economies, with disastrous effects. Peasants continued to have faith in their own deities, shamans, and ancestors and indeed turned to them in times of trouble. Yet given the turmoil of the modern era, it is not hard to imagine that countless rituals failed and a great many prayers went unanswered. For all these reasons, the modern era in East Asia is marked by the unprecedented flowering of "new religious movements" that did not rely on old practices or old deities. Most often, they arose from the lower classes through sects entirely independent of the traditional institutions of Daoism, Buddhism, and (premodern) Shinto.

✤ Taiping Rebellion in China (1850–1864)

Beyond the challenges provoked by the foreigners in their midst, a rebellion led by a Chinese convert to Christianity nearly ended Manchu rule a half century before their Qing dynasty was overthrown by revolutionaries led by Sun Yat-sen. The nineteenth-century rebellion began with a humble and failed village scholar, **Hong Xiuquan** (1814–1864).

After an illness during which he was delirious for several weeks, Hong, with the help of an American Southern Baptist missionary, interpreted his fevered visions as Christian revelations. Despite limited knowledge of the Bible, Hong proceeded to found his own form of Christianity, convinced that he had seen God, who had charged him with saving humanity and destroying demons, and that he had met Jesus, who was revealed to be Hong's "older brother." A charismatic preacher whose apocalyptic predictions captured the imagination of many, Hong organized his followers into a militant sect called the *Taipings*. To them he offered a prophetic, utopian vision of a future "Heavenly Kingdom of Great Peace" based on egalitarianism, shared property, and gender equality. One of his Old Testament–inspired proclamations was that all idols be destroyed, be they Buddhist, Daoist, or even Confucian ancestor tablets. He also insisted that those joining his group adopt a puritanical moral code, abstaining from alcohol, tobacco, and opium.

Hong vilified the Manchu elite as demons standing in the way of the sect's radical transformation of China. The Qing state, in turn, persecuted the group, stepping up its efforts after 1850, by which time the Taipings had over 10,000 members. Thus provoked, Hong gathered an army whose bloody campaigns likely comprised the most destructive civil war in world history. Most of China was affected, and an estimated 20 million people perished.

China had already been humiliated and weakened by the European powers, which offered many reasons for discontent in addition to those initially proposed by Hong, and the forces of rebellion mushroomed. The Taiping army captured Nanjing in 1853 and occupied it for ten years, establishing a separate regional state ruled by Hong and his neo-Christian ministers.

Ultimately, however, the movement fell apart, owing to internal divisions, refusal to cooperate with potential allies, the leadership's ruthless brutality and paranoia in governing the Taiping community, and their hostility to the Confucian elements deeply embedded in China's population. Nanjing was retaken in 1864, all Taiping leaders not killed in battle were executed, and the first Asian-Christian "new religion" was utterly eradicated.

❖ *"Religion of the Heavenly Way": Ch'ondogyo in Korea*

The **Ch'ondogyo**, which merges elements of Confucianism, Daoism, shamanism, and Roman Catholicism, was founded by Ch'oe Suun (1824–1864) in 1860. Its original name, *Tonghak* ("Eastern learning"), signals its origins as an indigenous response to the challenge of newly imported Christianity (called "Western learning" in Korean). According to the sect's scriptures, Suun received a direct revelation of a new "Heavenly Way" (*Ch'ondo*) designed to awaken each person to the totality of life in the universe and the divinity immanent in each person and all creation. Ch'oe was inspired to reverence the Ultimate Reality, most commonly called *Hanullim,* an impersonal force with whom each person can have an intimate, impersonal encounter.

The essential path to individual realization is through repetitive private and communal chanting. To invoke Hanullim to enter into personal awareness, this "21-syllable Incantation" is intoned:

> Ultimate Energy being all around me, I pray that I feel that Energy within me here and now. Recognizing that Hanullim is within me, I will be transformed. Constantly aware of that divine presence within, I will become attuned to all that is going on around me.[10]

Drawing on Confucianism for ethical principles and on Korea's folk religion for the communal rituals, Suun organized his movement on the notion that those who shared belief in that one God constituted a separate and distinct community within Korean society. Suun attracted a large following but was martyred by the government. The Ch'ondogyo continued to grow under Suun's successors, becoming one of the major religions of the Korean peninsula. Like Korean Christians, Ch'ondogyo members were active in resisting Japanese rule. Although banned in North Korea since 1949, recent reports mention its survival there; the group remains very popular in the south. There is an institutional center in Seoul, and in 2005 its membership, governed by an elected body, was reported to number over 3 million.

The collected writings of the first three leaders became the sect's chief scriptures. Ch'ondogyo's theology is simply expressed in one phrase, "Humans bear divinity." The ethics of the sect emphasize respecting this universal divinity in others. The injunction "Treat others as divine" seems tame today but was revolutionarily democratic in the status-conscious Korea of the late nineteenth century. Ch'ondogyo appealed especially to the lower classes, who were told that they, along with scholars and high officials, could achieve salvation through disciplined effort. There is reason to believe that Ch'ondogyo had an important role in the development of democratic and antiauthoritarian thought in Korea. The group's goal is to achieve a heavenlike earthly existence marked by widespread social cooperation.

❖ The Older "New Religions" Arising in Pre-Meiji Japan

By the end of the Tokugawa era, the medieval social order in Japan had begun to break down, and for some the vitality of Buddhism and traditional Confucianism had waned. Of the several dozen spiritual movements that arose in this period, three grew to become denominations among the postmodern "new religions" of the early twenty-first century.

Each of these movements began with a charismatic individual who experienced extraordinary revelations after a serious illness. Having shared their discoveries with others, these leaders began building communities of followers who felt the teachings helped them reorder their lives on new spiritual principles. Almost every "new religion" thus offered a singular path to salvation out of the maze of choices that had developed along the way of Japanese religious history: Buddhism, neo-Confucianism, elements of Daoism, Shinto. All later were harmonized with the Meiji state's neo-Shintoism, eventually becoming regarded as "Shinto sects."

> "True Sincerity is the one thing we must be most thankful for; with sincerity alone the Earth can be a family.
>
> In this world of ours we have come together to form a circle; let us pray to be joined by The Heart of all our hearts."
>
> —Munetada, founder of Kurozumikyo

Kurozumikyo Kurozumikyo ("Kurozumi's religion") was founded by Kurozumi Munetada, a charismatic teacher who in 1815 was possessed by the central Shinto deity, the sun goddess, Amaterasu, whom he asserted really to be the single Lord of the Universe. Although Kurozumi did not register his group until 1842, soon after his initial experience he began preaching and attracting disciples, who spread his revelations across Japan.

Followers of Kurozumikyo believe that all humans are emanations of the kami and that individual believers may become kami, or become one with them, securing eternal life, by adopting the moral and spiritual practices of these Japanese deities. The potential for all to realize the divine state explains the Kurozumikyo emphasis on the equality of all people, a radical idea in pre-Meiji Japan, where class completely determined individual destiny. Kurozumikyo grew dramatically after winning Meiji recognition. Its leaders had a central shrine established in Okayama City, and the group numbered perhaps 700,000 by 1880. In 2005, 330 centers were counted in Japan, and its membership had dropped to just more than 250,000.

Tenrikyo Tenrikyo ("Religion of Heavenly Wisdom") began with messages its founder, Nakayama Miki (1798–1887), received while in a trance. The source of these communications, he reported, was a spirit Nakayama called "God the Parent" (Oyagami). Regarded by followers as the one true god of the universe, Oyagami commanded Nakayama to be his medium and to further his mission through healing and preaching. Tenrikyo claimed that its newly released universal doctrine of harmonious living would usher in a new world order, a divine kingdom in which humanity would enjoy blissful union with God the Parent. In the sect's view, the "one, true kami" in the universe had created humanity to see it find harmonious life and then entered into creation in the form of ten other kami. Tenrikyo adherents believe that Oyagami made his new revelation to Nakayama to rectify growing human selfishness, a shortcoming that has undermined the original divine intent.

The Tenrikyo belief system accepts reincarnation until the heart is purified of the "eight dusts" (grudges, covetousness, hatred, selfish love, enmity, fury, greed, arrogance). Essential for salvation are a dance ritual, an initiation ("receiving the holy grant"), and performance of daily social service for others. Tenrikyo became a recognized Shinto sect in 1838 and rapidly spread throughout Japan. Its members carried missions to the United States in 1896, Taiwan in 1897, Korea in 1898, and China in 1901. Like the other Shinto-related sects, after the Second World War the group made efforts to "purify" Tenrikyo of its Shinto and nationalist associations. By 2000, there were over 2.3 million members, who had established over 16,000 centers in Japan, with an additional 20,000 missions worldwide.

❖ Nichiren-Related Sects of the Meiji Era

As the Meiji reforms opened and transformed Japanese society after 1867 and government calls to modernize Japan multiplied, the spirit of renewal found religious expression as well. In some cases, the sects arising passed beyond what the state found tolerable, and thus followers were persecuted and pressured to modify their teachings. Other groups became vehicles of resistance to the state's militarism and nationalism. Numerous laity-led groups arose because the Buddhist "establishment" gave few openings for those wishing to reinterpret the doctrines or apply them in the context of modern scientific discoveries from the West.

Many modern groups formed in association with Nichiren-shu, a Kamakura-era Buddhist school created by the charismatic thirteenth-century monk and introduced in Chapter 7. Directly stemming from this school is the largest new religion of modern Japan, the lay organization called *Soka Gakkai* ("Value Creation Society"). Established in 1930 by the Nichiren disciple and educator Makiguchi Tsunesaburo (1877–1944), the Soka Gakkai aims to foster a "Third Civilization" based on Nichiren's teachings, one in which the true Buddhism would spread throughout the world. Its members believe that repeatedly chanting the *Nam-Myoho-renge-kyo* (the name of the great Buddhist text, the *Lotus Sutra*) is "medicine for the soul" and a means for changing the world. The Soka Gakkai also considers its mission to work for world peace and human welfare, and after 1960 it established a political party in Japan (the Komeito) to implement specific government programs to achieve this goal in Japan. It has also sent missionaries to every major country of the world. By 2005, the Soka Gakkai had registered 12 million Japanese members and claimed 1.2 million international adherents.

Also originated by and for Nichiren laity, *Reiyukai Kyodan* ("Spiritual Friends Association") was intended to support the school's regular practices and to exert beneficial influences on Japanese society. Founded in 1925 by Kubo Kakutaro (1890–1944) and Kotani Kimi (1901–1971), the group stressed the need for ancestor worship by the laity and attributed the upheavals of the era to ancestral distress over the ineffectiveness of the contemporary Buddhist leaders. Only when ancestors achieve peace and salvation through lay rituals utilizing the *Lotus Sutra* can the living really find spiritual grace. The Reiyukai also emphasizes conservative social values and expects its members to work hard to strengthen the Confucian "three bonds" (between ruler and minister, father and son, and husband and wife). The Reiyukai are also strong supporters of imperial veneration and other conservative causes in Japanese society. One of the most active proselytizing new religions, the Reiyukai by 1990 had 3 million members and centers abroad in fourteen countries.

East Asian Religions and Postmodern Trends in a Postcolonial World

Practitioners have pushed back at every religious barrier that the states of East Asia erected in the modern era. In Korea and Japan, this return to religious freedom opened the way for reformers of ancient traditions as well as charismatic innovators founding "new religions." The coming of the Marxist state to mainland China in 1949 and the imposition of totalitarian rule by the officially atheistic Communist Party began an era of sustained religious repression. Chinese religions suffered the destruction of properties and religious institutions through concerted governmental attempts—unprecedented in world history—to exterminate any vestige of traditional religious teaching or spiritual training. In China, this lasted for almost two generations, until 1976.

But as we pointed out in Chapter 1, such repression and persecution have not led to the end of religion in China. Far from it. State-sponsored substitution of modernist Marxist ideologies, utopian mythology, and the orchestration of a personality cult centered on Mao Zedong represented attempts to substitute a communist Chinese civil religion for Confucianism, Daoism, and Buddhism (see Chapter 9). The effort failed, though it did weaken the bond between most mainland Chinese and their traditional organized religions.

Since the reform era that began soon after the death of Mao in 1976, the restoration of religion in China has been very gradual and has proceeded under the supervision of the state. A popular upsurge of practice at Daoist temples, family graves, Buddhist monasteries, Christian churches, and mosques is evident, however. Despite reverses, over the last decades, as the door has been cracked open, countless Chinese have rushed through to make pilgrimages, reopen shrines, and resume the ritual practices of their ancestors. We discuss here both the surviving traditions and new religions that have even further multiplied the pluralism characteristic of the postcolonial era.

CONTINUITIES AND TRANSFORMATIONS IN THE EAST ASIAN RELIGIONS

❖ *The Reality of Gods and Spirits in China*

Chinese myths dating back to the Zhou era (700 BCE) mention deities of mountains, rivers, rain, and the earth that have remained part of the diffuse Chinese religion. Interestingly, most deities appearing later in East Asia have human origins, as heroic ancestral spirits have become gods who have won renown beyond their own kin. This is true of **Guan Yu**, the god of war (in life, a Han general), various deified statesmen, Confucius, and even, in recent years, Mao Zedong. Most other important deities have been Buddhist in origin.

In regional and local contexts, the East Asian pantheon has always been in flux as new heroes arise and the deities are obliged continuously to show their power (ling), perhaps through healing or in dramatic shamanic displays of possessions, to prove themselves worthy of the investment of further offerings. Those manifesting strong healing powers or success in responding to popular appeals win devotees, patrons, new temples. Alternatively, other deities have lost favor and efficacy and so have faded from popularity. Thus, the East Asian understanding of and experience with divinities has not been based so much on faith as on dramatic experiential encounters and proven long-term potency at providing cures and other beneficial results.

Image of Mazu, the protective deity worshiped along the Chinese seacoast.

Who are the most common deities found on the typical altars in a Chinese community? Ubiquitous in Chinese homes and temples are icons of the *triple gods: Longevity,* in the form of a vigorous old man; *Wealth,* embodied by a Confucian official; and *Blessings,* symbolized by a male god holding male progeny.

Another prominent deity, Tian Shang Sheng-mu ("Holy Mother in Heaven"), is popularly known as *Mazu* ("Grandmother"). Her origins can be traced to a girl born in the ninth century, in coastal Fujian, who saved her father and brothers at sea by exercising magical powers acquired via Daoist practice. She died young, and soon apparitions and miracles attributed to her were reported. By the mid-twelfth century, the state had recognized Tian Shang Sheng-mu and Mazu cult and temples that spread along the eastern coast of China, where the goddess remains popular today.

In every traditional Chinese and Korean home (but not in Japan) will be another deity, Zao Wangye, the "**kitchen god**." From the kitchen hearth, he records the household goings on and composes a yearly report right before New Year's Day. Folk belief is that Zao Wangye can even determine the length of every household member's life. As early as the Ming era, this popular notion was part of a more systematic articulation of the pantheon (reflecting China's urban centers and government bureaucracy), by which the kitchen gods and earth gods of each locality were viewed as reporting to the nearby city gods, who in turn informed the celestial Jade Emperor on New Year's Day. This notion of a divine, hierarchical officialdom shaped the popular understanding in China of what happens when a person dies: The earth god of the locality reports to the city god, who then escorts the soul to the underworld to appear before ten judges who determine punishments and karmic destiny. It is to these divine "magistrates" that the family addresses prayers and sends bribes ("spirit money"), the latter consisting of specially purchased paper "currency" that is burned to expedite its magical, otherworld delivery.

Items for burning to be sent to the dead by the affluent Chinese of Singapore.

❖ Ritual Practices

In many respects, East Asia derives its unity as a religious and cultural area less from a common set of beliefs than from the shared ritualism within its temples and at family graves. These core rituals are simply an extension of the human custom of feasting an honored guest, in these cases an ancestral spirit or a deity. The foods offered in temples, which are those humans consume, including alcoholic drinks, are not wasted: Once the deities are thought to have consumed their essence, the humans eat the material leavings. Other items presented in East Asian rituals include candles, flowers, oil lamps, and incense. In keeping with the idea that the deities are senior but essentially human is the practice of full prostration (*ketou,* or "kowtow") before icons or tablets, an obeisance that junior kin also make before their living elders at festival times.

For most occasions in daily life, priests (be they Daoist, Buddhist, or shamans) are not needed. This is because senior householders and state officials, even at the highest level, have ritual tasks to perform according to their status. Such tasks are particularly well defined at the time of death. In particular, Confucian filial piety is shown at a parent's death through careful carrying out of the appropriate rituals. The reward is the soul-spirit's blessings and the promise of a reunion with kin after the children's own demise.

Death is indeed a crisis, and at funerals people show their loyalty and love to the departed. In East Asia, a long period of time is traditionally set aside to honor the dead. Further, participation in a funeral is one of the key events binding families and transmitting family values: All the relatives of the deceased remove jewelry, wear rough mourning garments, and wail ritually during specific times until actual burial. Burial will be after two days, with a longer wait in well-to-do families. The funeral itself involves the largest and most ostentatious procession that can be afforded, with musicians and mourners carrying large paper replicas of items the deceased is expected to need in the afterlife.

The traditional death rituals end in establishing the soul in two places for future worship, both in common with those who long ago expired. The cremation remains are taken out in a procession to the family grave or clan temple. Here they are left in an urn, and a grave tablet with the deceased's name is fixed. The yin (earthly) soul stays with these remains. The yang (heavenly) soul is carried to the family's home placed on a sword-shaped paper brought from the graveside. It is then ritually installed on the family altar as a permanent tablet inscribed with the person's name set in place. Placed near other senior kin and the various images of the deities, this spirit receives all the offerings made to the gods. Moreover, any important event in the family is announced to the tablets as if the ancestors resided there.

Although not all families can afford family grave sites, all wish to have them, since with such a burial the family can most directly ensure the happiness of the earthbound souls. Families possessing graveyards go to them on two occasions each year to tidy them, make sacrifices, and then eat and drink among the family's ancestral graves. The cemeteries in East Asia are not dreaded locales but places one can go to feel close to one's deceased parents and grandparents as well as to conform to the basic Confucian requirement of caring for them after death.

❖ *The Religious Institutions: Monasteries, Temples, Shrines*

The religious institutions that sustain the three traditions in East Asia vary widely. For their surrounding householder communities, Buddhist monasteries have temples with images of compassionate bodhisattvas and include monks who specialize in healing and death rituals. The temple in all these religions is considered as simply a house for humanlike divinities. They can be modest roadside boxes where humble images or cheap lithographic prints are kept, or they can be massive palaces with halls and side buildings, housing gilded images flanked by hosts of attending demigods.

Some deities, such as the earth god (*Tudiye*) found in most agricultural settlements, can be worshiped in a simple manner outdoors on a raised mound of decorated earth. Small temples are merely rooms made of wood or cement, housing a simple tablet with the name of the deity inscribed on it. Traditional Chinese towns had communities marked by a profusion of such shrines and larger temples, making it hard to understand the assertion by Westernized Chinese that "Chinese have no religion!"

The larger temples share certain characteristics. The greatest temples contain all the major deities of the pantheon, giving devotees "one-stop" access to the supernatural world. The entrance always opens to the south, an auspicious direction, and is guarded by statues of protectors in fierce poses. In larger establishments these guardians are lodged in a gatehouse through which all visitors must pass. The areas devoted to multistory pagoda temples in many cases reflect attention to geomancy calculations, complete with artificial mountains to channel positive energy to the site. In larger compounds, the main deity will be in the last hall on the same axis as the entrance, with halls containing lesser deities arrayed on the same line and separated by courtyards.

Chinese temple, the home of the gods, featuring the ornate pillars and roof tiles of the palace style.

Before each icon is an altar for receiving offerings, most commonly candles or incense sticks that go into large braziers. Kneeling cushions are supplied as well as a means of divination for the use of those posing questions to a deity: Two half-moon wooden blocks are thrown to derive a "yes" or "no" answer, based on their resting alignment.

The aesthetic in contemporary Chinese temples can be described as highly baroque. The temples, with their curving roof lines, eaves, and finials, are full of bright colors, from roof beams to columns to the decorated vestments adorning the deities.

The larger Daoist temples are usually served by a resident priesthood and by *fa-shi*, mediums who serve in temples. The mediums specialize in exorcisms and help private clients make simple offerings. Resident priests, called *dao-shi*, may assist in rituals such as exorcisms but have also mastered complex Daoist death liturgies and wear more formal attire.

❖ *Shinto Shrines:* Jinja

Equipped and arrayed in keeping with norms similar to those of the Chinese temple but in sharp decorative contrast are the Japanese Shinto shrines, *jinja*. They are notable for their natural wood, plain roof tiles, and restrained aesthetic. Every jinja is also marked by a gateway called a *torii*. Given the high emphasis on purification in Shintoism, water sources for rinsing the face and mouth are always present where devotees

A small Shinto shrine (jinja) dedicated to the protector of cows, the cow kami.

approach the main shrine. These distinctive features of Japan's Shinto architecture delineate a transition from the ordinary world into sacred space.

After purification, devotees proceed to the main and subsidiary shrines. Facing the main icon, they go before it to present their petitions. Before making a request, a visitor can pull on long, thick ropes to ring a shrine bell. Ending the ritual by clapping shows respect.

❖ The Diffuse Religion in Practice: The Major Religious Festivals

In our collective discussion of the religious practices of China, Korea, and Japan, we have pointed to the "diffuse religion" that gives the region a characteristic unity, drawing on elements of the three traditions. The festivals express this diffuse religion most clearly, since Confucian, Daoist, and Buddhist elements have clearly been woven into the yearly cycle of life. Only continued reliance on the ancient Chinese calendars in some areas of these countries has led to complications. Officially, all East Asian nations have adopted Western calendar days and selected celebrations: China from its connections with international communism, Korea and Japan through Christian influences. Yet, the Chinese system of twelve-year cycles, lunar days, and solar seasons is still used in many areas and has been intermixed with the Western calendar. Since Japan shifted many of its holidays away from the Chinese calendar and to fixed "Western" days, Japan's dates for the festivals it shares with the East Asian region are most often not on the same calendar day observed elsewhere.

National holidays have grown out of a variety of origins: mythic events or deities indigenous to the particular nation, days accentuating Confucian values, or relatively

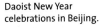

Daoist New Year celebrations in Beijing.

recent events that the nation's leaders wish to mark in the country's "civil religion." For example, Japan celebrates the Cherry Blossom Festival (April 1–8) to thank the kami of the forests for the renewal of life seen in the blossoming of the trees.

Every major deity in every locality is thought to have a "birthday," either a day celebrated nationally or the day a more local deity's temple was first established. On these annual occasions, which usually last for two or three days, the priests and temple supporters arrange for extravagant ritual performances, local devotees come to make their most elaborate yearly offerings (and petitions), merchants and artisans set up their wares to create a temporary fair, and in the evenings theatrical performances are staged to entertain deity and devotees alike.

Most common festivals of East Asia have Chinese or Buddhist origins and can be mentioned only in passing. New Year's Day (by either calendar) is a time for gathering family and friends, settling debts, and seeking blessings and divine protection for the year ahead. The day in China and Korea is called *Spring Festival*, although it falls usually just after the middle of winter. In traditional preholiday rites, householders send the Kitchen God (Zao Wangye) off to heaven by burning his paper icon and installing a new paper icon; they also post ancient characters on doorways to invite prosperity

Scene from the Qing-Ming festival, the yearly family ritual for feasting and honoring the ancestors.

for the year ahead. The essentials of Confucian family life are marked in sacrifices offered to ancestors at their tablets. It is customary for junior family members to kow-tow to seniors, who then in turn receive gifts of money in special red envelopes.

Ancestor's Day, or **Qing-Ming** ("Pure Brightness Festival"), is the first of two dates over the year when families must visit the ancestral graves to maintain them, make sacrifices, and feast together there with the departed spirits, usually in early April. In Japan, this festival has been fixed as the vernal equinox (March 21) and is called *Higan* ("Further Shore"), with a second Higan on the autumnal equinox. In the Chinese manner, families visit family graves together. Buddhist priests are also expected to come to the home on a short visit, during which they recite sacred scriptures. The merit earned for this good deed is dedicated to the dead.

Japanese Buddhists mark the Buddha's birthday on April 8, when people anoint images of baby Buddha with flowers and scented water, just as the texts describe the local deities doing at the actual birth of Siddhartha. Chinese and Korean Buddhists do the same on the eighth day of the fourth lunar month. Confucius' birthday is celebrated today only in Korea and always on September 28. In Taiwan, on Teacher's Day, Confucius is honored with colorful rituals and elaborate sacrifices laid out before the sage's temple tablets.

All Souls Festival is a summer event when the gates of purgatory are thought to be held open. On this occasion, families integrate practices from all three traditions to connect the living members with their departed kin. Buddhist and Daoist priests perform rituals to aid families in their effort to ensure their ancestors' comfort in the afterlife.

The early fall **Full Moon Festival** is a time to worship the harvest moon with special sweet "moon cakes." All are urged to take sight of the "full rabbit moon," an association derived from both Buddhist and Daoist traditions: In the popular Buddhist scriptures, the Buddha was once born as a rabbit who rendered such extraordinary service to his fellow animals that the gods placed his image on the moon's surface; in the Daoist perception, a rabbit can be seen on the moon, using a pestle to pound the herbs of immortality in a mortar. Across East Asia, people view the rising moon on this night to ask for blessings that in rural communities include a good rice harvest in the month ahead.

THE RETURN OF RELIGION TO CHINA: CASE STUDIES

We began the discussion of modern Hinduism with the comment that South Asia is a region of many subcultures and regional differences. The same reminder is applicable to East Asia, with a brief digression to note that China's breadth of variation is in certain respects much less pronounced now than in the past. Between 1949 and 1976, the heavy hand of the Communist Party–led government succeeded in disestablishing almost every public religious institution that anchored the "three faiths." It dispersed the religious specialists (monks, nuns, and priests) and destroyed much of the formal infrastructure of the organized religions of China, demolishing Buddhist and Daoist monasteries and image shrines as well as the nearly countless deity temples that before 1949 could be found in every community. The party also pushed the devout underground, since in the most active phase of the **Cultural Revolution** (1966–1969), any attempt to pray, meditate, or read religious literature was a serious offense, a sign of being "reactionary" or an "enemy of the revolution," a potentially capital crime. We now examine a few examples in pursuit of understanding the extraordinary phenomenon of religion's return to the People's Republic of China.

❖ Mao in the Rearview Mirror

Suppose you arrive in Beijing on your first visit to China and decide to go to the former imperial palace, the Forbidden City, the immense, walled complex from which the Yuan, Ming, and Qing emperors ruled all of China. It was at the top of the palace's southern gateway, called the Gate of Heavenly Peace (Tian'anmen), that Mao Zedong proclaimed the establishment of the People's Republic of China in 1949. Despite all the changes that have swept China since Mao's death in 1976, you would easily see from your taxi window the immense painted portrait that hangs over that gateway. The image commemorates the "new beginning" of China then and serves as a constant reminder of Mao's heroic and determined role in leading the Communist Party's triumphant success.

The style of the Tian'anmen Square portrait suggests that Mao is the ascetic servant of the people, a true communist leader whose deeds are legendary. He bravely fought the Japanese, and in the Long March of 1934 he led the troops in strategic retreat halfway across China. Later he exposed the internal enemies that had kept China backward, poor, and subjugated. Inspired by Marx, Engels, and Lenin, Mao identified these enemies as the landlords who oppressed the peasant masses, religious ideas and institutions, and Western capitalism, all of which kept the people from rising up and forcing China to become a just society. For Mao and so for the early Chinese Communist Party leaders, religion and religious institutions were "enemies of the people." Mao was a rationalist who critiqued "superstitious" religious ideas that allegedly blocked the people's attempts to understand the world; he never ceased to highlight the classic modernist goal of setting the world free from the wrong thinking stemming from belief in supernatural "magic."

Like Marx, Engels, and Lenin, Mao believed a true communist utopia was not obtainable in a society with strong religious traditions. Although official Chinese historians have by now admitted that Mao's own blind faith in communist ideology led to blunders causing the death of millions (especially in the 1958–1960 famine), the massive Tian'anmen portrait still hangs today as an icon of communist China. (Occasionally iconoclasts are caught defacing this portrait. Even in recent incidents, offenders have typically received multiyear prison terms.)

People who grew up during the decades of Mao's dictatorship later painfully realized how full of "superstition" they had been in uncritically following the Communist

Contemporary Mao amulet, inscribed with prayers for good fortune and safe travel, of the kind found widely in China today adorning rearview mirrors in cars.

Party and especially in showing reverence for Chairman Mao. Yet today, nearly thirty years after his death, for many Chinese, party members and nonparty members alike, Mao retains his standing as a sincere and uncorrupted champion of China's renewal who tried (however erringly) to seek justice and the common good. But regard for Mao endures in ways that even he did not anticipate.

As your taxi driver turns the corner on the great square near the stolid mausoleum where Mao's remains lie embalmed in a glass-enclosed tomb, you notice on the windshield mirror a gold-colored frame, decorated with red and yellow tassels. You immediately recognize the back-to-back portraits of Mao, a youthful one and one from middle age (similar to that overlooking Tian'anmen Square). You ask your interpreter what the object is and what it means. The answer, from the 30-something driver of a government-owned vehicle, takes a few moments to register: *"Ta shi shen"* ("He is a deity"). The driver then adds with unconcealed fervor that with so many more cars on the road, his work is quite dangerous, but this deity's amulet makes him feel safe. His income as a driver in fact has multiplied since he put it up, just as his fellow drivers in the work unit had promised. On later outings, you question other drivers who display similar icons, you learn that many believe that the icon—and Mao's spirit—have helped them in business. The transformations under way in China today and the restoration of religion among the Chinese people are embedded in this striking turn of fate: The most powerful man in East Asia, while alive an atheist who suppressed religion, is in death a powerful spirit.

While his transformation to a revered protective spirit and god of wealth would doubtless have dismayed Chairman Mao, it does demonstrate the global pattern of religious traditions responding to the exigencies of local life. As the state and party have moved since the early 1990s away from collectivist policies to emphasize individual and private enterprise, leaders have exhorted the Chinese people that "to get rich is glorious." At the same time, the government has retreated from promises of guaranteed state employment, pensions, and universal medical care. So is it really surprising that an unassailable icon would be adopted as the very needed god of personal protection and wealth?

✤ *The Force of Feng Shui*

Ideas about what constitutes "religion" in China not only fascinate modern scholars but have been repeatedly debated by officials of the Communist Party. In the reform era, as pressure has been exerted to reintroduce almost every sort of former spiritual practice, the East Asian organized religions, with their potential for reestablishing nationwide institutional networks, have had to deal with deliberate governmental attempts aimed at controlling and regulating them. A few ancient practices, however, were left almost entirely unmolested. One of these is *feng shui,* the school of applied religious Daoism that seeks to maximize human flourishing in natural and man-made environments. (The name, which means literally "wind-water," refers to the principal bearers of environmental energy used in geomancy.)

Feng shui consultants are today found everywhere across mainland China. Masters from overseas Chinese communities have returned to advise those building the myriad new hotels, residences, and factories rising so quickly across the PRC. The goal of feng shui is to determine the best sites, architectural designs, and living arrangements. Both private concerns and state ventures with party approval now take the "science" of mapping the qi, the inherent energy of a place, quite seriously. In mainland China today one can hear both success and disaster stories pointing to the advisability of consulting a feng shui expert before embarking on any construction project.

The state's support of the return of feng shui has given credence to the classical religious worldview regarding humanity and the environment. It is based on Daoist principles of balancing yin and yang, channeling the subterranean and atmospheric flow of their qi, and pursuing health and prosperity through expert arrangement of harmonious design features. The government's policy reflects the perennial Chinese emphasis on religion's practical, this-worldly benefits, which is visible elsewhere in society, too. Throughout the modern and postmodern eras, for example, doctors have had unobstructed leeway to practice acupuncture and other healing arts based on Daoist principles applied to the human body.

Nor is mainland China the only area to see the effect of this revival of the ancient worldview: As significant numbers of Chinese people have migrated overseas, real estate brokers from London to San Francisco are having to take account of feng shui analysis in marketing their properties. Feng shui's ideas about interior decorating have likewise entered into the ken of new age religion, where concern for fixing "the wealth corner" in one's house, situating decorations recognized for their "harmonious vibrations," and the plotting of energy flow from front door to back have been borrowed from this Chinese system of thought.

With the allowance for religious freedom after the Cultural Revolution, traditional Daoist priests have enjoyed their restoration to temple service across China.

✤ Ancestor Veneration and the Return of Traditional Funerals

In its zeal to end wasteful expenditures on the rituals of death and ancestor veneration, which for some traditional families meant going into nearly inescapable debt for extravagant funerals, the Communist Party in 1956 issued strict regulations limiting funeral observances and—a radical break from the past—required secular cremation while also prohibiting rituals at ancestral graves. This attempt to break with the Confucian tradition went even further during the periods of greatest excess in the Cultural Revolution, when the young revolutionaries called Red Guards ransacked and destroyed grave sites throughout China, including parts of the great imperial tombs, some of which had been in use for several thousand years. In loosing these energetic young zealots on the countryside, Mao was trying to destroy the familial tradition, which he saw as dividing "the people" and so undermining the party's quest to promote the collective good.

Beginning in the early 1990s, the practices of traditional funeral processions and burial of the dead in family graves slowly began to return, largely in villages and smaller towns and hardly at all around major cities such as Beijing. Graves are now increasingly visible, and across the rural areas, usually on sites unsuitable for agriculture, one sees burial places of elaborate design, including permanent brick structures with nameplates affixed. Also, official prohibitions on the burning of paper money or artificial gold ingots at gravesides have been dropped. Until 1996, government road signs still threatened punishment for those engaging in this practice, but since then even government-owned shops can be found selling the paper currency used in this exceedingly popular observance.

❖ Nationalism and Confucianism Revived

Perhaps even more striking than the abandonment of attempts to stamp out long-favored cultural practices is the return of Confucius to an honored position in modern China. In the retreat from socialist collectivism and having tacitly recognized the failure to convert the Chinese masses to the worldview of Marxist–Maoist communism, China has been beset by corruption accompanying its hastily instituted market reforms. Many Chinese writers have pointed out the crisis in faith and values that has gripped China, as the profit-seeking motive has been unleashed over the last two decades. As one of China's first rock stars, Cui Jian, sings in a popular album entitled *Eggs Under the Red Flag,* "Money is fluttering in the wind. We have no ideals."

The Communist Party, in apparent recognition of this potential source of chaos, recently embarked on another great reversal: It has turned back to Confucius. While the party publicly ignores its failure to make communist ideology the common foundation of postwar China, the restoration of Confucius to respectability is part of its promotion of a more primordial Chinese tradition on which to anchor its permanent power base: staunch nationalism.

Regardless of whether they support the communist government, Chinese people widely share a certain pride in their civilization and its culture. Party strategists see the world economy as developing in a direction leading to eventual domination by China. Thus, in the interest of guiding the country to reach this pinnacle, they are trimming their demands that the people accept ideologies counter to millennia of Chinese tradition.

Sales clerk at an ancestor worship shop, Shanghai. Once prohibited by official regulations, government shops across China now sell the paper money, candles, and incense needed for this ancient practice.

The PRC has readmitted Confucianism to the ideological stage in order to evoke nationalistic pride, another ironic turn by the Communist Party leadership. During the Cultural Revolution, Mao required Red Guards to denounce Confucius and his sons specifically as "villainous slave owners," tarring the master as an apologist for feudalism and exploitation, a symbol for all the traditions that the Communist Party was out to replace.

Yet the hated excesses of the Cultural Revolution may have sparked renewed interest in Confucian thought in China. In 1994, to mark the 2,545th birthday of the great sage, the party launched an initiative to revive Confucian thought. An international conference was convened, the Confucian temple in Beijing was restored and reopened to the public, and Confucius' home temple in Qufu was celebrated as a place to visit. By the year 2000, China's president, Jiang Zemin, was frequently quoting from Confucius in his public speeches; in 2006, one of the best-selling books in China was an introduction to Confucian thought and its applications to contemporary life.

❖ Qi Gong

Another area in which the spiritual has returned to mainland China in the guise of applied therapy is in the practice of **qi gong.** This healing art, like feng shui, draws on Daoist theories of vital energy in the body and on techniques of awakening its force in practitioners, both of which have their origins in religious Daoism's ancient paths to achieve immortality. It is now quite common in major cities for qi gong practitioners to open shops in the precincts of Buddhist or Daoist monasteries, with banners and posters unfurled outside their entranceways explaining the theory and practice as well as testimonials from people cured of various maladies. In most instances, a qi gong master uses his own body to concentrate healing energy and project it outwardly (through the hands) to affect the flow of energy in the patient. In the famous Great Goose Pagoda in Xi'an, the Buddhist committee since 1993 has rented a side assembly hall to a qi gong practitioner. This master draws a steady stream of interested people who can listen to an introductory lecture and, for a modest fee, take their first treatment.

In some governmental circles, there is ambivalence about such applied spirituality. Although the modern official press features an occasional article, often by a prominent scientist, that denounces "phony qi gong" as "harmful" and criticizes individual practitioners for "feudal and superstitious activities which use the flag of qi gong as a cover for swindling others," it continues to allow the practice to flourish, even in state-controlled temple precincts. Thus, while this medically oriented practice is mixed with other therapies (Chinese and Western), qi gong, like feng shui, now affirms the credibility of the most elemental ideas of classical Daoism.

⚶ Shrines in Chinese Village Squares, Shops, and Front Doors

Across mainland China since 1976, there has been the slow, hesitant, but unmistakable movement by devotees to reestablish shrines, temples, and the ritual practices destroyed or prohibited under government orders dating back to 1949. Exactly where the Communist Party's line of toleration lies has varied according to the region and its succession of officials. Tensions still exist over what is "superstition" (*mixin*), which is strongly discouraged by the government, versus what is considered "religion" (*zongjiao*). Individuals have a constitutional right to practice a religion, but the state reserves the right to grant or withhold this designation for a given belief system.

Women performing a qi gong ritual, with gestures designed to cultivate and concentrate the qi energy in the body.

Rituals performed at a Daoist temple in Xi'an.

Even so, the return of temples to the public domain for ritual use is in evidence almost everywhere. Daoist and Buddhist shrines are surrounded by flourishing votive markets, usually owned by or rented from the temple itself. Incense, candles, printed texts and scrolls with spiritual exhortations, souvenirs, and amulets are among the items sold. Many devotional traditions are flourishing, in forms that were popular centuries earlier.

Accounts of village life cite the near-universal attempt of rural peasants to use part of their new earnings to build (or rebuild) the public temples that house the local and regional gods. None is more telling than the practice of making offerings to the local earth gods (*tudi gong*). In pre-PRC China, the humble earth god shrines were found in every locality, possessing in fact a multiple presence according to the settlement: Tudi shrines were found in homes, in neighborhoods, in villages, in government offices (where they received offerings from state officials), and even in Buddhist monasteries. All deaths, births, and troubles were reported to them, and the simple icon or tablet was taken out of the temple to "inspect" sites suffering from severe problems. People believe that, if petitioned properly and sincerely, the earth gods protect against locusts, mildew, disease, and other obstacles to a rich harvest as well as solve any other difficulties in their domain. These shrines and this cult have returned everywhere.

The restoration of shrine and ritual has gone ahead even in restaurants and homes. After several attempted crackdowns by the government, restaurants have succeeded in reinstalling small altars to the local gods of wealth and protection. In private homes, the Chinese New Year has been increasingly observed with the traditional pasting of calligraphic good-luck icons, including the word for good fortune (*Fu*) placed upside down to indicate the sound of good fortune's arrival.

It is in connection with the Fu symbol that we see a further example of the government's acceptance of China's diffuse religion. Here again, by being sensitive to the importance and meaning of religion, we can comprehend the profundity of changes sweeping China: As the party expands economic opportunity but ends communal social safety-net programs, people feel that to prosper, they need all the luck they can attract. Accordingly, the quest to satisfy the perceived need for good fortune is so intense that the official proponents of communist doctrine are reluctant to suppress practices many party members consider to be superstitious.

JAPAN: OLD TRADITIONS AND NEW

Whereas in China the Cultural Revolution postponed the expression of religious awakening until after Mao's death in 1976, in Japan this era of innovation commenced in 1945, with the necessity of rebuilding the war-ravaged country both physically and spiritually. For seven years occupied and ruled by the Allied powers (principally the United States), Japan had to reinvent a form of government, redesign its economic system, and rebuild its major cities without reference to the emperor as their divine leader. Japan's surrender in 1945 was spoken by Emperor Hirohito in his own voice, and during the occupation he was compelled to renounce his divinity (as a Shinto kami) explicitly and to underscore his purely ceremonial presence in Japan's political future.

The state system of neo-Shintoism, which was integral to the modernizations that had begun in 1867, was also discredited and discarded. Shinto then survived largely in its myriad shrines dedicated to divinities in neighborhoods, villages, and regions and attended to by hereditary priests. Establishment Buddhism, like the rest of Japan's cultural institutions, also had to rebuild its physical and social presence, overcoming the stigma of having uncritically supported the fascist state. As the economic system flourished, the country's wealth eventually was used to rebuild these institutions, accelerating the traditional religion's material recovery and, in some cases, expansion.

✤ The Claim of "Having No Religion" and the Reality of New Year's Rituals

Educated Japanese and oftentimes their friends in intellectual Western circles are fond of proclaiming that the Japanese are "lacking in religion," an Enlightenment attitude common among educated East Asians. Some try to project an image of Japan as a modern society comparable to Europe or North America in its scientific sophistication. While few Japanese today care to learn much in depth about Shinto mythology or Buddhist doctrine, widespread indifference does not prove that Japan "lacks religion."

Beyond the unprecedented growth of the new religions, one has only to know where and when to seek a wealth of examples that dispel this widespread stereotype about a Japanese people somehow being different from everyone else. While it is foolish to ignore the force of skepticism, scientific theory, and cynicism in any modern society, it is also naive to judge "religiousness" by formal institutional measures alone. Contemporary New Year's Day observances provide an example of the strength of "diffuse popular religion" in modern Japan.

During the Meiji era, Japan had legislated a shift away from the Chinese lunar calendar's determining the date of the "new year" festival and adopted the Western (or Gregorian) system that has the year begin on January 1. On this day and days around it, Japan shuts down its industrial economy. Families begin the process of renewal through a special cleaning of the house (*susuharae,* "soot and cobweb clearing"). On New Year's Eve or early New Year's morning, a visitor to any Shinto shrine—even in the most modern Tokyo urban neighborhood—will see long lines of family members coming for *hatsu-mode,* a formal visit to pay their respects to their neighborhood's kami. The people then consign to the carefully laid bonfires all the family amulets accumulated over the past year. That evening or the next day, a family member will purchase new amulets that will be carefully set up on the newly purified family altar. Many temples plan their annual festival for this period, when crowds throng to temple precincts to buy amulets and attend the priestly rituals empowering them. In nearly every shop and house are decorations dedicated to the kami residing in the neighborhood. On New Year's morning, too, families gather at their household altars to worship the Buddhas, Kannon, and local gods. Thus, in the renewal of the family shrine at the year's turning, by "being careful" with local divinities, in sacralizing family ties, and by suspending the profane activities of markets and business activities, contemporary New Year's Day traditions in Japan fit perfectly into the "religion" framework we introduced in Chapter 1. In 2006, press reports in Tokyo noted that due to the discomforts of joining the usual crowd of 4 million people who traditionally visit the Meiji Shrine on New Year's Day, this shrine, like many across Japan, has established a website. Without leaving home, a virtual visit can be made: Cyber-visitors can click onto the site, bow twice, clap their hands, and bow again, after which they can express their request to the shrine's kami and order auspicious amulets online. (For an online index, see for example: http://www.japan-guide.com/e/e2059.html.)

✤ Continuing Support for Shinto Shrines

Most Japanese—housewives, salaried workers, artisans—still widely believe that wherever one lives and certainly wherever one's family still has an ancestral residence, one has loose ties to the shrine that houses the deity of that locality, the *uji-kami.* We've seen that on New Year's Day at least, paying respects to that kami remains a very popular observance. Almost equally popular in most parts of Japan is the ritual of bringing newborn babies to "meet" the kami and to pay their own respects, requesting protection. There is also a yearly Shinto festival dedicated to the well-being of children.

When we try to understand the typical individual today visiting a Shinto shrine, it is nearly impossible to separate the spiritual from the habitual or the recreational. In a recent survey of those who visited shrines, 65 percent of men and 75 percent of women reported experiencing *aratamatta kimochi,* "a feeling of inner peace," afterward.[11]

Honoring the kami at a
Shinto shrine in Kyoto .

The observer at the shrine finds many ritual activities that seem to indicate religious conviction—clapping the hands together, bowing before an image, making an offering, buying an amulet.

A modern exponent of Shinto's relevance in contemporary Japan would certainly note that, although some Shinto shrines may be neglected, there are over 100,000 such holy places, and none of them is in ruins.

✤ The Zen of Daruma-san

If any single religious icon could be said to embody all the mind-boggling complexities and paradoxes of religion in Japan today, it might be **Daruma-san.** The name and identity of this figure derives from Bodhidharma, the sage renowned as the transmitter of the Buddhist meditation tradition from India (around 600 CE) that became Ch'an in China and Zen in Japan. Daruma-san became a Zen saint, and legends about him are part of the scriptural lore of this school. They celebrate his unbending commitment to meditation retreats and his terse, no-nonsense replies to students and patrons. From the Kamakura period in Japan, when Zen schools were imported from China, Daruma-san became a favorite subject for painters and sculptors. Images of Daruma-san came to be popular in Japanese folk traditions as well: His visage adorns kites, toys, knockdown dolls, sake cups. Several dozen major Buddhist temples feature his icon and offer a full range of amulets.

Today, the most widely used images of Daruma-san are limbless round papier-mâché icons called *okiagari* that are employed for making vows or proclaiming formal wishes. The standard ritual consists of making a wish and coloring in one eye of the

statue, which is then placed on the family altar. When there is success in the matter wished for, the other eye is colored in and the doll (like all other amulets) is eventually discarded, fueling the next New Year's temple bonfire. The Daruma-san icon is used in the same manner by businesspeople undertaking new ventures and politicians beginning election campaigns.

Thus with Daruma-san we witness the domestication into popular Japanese ritual life of the founding saint of Zen Buddhism, a fiercely ascetic meditation master who has become transmuted into an ostensibly comic figure, who nonetheless commands a following of millions. The subtle meanings of Daruma-san stand in stark contrast to the extreme teachings of a recent Japanese cult, one that attempted to use the Buddha's Four Noble Truths to rationalize a premeditated attack with nerve gas on innocent citizens.

Shinto shrines remain reference points for many modern Japanese today

✤ The Rise and Fall of the Aum Cult

In March 1995, as government investigators were about to arrest its leaders, at least ten determined members of the Aum Shinrikyo sect executed a terrorist attack in the centrally located Kasumigaseki Station of the Tokyo subway. Twelve people were killed, and 5,500 were injured. The terrorist disciples were acting on the orders of the sect's

Zen painting depicting Bodhidharma, founder of the Ch'an/Zen Buddhist school.

guru, Shoko Asahara, a semiblind 40-year-old who claimed to be an incarnation of Jesus and a spiritual master who had distilled the final truths of tantric Buddhism, Hindu yoga, the LSD psychedelic experience, New Age astrology, and the self-proclaimed sixteenth-century seer Nostradamus. In 1989, Asahara applied for and received registration as a tax-exempt religious organization for Aum Shinrikyo ("the True Teaching of Aum"). Then he set about building his sect around a core of commune-living disciples, many of whom were highly educated, successful people who commanded considerable wealth. Devotion to Asahara himself reached fanatical cultic proportions, with Aum members buying bottles of his bathwater.

In the aftermath of the attack, the Japanese cultural elite and the media engaged in a long period of self-reflection: What does this group's success say about the moral and cultural state of the nation? What did it say about Japan's educational system that among Aum's inner circle were some of the better minds of a generation, including standouts in law and science? What manner of brainwashing could have induced cult members to accept such an unlikely collection of ideas? Why did they abandon their families and all their possessions to follow a pudgy dropout who made the bizarre claim to be both Buddha and Jesus? Why did they adopt Asahara's paranoid doomsday doctrine, which led them to express murderous hatred against innocent fellow citizens? Why do followers keep the organization going, under its new name, Aleph?

Leading commentators noted that Asahara and his followers were members of the generation born after World War II. They described cult members as frustrated with the laborious old Japan of business cartels that closed off new competitors, of the nation's intricate interpersonal ritual gestures, and of fathers who saw no avenue for success in life outside the Confucian code of work, hierarchy, and "waiting your turn."

The Aum tragedy also brought to popular attention the thousands of post–World War II "new religions" that claim the loyalty of an estimated 20 percent of modern Japanese; our survey of religion in Japan today concludes with a sampling of them.

❖ The New "New Religions" in Japan

A generation of Japanese spiritual leaders has arisen to form independent groups that have met the new yearnings, none bearing deadly fruit like the Aum attack. Still, the attraction of "new religions" must be kept in perspective: Most Japanese today have not joined them. The majority find the older traditions or being nonreligious more to their liking.

Some of the new "new religions" were synthesized by charismatic founders from Japan's long-extant traditions along with aspects of modern nationalism, elements of Christianity, or scientific principles. Many of the "new religions" began in some measure as responses to the dislocations that shook Japanese society during its sudden opening to the outside world in the late nineteenth century and the headlong modernization and Westernization of the Meiji era. Almost every older "new religion" splintered with the passing of its founder and the struggles of interpretation and succession that followed, adding to the number of groups. But most of the popular "new religions" today are more recent in origin, attracting followers who find themselves disconnected from the old pattern of melding Shintoism and Buddhism that satisfied their ancestors.

The lives of the Japanese people are changing in many dimensions—through migration from rural homesteads to burgeoning cities, with the concomitant separation from extended families and loss of community in newly built urban enclaves, and as travel and media have engendered an awareness of every portion of the world. In this new and often-chaotic environment, many individuals have been drawn to the "new religions" to find original answers to life's perennial questions.

In 1999 there were no less than 40,000 "new religion" organizations officially registered with the Japanese government. The great majority are exceedingly small in size, inconsequential, and for the most part rarely active. Many are hard to distinguish from poetry circles, philosophy clubs, or groups formed around health practitioners. The major new religions, however, are an important part of today's spiritual landscape; roughly 20 percent of Japanese people surveyed in recent years reported that their predominant religious affiliation is with one of the "new religions."[12]

While Aum's mass murder plot is completely atypical of the new religions, other aspects of this cult are not. Most form around a charismatic leader whose personal struggle to find the truth becomes paradigmatic for disciples drawn to the movement. Some sort of shamanic experience or performance is the most common ritual. In addition, members of most are taught to reject the diffuse eclecticism of Shintoism or Buddhism, and their gurus insist that one practice and one singular revelation are definitive. Yet many of the "new religion" worldviews draw on ancient traditions such as Buddhist karma and reincarnation doctrines, Confucian moral teachings and ancestor rites, or Shinto styles of worship. Some also import practices from the West (e.g., older psychologies like "new thought" or Norman Vincent Peale's "power of positive thinking") or from India (e.g., Hindu yoga). Each new religion also tends to be this-worldly in its goals (especially emphasizing healing) and imbued with the mission of ushering in a new divine era.

The most successful sects are built around a new "sacred center," a shrine that expresses the sect's mission and a priestly-bureaucratic administration that manages the organization. Membership in most new religions is quite open, but there is typically an initiation that requires individuals to make a personal commitment to the group, following what in the Abrahamic faiths would be called a "conversion experience."

Japan's new religions can be conveniently arranged according to their chronological emergence. The earliest, which are "new" only in relation to Japan's long history, are those that began in the nineteenth century and were eventually aligned with Shintoism. The most popular among them, the Kurozumikyo and the Tenrikyo, discussed earlier, have survived into the present. The most prominent of the second-tier group, which arose during the Meiji era (post-1867), remain among the largest new religions today: the Buddhist-derived Soka Gakkai and Reiyukai Kyodan and the Seicho no Ie, a group we have not mentioned, which teaches the unity of all religions. These now-established religions have followed a standard pattern: The religions that began in pre-war Japan have evolved through tumultuous times, and the survivors long ago abandoned their rebellious teachings to fit into the mainstream society. That these formerly angry sectarians have made their peace with Japanese society is demonstrated in most cases by policies that now allow families to participate in once-prohibited rituals to the Shinto gods and at Buddhist temples.

The most successful new religions have built schools, colleges, and hospitals; some offer residential communities and athletic facilities to sustain their members from cradle to grave. These resources are also useful for proselytizing purposes and for demonstrating the power and success of the new path itself. The Tenrikyo, for example, one of the most successful new religions, has centers in every urban area of Japan; its headquarters, called Tenri City (near Nara), is a center for pilgrimage comparable to Salt Lake City for Mormons.

Sociological surveys have shown that devotees of the new religions are most commonly those excluded from dominant avenues to prestige in modern Japan. That is, with certain exceptions, such as the high-achieving followers of Asahara, members do not typically have prestigious jobs in the large corporations but run small family businesses. Within the group there are characteristically hierarchies and internal ranks to which individuals can aspire. Women typically outnumber men in membership and serve as leaders; their proselytizing is notable for its distinctly maternal style.

The new religions assume a common outlook (hence social posture) in presenting themselves as experts at solving human problems. Whatever their supernatural beliefs, all hold that sickness, economic failure, and all interpersonal relations can be fully under individual control. Life will improve, they assert, if devotees will only discipline themselves in realizing the core values of Japanese culture: harmony, loyalty, filial piety, selflessness, diligence, ritual service. Problems can be solved by making a concerted effort to practice these virtues, to perfect the self, and to harmonize it with all levels of life (from personality integration to reconciliation with one's family, society, nature, ancestors, and the supernatural). The sects differ astoundingly in the prescriptions for accomplishing these goals, and we can give here only a representative sampling of the "new, new religions," groups formed in the postmodern era.

Perfect Liberty Kyodan Among the most popular groups is the Perfect Liberty Kyodan (P. L. Kyodan, or PL), whose primary slogan, "religion is art," indicates its emphasis on the spiritual value of practicing the fine arts in everyday life. Its focal practice is liturgical, that is, prayers choreographed with stylized prostrations, gestures, and offerings. The theology is monotheistic, but there is a strong emphasis on the human mind's central role in discerning divine warnings (*mishirase*) and receiving divine instruction (*mioshie)* through the sect's training. PL claims 500 churches in ten different countries, with more than 2.6 million members; its official aim is, according to its website, "to make true world peace a reality by inspiring people to understand and appreciate their power to create and plan, judge and decide, and make the world a true utopia."

Rissho Koseikai ("Society Establishing Righteousness and Harmony") Rissho Koseikai was founded by Reiyukai member Niwano Nikkyo (1906–1999), who retained the Nichiren Buddhist school's focus on the *Lotus Sutra*. After 1969, the group's focus shifted to the individual's personality development through special counseling sessions (*hoza*) led by trained lay "teachers" and the goal of world peace. In them, hoza members sit together in a circle, creating a warm, intimate atmosphere for open discussion. The range of problems and questions raised in the hoza varies from personal problems at home or office, through problems of human relationships, to questions of religion and ethics. Rissho Koseikai teachers are trained to bring the Mahayana teachings, particularly those highlighting the universal Buddha-nature within all beings, to bear on all problems. The member's vow, repeated daily, shows its Buddhist center and its commitment to bring the teachings to life in the modern world:

> We, members of Rissho Koseikai,
> Take refuge in the Eternal Buddha Shakyamuni,
> And recognize in Buddhism the true way of salvation,
> Under the guidance of our revered founder, Nikkyo Niwano.
> In the spirit of lay Buddhists,
> We vow to perfect ourselves
> Through personal discipline and leading others
> And by improving our knowledge and practice of the faith,
> And we pledge ourselves to follow the bodhisattva way
> To bring peace to our families, communities, and countries and to the world.[13]

The group does not forbid members to join other religious groups or to participate in their rituals. International missionary movements have brought Rissho Koseikai to Korea, Brazil, and the United States. As of 2007, the Koseikai was Japan's second-largest new religion, organized uniquely according to government unit lines and claiming over 6 million members.

Agonshu A new religion founded in 1971, Agonshu also has a Buddhist identity. The group was founded by Kiriyama Seiyu (b. 1921–), a charismatic spiritualist who declared that he had "cut off" his own karma and that through visits by Buddhas and deities, the true and original teachings of Shakyamuni Buddha were revealed to him. Kiriyama's distilled "essence of Buddhism" is that the ancestors must be properly "turned into realized Buddhas" through performing special rituals for them in the afterlife, a belief that would be disputed by traditional Buddhist monks and scholars. Agonshu teachings attribute the world's current troubles to the influence of the restless dead, who afflict the living to protest neglect. In the group's view, Kiriyama has rescued for the good of the entire world esoteric practices to pacify and enlighten the dead, particularly through fire rituals kept secret for centuries by the tantric Buddhist school in Japan called *Shingon*. The greatest yearly practice of this Agonshu rite, called *hoshi matsuri,* or "star festival," has become one of the most spectacular events in modern Japanese religion, attracting a half-million pilgrims to the site, while millions watch the spectacle on television. Each year Agonshu priests set massive twin fires, one to benefit the ancestors, the other to promote the personal welfare of all participants, who contribute millions of small boards to fuel the flaming blazes.

The goal of world peace has also in the last decade been featured as part of the sect's mission; Kiriyama has been photographed with Pope John Paul II and with the Dalai Lama to highlight Agonshu's intention of acting on the world stage for that end. Even with its outward missionizing, like many other new religions the group does not neglect fostering benefits for its individual disciples. Members are urged to chant the following five lines daily, the same words used to conclude Agonshu rallies:

> Let's do it!
> I will certainly succeed!
> I am blessed with very good luck!
> I will certainly do well!
> I will definitely win![14]

Sukyo Mahikari The group called Sukyo Mahikari, founded in 1963, provides an example of a more ethnocentric new religion that affirms fascist prewar values and presents a more narrow, sectarian view of salvation. It teaches that the postwar occupation unnaturally imposed democracy and materialism on the Japanese people, causing them to be possessed by evil spirits angry over the corruption of the country. Then communism was sent by the gods to warn humanity of a coming ordeal, or "baptism by fire," that will claim all but the elect, who must restore patriotic ties to the emperor and demonstrate their loyalty to other Confucian relationships (between parents and children, husbands and wives). Those who follow this vision set forth by the founder, Okada Kotama, will be the "seed people" to restart the world in its proper order, as set forth in a myth that foretells the leadership of Okada. This group's social programs without subtlety evoke a religious expression of prewar fascism by sponsoring military-style parades during which troops of disciples honor their founder with extended arms, a replica of the Nazi salute. Since the founder's death and the succession of his daughter to leader, the group has established branches in seventy-five countries and its aims have become more global. As its website proclaims: "Sukyo Mahikari strives to manifest a heavenly world: a civilization of peace, abundant health, and material well-being. It endeavors to reestablish a pristine and pollution-free world."

A STRONG CONFUCIAN TRADITION ACCOMMODATES KOREAN DIVERSITY

With the strong living tradition of Confucianism entrenched in family rituals, marriage arrangements, and the moral education programs in the public school curriculum, South Korea today is by all accounts the "most Confucian" nation in East Asia. Institutions dedicated to Confucian studies thrive in Korea, and exponents use the mass media to preach Confucian values. A common message is that by being true to its Confucian identity, Korea has a key role to play in achieving a harmonious "meeting of West and East."

Some among the Korean political elite (like many others in East Asia) believed Confucianism to be harmful to the nation, hindering its progress in the modern world. For those espousing this viewpoint, Westernization, agnosticism, and/or Christianity served as an antidote. However, Confucianism as the cultural center of Korea has endured even among Christian converts, most of whom openly observe their family's older rituals in honor of ancestors. South Korea adopted national economic goals in a Confucian framework: The central government takes responsibility for the citizenry's education and economic well-being, supports the family as the basis for social stability, accepts the intelligentsia as the conscience of the nation, and invests in education as the essential foundation for both material and cultural progress. The government has likewise supported major institutions dedicated to Confucian studies.

In the nation of North Korea, a strong if archaic emphasis on communist civil religion remains. Much as in the Maoist era, citizens are expected to renounce the culture of the past, sacrifice themselves for the common good, and participate in the "cult of personality" centered on the modern nation's ruling patriarch, Kim Jong Il.

As with Japan, we highlight groups that are shaping the diverse religious environment in modern South Korea.

❖ *Confucian Revival: The T'oegyehak Movement*

Since learning the lessons of history is a strong Confucian value, it is not surprising that an important South Korean group emphasizes a prominent figure in its own historical tradition, the philosopher Yi T'oegye (1501–1570). Master T'oegye developed the ideas of the most famous neo-Confucian Chinese thinker, Zhu Xi, whose Second Epoch leadership we have discussed, and T'oegye was responsible for making his system of thought prominent in Korea. To this end, he wrote treatises on the works of Zhu Xi and other neo-Confucians; all these texts were especially influential in the realm of state law and in focusing on ancestor ritualism.

The extraordinary industrial leader Lee Dong-choon (1919–1989) started the traditionalist **T'oegyehak** movement group by publishing the prolific writings of Master T'oegye. The T'oegyehak, which is a presence not only across East Asia but among East Asians living in the West, has tapped Lee's personal fortune to promote detailed studies of the Confucian values as interpreted by Chinese and Korean masters. The organization has sponsored numerous conferences and made low-cost copies of the Confucian classics available across the globe.

❖ Buddhist Revival

Despite many setbacks over the last century, the surviving Korean Buddhist institutions remain well endowed with landed income. As a result the major schools have established an important niche in Korean society through the monastery schools and lay institutions they founded. The Son Buddhist school, the Korean version of Zen, has sent several prominent teachers to the West, winning international support and renown.

A new school calling itself **Won Buddhism** arose in 1924, founded by Soe-Tae San (1891–1943), a teacher who claimed to have been enlightened from his own independent ascetic practices. He and his disciples sought to revive Buddhism by simplifying its doctrines and combining Pure Land and Zen teachings. The sole Won ritual involves the worship of a picture of a black circle in a white background, symbolizing the *dharmakaya,* the cosmic body of the Buddha. From this is derived the name of the group: *Won* is the Korean reading of the Chinese character "round."

Only after the death of San and the lifting of Japanese occupation did the group find popular acceptance across Korea. Typical of reformist "Protestant Buddhist" groups elsewhere in Asia (see Chapter 7), Won Buddhism has been especially popular in major urban areas and emphasizes that Buddhist doctrines are compatible with modern thought. It also makes Buddhism attractive to the laity by translating classical texts into vernacular Korean and through weekly congregational worship involving chanting, simple rituals, and sermons. The group encourages women to be leaders and active participants. Won Buddhist monks or nuns, who lead the ritual services, can marry.

Another aspect of Won Buddhism that resembles reform Buddhism as practiced outside Korea is the encouragement of lay meditation and social service. For the former, members try to cultivate the "Buddha nature in all things" and bring this awareness to all work done in everyday life, an exercise known as *Zen without time or place.* For Won social engagement, the Buddhist ideal of nonself (*anatman*) is sought through service offered to the public, and these activities are also seen in classical terms as a means to address the universality of suffering. The primary form of service by Won Buddhists has been in building schools, from kindergartens to universities. Its moral emphasis is also quite Confucian, emphasizing filial relations as the proper vehicle for Buddhist ethical aspiration.

By 2005, this school claimed 430 temples and 950,000 followers; it had built a grand central headquarters in Iri in southwest Korea and a convention center in Seoul.

The group has also spread to fourteen countries and the United States by way of immigrants, who have built many branch temples. Won Buddhists have shown increasing interest in ecumenical relations with other faiths, both in Korea and with Japanese Buddhist groups.

❖ Christianity in Korea

An alert observer of religion living in North America will be aware that significant numbers of native Koreans are Christians; signs with Korean characters dotting the landscape of many U.S. and Canadian cities announce that these congregations exist and sometimes share church sanctuaries with English-speaking Christians. As of 2000, approximately 30 percent of the South Korean population was Christian, with Protestants outnumbering Catholics by 4 to 1.

What makes Korea a unique stronghold of Christianity in Asia? Similarities between emotional Protestant rituals and the *mudang* tradition have been suggested as well as several elements unique to the recent Korean historical experience, such as the Buddhist cooperation with Japan's imperial rulers, churches' prominent involvement in the struggle against Japanese occupation (1910–1945), and Korean Christians' subsequent leadership in human rights activism. With the exception of some churches tolerating shamanism and reinterpreting ancestor ritualism within a Christian framework, there has been little doctrinal innovation outside the traditional denominational frameworks.

❖ Shamanism

Amid a rising number of Christian converts and modest revivals under way among the various Buddhist schools, old and new, one finds a steady and unmistakable reliance on shamans, or **mudang,** in South Korea. As discussed in Chapter 2, shamans in Korea enjoy uniquely high status and popularity in the East Asian region. Once demonized by Christian missionaries and denounced as charlatans by the early post–World War II South Korean governments, in 2007 shamans are lauded as bearers of "intangible cultural assets" and now have a growing following. An estimated 300,000 shamans exist in South Korea, and many now have commercial websites. Scholars speculate that it is shamanic traditions that have helped foster Korea's harmonious and richly pluralistic religious culture.

❖ Korean "New Religions"

As in Japan, the collapse of the traditional order in the nineteenth century precipitated a host of religious responses, and the one major avenue was the "new religions," formed to meet a three-part challenge: rebuilding the nation, restoring its spiritual center, and supporting individuals who were coping with rapid and often-traumatic changes.

Peak times of sociopolitical turmoil—for example, the years immediately following World War II—saw an especially great upsurge in these movements. Also conforming

Shamans have thrived in modern Korea through dramatic rituals such as this one, in which the mudang subdues a troublesome local spirit.

to the pattern seen in Japan's new religions, most Korean groups have been founded around men who claim a new supernatural revelation, usually a reassemblage of traditional doctrines from Buddhism, Daoism, Confucianism, or Christianity. Korean new religions likewise focus on this-worldly problems rather than the afterlife; some also imagine their playing a leading role in establishing Korea as humanity's global leader and/or creating a utopia on earth. Most have developed their doctrinal teachings into a comprehensive worldview and have created supportive social institutions. The total number of new religion adherents was last determined in 2003 by the government to number about 1 million, or 5 percent of the South Korean population. (We discuss the most prominent Korean new religion, the **Unification Church**, in the next chapter.)

 ## Conclusion

Our study of the religions of East Asia, past and present, has shown conclusively that contrary to assertions of many among the modern elites of China and Japan as well as numerous Western scholars, religious beliefs and practices are central to the life and culture of the region. East Asians are by no means an exception to the human condition, namely, that in every known society there are religious traditions at the center of its cultural life. Moreover, only by understanding the religious dimensions of Shintoism and Confucianism can one comprehend the nationalism and cultural foundations of Japan's recent economic success. Likewise, only by recognizing the religious dimensions of Maoist communism is it possible to fathom how in China the Communist Party has sustained its place of power since 1949, a topic we'll return to in Chapter Nine.

Nevertheless, Confucianism and Daoism present a challenge to the Western monotheistic model of "being religious," with some scholars claiming that these belief systems are not "religions" at all. Of course, in no manner is either monotheistic. Rather, their diverse aspects, as we illustrated, suggest another way for humans to be religious: not centering the sacred on a single God above but seeing as sacred this world "below," in which humans live together and within nature. Respect and reverence are the central religious emotions here. Confucianism and the diffuse religions of East Asia have both cultural and supernatural dimensions. They create in each society circles of reciprocal relatedness, making social relations sacred, harmonizing human existence with vital energies of nature, and respecting the creative power of the universe. In the supernatural dimension, they envision a world affected by deities and reverence the survival of ancestors as spirits with whom relations can endure forever.

Both attributes of religion outlined in Chapter One—"being bound to others" and "being careful"—are abundantly highlighted across the diverse landscape of East Asian religions. The general ethos promoted by all East Asian religions, old and new, can be characterized as optimistic toward human life and human potential, seeing the improvement of the individual and improvement of society as sacred goals. Respect for the multiple threads of the past serves to uphold acceptance of pluralism and the tolerance of religious diversity. The "diffuse religion" supports family cohesion as the center of a moral society, and the Confucian core of East Asia supports education for its role in cultivating character and in the acquisition of practical knowledge. This sort of "pragmatic idealism" calls for improving the world for the sake of this-worldly concerns, not as the dictate of a transcendent deity. The success in the modern global marketplace of this complex of religion and culture has given the lie to Western scholars who

The vibrant religious and philosophical ferment felt by many Chinese is clearly visible in the new art being produced by artists such as Zhang Huan.

had argued that East Asian religions were obstacles to modern economic development. New syncretistic religious understandings, informed by growing global connections, seem destined to develop further in China, as seen in new artistic movements.

CONTINUED RELIGIOUS REVIVAL IN CHINA: PROBLEMS AND POSSIBILITIES

In the face of determined government efforts by the Chinese communists to extirpate religion from society and despite three decades (1950–1980) of unchallenged propaganda in support of this goal, the reemergence of religion in China is powerful proof that Marx erred when he consigned religion to the "dustbin of history." Moreover, religion is gaining importance in the country, including underground Christian church movements, even as modern science, technology, and nationalism advance. The following census figures reveal the official reckoning of the scale and variation of organized religions in China today:

Table 8.1 Five Permitted Religions in the People's Republic of China			
Religion	**Adherents (millions)**	**Clergy (thousands)**	**Places of Worship**
Buddhism	100	200	20,000
Islam	20	40	30,000
Daoism	NA	25	1,500
Christianity: Protestantism	16	18	55,000
Christianity: Catholicism	5	4	4,600

SOURCE: China Daily, Chinese Foreign Ministry, 1997 [latest available official statistics].

If the Confucian system of family/ancestral devotion is regarded as the central pillar of Chinese tradition, then it is clear that it, too, has survived the criticisms and persecutions and that it has done so strongly. What is remarkable is that this has happened largely independent of any formal institutions and simply through the family relations that continued even amid fierce totalitarian attempts to suppress Confucianism.

It is possible that the future revival of religion in China will threaten regional stability. A large state trying to hold together diverse groups and disparate regions faces certain inherent problems, and difficulties loom large in the present relationship between communist China and its principal minorities. In particular, it is across religious issues that major fault lines affecting modern China are to be found—with Muslims in Xinjiang Province and with Buddhists in the Tibetan cultural region.

FALUN GONG

In general, there has been a marked lack of "new religions" in the PRC under communist rule; but barely a quarter century after Mao's death, the party leadership discovered that its relaxation of earlier repressive policies had allowed the formation of a powerful new Chinese religion called Buddhist Law Power (*Falun Gong* or *Falun Dafa*). After Falun Gong had spread to millions across China—young and old, party members and poor migrating laborers alike—and built an organization across the nation, its leaders began to attract government criticism, and its members suffered episodes of forceful intimidation. In late April 1999, the group staged a protest against these actions, with 10,000 members surrounding the Communist Party leadership compound in central Beijing. Arriving undetected, Falun Gong followers sat in silent, nonviolent protest throughout the day and then dispersed without incident. The massive sit-in baffled and unsettled the government, provoking an official warning against future protest actions. By summer, an all-out propaganda offensive was directed against it, capped by the arrest of Falun Gong leaders, who were charged with antigovernment subversion. By the fall, the group had been outlawed as "pernicious superstition." Thousands of members in small groups now stage protests against this persecution, fully aware that some of their number have been imprisoned and tortured and some have disappeared.

Falun Gong resembles the new religions we have described in Korea and Japan: Its doctrines comprise an original recombination of Buddhist and Daoist doctrines, and its founder, a charismatic leader named Li Hongzhi, claims supernormal status, "on a level the same as Buddha and Jesus." Its principal practice of qi gong exercises promises to promote individual health and spiritual transformation through the generation of extraordinary energy, in line with Daoist traditions at least two millennia old. Claiming 100 million followers in China and thirty other countries, Master Li from his exile in the United States has written texts and used mass media (videos, audiotapes, and Internet websites) to maintain connections between himself and his disciples. Falun Gong is an apt example of a new East Asian religion in the age of media technology, when faiths are becoming global. Such an organization, built on a now-shut-down network of centers across China, is one that China's communist government will never allow to form again. It is also certain that members of Falun Gong will continue to use their international ties and the Internet to protest across the globe their persecution by the Chinese government, including claims that imprisoned sect members have been tortured and used for involuntary organ transplants in prison.

A THIRD CONFUCIAN EPOCH?

Ascribing East Asia's economic revival mainly to its Confucian roots remains, for some, a contested position. However, there are signs of Confucian renewal in each country, as societies have modified traditions to foster modernity without abandoning classical

Confucian schools pro-
moting the classical
Confucian humanities
are being reinvented in
China in the twenty-
first century.

roots. According to "Third Epoch" proponents, the traumas of the modern era succeeded in liberating the Confucian worldview from the trappings of power that had
developed in the imperial systems of China, Korea, and Japan. Under them, the application of the highest Confucian ideals had been corrupted by government officials and
the organized religious academies that turned "mastery" of the classics into a mere
exercise in memorization needed to pass imperial examinations.

Now the Confucian revival movement seeks to return to the basic teachings of the
early sages (Confucius and Mencius, of the First Epoch) and do what Master Zhu Xi
and other reformers did in their time (Song Dynasty, 960–1279), when they revived,
reinterpreted, and adapted the tradition to the challenges of their era posed by Daoism
and Buddhism (the Second Epoch of neo-Confucianism). Believers in "Third Epoch"
Confucianism, working in the states on the periphery of China and finding growing
supporters in mainland China as well, are now addressing the challenges of economic
and cultural globalization.

Such efforts to revive this spiritual tradition have made "Third Epoch" Confucians
critical of the global modernizing process, especially insofar as it has caused the
extreme fragmentation of society, promoted the vulgarization of social life, disregarded
the public good, or overglorified wealth. The vast majority of modernist Confucians
adopt this critical stance while also being committed to empirical science, democratic
politics, gender equality, and the economic development in their own countries. In

early twenty-first-century China, interest in promoting Confucianism as a means of forming the character of citizens is winning widespread support among intellectuals and parents and even within the Communist Party itself. A host of newly approved schools include in their curriculum the study of traditional Confucianism; "Harmonious Society," the 2002 slogan for the nation's future that has been adopted by Hu Jintao, the new Communist Party president, has Confucian overtones. In 2007, a book on Confucian thought published in China became a best seller: *Yu Dan's Reflections on the Analects* sold over 10.2 million copies in the first year, and the author became a media celebrity starring in a show covering the basic teachings. Though some traditional scholars have criticized her simplified, selective interpretations of how the Analects provide advice for "stress reduction, forgiveness, simple living, friendship, and achieving one's dreams,"[15] the success of this book signals how far the culture of China has shifted again toward its great classical heritage.

Yet the global vision of "Third Epoch" exponents is to bring the Confucian tradition into the debate about how the twenty-first century's global order should be conceived. They aim to foster dialog between the Confucian worldview and the ideologies of sociopolitical modernization and consumerism prominent in the Euro-American world. One "Third Epoch" Confucian summarized this goal as follows:

Professor Yu Dan, author of the first best-selling book on Confucianism in modern China.

> Copernicus decentered the earth, Darwin relativized the godlike image of man, Marx exploded the ideology of social harmony, and Freud complicated our conscious life. They have redefined humanity for the modern age. Yet they have also empowered us with communal, critical self-awareness, to renew our faith in the ancient Confucian wisdom that the globe is the center of our universe and the only home for us and that we are the guardians of the good earth, the trustees of the Mandate of Heaven that enjoins us to make our bodies healthy, our hearts sensitive, our minds alert, our souls refined, and our spirits brilliant. . . . We are Heaven's partners, indeed cocreators. . . . Since we help Heaven to realize itself through our self-discovery and self-understanding in day-to-day living, the ultimate meaning of life is found in our ordinary human existence.[16]

Informed by very different notions of religious truth and by ethnocentric visions of their own central places in the cosmos, will the world's people outside East Asia be interested in such a dialog?

Discussion Questions

1. What beliefs from each of the three religious traditions of the region might explain the East Asian peoples' unique capacity for sustaining the three without choosing just one?

2. How is the cult of ancestor veneration related to the norms of Confucian family morality?

3. A Chinese novelist in the colonial period described the Chinese family as "a prison ward" that denies basic rights to the individual, exploits women, and wastes the energy of the young. How would you defend Confucian ideals against these criticisms?

4. What Daoist teachings would explain why many Chinese people over the ages have embraced Buddhism, which originated in India, despite strong teachings about the inferiority of non-Chinese people?

5. How might neo-Confucianism be seen as an attempt to harmonize Buddhism, Daoism, and early Confucianism?

6. Why, from the Daoist perspective, are disasters in the natural world taken so seriously by politicians in East Asia?

7. Why do purity and brightness sum up the ethos of Shintoism?

8. Are the twenty-first-century depictions of Daruma-san a reflection of how irrelevant Zen ideals have become in the popular imagination? Or are these an apt cultural reminder, embedded in the "diffuse popular religion," of Zen Buddhism's embrace of a spirituality that connects the transcendent with the cosmic?

9. Critique the following proposition: China's religious revival was postponed by the Chinese communists, who imposed a "forced conversion" of the nation to Marxism–Leninism, the "new religion" it had imported from Europe.

10. For all the nations of East Asia, the colonial era was very destructive. But certain individuals fused ideas from global culture with older beliefs, creating new and original religious understandings. Cite an example of this process in China, in Korea, and in Japan.

11. What influences from the West might have influenced elites in East Asia to claim that the Chinese (or the Japanese) are "not religious"?

Key Terms

All Souls Festival
Amaterasu
Analects
ancestor veneration
Ch'ondogyo
city god
Confucianism
Confucius
Cultural Revolution
Dao
Daoism, philosophical
Daoism, religious
Daoist
Daruma-san
de
diffuse religion
Five Classics
Full Moon Festival
Guan Yu
Hong Xiuquan
kami
"kitchen god"
Lao Zi
li
ling
mappo
Master K'ung
Mencius
mudang

neo-Confucianism
neo-Shintoism
"new religions"
Nichiren
philosophical Daoism
qi
qi gong
Qing-Ming
religious Daoism
ren
shamanism
Shang-di
shen
Shinto
Soka Gakkai
Taiping Rebellion
Tenrikyo
"three faiths"
Tian di
T'oegyehak
Tu-di gong
Unification Church
Won Buddhism
wu-wei
xiao
yin-yang theory
Zhu Xi
Zhuang Zi

Suggested Readings

Buswell, Robert E. *Religions of Korea in Practice* (Princeton, NJ: Princeton University Press, 2007).

Earhart, H. Byron. *Japanese Religion: Unity and Diversity* (Belmont, CA: Wadsworth, 1983).

Gardner, Daniel. *The Four Books* (Indianapolis, IN: Hackett, 2007).

Kendall, Laurel. *Shamans, Housewives, and Other Restless Spirits: Women in Korean Ritual Life* (Honolulu: University of Hawaii Press, 1985).

Lancaster, Lewis R., ed. *Contemporary Korean Religion* (Berkeley, CA: Institute for East Asian Studies, 1992).

Lee, Peter H., ed. *Sources of Korean Tradition: From Early Times to the 16th Century* (New York: Columbia University Press, 1996).

Lopez, Jr., Donald S., ed. *Religions of China in Practice* (Princeton, N.J.: Princeton University Press, 1996).

MacInnis, Donald E. *Religion in China Today* (New York: Orbis, 1989).

Nelson, John K. *A Year in the Life of a Shinto Shrine* (Seattle: University of Washington Press, 1996).

Picken, S. D. B. *Shinto: Japan's Spiritual Roots* (Tokyo: Kodansha, 1980).

Reader, Ian. *Religion in Contemporary Japan* (Honolulu: University of Hawaii Press, 1991).

——— and Tanabe, Jr., George J. *Practically Religious: Worldly Benefits and the Common Religion of Japan* (Honolulu: University of Hawaii Press, 1998).

Reid, T. R. *Confucius Lives Next Door: What Living in the East Teaches Us About Living in the West* (New York: Vintage Books, 1999).

Thompson, Laurence G. *Chinese Religion: An Introduction,* 5th ed. (Belmont, CA: Wadsworth, 1996).

Welch, Holmes. *The Practice of Chinese Buddhism, 1900–1950* (Cambridge, MA: Harvard University Press, 1973).

Notes

1. In D. C. Lau, *Confucius: The Analects* (New York: Penguin, 1979), p. 63.
2. In D. C. Lau, *Mencius* (New York: Penguin, 1970), p. 191.
3. Quoted in Stephen Teiser, "Popular Religion," *Journal of Asian Studies* 54(2), 1995, 378.
4. In Wing-sit Chan, *A Source book of Chinese Philosophy* (Princeton, N.J. Princeton University Press, 1973), 86–87.
5. *Ibid.*, pp. 497–498.
6. Timothy Brook, "Rethinking Syncretism: The Unity of the Three Teachings and Their Joint Worship in Late-Imperial China," *Journal of Chinese Religions,* 21, 1993, 17.
7. *Ibid.*, 18.
8. *Ibid.*, 22.
9. Quoted in Wing-tsit Chan, *Instructions for Practical Living and Other Neo-Confucian Writings by Wang Yang-ming.* (New York: Columbia University Press, 1962), p. 272.
10. Robert Buswell, Jr., ed., *Religions of Korea in Practice.* (Princeton University Press, 2007), p. 450.
11. In Donald E. MacInnis, *Religion in China Today* (New York: Orbis, 1989), p. 206.
12. S. D. B. Picken, *Shinto: Japan's Spiritual Roots* (Tokyo: Kodansha International, 1980), p. 56.
13. http://www.rk-world.org/ (November 10, 2007).
14. Ian Reader, *Religion in Contemporary Japan* (Honolulu: University of Hawaii Press, 1991), p. 100.
15. "Modern Gloss on China's Golden Age," *New York Times,* September 3, 2007.
16. Ian Reader, "The Rise of a Japanese 'New New Religion,'" *Japanese Journal of Religious Studies* 15(4), 1988, 244.

Web Bibliography

http://www.kurozumikyo.com/index.html
http://www.tenrikyo.or.jp/kaiden/newsletter/index.html
http://www.reiyukai.org/
http://www.pl-usa.org/welcome.html
http://www.rk-world.org/
http://www.sukyomahikari.org/index.html

6

Islam in Asia

Overview

Islam is the second largest of the world's religions. The 1.3 billion Muslims of the world are spread across more than fifty-seven Muslim majority countries and within Europe and America, where Islam is the second- and third-largest religion, respectively. Despite its global profile, Islam still tends to be disproportionately identified with the Arab world or the Middle East. Yet the vast majority of Muslims live in Asia and Africa. The Muslims of Asia, almost two-thirds of the world's Muslims, constitute the largest Muslim communities in the world. More Muslims live in Indonesia, Pakistan, Bangladesh, and India than live in the entire Arab world.

In an Asian Islam context, South and Southeast Asia, which account for 52 percent of all Muslims, enjoy special importance, given their size and their diversity. South Asia has 470 million Muslims. Living in Afghanistan, Pakistan, India, Nepal, Bhutan, Bangladesh, Sri Lanka, and Maldives, they belong to different ethnic, linguistic, cultural, social, and economic groups. A rich variety of Muslim religious belief, practice, and politics can be seen in these countries, from the Taliban of Afghanistan to the more modern cosmopolitan societies of Malaysia and Indonesia.

Southeast Asia's 240 million people live in a "Muslim archipelago," extending from southern Thailand, through Malaysia, Singapore, and Indonesia, and north to the southern Philippines. Muslim-minority communities also exist in Burma (Myanmar), northern and southern Thailand, and Cambodia. Approximately 88 percent of Indonesia's more than 241 million people are Muslim. They represent the largest population of Muslims in any country of the world. Also noteworthy is Malaysia, where approximately 60 percent of its 24 million Muslims live in a multireligious and multiethnic society of Chinese, Indians, Hindus, Buddhists, and

Christians. Malaysia and Indonesia have experienced considerable economic development and achieved a measure of political democracy while continuing to emphasize their Islamic roots and culture.

Although many Asian Muslim countries (Indonesia, Pakistan, Bangladesh, Malaysia) are multireligious and multiethnic societies with a history and legacy of religious and political pluralism and tolerance, in recent years communal conflicts have challenged and threatened that legacy. In Indonesia, despite a majority of Muslims who have participated in democratic elections, violent organizations also exist. The multinational Jemaah Islamiyya, which has reported ties to al-Qaeda, has been responsible for bombings in Bali, Jakarta, and elsewhere. The now-defunct Laskar Jihad (charged with the death of thousands of Christians, particularly in East Indonesia) and the Islamic Defenders Front (which follows radical interpretations of Islam) do not support democratic and pluralist values, and the militant group Abu Sayyaf in the Philippines has contributed to sectarian violence between Muslims and Christians. Islam in Asia has also been used to legitimate self-proclaimed Islamic governments in Pakistan and the Taliban's Afghanistan and to mobilize armed opposition in Central Asia.

For majorities of Muslims in Asia, Islam is both faith and way of life, a source of guidance for private life and public life. Like Judaism and Christianity, it began in the Arab world and like Christianity quickly spread throughout the Middle East, Africa, and Asia.

The Dawn of Islam in Asia

From the earliest years of Islam, merchants, seamen, mystics (Sufis), and soldiers traveled to port cities as far as China, establishing mosques and spreading the faith. In southern Asia, Islam made its first appearance in 711 when Muhammad bin Qasim and his armies traveled by sea to Sind, in what is Pakistan today. However, Muslims were able to establish a permanent presence in South Asia only after 1000, when Muslim armies as well as émigrés began to arrive in India through the Khyber Pass, which now marks the border between Afghanistan and Pakistan. Muslim expansion led to the establishment of the Delhi sultanates, incorporating increasing swathes of North Indian soil into Muslim rule. More important than immigration or even Muslim rule was the conversion of many in the local population to Islam, largely through the efforts of **Sufis** (Muslim mystics) and Muslim traders. In the fifteenth century, Akbar (1556–1605), the first great Mughal emperor, expanded the Mughal empire through conquest and diplomacy, consolidating Muslim rule in all but south India, and thus became the chief political force in the Indian subcontinent. Islam's expanding cultural influence can be seen in the magnificent Taj Mahal in Agra, created for of the Mughal emperor Shah Jahan's

The Taj Mahal, the mausoleum built (1631–47) by the grief-stricken emperor Shah Jahan for his beloved wife, Mumtaz Mahal, who died in childbirth. Situated in a 42-acre garden, it is flanked by two perfectly proportioned mosque complexes. This crowning achievement, landmark of world architecture, symbolizes the wealth and splendor of the Mughal Empire. The project brought together craftsmen and calligraphers from the Islamic world who worked with Muslim and Hindu craftsmen from the empire.

wife, Mumtaz Mahal. One of the most beautiful and costly mausoleums in the world, it is the greatest Mughal architectural monument and one of the Seven Wonders of the Modern World.

Traders, Arab and Indian, as well as Sufis played an even greater role in bringing Islam to the Malay-Indonesian archipelago. Muslim tombstones dating as early as the eleventh century can be found in Java. However, large-scale conversion occurred only after Muhammad Iskander Shah, ruler of Malacca, embraced Islam in 1414. Malaccan power and state sponsorship as well as individual missionary activity resulted in the spread of Islam throughout the peninsula. Strong Muslim states such as Aceh in North Sumatra and Banten in Java arose in the sixteenth century, followed by a host of other inland states in the seventeenth century. These states soon became well integrated in international sea trade that linked them to the Chinese empire as well as to the Muslim Mughal and Ottoman empires. Southeast Asian Muslims also established religious and intellectual links by studying at the great Islamic centers of learning in the Arab world, such as Al-Azhar in Cairo, the leading source of religious education, scholarship, and authority in the Muslim world, and this trend has continued throughout Southeast Asian history. Despite their rich religious and cultural diversity, Muslims in Asia possess a common underlying unity of faith, a religious worldview and a way of life shared with Muslims throughout the world.

WHAT IS ISLAM AND WHAT DOES IT MEAN TO BE A MUSLIM?

The word *Islam* means "peace" and "submission" to God. Just as Jews use the greeting *Shalom* (peace), Muslims have a similar greeting: *Assalam wa alaykum* (peace be upon you), which is used when greeting a friend or saying goodbye. The word *Muslim* means one who serves or follows God's will. The religion of Islam is not only a faith but also a way of life and a global community. Every Muslim, regardless of his or her race, sex, or tribal, ethnic, or national background, is a member of a worldwide community of believers (**ummah**), bound together by a common faith and mission: to create a socially just society: As the **Quran**, the Muslim scripture, says, "You are the best community ever brought forth for mankind, enjoining what is good and forbidding evil" (Q. 3:110).

THE CHILDREN OF ABRAHAM

Islam belongs to the Abrahamic family of monotheistic faiths. Jews, Christians, and Muslims all view themselves as the children of Abraham, whose story is told in the Old Testament (Hebrew Bible) and in the Quran. While Jews and Christians claim descent from Abraham and his wife, Sarah, through their son Isaac, Muslims trace their religious roots back to Abraham (Ibrahim) through Ismail, his firstborn son by Hagar, Sarah's Egyptian servant.

Despite specific and significant differences, Judaism, Christianity, and Islam share a belief in one God, the creator, sustainer, and ruler of the universe, who is beyond ordinary experience.

> "Say: He is Allah, the One and only; Allah, the Eternal. He did not beget, nor is He begotten; and there is none like Him."
>
> —Qur'an, 112

All three faiths believe in prophets, revelation, angels, Satan, moral responsibility and accountability, divine judgment, and reward and punishment. For Muslims, Islam is the completion of earlier revelations of **Allah** (Arabic for "God") to Moses and Jesus.

A dynamic religion that interfaces and at times competes with other faiths, Islam has had a significant impact on world affairs. Throughout much of history, to be a Muslim was not simply to belong to a faith community or to worship in a given place but to live in an Islamic community/state or empire, governed (in theory if not always in practice) by Islamic law. Historically, Islam has significantly formed and informed Muslim politics and civilization, giving rise to vast Islamic empires (caliphates) and states (sultanates) as well as Islamic civilization.

From earliest times Muslims engaged in a process of understanding and interpreting the word of God (Quran), defining, redefining, and applying their faith to the realities of life. This process led to the development of Islamic law, theology, and mysticism. Islamic doctrines and laws addressed the political and social questions and issues that arose in the first centuries of Islamic history. Religious doctrines, laws, and practices resulted not only from clear prescriptions in sacred texts but from the interpretations of religious scholars that reflected their intelligence and political and social environments. For example, since interpreters of Islam were males living in male-dominated societies,

Mecca is the holiest city of Islam: the birthplace of the Prophet Muhammad, where the earliest revelations occurred and toward which Muslims turn in prayer five times each day. Muslims on pilgrimage gather near Mecca's Grand Mosque following Friday dawn prayers.

the development of Islamic laws relating to women and the family was influenced by patriarchal culture and values. Thus, while it is correct to say that there is one Islam, revealed in the Quran and the traditions of the Prophet, there have been many human interpretations of Islam, some complementing each other, others in conflict.

The Islamic Tradition

At the core of Muslim faith and belief are the Prophet Muhammad and the Muslim scripture, the Quran. As Christians look to Jesus and the New Testament, and Jews to Moses and the Torah, Muslims regard Muhammad and the Quran as the final, perfect, and complete revelation of God's will for humankind. In addition, because of the remarkable success of Muhammad and the early Muslim community in spreading the faith of Islam and the rule of Muslims, an idealized memory of Islamic history and of Muslim rule became the model for success, serving as a common reference point for later generations of reformers.

God is beyond or transcends our ordinary experience, cannot be known directly, but, Muslims believe, he can be known through his messengers and revelations. Thus, Muhammad and the Quran, the final messenger and message, were key in the formation and development of the Islamic tradition, its beliefs, laws, rituals, and social practices.

MUHAMMAD: PROPHET AND STATESMAN

While there is a great deal of information about Muhammad's life after he received his "call" to be God's messenger, the portrait of his early years is drawn from early Muslim writers, legend, and Muslim belief. Muhammad ibn Abdullah (the son of Abdullah) was born in 570 into the ruling tribe of Mecca, the Quraysh. Orphaned at an early age, Muhammad was raised by an uncle and later employed in Mecca's thriving caravan business. During the prime of his life, Muhammad had one wife, Khadija, for twenty-eight years, until her death. Much is recorded about Muhammad's relationship with Khadija, who was his closest confidante and comforter and strongest supporter. The couple had six children, two sons who died in infancy and four daughters. After Khadija's death, Muhammad married other women, all but one of them widows.

By the age of 30, Muhammad had become a prominent, respected member of Meccan society, known for his business skill and trustworthiness. Muhammad would often retreat to the quiet and solitude of Mount Hira to contemplate his life and society. Here during the month of Ramadan in 610, on a night Muslims commemorate as the Night of Power and Excellence, Muhammad the caravan leader became Muhammad the messenger of God. Through a heavenly intermediary, identified by later tradition as the angel Gabriel, Muhammad at the age of 40 received the first message, or revelation: "Recite in the name of your Lord who has created, Created man out of a germ cell. Recite, for your Lord is the most generous One, Who has taught by the pen, Taught man what he did not know."

Muhammad became a link in a long series of biblical prophets, messengers from God who served as a conscience to the community and as God's messenger. Like Moses, who had received the Torah on Mount Sinai from the God of the Hebrews, Muhammad received the first of God's revelations on Mount Hira: "It is He who sent down to you the Book with the truth, confirming what went before it: and He sent down the Torah and the Injil ["Gospel"] before as a guidance to the people" (Q. 3:3). Also, like Amos and Jeremiah before him, Muhammad served as a "warner" from God who admonished his hearers to repent and obey God, for the final judgment was near:

> Say: "O Men I am only a warner." Those who believe, and do deeds of righteousness—theirs shall be forgiveness and generous provision. And those who strive against our signs to avoid them—they shall be inhabitants of Hell. (Q. 22:49–50)

Muhammad continued to receive revelations for more than two decades (610–632); together these revelations constitute the text of the Quran (literally, "the recitation or discourse").

As Muhammad continued to preach his message, the situation in Mecca became more difficult. After ten years of rejection and persecution in Mecca, Muhammad and his followers migrated to Yathrib, renamed Medina, "city" of the prophet, in 622. Invited to serve as arbiter, or judge, for Muslim and non-Muslim alike, Muhammad became the religious and political leader of the community. Medina proved a new beginning, for the Muslim community prospered and grew.

The emigration (**hijra**) from Mecca to Yathrib, (renamed Medina the "city" of the Prophet) in 622 was a turning point in Muhammad's life and in Islamic history, the establishment of the Islamic community. The importance of this event was underscored by the decision to date the beginning of the Muslim calendar not from the birth of the Prophet or from his first revelation but from the creation of the Islamic community at Medina.

Muhammad did not create a new religion; rather, he was a prophet and reformer. His message proclaimed monotheism, the unity (**tawhid**), or oneness, of God. Muslims believe that, over time, the Jewish and Christian communities had distorted God's original revelation. Therefore, they see Muhammad (the last, or "seal," of the prophets (Q. 33:40) and the Quran, the complete, uncorrupted revelation, as a corrective, a restoration of the true faith and message of God. All were called by Muhammad to repentance, to turn away from the path of unbelief and false practice and toward the straight path (**sharia**) of God.

During the short decade that Muhammad led the community at Medina, he forged its identity, consolidated its political base, and established its basic religious law and

The courtyard of the Mosque of the Prophet in Medina, the first mosque in Islam, is among the most sacred sites in Islam. The original structure has been rebuilt and expanded several times.

practice. Muhammad skillfully employed both force and diplomacy to defeat the Meccans and then to unite the tribes of Arabia under the banner of Islam. Muhammad's resort when under siege to flight (hijra) or emigration, armed struggle (**jihad**), and diplomacy have remained a time-honored example throughout Muslim history.

THE MESSAGE OF THE QURAN

Muslims believe that the Quran is the eternal, uncreated, literal, and final word of God, revealed to Muhammad as guidance for humankind (Q. 2:185). Thus, Islam is not a new religion but rather the oldest, for Muslims believe that it represents the "original" as well as the final revelation of God to Abraham, Moses, Jesus, and Muhammad.

The text of the Quran is about four-fifths the length of the New Testament. The Muslim scripture consists of 114 chapters (**surahs**) of 6,000 verses, arranged by length, not chronology.

The God (Allah) of the Quran is seen as the creator, sustainer, ruler, and judge of humankind. He is merciful and just, the all-knowing and all-powerful, the lord and ruler of the universe. The Quran teaches that God's revelation has occurred in several forms: in nature, in history, and in scripture.

Muslims believe that the Quran, like the Torah and the Evangel (Gospel), is taken from a heavenly Arabic tablet, the mother, or source, of all revealed scriptures. From it, the teachings of the three Abrahamic faiths (Judaism, Christianity, and Islam) were taken and revealed at different stages in history. Indeed, many Muslims take their names from the biblical prophets Ibrahim (Abraham), Musa (Moses), Sulayman (Solomon), Dawud (David), Yahya (John), Mary (Maryam), and Issa (Jesus). Equally striking to many is the fact that the name of Mary, the mother of Jesus, is cited more often in the Quran than in the entire New Testament.

Throughout Muslim history, Jesus and Mary (Maryam), his mother, have been held in high esteem. Jesus enjoys a special place among the prophets in

> In matters of faith, He has laid down for you the same commandment that He gave Noah, which We have revealed to you [Muhammad] and which We enjoined on Abraham and Moses and Jesus: 'Uphold the faith and do not divide into factions within it".
>
> —Quran 42:13

God's word, as revealed in the Quran, is the final and complete revelation. It provides the primary and ultimate source of guidance, the basis for belief and practice in Islam. Study, memorization, recitation, and copying of the Quran have been central acts of piety. The noble art of copying the Quran has produced a rich tradition of calligraphy. This manuscript page provides a beautiful example.

Islam. The Quran affirms the virgin birth of Jesus, the promised Messiah," who declared from his cradle: "I am God's servant; God has given me the Book, and made me a prophet" (Q. 19:30).

SUNNI AND SHIAH ISLAM

Given the pivotal role of Muhammad in the life of the community, his death in 632 was a traumatic event. What was the community to do? Who was to lead?

Muhammad's senior followers, known as the Companions of the Prophet, moved quickly to name a successor and reassure the community. They selected Abu Bakr as **caliph** (*khalifah,* "successor or deputy"), who was not a prophet but rather Muhammad's successor as political and military leader of the community.

Although the majority of the community accepted the selection of Abu Bakr as caliph, a minority strongly disagreed. They believed that Muhammad's successor should come from the family of the Prophet, its senior male member, Ali, Muhammad's cousin and son-in-law. Although initially bypassed, Ali was eventually selected as the fourth caliph. However, almost immediately his authority was challenged by the rebellion of Muawiya, the governor of Syria. Arbitration proved inconclusive. When Ali was assassinated by a breakaway group of religious extremists, Muawiya seized power and established the Umayyad dynasty (661–750).

Because Muslims believe that the Quran is God's Word, or revelation, from an early age children are taught to read the Quran.

Opposition to Umayyad rule led to a rebellion by the followers of Ali and the two great branches of Islam, the **Sunni** majority and the **Shiah**, or Shii, minority. The followers (*shiah,* "partisans") of Ali had been thwarted twice: when Ali was not appointed as the first caliph, and later when Muawiya seized the caliphate from Ali, who had been the Prophet's fourth successor. In 680, when Yazid, the son of Muawiya, came to power, Husayn, the son of Ali, was persuaded by a group of Ali's followers in Kufa (a city in modern Iraq) to lead a rebellion. However, the support promised to Husayn did not materialize, and Husayn and his army were overwhelmed and slaughtered by the Umayyad army at the city of Karbala (also in modern Iraq).

The memory of Karbala and the "martyrdom" of Husayn resulted in a Shii worldview, a paradigm of suffering, oppression, and protest against injustice. It was reinforced by early Shii experience as a disenfranchised or disinherited minority, often in opposing and rebelling against Sunni rulers.. The memory and commemoration of Husayn's martyrdom at Karbala, with its belief that Sunni rulers were usurpers and that this injustice would eventually be corrected with the coming of a messianic figure (the Mahdi) has sustained the community throughout history; it became a major source of inspiration and mobilization during Iran's "Islamic" Revolution of 1978–79.

Sunni Muslims constitute 85 percent and Shiah approximately 15 percent of the global Islamic community. Although united in their common confession of faith in God, the Quran, and the Prophet Muhammad, their notions of leadership and history differ.

The reality of the dynastic Umayyad and Abbasid caliphates notwithstanding, in Sunni Islam the caliph ideally is the selected or elected successor of the Prophet. However, he serves only as political and military leader of the community, not as prophet. In Shiah Islam, the **Imam**, or leader, is not selected from among the members of the community but must be a direct descendant of the Prophet's family. He is not only the political but also the religiopolitical leader of the community. Though not a prophet, he is the divinely inspired, sinless, infallible, final authoritative interpreter of God's will as formulated in Islamic law.

As a result of their experiences, Sunni and Shiah also developed differing interpretations of history. For Sunni, the early success of Islam and the power of its rulers were signs of God's guidance, rewards to a faithful community that were seen as historic validation of Muslim belief and claims. In contrast, the Shiah saw the same events as the illegitimate usurpation of power by Sunni rulers. For Shiah, therefore, history is the theater for the struggle of a minority community, righteous but historically oppressed and disinherited, who must restore God's rule on earth.

ISLAMIC LAW AND MYSTICISM

In contrast to Christianity's emphasis on doctrine or theology, Islam, like Judaism, places primary emphasis on what believers should do, on religious observance of and obedience to God's law. Muslims are commanded by the Quran to strive, or struggle (the literal word for struggle is *jihad*), in the path (sharia) of God, to realize, spread, and defend God's message and community. They are to function as God's representatives, or stewards, on earth, promoting the good and prohibiting evil (Q. 3:104, 3:110). All Muslims are responsible as individuals and as a community for the creation of the good society. Despite vast cultural differences, Islamic law has provided an idealized blueprint that has instilled among Muslims throughout the ages a common code of behavior and a sense of religious identity.

Islamic law did not develop primarily from the practice of courts or from government decrees but through the interpretation of religious scholars, **ulama**, who set out a religious ideal, a moral blueprint, based on four sources: The Quran, the Sunnah, *qiyas,* and *ijma*.

The Quran, which Muslims believe is the very word of God, is the primary source of Islamic law. It contains approximately eighty prescriptions that would rank as legal in the strict sense of the term, but the majority of Quranic texts provide general principles and values, reflecting what the aims and aspirations of Muslims should be.

The **Sunnah** (example) of the Prophet consists of hundreds of thousands of narrative stories (*hadith*) about what Muhammad is reported to have said or done. The centrality of the Sunnah and hadith in Islam cannot be overestimated. As a distinguished contemporary Muslim scholar has noted: "They are associated with the person who is 'alive' here and now and who is as revered and loved by all Muslims now as he was fourteen centuries ago."[1]

The third source of law is **qiyas**, which means "analogical reasoning." When confronted by a question or issue not addressed specifically and clearly in the Quran or the Sunnah, jurists looked for similar or analogous situations or examples to identify principles that could be applied to a new case. For example, no specific text deals with the use of mind-altering drugs, but jurists, by looking at analogical situations or texts, justify the condemnation of such substances on the basis of sacred texts that plainly forbid the consumption of alcohol.

Finally, **ijma**, or "consensus," in theory was based on a statement traditionally attributed to the Prophet: "My community will never agree on an error." In reality, consensus has generally amounted to acceptance of or consensus about an issue from the majority of ulama, scholars, who represented religious authority.

Islamic law has two main divisions: duties to God, which consist of obligatory religious practices or rituals such as the Five Pillars of Islam, and duties to others or social relations, regulations that govern public life, from contract and international law to laws on marriage, divorce, and inheritance.

Though Islamic law is a source of unity and guidance, individual jurists and legal scholars from diverse social backgrounds and cultural contexts have differed in their interpretation of sacred texts and legal reasoning. We see these differences in official legal opinions or interpretations (*fatwas*) of Muslim jurists (*muftis*) who advised rulers, judges, and litigants. A modern example is that of Salman Rushdie. This author of *The Satanic Verses,* a novel, was condemned to death by a fatwa from the Iranian **Ayatollah** Ruholla Khomeini, who found Rushdie guilty of blasphemy. With a price on his head,

Rushdie went into hiding. Some muftis, however, while deploring the book, called for the writer to be tried by Islamic law. In the Gulf War of 1991, some muftis supported Iraq and others supported a U.S.-led armada that included troops from Egypt, Kuwait, and Saudi Arabia. Similarly, sharp differences have existed among religious leaders over the religious legitimacy or illegitimacy of suicide bombing in Israel–Palestine.

However different and, at times, contentious interpretations of Islam and Muslim politics have been throughout Islamic history, the Five Pillars of Islam unite all Muslims in their worship and following of God.

THE FIVE PILLARS OF ISLAM

If God, the Quran, and the Prophet Muhammad are the foundation, the Five Pillars of Islam are the essentials of belief and practice that unite all Muslims however ethnically, racially, or culturally diverse they may be.

1. *The Declaration of Faith.* A Muslim is one who declares, "There is no God but the God and Muhammad is the messenger of God." One need only make this simple statement, known as the **shahadah**, to become a Muslim. The first part of the shahadah affirms Islam's absolute, uncompromising monotheism, faith in the oneness, or unity (**tawhid**), of God. The second part is the affirmation that Muhammad is the messenger of God, the last and final prophet, who serves as a model, "the living Quran," for the Muslim community.

   The action or practice orientation of Islam is illustrated by the remaining four pillars or duties.

2. *Prayer.* Five times a day (dawn, noon, midafternoon, sunset, and evening), Muslims throughout the world are called to face Mecca and worship God. In many cities of the world, the quiet of the night or daily noise of busy city streets is pierced by the **muezzin's** call to prayer from atop the tower (*minaret*) of the mosque: God is Most Great (Allahu Akbar)! God is Most Great!

   > I witness that there is no god but God (Allah) . . .
   > I witness that Muhammad is the Messenger of God . . .
   > Come to prayer . . . come to salvation . . .
   > God is Most Great! God is Most Great! There is no god but God!

   Prayer (**salat**) is preceded by a series of ablutions to cleanse the body and to symbolize the purity of mind and body required for worshiping God. Muslims may pray in any appropriate place wherever they happen to be: at home, in an airport, on the road. They may do so as individuals or in a group. However, the Friday noon prayer is a congregational (*juma*) prayer that usually takes place in a **mosque** (*masjid*, "place of prostration"). A special feature of the Friday prayer is a sermon (*khutba*), preached from a pulpit (*minbar*). Since there is no priesthood in Islam, traditionally any adult male Muslim may lead the prayer. Although women can lead other women in prayer, in recent years, in a break with tradition, some Muslim women have led mixed genders in the juma prayer, a practice still not widely accepted.

3. *Almsgiving.* The third pillar of Islam is the **zakat**, almsgiving. Just as all Muslims share equally in their obligation to worship God, so too are they all duty bound to attend to the social welfare of their community by redressing economic inequalities. This is accomplished through an annual contribution, or alms, based on 2.5 percent of one's accumulated wealth and assets, not just on income. Strictly speaking, zakat is not charity, since almsgiving is not seen as voluntary but as a duty imposed by God, an act of spiritual purification and solidarity. Just as the Quran condemns economic exploitation, it warns against those who accumulate wealth and fail to assist others (Q. 3:180). Those who have benefited from God's bounty, who have received their wealth as a trust from God, are expected and required to look after the needs of the less fortunate members of the Muslim community.

Five times a day across the Muslim world, the faithful are called to prayer in Arabic by a muezzin.

4. *The Fast of Ramadan.* Muslims are required to fast from dawn to dusk during **Ramadan**, the ninth month of Islam's lunar calendar, to abstain from food, drink, and sex. The primary emphasis is less on abstinence and self-mortification as such than on spiritual self-discipline, spiritual reflection, and the performance of good works.

   The fast is broken at the end of each day by a light meal, called *breakfast* (breaking of the fast). Families exchange visits and share foods and sweets that are served only at this time of the year. Ramadan ends with the Feast of the Breaking of the Fast, Id al-Fitr, one of the great religious holy days and holidays of the Muslim calendar. Family members come from near and far to feast and exchange gifts in a celebration that lasts for three days and more.

5. *Pilgrimage to Mecca.* The pilgrimage season follows Ramadan. Every adult Muslim who is physically and financially able is expected to perform the pilgrimage (**hajj**) to Mecca in Saudi Arabia at least once in his or her lifetime. Those who are able may go more often. In the twenty-first century

"Alms are for the poor, the needy, and those employed to administer the (funds); for those whose hearts are bound together; as well as for freeing slaves and [repaying] debts; spending in the cause of Allah and for the wayfarer: thus Allah commands, and Allah is All-Knowing and Wise."

—Qur'an 9:60

almost 2 million Muslims gather annually from every part of the globe in Saudi Arabia for the hajj.

The focus of the pilgrimage is the Kaaba, the cube-shaped House of God that Muslim tradition teaches was originally built by the prophet Ibrahim (Abraham) and his son Ismail to honor God. Like salat, the pilgrimage requires ritual purification; in addition, no jewelry, perfume, or sexual activity is permitted. Pilgrims wear simple garments symbolizing that all, men and women, rich and poor alike, are equal before God. All worship together, with no segregation of the sexes.

When the pilgrims reach Mecca, they proceed to the Grand Mosque and circumambulate the Kaaba seven times, a ritual act that many believe symbolizes the angels' circling of God's throne in heaven. At the end of the hajj, they visit the Plain of Arafat, the site of Muhammad's last sermon, where pilgrims seek God's forgiveness for their sins and for those of all Muslims throughout the world.

The pilgrimage ends with the celebration of the Feast of Sacrifice (Id al-Adha), which commemorates God's testing of Abraham by commanding him to sacrifice his son Ismail (in the Jewish and Christian traditions it is Isaac who is put at risk). Commemorating God's final permission to Abraham to substitute a ram for his son, Muslims sacrifice animals (sheep, goats, cattle), not only in Mecca but across the Muslim world. The three-day Feast of Sacrifice is a time for rejoicing, prayer, and visiting with family and friends.

Breaking the fast of Ramadan. At dusk each day during Ramadan, families gather to break the fast and share a meal. This practice is called *breakfast*.

Jihad

The Quran commands Muslims to "struggle or exert" (the literal meaning of the word *jihad*) themselves in the path of God. Jihad refers to the moral struggle to be virtuous, to do good works. It also can mean fighting injustice and oppression, spreading and defending Islam, and creating a just society through preaching, teaching, and, if necessary, armed struggle. The two broad meanings of jihad, violent and nonviolent, are contrasted in a well-known tradition that reports that when Muhammad returned from battle, he told his followers, "We return from the lesser jihad to the greater jihad."

THE QURAN AND ARMED STRUGGLE

The earliest Quranic verses dealing with the right to engage in a "defensive" armed jihad were revealed shortly after the *hijra* (emigration) of Muhammad and his followers to Medina. At a time when they were fleeing from persecution in Mecca and forced to fight for their lives, Muhammad is told in the Quran: "Leave is given to those who fight because they were wronged—surely God is able to help them—who were expelled from their homes wrongfully for saying, 'Our Lord is God'" (Q. 22:39–40). The defensive nature of jihad is emphasized in 2:190: "And fight in the way of God with those who fight you, but aggress not: God loves not the aggressors." The Quran and Islamic law provide detailed guidelines and regulations regarding the conduct of war: who is to fight and who is exempted (48:17, 9:91); when hostilities must cease (2:192); and how prisoners should be treated (47:4). Verses such as 2:294 emphasize that warfare and the response to violence and aggression must be proportional: "Whoever transgresses against you, respond in kind." From the earliest times, it was forbidden in Islam to kill noncombatants as well as women and children and monks and rabbis, who were promised immunity unless they took part in the fighting.

But what of those Quranic verses, referred to as the *sword verses*, that call for killing unbelievers, such as "When the sacred months have passed, slay the idolaters wherever you find them, and take them, and confine them, and lie in wait for them at every place of ambush" (9:5)? This is one of a number of Quranic verses that are cited by critics to demonstrate the inherently violent nature of Islam and its scripture. These same verses have also been selectively used (or abused) by religious extremists to develop a theology of hate and intolerance and to legitimate unconditional warfare against unbelievers.

During the period of expansion and conquest, many of the ulama (religious scholars) enjoyed royal patronage and provided a rationale for caliphs to pursue their imperial dreams and, in the name of spreading Islam, to extend the boundaries of their empires. Many argued that the "sword verses (9: 5 and 9: 123) abrogated or cancelled earlier verses that limited jihad to defensive war, thus permitting unprovoked military action in the cause of God."[2] However, the full intent of the sword verse "When the sacred months have passed, slay the idolaters wherever you find them" is missed or distorted when quoted in isolation, for it is followed and qualified by: "But if they repent and fulfill their devotional obligations and pay the zakat [alms], then let them go their way, for God is forgiving and kind" (9:5).

THE INTERIOR PATH: ISLAMIC MYSTICISM

Islamic mysticism (**Sufism**), like Islamic law, began as a reform movement led by pious Muslims concerned that the phenomenal geographic expansion (conquest of the Byzantine and Persian empires, spread of Muslim empires with their power, wealth, and luxury) distracted from and compromised the religious message of Islam. To counter this trend, Sufis emphasized a life of asceticism and devotion to God.

The term *Sufism* comes from the coarse woolen garment (*suf,* "wool") worn by many of these early ascetics. Sufis were known for detachment from the material world, which they viewed as ephemeral, a transient distraction from the divine; repentance for sins; fear of God and the Last Judgment; and selfless devotion to the fulfillment of God's will.

Over the years, a variety of ascetic and ritual practices were adopted as part of the mystic way, including fasting, poverty, silence, and celibacy, although many Sufis are also married. Among Sufi techniques to "remember" God, who is always present in the world, are rhythmic repetition of God's name (*dhikr*) and breathing exercises that focus consciousness on God and place the devotee in the presence of God. Music and song as well as dance are also used to express deep feelings of love of God, to feel or experience his nearness, and to show devotion to God and Muhammad. The most well

Turkish Sufi order (Mawlawi **Tariqah**), founded by Jalal al-Din Rumi (d. 1273), one of the most famous Sufi mystics. Known as *whirling dervishes*, meditation rituals include a dance in which they revolve to the music of Sufi songs.

known use of dance is that of Turkey's *whirling dervishes*, who circle their master to imi-tate the divinely ordained motions of the universe.

By the eleventh and twelfth centuries, Sufism had become a mass movement that swept across much of the Islamic world. Sufi orders became the great missionaries of Islam, and Sufism, with its strong emotional and devotional component, became inte-gral to everyday popular religious practice and spirituality.

The Challenge of European Colonialism

From the seventh to the eighteenth centuries, Muslims lived under Muslim rule in an expanding world of caliphates and sultanates. However, by the nineteenth century, most Muslim areas were colonized by Europe: the French in North, West, and Equa-torial Africa and the Levant (Lebanon and Syria); the British in Palestine, Transjordan, Iraq, the Arabian Gulf, and the Indian subcontinent; and, in Southeast Asia, the British in Malaya (Malaysia, Singapore, and Brunei) and the Dutch in Indonesia. Muslim responses to colonialism and Western culture and ideas varied from rejection and con-frontation to admiration and imitation.

Colonialism had significant and far-reaching consequences for Muslims, altering the map, institutions, minds, and lives of many: Islamic and local customary laws were replaced by European legal codes; European educational systems replaced traditional Islamic edu-cation; traditional elites, political and religious, were sidelined and eventually replaced by a new class of modern, Westernized Muslims; European economic models replaced local practices. In short, the political, economic, legal, educational, and social penetration of the Muslim world by the West permanently altered Muslim societies.

The eclipse of Muslim political power and fortune and Western occupation and rule eventually led to the rise of independence movements, beginning in the early twentieth century. Islam often became a key rallying point in these anticolonial and nationalist movements.

In the Indian subcontinent, Islam was used in the Khalifat (Caliphate) movement, which attempted to save the Ottoman Empire from dismemberment by the European Allied powers after WWI. It played a central role in the blossoming of the Muslim independence movement when, in the 1930s, the Muslim League separated from the Hindu-dominated Congress Party and called for the establishment of a separate Mus-lim homeland, which resulted in the establishment of the Islamic Republic of Pakistan. Even those Muslims, including a majority of the Indian ulama (religious scholars) that called for a united India, used Islamic arguments.

In Southeast Asia, a nascent Indonesian nationalism was given organizational form with the establishment of the Sarekat Islam (Islamic Union) in 1912. Other religiosociopolitical organizations and parties, such as the Muhammadiyah, Masyumi, and Nahdatul Ulama, came into being, representing a wide spectrum of Islamic orientations, from conservative to modernist. In contrast, early Malay nationalism religion did not emphasize Islamic ideas. Only after Malay Muslim political dominance was threatened by a British colonial attempt to reorganize traditional Malay states and their sultans, with the resultant privileges it would give the country's large Chinese and Indian immigrant communities, did Malay Muslims increasingly use Islamic rhetoric and concerns to inform Malay nationalism.

The mid-twentieth century brought the end of colonial rule and the creation of modern Muslim nation-states. The struggle against colonialism resulted in the formation in a number of nation-states with large Muslim populations and varying degrees of state support for Islamic norms: Indonesia in 1945, Pakistan in 1947, Malaysia in 1957, and Bangladesh (after its secession from Pakistan) in 1971. A large Muslim minority also became incorporated into India upon its independence in 1947. China continued to boast a substantial Muslim minority as well.

The boundaries of many modern nation-states were arbitrarily drawn by the European states that had colonized the areas. Indeed, many Muslim rulers were appointed by colonial governments; others, often military officers or former officers, simply seized power. As a result, instead of elected governments, much of the Muslim world has been governed and influenced by a legacy of autocratic rulers not of their choosing.

THE ISLAMIC RESURGENCE

Although Iran's Islamic revolution of 1979–80 drew attention to the reassertion and power of Islam in society, in Egypt, Libya, Pakistan, Bangladesh, Afghanistan, Malaysia, and Indonesia, Islam had been reasserting itself in Muslim politics for more than a decade before 1979. Despite national independence, most Muslim countries had remained weak, underdeveloped, and dependent on the West. What went wrong? To regain their past power and glory, many believed that they must return to the straight path of Islam. The 1973 Arab oil embargo and, later, the Islamic revolution in Iran, reinforced the belief that Muslim economic and political power could be attributed to the resurgence of Islam in contemporary Muslim politics and society.

Islam enjoyed a higher profile in personal and public life, demonstrated by greater religious observance and Islamic dress as well as the growth of Islamic political and social organizations and institutions: banks, publishing houses, schools. In addition, many governments as well as reform and opposition movements and political parties used Islamic slogans and language to mobilize popular support. Muslim rulers (Egypt's Anwar Sadat, Libya's Muammar Gadhafi, Pakistan's Zulfikar Ali Bhutto and General Zia ul-Haq, Malaysia's Mahathir Muhammad, and Suharto's Indonesia) turned to Islam to enhance their legitimacy.

At the same time, Islamic activist organizations sprang up across the Muslim world. Islamic activists have led governments and served in cabinets and in the elected parliaments from Egypt and Jordan to Pakistan, Bangladesh, Malaysia, and Indonesia. In addition, radical Islamic organizations have engaged in violence and terrorism to undermine and topple governments. Extremists have left a legacy of kidnapping, hijacking, bombing, and murder, from Cairo to Jakarta, Bali, and Mindanao.

THE ROAD TO 9/11

The 1990s witnessed an increase in global terrorist attacks across the Muslim world and in the United States and Europe. Osama Bin Laden increasingly emerged as the "god-father" of global terrorism, a major funder of extremist groups, suspected in the bombing of the World Trade Center in 1993, the killing of eighteen American soldiers in Somalia in 1993, and bombings in Riyadh in 1995 and in Dhahran in 1996.

In February 1998, bin Laden and other militant leaders announced the creation of a transnational coalition of extremist groups, the World Islamic Front for Jihad against Jews and Crusaders. His own organization, al-Qaeda, was linked to a series of acts of terrorism: the truck bombing of American embassies in Kenya and Tanzania in August 1998 that killed 263 people and injured more than 5,000, followed in October 2000 by a suicide bombing attack against the U.S.S. *Cole*, which killed 17 American sailors.

September 11, 2001, would prove to be a watershed, signaling the extent to which Muslim extremists, in particular Osama bin Laden and al-Qaeda, had become a global threat. Al-Qaeda represented a new global terrorism, associated at first with the Muslims who had gone to Afghanistan to fight the occupying Soviets in the 1980s. It was also reflected in the growth of extremism and acts of terrorism in Central, South, and Southeast Asia, where it has often been attributed to the influence of Saudi Arabia and Wahhabi Islam.

Bin Laden and other terrorists transformed Islam's norms about the defense of Islam and Muslims under siege to legitimate the use of violence, warfare, and terrorism. Their theology of hate espouses a bipolar view of a cosmic struggle between the armies of God and of Satan, the forces of good and evil, right and wrong, belief and unbelief. Those who are not with them, whether Muslim or non-Muslim, are judged to be against them. Extremists appealed to the concept of jihad to legitimate acts of violence and terror.

GLOBALIZATION AND HIJACKING OF "JIHAD"

Since the late twentieth century the word *jihad* has gained remarkable political currency. On the one hand, the term's primary Quranic religious and spiritual meanings became more widespread: Jihad was the "struggle" or effort to follow God's path, to lead a moral life, and to promote social justice. On the other hand, the idea of jihad as a sacred armed struggle has been widely used by resistance, liberation, and terrorist movements alike to legitimate their cause and recruit followers. Thus the Afghan Mujahideen waged jihad in Afghanistan against Soviet occupation and then among themselves; Muslims in Central Asia, Malaysia, Indonesia, and the southern Philippines have fashioned their struggles as jihads. The Middle East's Hezbollah, Hamas, and Islamic Jihad Palestine, Indonesia's Laskhar Jihad and Jamma Islami, Tajikistan's Islamic Renaissance Party, the Islamic Movement of Uzbekistan, and Abu Sayyif in the Philippines, among others, have been part of a global jihad, targeting Muslim governments as well as the West.

Muslim terrorists go beyond classical Islam's criteria regarding the goals and means of a valid jihad: that the use of violence must be proportional; that innocent civilians, noncombatants, should not be targeted; and that jihad can be declared only by a ruler or head of state. Today, extremists from Madrid to Mindanao legitimate unholy wars in the name of Islam itself, bypassing the Quranic requirement that authorization for jihad be given by a nation's ruler.

While bin Laden and al-Qaeda have enjoyed support from a significant minority of Muslims and religious leaders, the majority of Muslims and major Islamic scholars and religious leaders across the Muslim world condemned such attacks as unjustified. For example, the Gallup Organization in mid-2005, early 2006, and 2007 surveyed thirty-five predominantly Muslim countries from Morocco to Indonesia as part of its new Gallup World Poll. The vast majority of all polled said the 9/11 attacks were unjustified; 7 percent said the attacks were completely justified. The Islamic Research Council at al-Azhar University, regarded by many as the highest moral authority in Islam, and other prominent religious leaders issued authoritative declarations (fatwas) against bin Laden's and other terrorists' initiatives:

> Islam provides clear rules and ethical norms that forbid the killing of noncombatants, as well as women, children, and the elderly, and also forbids the pursuit of the enemy in defeat, the execution of those who surrender, the infliction of harm on prisoners of war, and the destruction of property that is not being used in the hostilities.[3]

CONTEMPORARY ISLAM: ISSUES OF AUTHORITY AND REFORM

While the sacred texts of Islam, the Quran and the Sunnah of the Prophet, remain the same, the political, social, and economic contexts have changed. Thus, Muslims, like followers of other faiths, face issues of change and religious reform.

The primary question for contemporary Muslims is not change, for most accept its necessity. Rather, it is how much change is possible or permissible in Islam and what kinds of change are necessary: the relationship of religion to state and society, reform of Islamic law, political participation or democratization, the promotion of religious and political pluralism, and the rights of women.

As in the past, both the ulama, the religious scholars of Islam, and Muslim rulers continue to assert their right to protect, defend, and interpret Islam. The ulama persist in regarding themselves as the guardians of Islam, the conscience of the community, its only qualified interpreters. Many rulers, through cooptation and coercion, combine their obligation to protect and promote Islam with the state's power to influence, control, and impose a certain "brand" of Islam. In many countries, governments control and distribute funds used to build mosques, pay the salaries of religious officials, even determine the topics or outlines for Friday mosque sermons and appoint religious leaders and judges.

Today, many others argue that it is not rulers or the religious scholars but the laity and parliaments that should be major actors in the process of change. While the ulama base their authority on their training in traditional Islamic disciplines, lay Muslims counter that they possess the legal, economic, and medical qualifications necessary to address contemporary issues and should be counted among the "experts" along with the ulama.

A major challenge in Asia's multireligious and multiethnic Muslim-majority countries, such as Pakistan, Bangladesh, Indonesia, and Malaysia, is how to maintain interethnic and interreligious peace in the light of new religious, political, social, and economic developments in their country. How do Muslims redefine Islam's traditional doctrine of minority rights, characterizing non-Muslim **People of the Book** as "protected" people (**dhimmi**), with the right to practice their faith in exchange for paying a poll or head tax (*jizya*), to support notions of an equality of citizenship that transcends religious and sectarian differences? The issue is demonstrated by the fact that the reassertion or greater influence of Islam in state and society has spawned Sunni–Shii conflicts in countries such as Pakistan and Afghanistan as well as strained interreligious and interethnic relations in Malaysia and Indonesia.

The terrorist activities of Osama bin Laden and al-Qaeda and radical Asian Muslim groups also underscore the urgency of Islamic reform. Formidable challenges and obstacles must be overcome, including the discrediting of militant jihadist ideas and ideologies and the reform of some *madrasas* (seminaries) and universities that perpetuate a "theology of hate" and train jihadists. Another obstacle to reform, however, is the ultraconservatism of many (though not all) ulama, which hinders reform in the curriculum and training of religious scholars, leaders, and students.

Today the struggle of Islam is between differing and competing voices and visions of over a billion mainstream Muslims, who range from conservative traditionalist and fundamentalist to more liberal Islamically oriented as well as secular reformers and a dangerous but deadly minority such as Osama bin Laden and al-Qaeda and other, like-minded terrorists. While the extremists dominate the headlines and threaten Muslim and Western societies, the vast majority of Muslims, like other religious believers, pursue normal, everyday activities.

Muslim reformers, often a small but significant minority within their communities, interpret and reinterpret traditional principles, values, and norms to respond to the new demands and unprecedented issues of today's societies. They face powerful and entrenched forces : conservative religious establishments, with their medieval paradigms, as well as authoritarian regimes that often see reformers as a threat to their privilege who use their power to control or manipulate religion, education, and the media.

Conclusion

Asian Islam, like much of the Muslim world, is challenged by the impact of modernity and globalization and the challenges of religious, political, and economic development that result. The situation is compounded by authoritarian regimes, limited democracies, and religious extremism.

Muslims continue to grapple with the relationship of the present and the future to the past. However, in contrast to Judaism and Christianity, Muslims, due to centuries of European colonial dominance and rule, have had only a few decades to accomplish what in the West was the product of centuries of religious and political revolution and reform, a process that included the Enlightenment, Reformation, counter-Reformation, and French and American revolutions.

Like the process of modern reform in Judaism and Christianity, questions of leadership and the authority of the past (tradition) are critical. A critical question remains: "Whose Islam? Who leads and decides?" Is it rulers, the vast majority of whom are unelected kings, military, and former military? Or is it elected prime ministers and parliaments? Is it the ulama or clergy, who continue to see themselves as the primary interpreters of Islam, although many are ill prepared to respond creatively to modern realities? Or is it modern educated, Islamically oriented intellectuals and activists? Lacking an effective leadership, will other Osama bin Ladens fill the vacuum?

The second major question is: "What Islam?" Is Islamic reform simply returning to the past and restoring past doctrines and laws, or does it mean a reformation or reformulation of Islam to meet the demands of modern life? Some call for an Islamic state based on the reimplementation of classical formulations of Islamic laws. Others argue the need to reinterpret and reformulate law in light of the new realities of contemporary society.

Discussion Questions

1. In what countries are the four largest Muslim populations located?
2. In what ways did Islam come to and spread across Asia?
3. Identify and describe the Five Pillars of Islam.
4. Describe the diverse meanings of jihad. How has the concept been used by different Islamic movements to justify their activities?
5. What are the major differences between Sunni and Shii Muslims?
6. What are several major challenges or issues in Islamic reform today?

Key Terms

Allah	ijma	mosque	Ramadan	Sunni
ayatollah	imam	muezzin	salat	surah
caliph	Islam	mufti	shahadah	tariqah
dhimmi	jihad	mujaddid	sharia	tawhid
fatwa	khutba	Muslim	Shiah	ulama
hadith	Mahdi	People of the Book	Sufi	ummah
hajj	masjid	qiyas	Sufism	zakat
hijra	minbar	Quran	Sunnah	

Suggested Readings

Armstrong, Karen, *Muhammad: A Biography of the Prophet* (San Francisco: Harper, 1993).

Donohue, John, and John L. Esposito, eds. *Islam in Transition: Muslim Perspectives* 2nd ed. (New York: Oxford University Press, 2005).

Esposito, John L. *Unholy War: Terror in the Name of Islam* (New York: Oxford University Press, 2000).

———. *What Everyone Needs to Know About Islam* (New York: Oxford University Press, 2002).

———, ed., *The Oxford Encyclopedia of the Islamic World* (6 vols.) (New York: Oxford University Press, 2009).

———. *Islam: The Straight Path,* 3rd rev. ed. (New York: Oxford University Press, 2005).

———, ed., *The Oxford History of Islam* (New York: Oxford University Press, 2000).

———, John O. Voll, and Osman Bakar, eds. *Asian Islam in the 21st Century* (New York: Oxford University Press, 2008).

Fealy, Greg, and Virginia Hooker, eds. *Voices of Islam in Southeast Asia: A Contemporary Sourcebook* (Singapore: Institute of Southeast Asian Studies, 2006).

Gross, Max. *A Muslim Archipelago Islam and Politics in Southeast Asia* (Washington, DC: NDIC, 2007).

Hefner, Robert W. *Remaking Muslim Politics: Pluralism, Contestation, Democratization* (Princeton: Princeton University press, 2007).

Lings, Martin. *What Is Sufism?* (London: I. B. Taurus, 1999).

McAmis, Robert Day. *Malay Muslims: The History and Challenge of Resurgent Islam in Southeast Asia* (Wm. B. Eerdmans, 2002)

Nasr, Seyyed Hossein. *Ideals and Realities of Islam,* 2nd ed. (Chicago: Kazi Publications, 2001).

Robinson, Francis. *Islam and Muslim History in South Asia* (Oxford India Paperbacks, 2004).

———. *The New Cambridge History of India: Islam in South Asia* (Cambridge: Cambridge University Press, 2008).

The Quran: A Modern English Version, transl. Majid Fakhry (Berkshire, UK: Garnet, 1996).

Notes

1. Seyyed Hossein Nasr. Muhammad: Man of God (Chicago: Kazi Publications, 1995), p. 90
2. http://www.geocities.com/clintonbennett/Lectures/WarinIslam.htm?200713-_ftn7
3. *Al-Hayat,* Nov. 5, 2001.

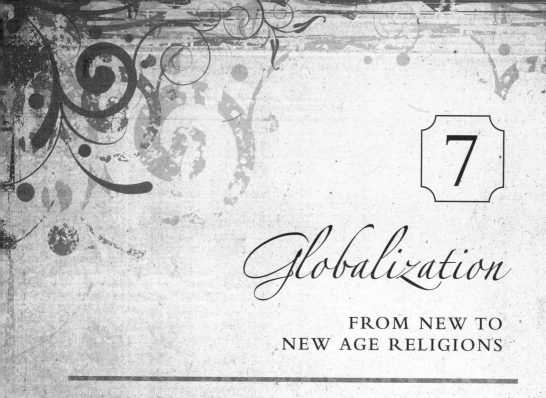

7

Globalization

FROM NEW TO
NEW AGE RELIGIONS

❧ Overview

Marie belongs to an Episcopal parish in Minneapolis, but she has other religious interests as well. Indeed, she regularly checks her astrological chart, and tonight she and her friend Allison are going to an introductory lecture on Transcendental Meditation. Last week, Marie's friend Jack talked her into going on a weekend retreat led by a psychic medium who offered to put people in touch with their dead relatives. In addition, Marie has been reading *Dianetics,* by Scientology founder L. Ron Hubbard, and she is thinking about responding to a questionnaire entitled "Are You Curious About Yourself?" Distributed by the local Church of Scientology, the flyer had come with the morning newspaper.

All these activities mark Marie as one of countless individuals who are on a personal quest that is typical of new age religion: They are eager to explore the mystery of the "self" and its perfection. Marie has another friend, Mark, who thinks she is too self-absorbed and needs to pay more attention to issues of social justice in a global culture that is shaped by mass media and multinational corporations and marred by racial and economic exploitation. Mark is trying to get her involved in a small interracial activist group inspired by the life and teachings of Martin Luther King Jr. All these approaches to life, and many more, as we shall see, could be grouped together under the heading of *new age religions.*

In this chapter we will first explore what we mean by "new" religions and then focus primarily on "new age religions"—the distinctive forms that new religions and new ways of being religious have taken in response to globalization. New religions represent the integration of influences from multiple religions and cultures, resulting in the creation of new variations and expressions of known religious practices. In one familiar pattern, a new prophet or sage reveals new understandings of an existing tradition, given to him or her in religious experiences or revelations.

In the past the messages of prophets and sages reflected primarily local situations—typically the incursion of elements imported from nearby religions and cultures. Today, however, many new religious movements reflect not just a response to local diversity—to this or that movement that has entered the environment of a relatively stable culture. Rather, they are indicative of an awareness of global religious diversity as a whole, past and present. This awareness is fostered by mass communications and widespread access to international transportation, made possible by modern science and technology.

A shamanistic ritual practiced at a new age conference in Long Beach, California.

It is in this new environment of the awareness of the diversity of human religious experience that the "new age" religions are emerging, both accommodating and integrating diverse elements of varying, often quite dissimilar, existing traditions. Some movements, however, represent the attempt to reassert particular forms of religious expression that adherents believe have been neglected but should be operative in the new age of global interdependence. Contemporary interest in shamanism and goddess worship would be examples of this. What these movements typically have in common is the belief that humanity is indeed entering a "new age" in which global harmony must be achieved, not only with other religions and cultures but also with the natural environment.

New Religions

OLD RELIGIONS AND NEW RELIGIONS IN THE HISTORY OF RELIGIONS

From a historical perspective, as this book has amply indicated, no religion has ever managed to remain unchanged. Indeed, while every chapter in this book began with an "overview" description of the religious beliefs and practices of the tradition, in every case we went on to say that such a snapshot was no more than a broad generalization that did not accurately reflect the tremendous diversity found among practitioners, yesterday or today. There is not one Judaism but many, not one Buddhism but many—likewise there are many Christianities, many Islams and Hinduisms, many Daoisms and Confucianisms.

New religions test and transform boundaries. Every tradition tolerates a tremendous amount of diversity. An emerging movement that at first is treated as a form of error may finally be accepted into the fold or at least tolerated as a distant cousin. It may, for example, by seen as a reform within the tradition to bring it back to its original purity. But then there are other movements, perhaps brought about by new religious experiences and extraordinary revelations, whose "errors" seem too great. Changes that had started out as reforms may present such a dramatic break with past beliefs and practices that they come to be perceived not as a continuation of the old tradition but as a fatal error—a deviation from the true path. The new tradition, of course, sees the error lying not in itself but in the old tradition, which had somehow lost its way.

Although before the common era there was more than one form of Judaism, Christianity, which began as a Jewish sect called the *Nazarenes*, came to be seen and, to see itself, as crossing a boundary that made it no longer a Jewish alternative but a "new religion." And while Christianity also encompasses tremendous diversity, when Islam emerged in Arabia in the seventh century it was seen by Christians as a new and

"The New Age is partially an offshoot of the Age of Science. . . . Children of the Age of Science, myself included, prefer to arrive firsthand, experimentally, at their own conclusions as to the nature and limits of reality. Shamanism provides a way to conduct these personal experiments, for it is a methodology, not a religion."

Source: Michael Harner, *The Way of the Shaman*.

heretical religion, even though Muslims recounted many of the same biblical stories and saw their faith as the continuation and culmination of God's revelations handed down through Moses and Jesus. Moreover, Islam developed two major branches, Sunni and Shiah, as well as many schools of theology and law. However, in nineteenth-century Persia, when the Baha'i movement claimed to bring a final revelation that included all the religions, East and West, it came to be viewed as "not true Islam," hence as a new belief system.

When we look at Asian religions we find the same pattern. Hinduism encompasses great diversity, and yet as Buddhism grew and developed it was seen, and came to see itself, as a "new religion." Buddhism, too, splintered into many Buddhisms, some claiming to be more advanced than others.

In every tradition, some movements emerged and then disappeared. Even so, in century after century, many of "today's" new religions become tomorrow's old and established religions. We can illustrate the character of new religions with a few examples before turning to our primary concern, examples of "new age" religions that have appeared in our emerging global civilization. The relatively recent history of Christianity in North American culture presents an interesting illustration of how a new religion comes to be.

In the 1800s, Christian denominationalism began to emerge as a way of moving beyond the hostile sectarianism that had divided Christians, and by the late twentieth century there was a broad spectrum of "acceptable" religious diversity in America. Nevertheless, a number of very distinctive religious movements that originated in the nineteenth century tested the limits of denominationalism. As a rule, contemporary mainline Christian denominations (i.e., those representing widely established, long-accepted church traditions in America, such as the Methodists, Presbyterians, and Episcopalians) regard these unique movements as having strayed beyond the boundaries of Christianity. Mormonism provides us with a good example.

❖ The Church of Jesus Christ of Latter-day Saints: A New American Christianity

The Church of Jesus Christ of Latter-day Saints, or Mormonism, was established on April 6, 1830, by Joseph Smith Jr. It appears to have arisen in response to the confusion and conflict created by the incredible sectarian diversity of nineteenth-century Christianity. Joseph Smith believed he had been led by angels to discover a revelation that would overcome this confusion. The new revelation, contained in the Book of Mormon, was understood by Smith and his followers as a continuation of the revelation given in the Bible. It was a revelation that had been given first to Native Americans, as descendants of the lost tribes of ancient Israel. Mormons believe that these tribes had migrated to the North American continent, where the risen Christ visited them and gave them new revelations. Eventually the book containing these pronouncements was buried by a Native American named Mormon, who was killed by tribesmen who rejected the new message and wanted to suppress it. It was these "pagan" natives who met Columbus in 1492. But the revelation could not be suppressed forever, and so Joseph Smith was guided by angels to find the Book of Mormon so that it could flourish once more.

Earlier we noted the incorporation into Christianity of traditions specific to Africa and Asia. Similarly, Mormonism links biblical religion to the history of an indigenous population—in this case producing a distinctively American Christianity, one that includes visits of the risen Christ and several of the risen apostles to a new land, to guarantee the purity of Mormon revelation and so set it apart from existing "human interpretations" of Christianity. The capstone of the message was the promise that at the end of the "latter days," Christ would return to establish a "New Jerusalem" in America. Mormonism, with its emphasis on family, community, and healthy, wholesome living, flourishes today, with well over 10 million members worldwide.

❖ Ahmadiyyat: A New Islamic Religion

The Ahmadiyyat is an example of a new religious movement in modern Islam. From its inception in 1899 in British India, it has been one of the most active, progressive, and controversial movements in Islam, rejected by many Muslims as heretical. Mirza Ghulam Ahmad, the founder, was born in Qadian, a village in the Punjab. He wrote prolifically, built and expanded the organization, and engaged in sometimes-heated debates with many Sunni ulama and Christian missionaries.

Ghulam Ahmad described his spiritual status and mission in both messianic and prophetic terminology. His claim to be a renewer of Islam, a mujaddid, fell within the boundaries of official Islam, or orthodoxy. When he assumed the titles of Mahdi and prophet, however, he was roundly condemned by the ulama and by prominent Muslim groups such as the Jamaat-i-Islami. Ahmad answered criticisms by saying that unlike legislative prophets, such as Jesus and Muhammad, who bring God's revelation and divine law to the people, he had a divine mandate to renew and reform the Islamic community. Thus, as a nonlegislative prophet, Ahmad could affirm the finality of the prophethood of Muhammad while maintaining that God continued to send religious reformers such as himself to provide prophetic guidance to the Islamic community.

The Ahmadis are great supporters of modern education and Islamic reform. As a global missionary movement they have established a large network of

Joseph Smith Jr. receiving the sacred plates of the Book of Mormon from the Angel Moroni.

mosques and centers and peacefully propagated their faith in Asia, Africa, Europe, and America.

✤ *Civil Religion in China and the United States*

Civil religions represent yet another form in which new religious traditions can play very traditional roles in a society. In most times and most places throughout the history of civilization, religion and politics permeated all of culture and were like two sides of the same coin. It was, as we have seen, modernity that introduced secular nation-states and the idea that government should not impose on citizens the obligation to join or practice any particular religion. But having removed religion as a legitimizer of their own authority, these modern states faced a new problem—winning loyalty from their citizens without the traditional appeal to religion. The result has been the creation of a distinct entity we shall call *civil religion*, which reintroduces religion under the disguise of "indigenous cultural history and tradition" to reinforce the authority of new and more secular political social orders.

Thus a civil religion is based on a sacred narrative of the state's founding, in which the development of the state is portrayed as a just, moral enterprise, in harmony with ideals of the religious traditions shared by most citizens. Typically, the state's leaders developed a set of national rituals and yearly holidays (holy days) that celebrate and allow the regular, solemn reliving of key events in the nation's history. Such civil religions come to expression in national anthems and patriotic songs, school textbooks that emphasize the righteousness of the country's founders, and war memorials honoring those who sacrificed their lives for the nation.

In many cases, the cultural pattern from one tradition (Christianity, Islam, Confucianism, etc.) clearly comes to underlie the nation's civil religion, though seldom to the extent of specific endorsement. What is striking is how nearly all the great ideas in the history of religions (e.g., sacrifice, sage, prophet, martyrdom, sacred center, "chosen people," rebirth, *millennialism*) (i.e., the belief in an age of peace and perfection at the end of time) have been adopted across the world in the service of creating and sustaining the civil religions that support modern nations. Two examples will illustrate this: Chinese communist civil religion and civil religion in the United States.

Chinese Communist Civil Religion When the Red Army gained control of the mainland of China in 1949, Communist Party leader Mao Zedong ascended the southern gateway to the emperor's old palace (the Forbidden City) to proclaim the creation of the People's Republic of China. This moment was later pictured on currency and in popular prints, and soon thereafter an immense portrait of Chairman Mao was mounted over the ancient gateway, where it hangs to this day. Over the next twenty-five years, the Communist Party drew on a variety of religious conceptions to legitimate its position in China and to wield power. The Communist millennial doctrine, imported from Russian revolutionaries but rooted in the prophetic biblical understanding, insisted that a paradise on earth was inevitable if the people changed their ways and lived in thoroughgoing cooperation. Citizens who sacrificed themselves for the common good were immortalized as "heroes of the people," their dying was said to hasten the arrival of the new age.

Early on, the government adapted ancient Confucian imperial doctrine to promote the cult of Mao himself as the sage-philosopher leader of the nation, whose words and teachings were pivotal for national salvation, whose character radiated the morality of communist truth. Statues of Mao were put up in public spaces around the nation, his portrait replaced images of family ancestors in home shrines, and during the Cultural Revolution (1966–1976) his "Little Red Book" became a sacred text to be memorized, followed, and always possessed. Officially, the Communist Party disavowed religion as superstition and railed at long-dead Chinese emperors as feudal exploiters of the masses. Nevertheless, it is not hard to see how party strategists adapted powerful religious ideas from both European and Chinese traditions to create a civil religion to confirm the legitimacy of the dictatorship.

American Civil Religion American civil religion as found in the United States develops from European colonization, justifying the history of American ancestors' claiming the land "from sea to shining sea" as being part of a divine plan unfolding in its "manifest destiny." God is said to have given America as a "promised land," to those who are his "chosen people" to foster the sacred values of freedom and democracy. Thus the narrative of American civil religion presents the United States as a "city on a hill," called by God to be a model for all nations.

Mao Zedong, founder of the People's Republic of China.

Although founded by those who consciously avoided the establishment of any state religion, American civil religion, according to sociologist Robert Bellah, appeals to George Washington as the "Father" of the country while Abraham Lincoln is its "Savior" who led the nation from the sin of slavery through the crisis of civil war, dying in the service of the sacred land and leading to its moral and spiritual renewal. National holidays such as Presidents' Day, the Fourth of July, Memorial Day, and Thanksgiving celebrate American civil religion. The rituals of these celebrations connect patriotism to the sacredness of the American way of life and God's special blessings on the United States.

As the record of the recent past makes clear, civil religion has had the effect of assimilating individuals and diverse ethnic groups into the world's new nations. But the rise of civil religions has also led to excesses, fueling genocidal campaigns by states on four continents against those who are not part of their sacred history.

New Age Religions

THE NEW AGE: MODERN AND POSTMODERN

The collapse of colonialism was followed by the emergence of globalization, fostered by the development of international corporations, global mass transportation, and global mass media, carrying modern science and technology around the world. Logically enough, then, since the 1960s and 1970s new patterns of religion have appeared that reflect a global consciousness. These religions shaped by science and technology as well as by the traditional considerations, although incredibly diverse, are often grouped together under the title *new age religions*. Not all new age religions are postmodern as

The age of globalization is well illustrated by this global map of transportation networks.

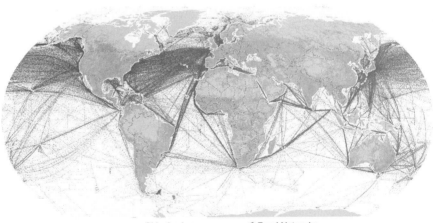

Shipping Lanes   Road Networks

we have defined that term. Indeed, many are content to continue the modernist pattern of privatization rather than seek a new public role for religion. But global consciousness has been a significant factor in the emergence of all new age religions. In this section and the next, we will look at examples of modernist and postmodernist new age religions.

The problem with a secular understanding of time, history, and society is that the significance and drama provided by the grand narratives of religions are missing. The resurgence of religions since the 1970s may well represent the need to fill the vacuum created by the tendency of secularization to purge events of meaning. Pluralism may have collapsed the grand metanarratives into smaller stories, but there is still a great hunger for such stories, and new age religions help people discover the meaning and significance of time and their place in it. New age religions provide a rich feast for the religious imagination as seekers attempt to penetrate the mysteries of their time and to explore the wonders it offers.

In the first chapter we cited Jean-François Lyotard's definition of *postmodernism* as the collapse of metanarratives, the grand stories or myths that gave each civilization a sense of meaning, purpose, and identity. The great metanarratives created a relationship of identity between religion and culture, giving us Hindu civilization, Christian civilization, Islamic civilization, and so on. Each civilization was centered in its own grand stories and the social practices that came from the vision of life the stories promoted. Modernism, with its myth of scientific progress, was a relatively recent addition.

Postmodern culture represents the loss of a normative center in every culture that has been touched by global mass media, international corporations, and global mass

This young Chinese Christian, Chen Yingjie, from Fujian province, participates in a phone prayer meeting with others he has never met face to face.

transportation. Postmodern culture is pluralistic, relativistic, and eclectic—seemingly without any public norms or standards. The choice between "truths" is said to be intellectually undecidable and so is decided pragmatically, in terms of "what works for me." Truth, goodness, and beauty are in the eye of the beholder. People mix and match beliefs, practices, and aesthetic choices to their own taste in all areas of life—whether music, clothing, architecture, intellectual beliefs, or religion.

Globalization provides the social context of postmodernism. Globalization "marbleizes" all cultures so that the world's religions are accessible in everyone's hometown. Today, much more than in the past, in the same community you will find Jews, Christians, Muslims, Hindus, Buddhists, and many others. Such pluralism is a powerful social force inducing the collapse of metanarrative, whereby a story that was once embraced by almost all people in a given culture is now simply one of many stories. In this situation religions are challenged first to relinquish their position of being identical with the culture and then to accommodate an existing cultural pluralism. In this context, almost all religious communities have had to embrace denominational identities, accepting the existence of other beliefs and practices, although fundamentalist communities strive mightily to resist such an accommodation. This denominational accommodation, we said, was what sociologist Peter Berger meant by saying that all religions have become "Protestant." But for most new age groups their religious practices have gone a step further, moving from organizational pluralism (denominationalism) to eclecticism.

Many of the "new age" religions, like older "new religions," represent the integration of the diverse influences from different traditions. The new age religions are not based solely on the great world religions; often they incorporate elements of primal religions, exhibiting a special interest in shamanism. Moreover, today these eclectic belief systems typically reflect not only global religious diversity but the global influence of science and technology as well.

New age religious movements can be divided into modernist forms, which continue to privatize religion, and postmodernist public forms of religious practice, which seek an active role, socially and politically, in transforming society. Most modernist new age religions are highly diverse in their practices and beliefs, with minimal organizational structure. Nevertheless, there are some very important instances of highly structured new age movements; as we shall see, Scientology is one. What unites new age seekers, despite their diversity, however, is the quest for the perfection of the self. Their goal is to realize a "higher self" through intense personal experiences of transformation.

Many new age seekers are not interested in joining religious organizations. They typically integrate a variety of interests into their personal style of spiritual practice. Many read "spiritual" books and go to workshops and seminars intended to guide them to self-realization. Modernist "new agers" are interested in such shamanistic practices as channeling information from other-worldly spiritual beings, contacting the dead through mediums, spiritual healing, and the cultivation of ecstatic out-of-body experiences (sometimes referred to as *astral projection*). They are also interested in the mystical traditions and meditation practices of all religions as well as the ancient divination practice of astrology. Some combine these interests with the teachings and practices of transpersonal psychologists such as Abraham Maslow (1908–1970) and Fritz Perls (1894–1970); others embrace speculative visions that combine the "new physics" with religion, believing that science itself is finally coming to discover and affirm ancient religious and metaphysical insights. The final test of each seeker's synthesis is personal experience and pragmatically evaluated usefulness.

Modernity, we learned in Chapter 4, on Christianity, emerged out of the splitting of the medieval unity of faith and reason into the *via moderna* of empirical rationality and the *devotio moderna* of personal emotional experiences of transformation (mysticism, pietism, and the experience of being "born again"). The first path became dominant in the Enlightenment and the second in the Romantic movement, as a reaction to the Enlightenment. The growth of new age religiousness is deeply rooted in this Romantic reaction to the rationalism of the Enlightenment.

The Enlightenment emphasized universal rationality (i.e., the sameness of human nature), science, and progress. Its philosophers rejected the ancient, the archaic, the traditional, the idiosyncratic, and the nonrational. The Romantic reaction did just the opposite, embracing in all their diversity the emotional, the experientially transformational, the historically unique and particular, as well as the "primitive" and traditional aspects of human history.

Like fundamentalist evangelical Christianity, modernist forms of new age religions are expressions of the human need for transformative experience, a need as old as shamanism and as recent as the Romantic reaction to Enlightenment rationalism. Both deemphasize rationality and focus on the experiential transformation and perfection of the self through deeply emotional experiences of the kind we have called religious. And both share the conviction that all social change begins by changing the self (i.e., by being born again).

THE AGE OF APOCALYPSE OR THE AGE OF AQUARIUS?

Two new age models of religious meaning are playing a role in our emerging global civilization—the apocalyptic and the astrological. These models share a vision of the conflict and discord of the past and present giving way to a future era of global peace and harmony. Among Christian evangelicals the popularity of the belief that the end of time is near is evidenced by sales of tens of millions of books such as Hal Lindsey's *The Late Great Planet Earth* and the *Left Behind* series of novels. As indicated by the popularity of biblical prophecies of the end times among evangelical Christians, there are still many heirs to the apocalyptic religious vision of the medieval monk Joachim of Fiore, who anticipated a "third age" (the age of the Spirit) as a time of global peace and harmony. However, the third age will be preceded by the biblical apocalypse, which in turn will bring the cataclysmic end of time. The belief that there will be a cataclysmic end to time followed by a new age of peace and harmony is also illustrated in such late-twentieth-century movements as the Unification Church and Aum Shin-rikyo, to be reviewed shortly. But first we will turn to the alternative vision—the astro-logical vision of the age of Aquarius.

A gentler vision of the new age, the age of Aquarius, has been offered by some astrologers in recent decades:

> We are passing out of 2,000 years of Piscean astrological influence into the influence of Aquarius, which will affect all aspects of our culture as we move from Piscean structures of hierarchical devotion to more fluid and spontaneous relationships that dance to an Aquarian rhythm.[1]

Predictions of the coming of a new age by others not of the apocalyptic tradition include the writings of Jose Arguelles. In his book *The Mayan Factor,* this new age author used ancient Mayan and Aztec astrology to calculate that the age of Aquarius would begin in 1987, on August 16 or 17.[2]

In these Aquarian times, many forms of new age religion tap into a very ancient type of religious experience found in primal animistic and early urban polytheistic religious practices—that of the shaman. As we saw in Chapter Two, in his or her ecstatic or out-of-body experiences, the shaman explores the spirit world, the realm of contact with spiritual beings and dead ancestors.

Everywhere in the world, shamanism appears to be the earliest form of religious experience. And everywhere, the great world religions emerge with the discovery that the shaman's realm is really an intermediate spiritual realm between the earthly phys-ical world and a higher unitary reality. For example, in the Vedas of Hinduism the high-est realities are the many gods and goddesses of nature, but in the Upanishads the dis-covery is made that the gods are part of the order of this world of samsara and that there is a higher power beyond their realm, the reality of Brahman.

The emergence of monotheism out of polytheism in the Mediterranean world (in Judaism, Christianity, and Islam) provides another example. The polytheistic realm of the gods was not denied. It could not be denied because many people continued to have shamanistic-type experiences of another realm, inhabited by spiritual beings. So this realm of the deities was reassigned to a different kind of spiritual being and renamed the realm of angels and demons. Like the devas or gods of Hinduism, angels were recognized as spiritual beings, yet they were part of the cosmic order created by a higher reality, God. In China this concept of a higher unitary reality was given the impersonal name of Dao.

For all the differences between ancient urban religious cultures and religions in postmodern society, there is at least one profound similarity between them: Both pre-modern urban society, as typified by the polytheistic culture of ancient Rome, and postmodern society, with its myriad eclectic religious practices, lack an integrating center. In both, being religious is not so much about belonging to "a religion" as it is about selecting from the chaotic variety of available beliefs and practices, a mix that will serve the pragmatic purposes of finding health, happiness, and meaning, that is, of having the unseen powers that govern your destiny on your side.

WICCA AND THE RESURGENCE OF GODDESS WORSHIP

Determining how many people "practice new age religion" is next to impossible. This is because it is quite common for nominal adherents to one of these belief systems to practice several different forms in their private life while perhaps also belonging to a traditional church or synagogue. One form this eclectic spirituality can take is sometimes called *neopaganism*, which is vividly exemplified in a return to the practice of witchcraft, or attunement to the sacred powers of nature, a pattern found in all premodern societies. The most prominent such practice today is Wicca, which appears to be a self-conscious reconstruction of ancient pagan religious practices. The Wiccan movement can be traced back to England in the 1940s and the writings of Gerald Gardener, who claimed to be an initiate of a Wiccan coven, authorized to reveal its teachings and practices to the public. Two students of Gardener's brought the practice to America in the 1960s. By 1965 a church of Wicca was established in Mississippi, and by 1978 the handbook for U.S. military chaplains included Wicca in its list of religions.

Wiccans see the world ordered by sacred forces that can be accessed through ritual magic. These powers are personified as gods and goddesses. Wiccan rituals involve the elaborate use of chant, dance, drumming, and meditation. By following the ancient Celtic agricultural cycle of festivals for the seasons of the year, these rituals enable Wiccans to reconnect with the rhythms of nature and to experience its hidden unity. Many tend to see their ritual practice as an outward expression of the fundamental truth of the interconnectivity of all things, a view that they believe modern science also affirms. One strand of Wicca, Dianic Wicca, presents itself as a feminist religion that rejects references to gods in favor of goddess worship and has radicalized its practice by banning male membership.

A Wiccan ritual celebrating harmony with nature.

THE CONVERGENCE OF SCIENCE, TECHNOLOGY, AND RELIGION: THE PATH TO SCIENTOLOGY

The precedents for Wicca and many other forms of new age religion go back to the interest in esoteric religious beliefs and practices that flourished in the nineteenth century when historical and ethnographic researchers were just beginning to catalog the diverse practices of primal (tribal) and archaic (early urban) religions. From Europe, the teachings of Emanuel Swedenborg (1688–1772) and Franz Anton Mesmer (1734–1815) spread belief in the validity of the shamanistic experience of other worlds and in the animistic unity of all things, which made spiritual healing possible. In America, Ralph Waldo Emerson (1803–1882) and others popularized a school of thought called *transcendentalism*, which integrated certain Asian religious beliefs (especially Hinduism) with American philosophy, affirming the existence of a "world soul" that all beings shared. In this context the practice of spiritualism also flourished, with psychic mediums performing in private séances the ancient shamanistic rituals for contacting spirit beings and dead relatives.

One of the most important movements to emerge at this time was *theosophy*, founded in New York by Helena Petrovna Blavatsky (1831–1891) in 1875. Like the transcendentalists, theosophists found great spiritual wisdom in esoteric teachings, especially in the ancient teachings of Hinduism, with their focus on the interconnectedness of all beings through the universal Brahman. In the theosophical view, all world religions have a hidden unity of message and metaphysical reality, which could be sought through the truths of esoteric texts as well as through the help of leaders who claimed to receive guidance from "living masters," residing in the Himalayas. As we saw in Chapter 7, the theosophists had considerable influence among Asian reformers who were trying to modernize Buddhism. This growing interest in global religious wisdom is illustrated by the first Parliament of World Religions in Chicago in 1893, at which representatives of all the world's religions convened to share their views.

Madam Helena Petrovna Blavatsky, founder of the theosophy movement.

This historical milieu gave birth to two important nineteenth-century precursors of new age religion, both with roots in the New Thought movement: the Church of Christ, Scientist (Christian Science) and the Unity School of Christianity. Women were leaders in both movements. Mary Baker Eddy was the founder of the Christian Science movement, and Emma Curtis Hopkins, a former disciple, broke with Eddy to form the Unity School. The two movements drew on popular forms of philosophical idealism, and the Unity School emphasized Hindu teachings, as well. These influences were integrated with an aura of "science" to affirm the higher reality of mind over matter and therefore the possibility of spiritual healing and spiritual control over the events of one's life.

As the new age religions began to appear in the twentieth century, the religious fascination with the authority of "science" broke free of its earlier linkage to Christianity in movements of the "Christian Science" type. One result was the emergence of *Scientology*, founded by L. Ron Hubbard (1911–1986). In 1950 Hubbard published *Dianetics: The Modern Science of Mental Healing,* in which he claimed to have discovered a cure for all human psychological and psychosomatic ills through the realization of a state of mind he called "Clear." Hubbard went on to establish the Hubbard Dianetic Research Foundation in Elizabeth, New Jersey. Later he moved the organization to Phoenix, Arizona, where the Hubbard Association of Scientologists was founded in 1952.

Scientology goes beyond the psychological orientation of Dianetics to develop an elaborate mythology according to which all humans were once advanced beings Hubbard called *Thetans*: all-powerful, eternal, and omniscient. The first Thetans relieved their boredom by playing mind games in which they used imagination to create different physical worlds. However, they soon forgot their true identity as creators and found themselves trapped in these worlds, living as mortals who died, only to be reincarnated again and again. At each reincarnation, people accumulated more psychological baggage, which Hubbard called *engrams*. To be liberated from this pattern and realize one's true identity, it is necessary to gain insight into one's engrams. Upon finally achieving the "Clear" state of mind, a person gains control over both mind and life. The auditing process that leads to this liberation came to involve the use of a machine that works somewhat like a lie detector. This device, the E-meter, it is believed, measures reactions of resistance to words and other symbols that reveal undissolved engrams. After achieving "Clear," one can go on to higher states that involve out-of-body experiences.

In 1954 Hubbard established the first Church of Scientology in Washington, D.C., and in 1959 he started the Hubbard College of Scientology in England. Whereas many new age religious movements stress individualism and are quite loosely organized, Scientology has an elaborate global organization; bureaucratically and hierarchically, it is not unlike Roman Catholicism or Mormonism. Perhaps an even better analogy is to the modern international business corporation, with its penchant for technical language, efficient organization, and the dissemination of polished communications to interface with the world. And yet all this organization and efficiency is focused on bringing about a powerful experience of enlightenment or rebirth that perfects the self and opens it to the spiritual world that shamans have traversed throughout the ages. Scientologists have also shown a keen interest in Buddhist teachings, and of course the parallels of the auditing practices to depth psychology are obvious. The achievement of "Clear" shows the movement's affinity with both Western experiences of being "born again" and Eastern experiences of enlightenment.

Scientology is, in many ways, the perfect illustration of the global eclectic integration of the elements that make up new age religions: science (especially psychology), technology (corporate and technical structure), Asian religions (reincarnation and the quest for liberation), and shamanism (out-of-body spiritual explorations). A Thetan,

> "The lofty reasonings of Science are the sunshine of the Spirit. They are the works of Truth. Truth is in us. Let it shine. Truth performs great tasks. Let it shine on miracles of health, cheering, enlightening the nations."
>
> —Emma Curtis Hopkins

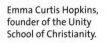

Emma Curtis Hopkins, founder of the Unity School of Christianity.

according to Hubbard, goes "through walls, barriers, vanishes space, appears anywhere at will and does other remarkable things."[4]

EAST GOES WEST: TRANSCENDENTAL MEDITATION

Transcendental Meditation (TM) is an example of an Asian religion moving West, yet another manifestation of the globalization process inherent in new age religion. The mantra system known by its trademarked name, Transcendental Meditation, first came to global public attention in the 1960s when its founder, Maharishi Mahesh Yogi, became the guru of the Beatles, then at the height of their popularity.

The Maharishi taught a kind of spiritual hedonism, according to which our desire to enjoy life is natural, holding that TM offers the most efficient path to this joy. One need not become an ascetic, fasting and meditating for endless hours: Twenty minutes, twice a day, could suffice to bring spiritual transformation. Drawing on traditional teachings from Vedantic Hinduism, the Maharishi taught that happiness could be achieved by tapping into one's naturally serene self, a fragment of the universal Brahman self that all beings share. This is accomplished by stopping all distracting thoughts so that one's consciousness can reach its true center.

Becoming a practitioner was made fairly easy. There is an introductory lecture on the philosophy and scientific benefits of TM. Then in a second meeting, more advanced information is provided and the seeker is initiated. A short period of fasting precedes the initiation, and an offering of fruit, flowers, and money is brought to the event. Then the seeker is given a personal mantra, a secret Sanskrit phrase attuned to the individual's unique needs and temperament, that is to be chanted silently in daily meditation. This mantra must never be revealed to anyone. The initiation rites are followed by three days of supervised meditation and small-group discussions. After ten days the initiate returns for checking by his or her teacher and after that returns once a month.

Initially a countercultural protest against the commercial techno-bureaucracy ("the system") of modern society, TM soon adapted itself to this bureaucracy. In the 1970s the movement began to market itself to corporations, presenting workshops to upper-level managers as a way of creating more efficient and happier professionals on and off the

> "Philosophic knowledge is only valuable if it is true or if it works. . . . A philosophy can only be a *route* to knowledge. It cannot be crammed down one's throat. If one has a route, he can then find what is true for him. And that is Scientology."
>
> —L. Ron Hubbard

Mary Baker Eddy, founder of the Church of Christ, Scientist (Christian Science).

L. Ron Hubbard

L. Ron Hubbard, founder of Scientology.

Scientology was founded by L. Ron Hubbard (1911–1986). Although born in Tilden, Nebraska, Ron Hubbard was exposed to Asian religion and culture as a child because his father was in the navy. As a young man with an adventurous spirit Hubbard was involved in three Central American ethnological expeditions. He received a commission in the navy during World War II, during which service he was pronounced dead twice. In one instance he apparently had something like a shamanistic out-of-body experience in which he acquired spiritual knowledge that gave him his life's mission.

In 1950 Hubbard published *Dianetics: The Modern Science of Mental Healing,* which became the foundation for Scientology. According to *Dianetics,* the mind is made up of two parts, the analytic and the reactive. Traumatic experiences in early life or even in the womb are said to imprint themselves on the reactive mind as *engrams,* which cause psychological and psychosomatic problems if they are not dissolved. The way to dissolve these traumatic impressions is to work with a counselor called an *auditor,* who leads the individual into reenacting the events that caused the trauma, thus releasing or liberating the individual from the engrams' negative effects. Hubbard called this state of release "Clear," and devotees of Scientology work hard to attain it.

job. To achieve scientific legitimacy the movement attempted to accumulate hard evidence that twenty minutes of meditation twice a day improved sleep, resulted in greater oxygen consumption, and made one more creative and happier in life as a result of lower metabolism.

Like many of the new age movements and perhaps more than most, TM offered a new "Methodism" for a new age. It provided a minimal set of required beliefs and a

Tales of Spiritual Transformation

A Scientologist's Account of Achieving "Clear"

As with other religious movements throughout history, Scientologists seek to undergo spiritual death and rebirth, or being "born again." In such rebirth experiences the old way of experiencing the world is replaced by a dramatically new one. The following example is taken from a publication of the Church of Scientology of California dated 1970.

There is no name to describe the way I feel. At last I am at cause. I am Clear—I can do anything I want to do. I feel like a child with a new life—everything is so wonderful and beautiful. Clear is Clear! It's unlike anything I could have imagined. The colors, the clarity, the brightness of everything is beyond belief. Everything is so new, I feel newborn. I am filled with the wonder of everything.

Source: Quoted in Robert S. Ellwood and Harry Partin, eds., *Religious and Spiritual Groups in America,* 2nd ed. (Upper Saddle River, NJ: Prentice Hall, 1988), p. 140.

Maharishi Mahesh Yogi

The Maharishi Mahesh Yogi, who had once studied physics in India, abandoned his academic courses to learn yoga from a master known as Guru Dev. Urged by his guru to take the teachings of yoga to the West, Maharishi journeyed to the United States, where he was able to tap the growing interest in Asian religions that was part of the cultural scene of the 1960s. He gave lectures to crowds all across America, hired a PR firm, made the TV talk shows, and drew a following among prominent actors and rock musicians. In the 1970s he founded the Maharishi International University in Fairfield, Iowa. In addition to the more conventional curriculum, the school offered a doctorate in the neuroscience of human consciousness, and all students and faculty met twice a day to practice Transcendental Meditation.

simple, methodical set of practices aimed at self-perfection, all attuned to the needs of busy individuals in a modern scientifically and technologically oriented culture.

WEST GOES EAST: THE UNIFICATION CHURCH OF SUN MYUNG MOON AND THE AUM SHINRIKYO MOVEMENT

The new age religions we have looked at so far have been more Aquarian than apocalyptic. They have been rooted in the nature-oriented religions deeply attuned to the cycles of nature, like the astrological tradition that posits the Aquarian age. But other new age religions reflect the pattern of the eastward migration of biblical apocalyptic traditions, leading to some interesting integrations of West and East. The Unification Church, originating in Korea, is one such example.

❧ Unification Church

The Unification Church reflects the impact of globalization, for it is the product of colonialism and the very successful impact of Christian missions in Korea, as noted in Chapter 4, on Christianity, and Chapter 8, on East Asian religions. But, even more, it is an example of the transformation of Christianity in a new cultural environment, followed by the exportation of this new form of Christianity back to the West, especially to the United States.

The founder of the Unification Church, Sun Myung Moon, established a religion of divine principle called *Tong Il*. Eventually, Tong Il became known in the West as the Unification Church. In its earliest form this movement drew heavily on Korean shamanism, emphasizing out-of-body travels, healing, communication with spirits, and so on. As the religion moved from East to West, these elements have been downplayed. The church's global outreach really began with the emigration of Sun Myung

Sun Myung Moon

Sun Myung Moon, the founder of the Unification Church, was born in 1920 in northern Korea, where his family joined the Presbyterian church. Moon's experience presents striking parallels to that of Joseph Smith and the emergence of the Church of Latter-day Saints (Mormonism) in the United States. In both cases, the risen Christ visits a country far from the Middle East to establish it as the new center of salvation history.

Sun Myung Moon says that when he was 16 years old, Jesus appeared to him on Easter Sunday and told him to "complete my mission." Over time, Moon says, he also was visited by other great religious figures, including Abraham, Moses, and Buddha. For nine years

he struggled against "satanic forces," and as he began to draw a small following, he was arrested, imprisoned, and tortured by the Communists—an ordeal his followers see as divinely ordained suffering that will lead to the redemption of the human race from the sin of the first parents, Adam and Eve.

Moon was liberated from his imprisonment during the Korean War and took refuge in the southern part of the peninsula. There he established a "religion of divine principle" called *Tong Il*. It soon became known in the West as the Holy Spirit Association for the Unification of World Christianity, or the United Family, and finally as the Unification Church.

Moon to the United States in 1971. Like Scientology (and to a lesser degree like TM), the movement showed a penchant for organization and public relations. Just as Scientology developed a reputation for attracting famous entertainers, the Unification Church courted political and academic figures with some success.

Unification's teachings are based on Moon's book, *Divine Principle,* which is really a kind of Asian or Daoist interpretation of the Bible in terms of polarities, or opposites (divine-human, male-female, etc.), beginning with the polarity of male and female in God. As in the Confucian traditions, these polarities are arranged hierarchically. The proper fourfold foundation of social order puts God at the top, then male and female as equals, with children at the bottom. The lowest order shows deference to the next higher, and all defer to God.

According to Moon's teachings, the "original sin" was Lucifer's spiritual seduction of Eve, leading her to rebel against God, after which she seduced Adam, who had intercourse with her before the time God intended, undermining the proper order of love and deference. To restore the sacred order, says Moon, God has repeatedly sent great prophets—Abraham, Moses, Jesus—but none were able to succeed. If Jesus, for instance, had not been destroyed by his enemies, he (as the second Adam) would have married a second Eve and reinstituted the right order of family and society.

Moon teaches that God has sent three "Israels" to attempt to redeem the world. He chose first the Jews and then the Gentiles. In the twentieth century he chose a third, the Koreans, as the people of salvation, and a Korean (Moon himself) is the third Adam. Just as the early Hebrews, the first Israel, suffered persecution at the hands of the Babylonians and the second Israel, in the days of the second Temple, at the hands of the

Romans, so Koreans, as the third Israel, suffered at the hands of the Japanese during World War II. Finally, in Korea Satan is making his last stand. For in Korea the forces of God and Satan (democracy and communism) are engaged in the final apocalyptic conflict. But God has chosen as the divine center for the salvation of the world Korea, where East and West have met. Confucianism, Buddhism, and Christianity have come together, and now God has sent Rev. and Mrs. Moon, a third Adam and Eve, to restore the human race and complete the unification mission.

Moon's followers generally believe that Moon is the new Messiah and that he and his wife are the new and true parents who are regenerating the human race. To effect this regeneration, Sun Myung Moon chooses marriage partners for his followers and then, with his wife, officiates at mass wedding ceremonies, which have attracted considerable media attention. For the movement, every new crop of married couples furthers the struggle against the Communists, Satan's representatives on earth, who Moon depicts as arrayed against himself as demonic agents in a lifelong cosmic battle. Though famous globally, the Unification Church claims only a modest number of adherents in Korea.

Rev. Sun Myung Moon and his wife officiate at a mass wedding of 2,000 couples in Madison Square Garden in 1998.

Shoko Asahara (Chizuo Matsumoto)

Cult of Doom

A poison-gas attack triggers fears about extremists using homemade weapons of mass death

As a child in a school for the blind, Aum Shinrikyo founder Chizuo Matsumoto boasted that he would one day be prime minister of Japan. Yet the early years of the severely sight-impaired youth were not promising. After two failures to enter the Japanese university system, he joined a new religious movement called *Agonshu*, which mixed Buddhist, Daoist, and Hindu teachings. In 1984 he broke with Agonshu and developed a personal religious vision, integrating elements of Hindu yoga, Buddhist meditation, and Christian apocalyptic beliefs. He visited India in 1986 and had what he believed to be a powerful enlightenment experience. Convinced that he was destined to be a great spiritual master, Chizuo Matsumoto, then the leader of his own small movement, took on the name of Shoko Asahara and changed the name of his group to Aum Shinrikyo.

Shoko Asahara, founder of Aum Shinrikyo.

❖ *Aum Shinrikyo*

An apocalyptic new age vision has also taken root in Japan, and members of one cult, Aum Shinrikyo, achieved global notoriety and terrorist status when they released deadly sarin gas into the Tokyo subway system in 1995.

The Aum Shinrikyo ("Supreme Truth") movement is the creation of Chizuo Matsumoto, who in 1986 changed his name to Shoko Asahara and registered his two-year-old group as a religion with the Japanese government. Having done this, he attracted additional followers by writing extensively in his country's new age religious publications, promising to teach seekers out-of-body shamanistic skills such as clairvoyance and teleportation. He had a charismatic personality, and his movement, which has had an extraordinary appeal to the university-educated professional class, quickly became one of the fastest-growing new religions in Japan.

Through a well-developed bureaucracy, with Asahara at the top, Aum Shinrikyo established monastic-like separatist communities throughout Japan, where the most devoted followers congregated, having left their families and given all their earthly belongings to the movement. Descriptions of the initiation rituals have mentioned the heavy use of hallucinogens, the drinking of vials of Asahara's blood, and a total surrender to Asahara as the spiritual master.

In the beginning Asahara taught that the world would end soon and that it was the task of his followers to save humanity through their hard work in Aum business ventures and through purification by personal spiritual practices. After Asahara and some of his handpicked leaders were decisively defeated in an attempt to win seats in Japan's parliament in 1990, Asahara's teachings took a darker turn, seeking to destroy what he believed were the demonic forces that opposed his movement.

By 1993 Aum Shinrikyo had plants producing automatic weapons as well as chemical and biological weapons, ostensibly to protect Japan against its enemies. Believing that the United States was about to trigger an apocalyptic nuclear war, Aum scientists traveled to Russia and Africa in search of biological and nuclear weapons. Aum Shinrikyo's following in Russia by 1995 was estimated at 30,000, roughly three times its membership in Japan. The group's terrorist plans, however, were known only to a small, mostly Japanese, elite.

Asahara came under legal scrutiny for his varied activities, especially after authorities learned that the worth of Aum's assets exceeded $1 billion. In 1994, convinced that the Japanese government's special police force had set out to destroy him, Asahara ordered the assassination of three judges by releasing poison gas in their neighborhoods. The judges survived, but some innocent bystanders were killed. The next year, after the Tokyo subway gassing, he was arrested.

Asahara integrated Japanese Shinto beliefs with Hinduism and Tibetan Buddhism in a way that appealed to many young Japanese professionals (including scientists) by calling into question modern materialism as well as the stress and decadence of modern life. Indeed, influenced by the science fiction of Isaac Asimov, Asahara developed a vision of the role of scientists as building an elite secret society that would save civilization from cataclysmic wars. To this he added a strong dose of Christian apocalyptic expectations (mixed with the predictions of Nostradamus) about the imminent end of the world in a battle between good and evil. He justified his murderous assaults on his fellow citizens by pronouncing that killing those who are creating bad karma was actually doing them a spiritual favor, since it stopped them before they produced even more negative karma.

To his followers, Asahara declared himself to be Jesus Christ, come to bring judgment on the world. In preparation for the global nuclear war he believed the United States was plotting, he bought land in Australia. There his followers could start to build a new civilization as they waited out the years of lethal radiation in a devastated Northern Hemisphere. Ultimately, Asahara was convicted for having masterminded the Tokyo sarin gas attack. He was sentenced to death in 2004, and the movement, which regrouped under the name *Aleph* ("the beginning"), still reveres him as its spiritual leader.

Like Scientology, Aum Shinrikyo illustrates the integration of shamanism and Eastern mysticism with scientific research and technological applications organized by a highly efficient globally oriented bureaucratic organization. The difference between them is equally important, for Asahara's eclectic religious vision adds elements of Western apocalyptic thought colored by his own paranoid vision of himself as the rejected prophet and spiritual master. The result was dangerously violent.

Religious Postmodernism and Global Ethics

THE CHALLENGE OF POSTMODERN SECULAR RELATIVISM

As explained in Chapter Four, on Christianity, the difference between fundamentalists and modernists stems from an argument about the impact of science on traditional religious beliefs. Fundamentalists often seem to believe they must oppose science to reaffirm traditional religious beliefs, whereas modernists seem to embrace science, preferring to adapt religious beliefs to the changing understanding science brings.

Fundamentalists generally had no objection to the use of science to invent things like the automobile or for the creation of better medications. When science impinged on religious beliefs concerning the origins of humanity and the right way to order society, however, many drew a line. If the human self and society do not have sacred origins but are the result of biological evolution and human decisions, then the human self and society seem to be set adrift in a world without meaning, purpose, or ethical norms.

As modern science and technology—and the worldview they foster—were carried around the world by colonialism, the impact of modernity was felt in different ways in different societies and cultures. Not every religious tradition emphasizes orthodoxy ("right beliefs") the way Christianity does. For example, Hinduism, Judaism, and Islam place far more emphasis on orthopraxy ("right actions"), the maintenance of a sacred way of life. Thus the most common feature of the fundamentalist reaction to modernity across religions and cultures is the desire to preserve the premodern sacred way of life against the threat of secularization and the normless relativism it seems to engender.

The social sciences of the nineteenth century promoted a technological understanding of society. According to this understanding, society itself can be redesigned through public policy decisions, just as engineers periodically redesign cars. While the use of scientific and technological inventions per se was relatively uncontroversial, many rejected treating the social order in a secular and technological fashion, as if society could or should be shaped and reshaped by human choices, without regard to the sacred ways of one's ancestors.

In our chapter on Christianity, we pointed to the emergence of existentialism as a watershed moment in the history of modernization, opening the door to postmodern relativism by calling into question the idea of *human nature*. For many, this seeming disappearance of human nature is terrifying, suggesting that we as human beings know neither who we are nor what we ought to do. This is the mindset Nietzsche was addressing when he said that "modern man" had murdered God and so now wandered the universe without a sense of direction. For many today, it seems that the secular "technologized" understandings of self and society can only lead to moral decadence—a decadence in which the family and the fabric of society will be destroyed. Those who believe that secularization is robbing humanity of an understanding of its sacred origins and destiny reject technologized understandings of self and society. As an antidote, they favor a return to the fundamental truths about human nature that governed life in premodern times.

Modernization is often presented in terms of a story about the secularization of society, that is, the liberation of the various dimensions of cultural life from the authority of religion. Since religion in premodern societies preserves the sacred by governing every aspect of life, modernization and secularization are threats to traditional societies everywhere.

Nevertheless, sacralizing society to protect a divinely ordered way of life is not the only role religion has played in history. The great sociologist Max Weber pointed out that religion not only sacralizes and reinforces the unchanging "routine" order of society, sometimes it also "charismatically" desacralizes and transforms society. Brahmanic Hinduism sacralized caste society in ancient India, but Buddhism began as a movement to desacralize the priestly elite and see all persons in the caste system as capable of achieving spiritual deliverance. Sacralization is total and readily accommodates hierarchies (e.g., a caste system, a multitiered social order), whereas desacralizing breaks with caste, inviting pluralism and equality.

Because religions (even in the same traditions) often manifest dramatically opposing values and orientations, the sociologist Jacques Ellul has argued that it is helpful in understanding the role of religion in society to distinguish between two terms that are typically used interchangeably: *sacred* and *holy*. In his view, the experience of the sacred leads to a view of society as an order that is itself sacred and must be protected from all profane attempts to change it. The experience of the holy, on the other hand, calls into question the very idea of a sacred order. It desacralizes (or secularizes) society and seeks to introduce change in the name of a higher truth and/or justice. According to this view, the same religious tradition can express itself in opposite ways in different times and places. In the East, early Buddhism called into question the sacred order of Hindu caste society, but later Buddhist societies developed their own sacred orders. Early Daoists in China called into question the sacred hierarchical order of Confucianism but later also integrated themselves into the sacred order of Confucian society by means of a neo-Confucian synthesis.

In the West, early Christianity, sharing a common ethos with Judaism, called the sacred order of Roman civilization into question, but medieval Christianity resacralized Europe. Then later, Protestantism desacralized the medieval European social order and unleashed the dynamics of modernism. From this perspective, the struggle between fundamentalism and modernism in the modern world that we have surveyed in this textbook is an example of the conflict between the sacralizing and desacralizing (secularizing) roles of religion.

Religious fundamentalists express the desire to preserve the sacredness of human identity in a rightly ordered society against what they perceive as the chaos of today's decadent, normless secular relativism. To restore the sacred normative order, therefore, they tend to affirm the desirability of achieving the premodern ideal of one society, one religion. They remain uncomfortable with the religious diversity that thrives in a secular society.

Religious modernism as it emerged in the West rejected the fundamentalist ideal, adopted from premodern societies, of identity between religion and society. Instead of dangerous absolutism, modernists looked for an accommodation between religion and modern secular society. They argued that it is possible to desacralize one's way of life and identity in a way that creates a new identity that preserves the essential values or norms of the past tradition, but in harmony with a new modern way of life. Modernists secularize society and privatize their religious practices, hoping by their encouragement of denominational forms of religion to ensure an environment that supports religious diversity.

What we are calling religious postmodernism, like religious modernism, accepts secularization and religious pluralism. But religious postmodernism, like fundamentalism, rejects the modernist solution of privatization and seeks a public role for religion. It differs from fundamentalism, however, in that it rejects the domination of society by a single religion. Religious postmodernists insist that there is a way for religious communities in all their diversity to shape the public order and so rescue society from secular relativism. The chief example of this option is the model established by Mohandas K. Gandhi. Because his disciples rejected the privatization of religion while affirming religious diversity, Gandhi's movement is a postmodern new age religious movement rather than a modern one.

EXPLORING RELIGIOUS DIVERSITY BY "PASSING OVER": A POSTMODERN SPIRITUAL ADVENTURE FOR A NEW AGE OF GLOBALIZATION

All the great world religions date back a millennium or more, and each provided a grand metanarrative for the premodern civilization in which it emerged—in the Middle East, in India, and in China. In the past these world religions were relatively isolated from one another. There were many histories in the world, each shaped by a great metanarrative, but no global history.

The perspective of religious postmodernism arises from a dramatically different situation. We are at the beginning of a new millennium, which is marked by the development of a global civilization. The diverse spiritual heritages of the human race have become the common inheritance of all. Modern changes have ended the isolation of the past, and people following one great tradition are now very likely to live in proximity to adherents of other faiths. New age religion has tapped this condition of globalism, but in two different ways. In its modernist forms it has privatized the religious quest as a quest for the perfection of the self. In its postmodern forms, without rejecting self-transformation, it has turned that goal outward in forms of social organization committed to bettering society, with a balance between personal and social transformation.

Leo Tolstoy, the famous Russian novelist, whose writings on Jesus' Sermon on the Mount inspired Gandhi.

The time when a new world religion could be founded has passed, argues John Dunne in his book *The Way of All the Earth.* What is required today is not the conquest of the world by any one religion or culture but a meeting and sharing of religious and cultural insight. The postmodern spiritual adventure occurs when we engage in what Dunne calls *passing over* into another's religion and culture and come to see the world through another's eyes. When we do this, we "come back" to our own religion and culture enriched with new insight not only into the other's but also our own religion and culture—insight that builds bridges of understanding, a unity in diversity between people of diverse religions and cultures. The model for this spiritual adventure is found in the lives of Leo Tolstoy (1828–1910), Mohandas K. Gandhi (1869–1948), and Martin Luther King Jr. (1929–1968).

Two of the most inspiring religious figures of the twentieth century were Mahatma Gandhi and Dr. King. They are the great champions of the fight for the dignity and rights of all human beings, from all religions and cultures. Moreover, they are models for a different kind of new age religious practice, one that absorbs the global wisdom of diverse religions, but does so without indiscriminately mixing elements to create a new religion, as is typical of the eclectic syncretism of most new age religions. Yet clearly these religious leaders initiated a new way of being religious that could occur only in an age of globalization.

Martin Luther King Jr. often noted that his commitment to nonviolent resistance, or civil disobedience, as a strategy for protecting human dignity had its roots in two sources: Jesus' Sermon on the Mount and Gandhi's teachings of nonviolence derived from his interpretation of the Hindu sacred story called the *Bhagavad Gita.* Gandhi died when King was a teenager, but Dr. King did travel to India to study the effects of Gandhi's teachings of nonviolence on Indian society. In this he showed a remarkable openness to the insights of another religion and culture. In Gandhi and his spiritual heirs, King found kindred spirits, and he came back to his own religion and culture enriched by the new insights that came to him in the process of passing over and coming back. Martin Luther King Jr. never considered becoming a Hindu, but his Christianity was profoundly transformed by his encounter with Gandhi's Hinduism.

Just as important, however, is the spiritual passing over of Gandhi himself. As a young man, Gandhi went to England to study law. His journey led him not away from Hinduism but more deeply into it, for it was in England that Gandhi discovered the *Bhagavad Gita* and began to appreciate the spiritual and ethical power of Hinduism.

Having promised his mother that he would remain a vegetarian, Gandhi took to eating his meals with British citizens who had developed similar commitments to vegetarianism through their fascination with India and its religions. It is in this context that Gandhi was brought into direct contact with the nineteenth-century theosophical roots of new age globalization. In these circles he met Madam Blavatsky and her

"I simply want to tell the story of my numerous experiments with truth, and my life consists of nothing but these experiments. . . . They are spiritual, or rather moral; for the essence of religion is morality."

—M. K. Gandhi

disciple Annie Besant, both of whom had a profound influence on him. His associates also included Christian followers of the Russian novelist Leo Tolstoy, who, after his midlife conversion, had embraced an ethic of nonviolence based on the Sermon on the Mount (Matthew 5–7).

At the invitation of his theosophist friends, Gandhi read the *Bhagavad Gita* for the first time, in an English translation by Sir Edwin Arnold, entitled *The Song Celestial.* It was only much later that he took to a serious study of the Hindu text in Sanskrit. He was also deeply impressed by Arnold's *The Light of Asia,* recounting the life of the Buddha. Thus, through the eyes of Western friends, he was first moved to discover the spiritual riches of his own Hindu heritage. The seeds were planted in England, nourished by more serious study during his years in South Africa, and brought to fruition on his return to India in 1915.

From his theosophist friends, Gandhi not only learned to appreciate his own religious tradition but came to see Christianity in a new way. For unlike the evangelical missionaries he had met in his childhood, the theosophists had a deeply allegorical way of reading the Christian scriptures. This approach to Bible study allowed people to find in the teachings of Jesus a universal path toward spiritual truth that was in harmony with the wisdom of Asia. The power of allegory lay in opening the literal stories of the scripture to reveal a deeper symbolic meaning based on what the theosophists believed was profound universal religious experience and wisdom. From the theosophists, Gandhi took an interpretive principle that has its roots in the New Testament writings of St. Paul: "The letter killeth, but the spirit giveth life" (2 Corinthians 3:6). This insight would enable him to read the *Bhagavad Gita* in the light of his own deep religious experience and find in it the justification for nonviolent civil disobedience.

Gandhi was likewise profoundly influenced by Tolstoy's understanding of the Sermon on the Mount. The message of nonviolence—love your enemy, turn the other cheek—took hold of Gandhi. And yet Gandhi did not become a Christian. Rather, he returned to his parents' religion and culture, finding parallels to Jesus' teachings in the Hindu tradition. And so he read Hindu scriptures with new insight, interpreting the *Bhagavad Gita* allegorically, as a call to resist evil by nonviolent means . And just as King would later use the ideas of Gandhi in the nonviolent struggle for the dignity of blacks in America, so Gandhi was inspired by Tolstoy as he led the fight for the dignity of the lower castes and outcasts within Hindu society and for the liberation of India from British colonial rule.

Gandhi never seriously considered becoming a Christian any more than King ever seriously considered becoming a Hindu. Nevertheless, Gandhi's Hindu faith was profoundly transformed by his encounter with the Christianity of Tolstoy, just as King's Christian faith was profoundly transformed by his encounter with Gandhi's Hinduism. In the lives of these twentieth-century religious activists we have examples of "passing over" as a transformative postmodern spiritual adventure.

Mohandas K. Gandhi, whose techniques of nonviolent civil disobedience led to the liberation of India from British colonial rule in 1947.

Martin Luther King Jr., who led the civil rights movement for racial equality in the United States, using the techniques of nonviolent civil disobedience inspired by Gandhi.

Whereas in the secular forms of postmodernism all knowledge is relative, and therefore the choice between interpretations of any claim to truth is undecidable, Gandhi and King opened up an alternate path. While agreeing that in matters of religion, truth is undecidable, they showed that acceptance of diversity does not have to lead to the kind of ethical relativism that so deeply troubles fundamentalists. For in the cases of Gandhi and King, passing over led to a sharing of wisdom among traditions that gave birth to an ethical coalition in defense of human dignity across religions and cultures—a global ethic for a new age.

By their lives, Gandhi and King demonstrated that, contrary to the fears raised by fundamentalism, the sharing of a common ethic and of spiritual wisdom across traditions does not require any practitioners to abandon their religious identity. Instead, Gandhi and King offered a model of unity in diversity. Finally, both Gandhi and King rejected the privatization of religion, insisting that religion in all its diversity plays a decisive role in shaping the public order. And both were convinced that only a firm commitment to nonviolence on the part of religious communities would allow society to avoid a return to the kind of religious wars that accompanied the Protestant Reformation and the emergence of modernity.

The spiritual adventure initiated by Gandhi and King involves passing over (through imagination, through travel and cultural exchange, through a common commitment to social action to promote social justice, etc.) into the life and stories and traditions of others, sharing in them and, in the process, coming to see one's own tradition through them. Such encounters enlarge our sense of human identity to include the other. The religious metanarratives of the world's civilizations may have become "smaller narratives" in an age of global diversity, but they have not lost their power. Indeed, in this Gandhian model, it is the sharing of the wisdom from another tradition's metanarratives that gives the stories of a seeker's own tradition their power. Each seeker remains on familiar religious and cultural ground, yet each is profoundly influenced by the other.

TOLSTOY, JESUS, AND "SAINT BUDDHA": AN ANCIENT TALE WITH A THOUSAND FACES

Although at first glance the religious worlds of humankind seem to have grown up largely independent of one another, a closer look will reveal that hidden threads from different religions and cultures have for centuries been woven together to form a new

Teachings of Religious Wisdom

John Dunne on "The New Spiritual Adventure"

In 1972, as a new age of religious resurgence was just getting under way, John Dunne, a professor at the University of Notre Dame, published The Way of All the Earth. *While others were puzzling over the meaning of the religious eclecticism of "the new age" and "globalization," Dunne saw these developments as a new turning point in the history of religions and cultures. In this excerpt from the Preface he identifies the unique spiritual adventure that belongs to an age of globalization.*

Is a religion coming to birth in our time? It could be. What seems to be occurring is a phenomenon we might call "passing over," passing over from one culture to another, from one way of life to another, from one religion to another. Passing over is shifting of standpoint, a going over to the standpoint of another culture, another way of life, another religion. It is followed by an equal and opposite process we might call "coming back," coming back with new insight to one's own culture, one's own way of life, one's own religion. The holy man of our time, it seems, is not a figure like Gautama [Buddha] or Jesus or Mohammed, a man who could found a world religion, but a figure like Gandhi, a man who passes over by sympathetic understanding from his own religion to other religions and comes back again with new insight to his own. Passing over and coming back, it seems is the spiritual adventure of our time.

Source: John Dunne, *The Way of All the Earth* (Notre Dame, IN: University of Notre Dame Press, 1972), p. ix.

tapestry, one that contributes to the sharing of religious insight in an age of globalization. In *Toward a World Theology,* Wilfred Cantwell Smith traces the threads of this new tapestry, and the story he tells is quite surprising.[5] Smith notes, for example, that to fully appreciate the influence on Gandhi of Tolstoy's understanding of the Sermon on the Mount, it is important to know that Tolstoy's own conversion to Christianity, which occurred in a period of midlife crisis, was deeply influenced not only by the Sermon on the Mount but also by the life of the Buddha.

Tolstoy was a member of the Russian nobility, rich and famous because of his novels, which included *War and Peace* and *Anna Karenina.* Yet in his 50s, Tolstoy went through a period of great depression that resolved itself in a powerful religious conversion experience. Although nominally a member of the (Russian) Orthodox Church, Tolstoy had not taken his faith seriously until he came to the point of making the Sermon on the Mount a blueprint for his life. After his conversion, Tolstoy freed his serfs, gave away all his wealth, and spent the rest of his life serving the poor.

As Wilfred Cantwell Smith tells it, a key factor in Tolstoy's conversion was his reading of a story from the lives of the saints. The story was that of Barlaam and Josaphat. It is the story of a wealthy young Indian prince by the name of Josaphat who gave up all his wealth and power and abandoned his family to embark on an urgent quest for an answer to the problems of old age, sickness, and death. During his search, the prince comes across a Christian monk by the name of Barlaam, who tells him a story. It seems that once there was a man who fell into a very deep well and was hanging onto two vines for dear life. As he was trapped in this precarious situation, two mice, one white and one black, came along and began to chew on the vines. The man knew that in short order the vines would be severed and he would plunge to his death.

The story was a parable of the prince's spiritual situation. Barlaam points out that the two mice represent the cycle of day and night, the passing of time that brings us ever closer to death. The paradox is that like the man in the well, Josaphat cannot save his life by clinging to it. He must let go of the vines, so to speak. He can save his life only by losing it. That is, if he lets go of his life now, no longer clinging to it but surrendering himself completely to the divine will, this spiritual death will lead to a new life that transcends death. This story and its parable touched the deeply depressed writer and led him first to a spiritual surrender that brought about his rebirth. Out of this rebirth came a new Tolstoy, the author of *The Kingdom of God Is Within You,* which advocates a life of nonviolent resistance to evil based on the Sermon on the Mount.

The story of the Indian prince who abandons a life of wealth and power and responds to a parable of a man about to fall into an abyss is of course a thinly disguised version of the life story of the Buddha. Versions of the story and the parable can be found in almost all the world's great religions, recorded in a variety of languages (Greek, Latin, Czech, Polish, Italian, Spanish, French, German, Swedish, Norwegian, Arabic, Hebrew, Yiddish, Persian, Sanskrit, Chinese, Japanese, etc.). The Greek version came into Christianity from an Islamic Arabic version, which was passed on to Judaism as well. The Muslims apparently got it from members of a Gnostic cult in Persia, who got it from Buddhists in India. The Latinate name *Josaphat* is a translation of the Greek *Loasaf,* which is translated from the Arabic *Yudasaf,* which comes from the Persian *Bodisaf,* which is a translation of *Bodhisattva,* a Sanskrit title for the Buddha.

The parable of the man clinging to the vine may be even older than the story of the prince (Buddha) who renounces his wealth. It may well go back to early Indic sources at the beginnings of civilization. It is one of the oldest and most universal stories in the history of religions and civilizations. Tolstoy's conversion was brought about in large part by the story of a Christian saint, Josaphat, who was, so to speak, really the Buddha in disguise.

The history of the story of a great sage's first steps toward enlightenment suggests that the process leading to globalization goes back to the very beginnings of civilization.. Therefore the line between new religions and new age (globalized) religions may not be as sharp as previously assumed. We can see that the practice of passing over and coming back, of being open to the stories of others, and of coming to understand one's own tradition through these stories is in fact very ancient. Therefore, when Martin Luther King Jr. embraced the teachings of Gandhi, he embraced not only Gandhi but also Tolstoy and, through Tolstoy, two of the greatest religious teachers of nonviolence: Jesus of Nazareth, whose committed follower King already was, and Siddhartha the Buddha. Thus from the teachings of Gandhi, King actually assimilated important teachings from at least four religious traditions—Hinduism, Buddhism, Judaism, and Christianity. This rich spiritual debt to other religions and cultures never in any way diminished Martin Luther King Jr.'s faith. On the contrary, the Baptist pastor's Christian beliefs were deeply enriched, in turn enriching the world in which we live. The same could be said about Gandhi and Hinduism.

Gandhi's transformation of the *Bhagavad Gita*—a Hindu story that literally advocates the duty of going to war and killing one's enemies—into a story of nonviolence is instructive of the transforming power of the allegorical method that he learned from his theosophist friends. The *Bhagavad Gita* is a story about a warrior named Arjuna, who argues with his chariot driver, Krishna, over whether it is right to go to war if it means having to kill one's own relatives. Krishna's answer is Yes—Arjuna must do his duty as a warrior in the cause of justice, but he is morally obliged to do it selflessly, with no thought of personal loss or gain. Gandhi, however, transformed the story of Arjuna and Krishna from a story of war as physical violence into a story of war as active but nonviolent resistance to injustice through civil disobedience.

If the message of spiritual realization in the *Gita* is that all beings share the same self (as Brahman or Purusha), how could the *Gita* be literally advocating violence, for to do violence against another would be to do violence against oneself? The self-contradiction of a literal interpretation, in Gandhi's way of thinking, forces the mind into an allegorical mode, where it can grasp the *Gita*'s true spiritual meaning. Reading the *Gita* allegorically, Gandhi insisted that the impending battle described in the Hindu classic is really about the battle between good and evil going on within every self.

Krishna's command to Arjuna to stand up and fight is thus a "spiritual" command. But for Gandhi this does not mean, as it usually does in "modern" terms, that the struggle is purely inner (private) and personal. On the contrary, the spiritual person will see the need to practice nonviolent civil disobedience: that is, to replace "body force" (i.e., violence) with "soul force." As the *Gita* suggests, there really is injustice in the world, and therefore there really is an obligation to fight, even to go to war, to reestablish justice. One must be prepared to exert Gandhian soul force, to put one's body on the line, but in a nonviolent way. In so doing, one leaves open the opportunity to gain the respect, understanding, and perhaps transformation of one's enemy.

The lesson Gandhi derived from the *Gita* is that the encounter with the other need not lead to conquest. It can lead, instead, to mutual understanding and mutual respect. King's relationship to Gandhi and Gandhi's relationship to Tolstoy are models of a postmodern spirituality and ethics that transform postmodern relativism and eclecticism into the opportunity to follow a new spiritual and ethical path—"the way of all the earth"—the sharing of spiritual insight and ethical wisdom across religions and cultures in an age of globalization.

On this path, people of diverse religions and cultures find themselves sharing an ethical commitment to protect human dignity beyond the postmodern interest in personal transformation fostered by the modernist ideal of privatization. Gandhi and King were not engaged in a private quest to perfect the self (although neither neglected the need for personal transformation). Rather, each man embarked on a public quest to transform human communities socially and politically by invoking a global ethical commitment to protect the dignity of all persons. The religious movements associated with both men fit the pattern of the holy that affirms the secularization of society in order to embrace religious pluralism. Gandhi and King recovered the premodern ideal of religion shaping the public order but now in a postmodern mode, committed to religious pluralism.

THE CHILDREN OF GANDHI: AN EXPERIMENT IN POSTMODERN GLOBAL ETHICS

In April 1968, Martin Luther King Jr., sometimes referred to as "the American Gandhi," went to Memphis to support black municipal workers in the midst of a strike. The Baptist minister was looking forward to spending the approaching Passover with Rabbi Abraham Joshua Heschel. Heschel, who had marched with King during the voter registration drive in Selma, Alabama, three years earlier, had become a close friend and supporter. Unfortunately, King was not able to keep that engagement. On April 4, 1968, like Gandhi before him, Martin Luther King Jr., a man of nonviolence, was shot to death by an assassin.

The Buddhist monk and anti-Vietnam War activist Thich Nhat Hanh, whom King had nominated for a Nobel Peace Prize, received the news of his friend's death while at an interreligious conference in New York City. Only the previous spring, King had expressed his opposition to the Vietnam War, largely at the urging of Thich Nhat Hanh and Rabbi Heschel. King spoke out at an event sponsored by Clergy and Laymen Concerned about Vietnam, a group founded by Heschel, Protestant cleric John Bennett, and Richard Neuhaus, then a Lutheran minister. Now another champion in the struggle against hatred, violence, and war was dead. But the spiritual and ethical vision he shared with his friends, across religions and cultures, has continued to inspire followers throughout the world.

These religious activists—a Baptist minister who for his leadership in the American civil rights movement won the Noble Peace Prize, a Hasidic rabbi and scholar who narrowly escaped the death camps of the Holocaust, and a Buddhist monk who had been targeted for death in Vietnam but survived to lead the Buddhist peace delegation to the Paris peace negotiations in 1973—are the spiritual children of Gandhi. By working together to protest racial injustice and the violence of war, they demonstrated that religious and cultural pluralism do not have to end in ethical relativism and, given a commitment to nonviolence, can play a role in shaping public life in an age of globalization. The goal, Martin Luther King Jr. insisted, is not to humiliate and defeat your enemy but to win him or her over, bringing about not only justice but also reconciliation. The goal, he said, was to attack the evil in systems, not to attack persons. The goal was to love one's enemy, not in the sense of sentimental affection or in the reciprocal sense of friendship, but in the constructive sense of seeking the opponent's well-being.

Nonviolence, King argued, is more than just a remedy for this or that social injustice. It is, he was convinced, essential to the survival of humanity in an age of nuclear weapons. The choice, he said, was "no longer between violence and nonviolence. It is either nonviolence or nonexistence."

Truth is to be found in all religions, King said many times, and "injustice anywhere is a threat to justice everywhere. We are caught in an inescapable network of mutuality, tied in a single garment of destiny. Whatever affects one directly affects all indirectly."[6] The scandal of our age, said Abraham Joshua Heschel, is that in a world of diplomacy "only religions are not on speaking terms." But, he also said, no religion is an island, and all must realize that "holiness is not the monopoly of any particular religion or tradition."[7]

"Buddhism today," writes Thich Nhat Hanh, "is made up of non-Buddhist elements, including Jewish and Christian ones." And likewise with every tradition. "We have to allow what is good, beautiful, and meaningful in the other's tradition to transform us," the Vietnamese monk continues. The purpose of such passing over into the other's tradition is to allow each to return to his or her own place transformed. What is astonishing, says Thich Nhat Hanh, is that we will find kindred spirits in other traditions with whom we share more than we do with many in our own tradition.[8]

THE FUTURE OF RELIGION IN AN AGE OF GLOBALIZATION

Will the global future of religion and civilization be shaped by this Gandhian model of new age spiritual practice? It clearly offers an alternative to both traditional denominational modernist religions and the more privatistic modernist forms of new age religion. The Gandhian model also offers an alternative to the rejection of modernization and secularization, trends that fundamentalists fear can only lead to the moral decadence of ethical relativism. But the sharing of spiritual wisdom does require seeing the religions and cultures of others as having wisdom to share, and not all will accept this presupposition. Nevertheless, the emergence of religious postmodernism means that in the future, the struggle among religions will most likely be not between fundamentalism and modernism, as a conflict between the sacred and the secular (public and private religion), but between the sacred and the holy—religious exclusivism and religious pluralism as alternative forms of public religion.

Discussion Questions

1. What is the difference between a "new religion" and a "new age religion"?

2. How do modernist new age religious belief and practice differ from postmodernist new age religious belief and practice? Give an example of each.

3. How does new age religion relate to the split between faith and reason (the *via moderna* and the *devotio moderna*) that shaped the emergence of the modern world through the Enlightenment and the Romantic reaction it provoked?

4. In what sense is "civil religion" a new way of being religious, and in what sense is it a very old way of being religious?

5. In what way is the postmodern path of religious ethics opened up by M. K. Gandhi and Martin Luther King Jr. similar to fundamentalist ideals for society, and in what way is it different?

Suggested Readings

Bruce, Steve. *Religion in the Modern World* (New York: Oxford University Press, 1996).

Dunne, John S. *The Way of All the Earth* (New York: Macmillan, 1972).

Ellwood, Robert S., and Harry B. Partin, eds. *Religious and Spiritual Groups in Modern America,* 2nd ed. (Upper Saddle River, NJ: Prentice Hall, 1973, 1988).

Fasching, Darrell J. *The Coming of the Millennium* (San Jose, CA: Authors Choice Press, 1996, 2000).

————. "Stories of War and Peace: Sacred, Secular and Holy," in Sarah Deets and Merry Kerry, eds., *War and Words,* (Lanham, MD: Rowman and Littlefield, 2004).

————, and Dell deChant. *Comparative Religious Ethics* (Oxford: Blackwell, 2001).

Juergensmeyer, Mark. *Terror in the Mind* (Berkeley: University of California Press, 2000).

Kronerborg, Reender. *New Religions in a Postmodern World* (Aarhus, Denmark: Aarhus University Press, 2003).

Laderman, Gary, and Luis Leon, eds. *Religion and American Cultures,* Vol. 1 (Santa Barbara, CA: ABC Clio, 2003).

Lewis, James R., ed. *The Oxford Handbook of New Religious Movements* (New York: Oxford University Press, 2004).

Rothstein, Mikael, ed. *New Age Religion and Globalization* (Aarhus, Denmark: Aarhus University Press, 2001).

Notes

1. William Bloom, *The New Age: An Anthology of Essential Writings* (London: Rider/Channel 4, 1991), p. xviii. Quoted in Steve Bruce, *Religion in the Modern World* (Oxford and New York: Oxford University Press, 1996).

2. Sarah Pike, "New Age," quoted in Robert S. Ellwood and Harry B. Partin, eds., *Religious and Spiritual Groups in America,* 2nd ed. (Upper Saddle River, NJ: Prentice Hall, 1988), p. 140.

3. Quoted in Ellwood and Partin, eds., *Religious and Spiritual Groups in America,* 2nd ed. (Upper Saddle River, NJ Prentice Hall, 1988), p. 140, citing a publication of the Church of Scientology of California dated 1970.

4. L. Ron Hubbard, *Scientology: The Fundamentals of Thought* (Edinburgh: Publications Organization Worldwide, 1968); originally published 1950. Quoted in Ellwood and Partin, eds., *Religions and Spiritual Groups in America,* 2nd ed. (Upper Saddle River, NJ: Prentice Hall, 1988), p. 147.

5. Wilfred Cantwell Smith, *Toward a World Theology* (Philadelphia: Westminster Press, 1981), Chapter 1.

6. Martin Luther King Jr., "Letter from Birmingham Jail," in King, *I Have a Dream: Writings and Speeches That Changed the World,* James M. Washington, ed. (San Francisco: HarperSanFrancisco, 1992), p. 85.

7. Abraham Joshua Heschel, *Moral Grandeur and Spiritual Audacity: Essays [of] Abraham Joshua Heschel,* Susannah Heschel, ed. (New York: Farrar, Straus & Giroux, 1996), pp. 241, 247.

8. Thich Nhat Hanh, *Living Buddha, Living Christ* (New York: G. P. Putnam and Sons, Riverhead Books, 1995), pp. 9, 11.

Glossary

❖ *Introduction*

divine: representative of the gods

ethical: right action

fundamentalist: one who rejects important aspects of modernity and wants to go back to what he or she perceives as the purity of an "authentic" social/political order manifested in the sacred way of life of his or her ancestors

globalization: for the purposes of world religions, the idea that all the world's religions have members in every country or society. Anyone using the Internet can view the major temples, shrines, churches, mosques, or monasteries from around the world and offer ritual prayers or make monetary offerings to them

heretic: from the ancient Greek, meaning "to choose." In our postmodern world every religious person becomes a heretic, that is, one who is not simply born into a given religion or identity but must choose it, even if it is only to choose to retain the identity offered by the circumstances of his or her birth

metanarrative: a grand cosmic and/or historical story accepted by the majority of a society as expressing its beliefs about origin, destiny, and identity

modern: a civilization that separates its citizen's lives into public and private spheres, assigning politics to public life while restricting religion to personal and family life. A dominant scientific metanarrative provides the most certain public truths people believe they know. Society and politics are governed by secular, rational, and scientific norms rather than religion

myth: from the Greek *mythos,* meaning "story." A symbolic story about the origins and destiny of human beings and their world; myth relates human beings to whatever powers they believe ultimately govern their destiny and explains to them what the powers expect of them

orthodoxy: acceptance of "right beliefs" or "doctrines" based on sacred texts as formulated by religious authorities

orthopraxy: the practice of "right actions" or rituals as prescribed by sacred traditions

postmodern: a society typified by diversity in both beliefs and social practices that has no single dominant metanarrative (other than the narrative of diversity) and is skeptical of finding either certain knowledge or norms in any public form of truth, whether religious or scientific

premodern: a civilization in which there is no separation between religion and society. A dominant religious metanarrative provides the most certain truths people believe they know. By being a member of that culture, one automatically participates in its religious vision and lives by its religious norms

religion: from the Latin *religare,* meaning "to tie or bind" and the root *religere,* which has the connotation of "acting with care." It expresses a sense of being "tied and bound" by obligations to whatever powers are believed govern destiny—whether those powers be natural or supernatural, personal or impersonal, one or many. Ancient peoples everywhere believed that the powers governing their destiny were the forces of nature

ritual: actions that connect the individual and the community to the sacred

secular: nonreligious

sympathetic imagination: empathy. Necessary to understand the religious languages and messages of different religious traditions

transcendent: beyond all finite things

ultimate reality: that which is the highest in value and meaning for the group

via analogia: a way of knowing spiritual reality through the use of analogy, for example, "God is my shepherd"

via negativa: the mystical way of knowing the highest spiritual reality (God, Brahman, etc.) by negating all finite qualities and characteristics; Hindus, for instance, say Brahman is "neti . . . neti"—not this and not that (i.e., Brahman is not a thing, Brahman is no-thing and therefore is pure nothingness, Brahman is beyond imagination and cannot be imaged, Brahman can only be known by a mystical experience of unknowing)

❖ *Indigenous Religions*

aboriginal peoples of Australia: the indigenous nations of Australia

Ainu: indigenous people of Hokkaido Island in northern Japan

animism: religious tradition whose basic perception entails belief in an inner soul that gives life and ultimate identity to humans, animals, and plants and that places primary emphasis on experiential rituals in which humans interact with other souls

Bwiti: a West Central African religion that incorporates animism, ancestor worship, and Christianity into its belief system, along with a specially cultivated hallucinogen

circular time: the awareness, more prevalent in hunter-gather than in industrial societies, that life is governed by the rising and the setting of sun, the phases of the moon, and the seasons of the year

cosmogony: mythological account of the creation

Dani: indigenous agricultural group in highland New Guinea

"Dreamtime": in Aboriginal legend, the time when the world was being created

E.B. Tylor: see *soul belief*

Émile Durkheim: sociologist who theorized that religion's power to bind human communities together is what established it and keeps it central to human life

Ghost Dance: a shaman-led nationwide movement aimed at reviving the indigenous nations of North America. Ended in 1890 when the U.S. Cavalry massacred up to 300 of the men, women, and children gathered for the Ghost Dance at Wounded Knee, South Dakota

Homo religiosus: religious humanity. A term coined by comparative religions scholar Mircea Eliade to indicate that religious practice was universal to all humans

Kung San: a nomadic hunter-gatherer group in southern Africa

Lakota Sioux: indigenous nation in North America

mudang: Korean shamans, predominantly women, drawn into the role through either troubling personal experiences or inheritance

***Native American Church*:** a "Pan-American" movement among American Native peoples that has factions related in varying ways to Christianity but that are united in their ceremonial use of the cactus peyote as the group's own communal sacrament

numinous: the human perception of the sacred

shaman: ritual specialists, intermediaries who attempt to connect this world to another realm of being impinging on humanity. By these rituals, they knit together the community in the face of the chaos of disease, death, and discord

sorcerers: mediums who manipulate the spirit world and coerce the supernaturals without their consent, often for their own benefit and against community values

***soul belief*:** theory, articulated in 1871 by E.B. Tylor [1831–1917], that the human perception that there is an invisible soul or intangible spirit inside our visible, tangible bodies is universal

spirit flight: "soul journey." A shaman's attempt to locate another person's soul, perhaps because it has wandered off in this world or needs assistance to reach the afterlife dwelling place of the clan's ancestors

spirit medium: person who is believed to communicate with the dead

syncretism: the weaving together of alien and indigenous religious beliefs and practices; or the combining of elements from different practices to create a new religion

taboo: forbidden

totem: symbol taken from the natural world that stands for a social group possessing a common origin and essence

tutelary spirit: a supernatural agent, often an ancestral spirit, whose help is required by a shaman to perform the difficult soul journeys, negotiate with evil spirits, compel a soul to return, or increase the shaman's healing powers

"Venus" figurines: prehistoric Eurasian small stone sculptures of females with large breasts and hips, often with their genitalia emphasized, thought to indicate a worship of fertility in small communities

white shamans: Westerners who create global organizations propagating a purported "universal" shamanic tradition, charging high fees for tours, courses, initiations, and healing services, some pledging to use some of the proceeds to assist indigenous shamans

✤ *Hinduism*

Adi Granth: the scripture worshipped by Sikhs

ahimsa: nonviolence, the ideal of doing no killing, especially for its karmic effects

atman: in Hindu thought, the soul that resides in the heart, is the source of both life energy and spiritual awareness, and transmigrates after death

avatara: "incarnation" of the gods that descends to earth; avataras assume life-forms that aid creation, usually to defeat demons and overcome evil

Bhagavad Gita: Hindu scripture inserted into the great epic, the *Mahabharata,* extolling the divinity of Krishna as the ultimately real deity

bhakti: devotionalism to a divinity, a means to reach salvation from the world of rebirth

BJP (Bharatiya Janata party): Hindu nationalism party that rose meteorically in popularity in the 1990s and assumed national rule in 1998

Brahman: world spirit that arises at creation, which Hindus hold is either in impersonal form, nirguna Brahman, or human form, saguna Brahman

brahmin: member of the highest caste, innately possessing the highest natural purity; the men traditionally specialize in ritual performance, textual memorization and study, and theology

dharma: "duty" determined by one's caste and gender

guru: a teacher in matters spiritual and cultural, whom disciples regard as semidivine

gurudwaras: Sikh temples

Hindutva: Hindu-ness

Kali Yuga: the dark age the world has now entered, when human spiritual capacity is thought to be diminished; a view shared by some Hindus and Buddhists

karma: literally "action," but also meaning the effects of actions that, through a hidden natural causality, condition a being's future; Hindus fix karma as acting on the inborn soul, Buddhists define its effects on the consciousness and habits

Khalsa: Sikh organization for the defense of the faith, marked by their uncut hair (covered with a turban), short trousers, steel wristlet, comb, and sword

Maharishi Mahesh Yogi: (1917–2008), founder of the Transcendental Meditation movement

matha: monastery

moksha: "release" from samsara, freedom from future rebirth and redeath (i.e., salvation)

nirguna Brahman: see *Brahman*

OM: also written in full phonetic rendition as AUM, one of the most prominent symbols of Hinduism. Repeated as part of almost every mantra for offerings and meditation as well as written calligraphically on icons and other symbols

Om-kara: ("Divine One") and Sat Guru ("True Teacher"): Sikh terms for God

prasad: the remains of any substance (food, flowers, incense, etc.) used in a ritual offering, thought to be medicinal because it has been in contact with the divinity

puja: a ritual offering to a Hindu or bodhisattva deity, Buddha, or bodhisattva

puranas: texts extolling the histories, theologies, and necessary rituals for expressing the Bhakti faith for the different Hindu deities

Ramakrishna Mission: founded by Swami Vivekananda to further the teachings of his guru, Ramakrishna; an influential Hindu missionary and reform organization that today runs hospitals, schools, and temples and has centers in over a dozen countries

Ramanuja: an influential theologian (1025–1137) who argued that the ultimate reality humans could relate to was saguna Brahman

RSS (Rashtriya Svayamsevak Sangh): "National Union of [Hindu] Volunteers," a group that since 1923 has proposed a nativist definition of *Hinduism* as devotion to "Mother India"

saguna Brahman: see *Brahman*

samsara: "the world" of rebirth subject to the law of karma and the inevitable reality of death, a religious understanding shared by Hinduism, Buddhism, Jainism, and Sikhism

satyagraha: Gandhi's central principle of "grasping the truth." With roots in the Hindu and Jain doctrine of nonviolence (ahimsa) and in Christianity's injunctions to love one's enemy and turn the other cheek (as a reaction to being struck in the face), Gandhi required those opposing the government to confine their protests to nonviolent acts, to accept suffering for the cause, to love the opponent, and to be disciplined in personal life

Shaivite: devotee of Shiva

Shankara: Hindu philosopher (788–820) and monastic organizer, whose monistic interpretation of the *Upanishads* became the most influential expression of nirguna Brahman doctrine

tantra: the esoteric tradition common to both Hinduism and Buddhism that employs practices that defy caste and gender orthopraxy to lead individuals to moksha/nirvana quickly

Tattvabodhini Sabha: a colonial Hindu sect, powerful around Calcutta, that promoted the "modern Hindu's" adaptation to India's new economic and political realities. Merged the values of working hard, living honestly, saving rationally, and promoting altruism with the individual controlling personal desires. Along with Rammohan Roy (1772–1833), they saw reformed Hinduism now being led by the "godly householder," not the premodern elite of world-renouncing ascetics

TM (Transcendental Meditation): a movement founded by Maharishi Mahesh Yogi that brought mystical Hindu teachings to the West through mantra-centered meditation

Upanishads: appendices to the Vedas that record early Hindu speculations on Brahman, atman, the means to realize their identity, and moksha

Vaishnavite: devotee of Vishnu or his incarnations

Vedas: the collection of the earliest Hindu hymns directed to the pantheon of deities, including ritual directions and chanting notations for their use

Vishva Hindu Parishad (VHP): An organization of religious leaders founded in 1964 to promote the interests of Hindus

yoga: a term meaning "union" that refers to the various means of realizing union with the divine; earliest use of yoga refers to ascetic practices but expands to include the path of philosophical inquiry, bhakti, and tantra

Yoga Sutras: codification of yoga practices, attributed to Patanjali

❖ Buddhism

Amitabha/Amida: The most important and highly developed of the Pure Land schools created by a Chinese Buddha named Amitabha in Sanskrit (Amitofo in Chinese, Amida in Japanese), featured chanting Amitabha's name (*Namo A-mi-t'o Fo*) as a meditative act and communal ritual

anatman: "nonself," the doctrine denying the reality of a permanent, immortal soul as the spiritual center of the human being

arhat: an enlightened disciple, according to the Theravada school; an advanced disciple, according to the Mahayana

Avalokiteshvara: see *Guanyin*

bhikkhuni: nuns

Bodh Gaya: the site of Shakyamuni Buddha's enlightenment, under a tree

bodhisattva: a Buddha to be, either in the present life or in a future life; in the Mahayana tradition, all individuals should aspire to be Buddhas, hence the bodhisattva is the highest human role; some future Buddhas can be reborn as deities, hence in Mahayana Buddhism there are also bodhisattvas who can assist humans

Buddha-nature school: a Mahayana Buddhist belief that all beings have a portion of nirvana and so possess the latent potential for its realization. A reversion to belief in the soul that also reinforced the need for traditional meditation practices

Buddha: literally, one who has "awakened," ended karmic bondage, and will no longer be reborn; one who will enter nirvana

caitya: a term that can also signify any Buddha shrine. See *stupa*

Ch'an: a Mahayana Buddha-nature tradition in East Asia called Ch'an in China, Sön in Korea, and Zen in Japan

dana: one of the four merit-making activities in Buddhist culture, "self-less giving" to diminish desire

dependent origination: a twelve-part formula explaining how individuals are bound to future rebirth until they extirpate desire and ignorance

Dharma: the Buddha's teaching, one of the three refuges; more broadly, the truth at the center of Buddhism, the basis for realizing enlightenment

Eightfold Path: the eight qualities needed to reach nirvana, concerning morality, meditation, and salvific wisdom

engaged Buddhism: a reformist movement among global Buddhists seeking to relate the teachings to contemporary suffering

enlightenment: see *nirvana*

Four Good Deeds: a doctrinal formula guiding the laity on the uses of wealth, advising the pursuit of happiness, security, philanthropy, and ritual

Four Noble Truths: a doctrinal formula focusing on diagnosing the human condition as marked by suffering and distorted by desire and then prescribing the Eightfold Path as a solution

Guanyin: The most popular and universal celestial bodhisattva was Avalokiteshvara, known as Guanyin in China, Kannon in Japan, Chenrizi in Tibet, and Karunamaya in Nepal

karuna: compassion, the quality that motivated the Buddha to preach and the principal Buddhist social virtue

koan: a Buddhist spiritual riddle designed to foster spiritual growth, posed by monastic teacher to junior monks, such as "What is the sound of one hand clapping?" or "Does a dog have a Buddhist nature?"

Lotus Sutra: one of the earliest and most influential Mahayana Buddhist texts, which reveals the cosmological nature of a Buddha and the universal character of Buddhist truth

Madhyamaka: a Mahayana philosophical school that posits the provisional and incomplete nature of all assertions; its goal is to clear away attachment even to words, making realization possible

Mahayana: the "Great Vehicle" that was the dominant school of Buddhism in Tibet and East Asia; the Mahayana philosophical schools developed cosmological theories of Buddhahood and envisioned the universe as permeated by bodhisattvas, some of whom were like deities and the focus of ritual veneration

maitri: loving-kindness, a Buddhist ethical virtue and topic of meditation

merit: see *punya*

mizuko cult: a new form of Kannon devotionalism in Japan organized to seek the forgiveness of the spirits of aborted fetuses, until they fulfill their destiny and continue on to another human rebirth

nirvana: a blissful state achieved by individuals who have cut off their karma by ending desire, attachment, and ignorance; after death, they enter the final transpersonal state for eternity, free from future rebirth

Pali Canon: the only complete canon among the early collection of Buddha's teachings, in this case in the Pali language derived from Sanskrit; it is split into three divisions: *Vinaya* (monastic code), *Sutras* (sermons), and *Abhidhamma* (advanced teaching formula)

prajna: the "insight" or "wisdom" necessary for enlightenment in Buddhism, comprising the ability to "see clearly" into the nature of existence as marked by suffering, impermanence, and absence of a soul

"Protestant Buddhism": a term signifying a pattern of reform in which Buddhists protested colonial rule yet adopted perspectives and missionary techniques of Protestant Christianity

punya: merit, or the good karma that enters into the content of an individual's life, earned in Buddhist doctrine by moral practices, learning, and meditation

Pure Land: in Mahayana Buddhism, the belief that Buddhas and advanced bodhisattvas can through their inexhaustible merit create rebirth realms where humans can easily engage in Buddhist practices conducive to enlightenment

sangha: the Buddhist monastic community of monks and nuns

Shakyaditya: The "Shakya Daughters" is a group of Buddhist nuns dedicated to the restoration of the full ordination of bhikkhunis (nuns) among the Theravadins

shramana: wandering ascetics known at the time of the Buddha

skandha: an aggregate, used in Buddhist thought to identify each of the five components that define a human being: the physical body (*rupa*), feelings (*vedana*), perceptions (*samjna*), habitual mental dispositions (*samskaras*), and consciousness (*vijnana*)

Sthaviravadins: the traditionalists among the early Buddhist monastic schools, the only surviving school today being the Theravadins

stupa: the distinctive Buddhist shrine, a raised mound surmounted by a ceremonial pole and umbrella; contains the relics of a Buddha or enlightened saint, either the literal bodily relics or other items left behind, such as words in textual form or clothing items worn

Theravada: traditionalists, the last surviving Buddhist school of elders (Sthaviravadins) that is now dominant in South and Southeast Asia

Three Marks of Existence: the Buddhist terms for analyzing human reality as marked by impermanence, suffering, and no soul

Three Refuges: see *Triratna*

Thunderbolt Vehicle: see *Vajrayana*

Triratna: the "Three Jewels" that every Buddhist takes refuge in for all rituals: the Buddha, the Dharma, and the Sangha

Vajrayana: the Mahayana-derived Buddhist tantric "vehicle" of belief and practice that uses unorthodox means, including sexual experience, to propel individuals quickly toward enlightenment

vihara: a Buddhist monastery

vipashyana (vipassana): the widespread Buddhist meditation practice focusing on calming the mind and discerning the truly real

Zen: the Japanese Mahayana Buddhist school focused on meditation practice, as transmitted from and organized in China as the Chan

❖ *East Asian Religions*

All Souls Festival: a summer event when the gates of purgatory are thought to be held open. Families perform rituals to connect the living members with their departed kin and ensure their ancestors' comfort in the afterlife

Amaterasu: the kami of the sun and progenitor of the Japanese imperial line

Analects: collection of sayings attributed to Confucius

ancestor veneration: worship, feeding, and petitioning of the souls of dead ancestors at family graves, temples, or home altars

Ch'ondogyo: Korean movement reaffirming the truth of human dignity and the vitality of Daoism and Confucianism

city god: Chinese deity with influence on spirits living within city precincts, to whom every family's kitchen god reported at year's end

Confucianism: culture of the literate elite (rujia) informed by Confucius and his disciples, who mastered the classics and rituals; the moral tradition upholding the "three bonds" and the "three principles" as the basis of social life; the spiritual tradition of revering ancestors as part of the family bond

Confucius: see *Master K'ung*

Cultural Revolution: period from 1966 to 1976 when China's Communist Party, under the leadership of Mao Zedong, attacked religious traditions and practitioners

Dao: mysterious power that moves the universe and all beings

Daoism, philosophical: Chinese tradition advocating the way to harmony for individual and society based on understanding natural forces and flowing with life naturally

Daoism, religious: Chinese tradition that cultivates individual immortality through either alchemical infusions or meditative practices

Daoist: East Asian visionaries who advocated individualistic retreat, learning from the natural world, and noninterference by the state as the best way to ensure humanity's flourishing

Daruma-san: Japanese name for the monk Bodhidharma, who brought a meditation-centered Buddhist tradition to China, which would be called Zen in Japan

de: mysterious and spontaneous energy of the universe

diffuse religion: spiritual tradition centered on family and locality, informed by common ideas from Confucianism, Daoism, and Buddhism

Five Classics: Confucian canon attributed to Master K'ung: *Book of Changes* (*Yi-Jing*), *Book of Documents* (*Shu Jing*), *Book of Poetry* (*Shi Jing*), *Book of Rites* (*Li Jing*), and a historical work that uses events in the early Chinese state to show how to assess praise and blame

Full Moon Festival: an early fall festival to worship the harvest moon with special sweet "moon cakes." Across East Asia, people view the rising moon on this night to ask for blessings. Rural communities request a good rice harvest in the month ahead

Guan Yu: Chinese god of war, regarded as protector of merchants

Hong Xiuquan (1814–1864): charismatic instigator of the Taiping Rebellion, whose trance experiences led him to believe that he was the "younger brother" of Jesus, charged with establishing a new state in China

Huang-di: "Yellow Emperor," first immortal in religious Daoism

jun-zi: a Confucian gentleman who has cultivated character and learning

kami: deity of Japan associated with places, certain animals, and the emperor

kitchen god (Zao Wangye): deity residing in every household, thought to observe and report on family events to his celestial superiors yearly

Lao Zi (Lao Tzu): "Old Sage," reputed author of *Daodejing* and founder of *Daoism*

li: in Confucian thought, individual performances needed for personal development, including manners, service to others, and rituals

ling: spiritual force possessed by geographic places, such as rivers, mountains, caves, as well as by deities and charismatic sages

literati tradition: see *Confucianism*

mappo: Buddhist doctrine of the world in decline, especially that humans cannot practice meditation as well as in the time of the Buddha

Master K'ung: sage's (551–479 BCE) given Latin name to whom Catholic missionaries later gave the Latinate name Confucius

Mencius: first major disciple of Master K'ung, a systematizer of Confucian ideals who lived 371–289 BCE

Mizuko cult: the newly popularized Japanese tradition of ritual apology and merit transfer to the spirits of aborted fetuses

mudang: Korean shaman

nembutsu: repetition of the name of the Buddha Amitabha, for the purpose of making merit and gaining rebirth in the Pure Land

neo-Confucianism: tradition originating in the Song dynasty and developed subsequently by masters such as Zhu Xi who sought to harmonize early Confucian humanism with more cosmological theories of Daoism and karma doctrine of Buddhism, adopting meditation techniques from both

neo-Shintoism (or state Shinto): Meiji state's adoption of Shinto as state religion, with emperor as focal divinity, which lasted from 1868 to 1945

"new religions": sects arising in Japan from the early nineteenth century combining elements of Buddhism, Daoism, and Confucianism with ideas imported from abroad; term may be applied outside Japan

Nichiren: thirteenth-century Buddhist monk who taught that the *Lotus Sutra* was the sole true Buddhist text and that chanting its title was an essential salvation practice; founded new school based on these ideas

qi gong: discipline of cultivating the vital individual life force that can be used for worldly goals such as healing or to reach immortality

qi: vital force of life within individuals and in nature

Qing-Ming: yearly spring festival when Chinese visit and clean family graves and then feast after making offerings to the ancestors

ren: Confucian ideal of being "fully human" in ethics, manners, cultivation

shamanism: tradition by which human mediums are possessed by spirits and communicate with the living; in China called *wu/xi or fa-shih;* in Korea, *mudang*

Shang-di: Heavenly Lord, thought to preside over early Chinese pantheon; term Christians used to translate *God*

shen: usual term in Chinese for a kindly god or goddess

Shinto: indigenous religion of Japan that reveres the deities of the islands including the emperor

Soka Gakkai: Nichiren Buddhist offshoot, now global religion seeking world peace through Mahayana Buddhist teachings

Taiping Rebellion: nineteenth-century revolt in China led by converts to Christianity, who established a separate state in the city of Nanjing; resulting civil war was bloodiest in world history

Tenrikyo: Tenrikyo ("Religion of Heavenly Wisdom") was founded by Nakayama Miki (1798–1887) and became a recognized Shinto sect in 1838. Essential for salvation are a dance ritual, an initiation ("receiving the holy grant"), and performance of daily social service for others

"three faiths": Chinese grouping of the three great traditions: Confucianism, Daoism, and Buddhism

t'i: affection for siblings, in Confucianism a marker of character

Tian: "heaven," understood as impersonal yet responsive to human actions

Tian di: a supreme overlord believed to keep records on each individual soul, according to texts found in Han-era tombs in China

T'oegyehak: modern Korean Confucian group based on teachings of master Yi T'oegye (1501–1570)

Tu-di (or Tu Chu): "Earth Ruler," local god who controls earth's fertility

Tu-di gong: The cult of Tu-di Gong, the "earth ruler" who controls fertility, widespread among farmers in China during the millennium from the Zhou dynasty (1122–221 BCE) until the fall of the Han (206 BCE–220 CE)

Unification Church: Korean "new religion" founded by Rev. Sun Myung Moon, who claims to be completing the work of Jesus as a messiah by establishing a global community

Won Buddhism: A new Korean school of Buddhism founded in 1924 by Soe-Tae San (1891–1943). It ritualizes worship of a picture of a black circle in a white background, symbolizing the *dharmakaya,* the cosmic body of the Buddha. The group is named *Won* from the Korean reading of the Chinese character "round."

wu-wei: "noninterference" or "non-[forced] action," an ideal in Daoism

xiao: Confucian ideal of children honoring their parents, attitude that extends to the ruler

yin-yang theory: twin forces by which the Dao is known, each complementing the other (female–male, valley–mountain, etc.)

Zhu Xi: great Chinese master of neo-Confucian thought who integrated into Confucianism elements of Buddhism and Daoism and established core rituals of subsequent tradition

Zhuang Zi: second great Daoist classic

❖ *Islam*

Allah: God

ayatollah: literally, "sign of God"; title used by certain Shiah religious leaders who are widely reputed for their learning and piety

caliph (*khalifah*): successor of Muhammad as the political and military head of the Muslim community

dawah: call, missionary work, proselytization

dhimmi: literally, protected non-Muslim peoples; refers to Jews and Christians (later extended to others) who were granted "protected" status and religious freedom under Muslim rule in exchange for payment of a special tax

fana: in Sufi usage, annihilation of the ego-centered self

faqih (pl. _fuqaha_): jurist, legal scholar; one who elaborates _fiqh_

faqir: ascetic mendicant mystic ideal; Sufi _shaykh_

fatwa: legal opinion or interpretation issued on request by legal expert (mufti) to either judges or private individuals

hadith: narrative report of Muhammad's sayings and actions

hajj: annual pilgrimage to Mecca; all Muslims should make the hajj at least once in their lifetime, but it is recognized that individual circumstances may make compliance impossible

al-haram al-sharif: the noble sanctuary

hijra: migration; Muhammad's hijra from Mecca to Medina in 622 marks the first year of the Muslim lunar calendar

ijma: consensus; in Islamic law, refers to agreement of scholars on interpretation of legal questions; some have reinterpreted this principle to justify the right of a parliament to enact legislation

imam: in Sunni Islam, the prayer leader and the one who delivers the Friday sermon; in Shiah Islam, refers to Muhammad's descendants as legitimate successors, not prophets, but divinely inspired, sinless, infallible, and the final authoritative interpreter of God's will as formulated in Islamic law

Islam: submission or surrender to God

jahiliyya: unbelief, ignorance; used to describe the pre-Islamic era

jihad: to strive or struggle; exerting oneself to realize God's will, lead a virtuous life, fulfill the universal mission of Islam, and spread Islam through preaching and/or writing; defense of Islam and Muslim community; currently often used to refer to the struggle for educational and social reform and social justice as well as armed struggle, holy war

khatam: seal or last of the prophets; Muhammad

khutba: sermon delivered at Friday prayer session in the mosque

Mahdi: expected or awaited one; divinely guided one who is expected to appear at the end of time to vindicate and restore the faithful Muslim community and usher in the perfect Islamic society of truth and justice

masjid: mosque; Muslim place of worship and prayer

minbar: pulpit in the mosque from which the Friday sermon (_khutba_) is preached

mosque: Islamic temple, from _masjid,_ "place of prostration"

muezzin: one who issues the call to prayer from the top of the minaret

mufti: legal expert, adviser, or consultant; one who issues fatwas to judges and litigants

mujtahid: expert in Islamic law; one who exercises ijtihad, or independent reasoning, in legal matters; one capable of interpreting Islamic law

Muslim: one who submits or surrenders himself or herself to God and his will; one who follows Islam

People of the Book (_Ahl al-Kitab_): those possessing a revelation or scripture from God; typically refers to Jews and Christians, sometimes includes Zoroastrians

qiyas: legal term for analogical reasoning

al-Quds: the holy city (i.e., Jerusalem)

Quran: revelation, recitation, message; Muslim scripture

Ramadan: month of fasting; ninth month of the Muslim calendar

salat: official prayer or worship performed five times each day

shahadah: declaration of faith, witness, testimony; refers to the declaration of Muslim faith: "There is no god but God and Muhammad is His Messenger"

sharia: Islamic law; straight path

Shi or Shiah: follower(s), partisan(s); refers to those who followed the leadership of Ali, the nephew and son-in-law of Muhammad, as Muhammad's successor, those who believe that leadership of the Muslim community should belong to Muhammad's descendants

shirk: polytheism, idolatry, association of anyone or anything with God; the biggest sin in Islam

Sufi: literally "one who wears wool"; Muslim mystic or ascetic

Sufism: Islamic mysticism or asceticism

Sunnah: example; typically refers to Muhammad's example, which is believed by Muslims to be the living out of the principles of the Quran; *Sunni* is derived from this word

Sunni: those who accept the *sunna* and the historic succession of the Caliphs; the majority of the Muslim community

surah: chapter, particularly of the Quran

tariqah: path, way; used by Sufis to designate order to which they belong

tawhid: oneness, unity, and uniqueness of God; absolute monotheism

ulama (sing. *alim*): religious scholars

ummah: Muslim community of believers

zakat: almsgiving, one of the Five Pillars of Islam: 2.5 percent tithe on one's net worth to help the poor is required of all Muslim

✤ *Globalization*

civil religions the beliefs and rituals of modern "secular" societies that treat their social order as sacred due to the "cultural" influence of the religions that shaped their development

millennialism: beliefs about an age of peace and perfection (1000 years) at the end of time that have their origin in the New Testament book of Revelation

neopaganism: modern adaptations of ancient pagan (polytheistic and animistic) beliefs

new religions: religions that emerge by breaking with traditional beliefs and practices, often through the influence of other religions in their local environment

new age religions: religions that emerge by breaking with traditional beliefs and practices, typically through the influence of other religious practices around the globe due to the influence of global media and global travel

nonviolence: a strategy for dealing with the violence of others through nonviolent acts of civil disobedience

passing over: the act of imagination whereby one sees the world through the eyes of another's religion and thereby gains new insight into one's own religion

shamanism: the practice of leaving your body to enter the realm of the gods and spirits and learn higher spiritual truths and the arts of healing to bring back to one's people. Shamanism has its roots in ancient animistic and polytheistic cultures

Art Credits

Index